Publish It!® 2 Made Easy

Publish It!® 2 Made Easy

Paul Garrison

Osborne **McGraw-Hill**

Berkeley New York St. Louis San Francisco
Auckland Bogotá Hamburg London Madrid
Mexico City Milan Montreal New Delhi Panama City
Paris São Paulo Singapore Sydney
Tokyo Toronto

Osborne **McGraw-Hill**
2600 Tenth Street
Berkeley, California 94710
U.S.A.

For information on translations or book distributors outside of the U.S.A., please write to Osborne **McGraw-Hill** at the above address.

Publish It!® 2 Made Easy

234567890 DOC 9987654321

ISBN 0-07-881722-6

Publish It!® 2 Made Easy

Paul Garrison

Osborne **McGraw-Hill**

Berkeley New York St. Louis San Francisco
Auckland Bogotá Hamburg London Madrid
Mexico City Milan Montreal New Delhi Panama City
Paris São Paulo Singapore Sydney
Tokyo Toronto

Osborne **McGraw-Hill**
2600 Tenth Street
Berkeley, California 94710
U.S.A.

For information on translations or book distributors outside of the U.S.A., please write to Osborne **McGraw-Hill** at the above address.

Publish It!® 2 Made Easy

234567890 DOC 9987654321

ISBN 0-07-881722-6

Publisher

Kenna S. Wood

Acquisitions Editor

Elizabeth Fisher

Associate Editor

Wendy Goss

Project Editor

Laura Sackerman

Copy Editor

Ann Krueger Spivack

Proofing Coordinator

Kathy Krause

Proofreaders

Paul Medoff
Linda Medoff
Jeff Barash

Computer Designers

Patricia Jani Beckwith
Peter F. Hancik

Typesetters

Helena Charm
Marcela Hancik
Stefany Otis
Michelle Salinaro
Erick Christgau
Fred Lass

Technical Illustrators

Fred Lass
Lance Ravella

Word Processer

Valerie Haynes Perry

Cover Designer

Bay Graphics Design, Inc.

Contents

II Program Elements

Introduction

Desktop publishing, the technique of using your personal computer to design and prepare all manner of printed documents, might sound somewhat more intimidating than it needs to be. What desktop publishing does is eliminate the need for scissors and paste, and the often expensive services of a typesetter, replacing them with simple to learn and easy to manage computer operations, making the preparation of these and many other types of documents a breeze:

Letterhead stationery	Resumes
Envelopes	Fliers
Invoice forms	Reports
Business cards	Proposals
Business forms	Greeting cards
Newsletters	Catalogs
Brochures	Booklets
Announcements	Books

Until the introduction of Publish It!, efficient desktop publishing required some rather costly software that involved much time and effort to master.

Publish It! changed all that. It is a powerful program that rivals even the highest-priced competition in terms of its vast array of capabilities. And, best of all, it can easily be mastered in just a few hours.

About This Book

This book is for anyone who might be interested in desktop publishing, whether to produce just an occasional piece of letterhead stationery or a flier, or to create sophisticated, carefully designed documents, periodicals, or any other type of published material. It explains in considerable detail how to get the most out of using the various versions of Publish It! (1.1, 1.2, and 2.0) and of Publish It Lite!, the smaller version designed for those users who have no need for the more advanced features available with the full-featured versions. All illustrations in this book showing the computer screens, except those identified as being associated with Publish It Lite!, were produced using Publish It! version 2.0. Users of earlier versions will find that there are slight differences. The book includes a large number of actual examples of desktop publishing, representing the types of documents that are frequently produced by this method. Each of these can be edited to conform to the specific needs of the individual user.

You do not need to be an experienced computer user or programmer to use Publish It! or this book. Only the most basic knowledge of how to operate the computer and keyboard is expected.

Each chapter covers examples of desktop publishing projects in an easy-to-follow tutorial format along with detailed explanations. You will find that it is easy to progress from designing and producing simple one-page documents to the more specialized uses available with desktop publishing.

How This Book Is Organized

The book is divided into five parts. Part I, "An Overview," provides an introductory explanation of the way Publish It! and Publish It Lite! function.

It also includes a quick-start chapter for the impatient reader. Part II, "Program Elements," is the reference section. It discusses each feature of the two programs in detail. Part III, "Text and Graphics," furnishes the reader with hands-on experience in terms of producing different types of desktop publishing documents. Part IV, "Publishing," covers general subjects like layout and design, and such publishing requirements as multiple copies, distribution, and advertising. Part V contains the appendixes.

Part I, "An Overview"

Chapter 1, "Publish It! Basics," is an overview of the Publish It! and Publish It Lite! programs. It explains the principles of operating the two programs.

Chapter 2 is a quick tutorial, entitled "A Trial Run." It applies to either version and leads you through the production of a one-page document containing headlines, subheads, and text wrapped around a graphic image. Even though you'll still be unfamiliar with the program, all of this can be accomplished in less than an hour. It is designed especially for those of you who do not have the time to read all the instructions in detail.

Part II, "Program Elements"

Part II deals with the program elements. It covers all the commands, functions, and features of Publish It! and Publish It Lite! in great detail. This reference section can be referred to frequently when you are in doubt as to how to achieve a certain result.

Chapter 3, "The Screen Displays," covers the individual items that make up the work screen: the menu bar, the toolbox with its icons, the Library window, the work area, and more.

Chapter 4, "The Menus," presents the menus and the options offered by each. It includes illustrations of each menu and option and explains all functions in detail.

Chapter 5, "The Publish It! Libraries," covers the font, art, and sample publication libraries that are included in the software package. It illustrates the available fonts and describes how to use the clip-art library.

Part III, "Text and Graphics"

Part III deals with the many ways in which text and graphics can be generated from within the programs or imported, edited, and otherwise manipulated.

Chapter 6, "Importing and Manipulating Text," concentrates on the means of generating, importing, and working with text. It includes hands-on practice sessions that help you produce a variety of documents.

Chapter 7, "Importing and Manipulating Graphics," explores the different ways of generating, importing, editing, and otherwise manipulating graphics. It concentrates on graphics included with the Publish It! software and graphics produced directly in the <GRAPHICS> mode.

Chapter 8, "Hands-on Practice," helps you produce a variety of documents ranging from a party invitation to multipage documents and full-page ad layouts.

Chapter 9, "Using External Files," describes the use of files generated from external graphics programs, screen-capture software, scanners, and other sources.

Chapter 10, "Computer-Generated Artwork," covers computer-generated graphics. It includes examples that utilize various paint and computer-aided-design programs.

Chapter 11, "Special Tricks and Techniques," consists of helpful hints that are not immediately obvious. Included are means of combining documents, manipulating text and graphics frames, and more.

Part IV, "Publishing"

Part IV describes publishing in general.

Chapter 12, "Layout and Design," covers the principles of good layout and design. It includes numerous examples with explanations of how they are produced using Publish It!.

Chapter 13, "Peripheral Publishing Requirements," deals with the more mundane publishing needs, those that come into play when a document has been created but must be duplicated, distributed, marketed, and so on.

Part V, "Appendixes"

Appendix A, "Installation," explains how to install the program and the different ways in which the program can be started.

Appendixes B and C provide glossaries of terms and abbreviations used by Publish It! and in the publishing business in general.

Appendix D, "Quick Keys," lists the quick keys available with Publish It! and Publish It Lite!.

Appendix E, "External Program Sources," lists the names and addresses of the manufacturers whose software and other products are mentioned in the book.

Appendix F, "Publish It! Version 2.0," covers all the features of Publish-It! version 2.0.

Conventions

Publish It! 2 Made Easy uses the following typeface conventions to make it easier for you to accomplish the examples in this book.

Key names and key combinations are printed in uppercase and boxed: ENTER, END, CTRL-J, and so on. They either require that you press the indicated key or that you hold down the CTRL (or ALT or SHIFT) key while pressing the key to the right of the hyphen.

Quick keys are boxed together: ALT-A. Hold down the ALT key while pressing the letter key in either upper- or lowercase.

The mouse commands are click, double-click, hold down, drag, and release, always referring to the left mouse button.

Options selected by clicking the mouse button are enclosed in pointed brackets: <Open>, <Go to page>, <Import text>. Move the pointer to the desired menu *without* clicking the mouse button. As the options are displayed, move the highlighting to your selection and then click.

Modes to be selected by clicking on icons are in uppercase and enclosed in pointed brackets: <TEXT> mode. Move the pointer to the icon in the tool box and click.

Menu names start with a capital letter: File menu, Edit menu. Access menus by moving the pointer onto the menu name. Do *not* click.

Filenames are printed in all uppercase: FILENAME.DTP, PICTURE.IMG

Text to be typed by you is in bold type: **Desktop Publishing**.

The Equipment You Will Need

Publish It! and Publish It Lite! are designed to run on IBM PC, XT, AT, or PS/2 computers or compatibles. (A Macintosh version is also available.) Publish It! version 2.0 requires a minimum of 640K RAM, one 5 1/4- or 3 1/2-inch floppy drive, and one hard disk. Publish It Lite! and earlier versions of Publish It! can operate with 512K RAM, assuming a CGA graphics card is used. With other graphics adapters, 640K RAM is needed. In either case, a graphics card and two floppy drives or one floppy drive and one hard disk must be part of the system. A monochrome or color monitor can be used. A printer capable of printing graphics is needed. A mouse, while not a necessity, is recommended.

I

An Overview

1

Publish It! Basics

Desktop publishing, although still young, is rapidly revolutionizing virtually every facet of the publishing profession. At first glance, desktop publishing seems merely to simplify the tasks involved in publishing. A closer inspection, however, reveals that by eliminating the need to use scissors and glue for page composition, desktop publishing also spurs the imagination. But even with desktop publishing, in order to proficiently create and produce good quality published material, you still need the right tools and a reasonable degree of skill.

Basically, desktop publishing refers to the design and preparation of documents that, in most instances, will be reproduced and circulated using one of the conventional printing and distribution methods. In other words, desktop publishing refers to the preparation of what in publishing circles is known as *camera-ready copy*.

Desktop publishing is ideally suited to producing newsletters, fliers, announcements, letterhead stationery, business cards, form letters, business forms, invoice forms, display advertisements, in-house publications, technical reports, and educational material. It can also effectively produce brochures, booklets, manuals, directories, presentations, price lists, and technical documentation. Furthermore, it is not unusual for entire magazines and books to be produced using desktop publishing techniques.

The market is literally flooded with desktop publishing software. Some of the programs are easy to use, whereas you may need weeks or even months to become reasonably proficient in the use of others. Much of the appeal of Publish It! and Publish It Lite! is the simplicity of their basic operations. In fact, after working through Chapter 2, "A Trial Run," which should take you about an hour, you'll be ready to create simple documents. Publish It! and Publish It Lite!, despite their ease of use and reasonable price, are powerful and versatile programs. To be able to make full use of all the available features and functions will require study and practice.

Avoid demanding projects at first. If something doesn't seem to work the way you want it to, it could easily sour you on the whole process of desktop publishing. Therefore, begin by producing simple, short documents, and spend as much time as possible experimenting with different ways to use text and graphics. Nothing will be ruined if you make a mistake. You will be able to fix it or, if you worked yourself into what appears to be a dead end, simply abandon your work and start from scratch. The more time you spend playing around with the functions and features of the software, the better your results will be.

Operating Publish It!

This section teaches you how Publish It! and Publish It Lite! operate. You will also learn the principles involved in creating and importing text and graphics.

Frames

Basically, Publish It! and Publish It Lite! operate by creating a series of containers into which text and graphics are poured. The containers, called *frames,* are rectangular and can be any size and dimension—from a full page to a tiny speck just large enough to hold a single character. In addition, Publish It! version 2.0 lets you create all kinds of user-defined odd-shaped frames, capable of producing many unusual effects. (For more on this feature, see the "Text Runaround" portion in the "Options Menu" section in Chapter 4, "The Menus.") Figure 1-1 shows a Publish It! screen with standard rectangular frames in three different sizes. These frames are shown on the screen but do not appear in the printed document. If you want actual printed frames you use the options that create printed borders, which will be discussed in Chapter 2.

Frames can be created as your first step in designing and creating a new document. Then, since they are completely flexible, you can change their width and depth, manipulating them at will to experiment with different layout possibilities. Frames can overlap, thus obscuring part of one or more frames. They can also be stacked, allowing one frame to show through the other. These overlaps can be toggled back and forth to determine which produces the most pleasing result.

After you create the frames, you can select one and import either text or graphics into it. In most instances text and graphics materials are in separate files and are produced by external programs, such as word processors or graphics and computer-aided-design programs. Publish It! also has limited

Figure 1-1. *The Publish It! screen with three frames*

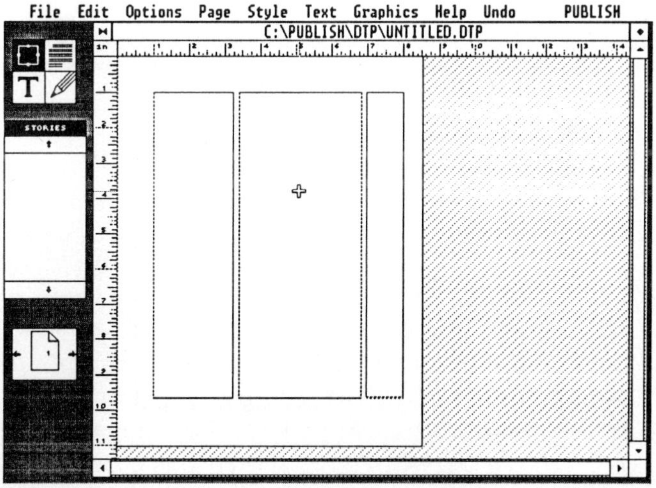

graphics functions that let you create original images and text functions that let you type or edit text in a frame and manipulate or adjust text that was imported from another source. Keep in mind that you can change the dimensions of any of the frames, including those with text or graphics, to accommodate the material and produce the best possible layout.

You can also import text and graphics before you establish frames. In that case the filenames of the imported matter are displayed in a Library window on the screen and then stored for future recall, as shown in Figure 1-2.

Master Pages

Publish It! lets you create *master pages* to use as templates for all pages of a document. Figure 1-3 is a typical master page on which five frames are established. This frame layout is repeated automatically on each succeeding page in the active document. You can produce different master pages for the right and left pages of documents that, because they will be bound, require different margins and possibly different placements of page numbers,

Figure 1-2. *The Library window displaying text filenames*

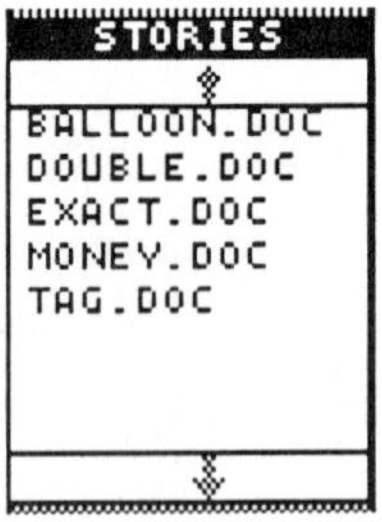

Figure 1-3. *A master page design*

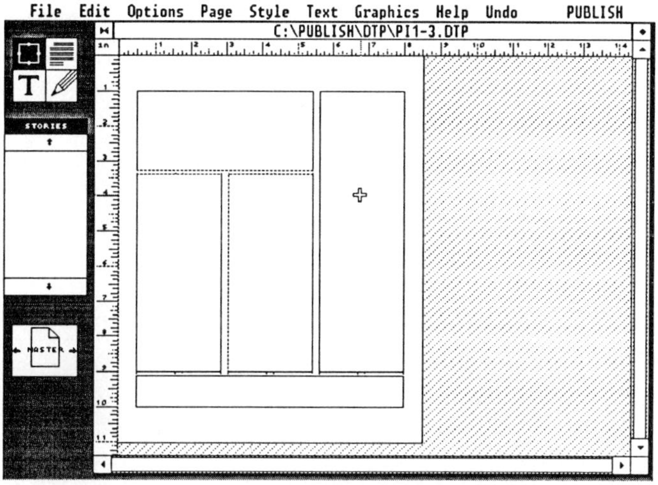

headers, and footers. Figure 1-4 shows typical left and right master pages. Once a master page has been associated with a given document, it is automatically saved with that document and retrieved along with it whenever the document file is opened. For more information on master pages, see Chapter 6, "Importing and Manipulating Text."

Master pages are not available with Publish It Lite!.

Style Sheets

Publish It! includes an option that creates a *style sheet.* Style sheets are files that retain information regarding paper size and *orientation,* that is, *portrait* orientation (with the long side of the paper vertical as is a portrait-style painting) or *landscape* orientation (horizontal). The style sheet file is automatically assigned a .STY extension and contains the commands that determine paper size and orientation. In Figure 1-5, landscape orientation was selected.

Figure 1-4. *Left and right master pages*

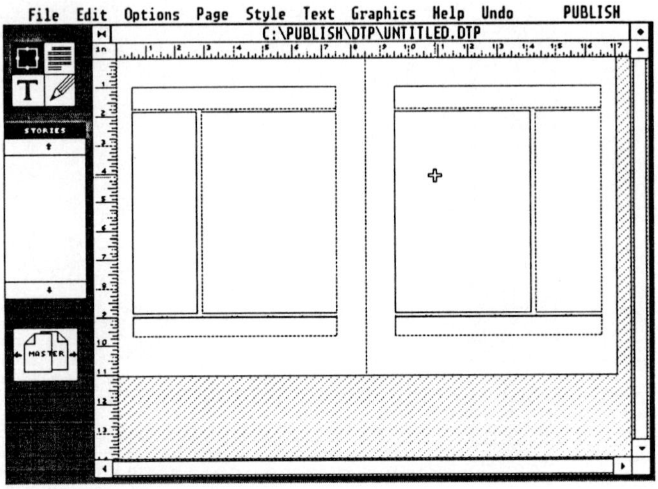

Figure 1-5. *A horizontal page layout*

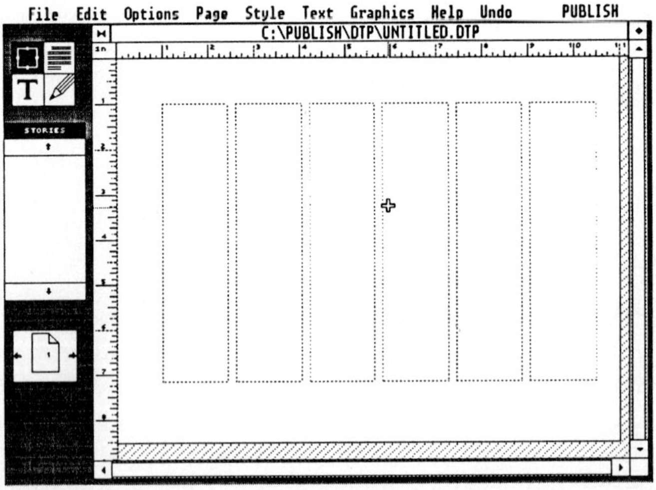

Style sheets also contain the definitions of all paragraph styles used in a document. This allows for a consistent look and style among documents that use the same style sheet. Paragraph styles include information about which type styles, fonts, and similar features you have used for the text in your document. Style sheet files cannot be printed, but they can be loaded at any time, thereby providing the specifications for a new document. For more information on style sheets, see Chapter 6, "Importing and Manipulating Text."

Style sheets are not available with Publish It Lite!.

The GEM/3 Environment

Publish It! and Publish It Lite! operate in the GEM/3 environment. GEM/3 Desktop is a program designed and marketed by Digital Research. Technically, GEM/3 Desktop is an *operating system interface.* It acts as a substitute for the DOS command line and allows you to move, copy, delete, and otherwise manipulate files by moving pictures around on the screen. These pictures, called *icons,* represent both files and directories from DOS. For example, by clicking on the picture of a *folder,* the GEM word for directory, you can display a list of the files in that directory, much like the DOS DIR command. All versions of Publish It! and Publish It Lite! include a ready-to-run version of GEM. As a result, most users will never see the complete GEM Desktop or activate Publish It! by clicking on its icon. Instead, usually you type **PUBLISH** at the DOS prompt.

The GEM operating system also works while a program is running to perform a variety of tasks, such as listing files, deleting them, or showing icons on the screen. Users who have GEM/3 Desktop can run it normally and start Publish It! or Publish It Lite! directly from it. For those who do not have GEM/3 Desktop, a run-time version is included with both programs and is installed automatically along with them. This run-time version takes care of all GEM functions in the programs, just as if the full GEM/3 Desktop were installed. For a detailed description of either type of installation, see Appendix A, "Installation."

Command Structure

Publish It! and Publish It Lite! are *menu driven,* which means they contain a series of menus offering related options. Once an option has been selected, it often produces a *dialog box,* which is a box containing one or more questions for you to answer. Selecting an option also may result in the display of an *item selector box,* which you use to select the name of a file to be accessed or to enter the name of a file you want to save.

Dialog boxes and item selector boxes eliminate the need to learn a lot of specialized commands. At times, however, it can be a bit tricky to figure out how to get to the particular box you need to produce the result you are looking for at the moment. Chapter 4, "The Menus," deals with each of the menus, dialog boxes, and item selector boxes in detail. It explains what they are used for and how each can be accessed.

Word Processors and Text Editors

Publish It! and Publish It Lite! include a <TEXT> option that lets you type text directly into the document. Using this option for anything other than headlines, subheads, picture captions, or very short paragraphs, however, is not practical. Text is best generated by an external word processor or text editor. The manufacturers of Publish It! and Publish It Lite! market Word Writer PRO and Beyond Word Writer, which can be used to generate text files. The different versions of Publish It! also support text produced by a variety of popular word processors:

Quintet	Publish It! 1.1, 1.2, Publish It Lite!
1st Word Plus	Publish It! (all versions)
DCA/RFT	Publish It! 2.0
Microsoft Word 4	Publish It! (all versions)
Microsoft Word 5	Publish It! 2.0
Microsoft Works	Publish It! 2.0
WordPerfect 4	Publish It! (all versions)
WordPerfect 5	Publish It! 2.0
Word Writer 3	Publish It! 2.0
WordStar	Publish It! (all versions)

All versions of Publish It! as well as Publish It Lite! also accept text in the ASCII format regardless of the text editor that was used to produce it. The *ASCII format* is a standardized format for storing plain text documents, allowing such text to be transferred from one program to another.

Editing Imported Text Files

The amount of editing and reformatting that is necessary once an external text file has been imported largely depends on the word processor that was used. Text produced by Word Writer PRO and Beyond Word Writer requires approximately the same amount of formatting as that produced by other types of word processors. Text imported into Publish It! from any of the supported word processors retains such style commands as bold, italic, underline, superscript, and subscript, but formatting such as centered or justified text or font styles and sizes is ignored (but can easily be reestablished using the paragraph options provided by Publish It!).

Text contained in ASCII files must be reformatted. When ASCII files are created, the end of every line that you typed is changed to a hard return (as if you had pressed (ENTER)). Publish It! ignores these hard returns when it imports an ASCII file. This prevents every line in your document from being treated as a separate paragraph. To create paragraphs where you want them, load the ASCII file into your word processor and save it in that word processor's basic format. By using these steps, the line and paragraph breaks are retained when the document is transferred from the word processor into Publish It!.

Text editors that are included in most programming language packages, such as Turbo Pascal, C, Turbo Prolog, Turbo BASIC, and Microsoft's QuickBASIC and QuickC, produce straight ASCII files. When such ASCII files are imported directly into Publish It!, hard returns are ignored (they must be doubled in order to be recognized). The entire text appears as one big mess that is then reworked by the <TEXT> option in Publish It!. For that reason you will always want to import such files into your word processor before using them with Publish It!.

There may be occasions when you want to use a text file that was produced in a format that is not supported by the version of Publish It! you are using. In that case, you could use one of the file-conversion programs that are included with some of the word processors. WordPerfect includes a program appropriately called CONVERT.EXE that converts ASCII and many other types of files to files that WordPerfect can handle. Beyond Word Writer includes a program called EXCHANGE that is used for this purpose. With a few exceptions, the files are converted in the format in which they were originally written, requiring a minimum of editing. The exceptions are some of the more esoteric features of programs like WordPerfect and WordStar, which don't seem to fare well during these conversion processes.

The Hardware

Desktop publishing places considerable importance on the *hardware*—the individual components constituting your computer system. For basic computer uses, such as word processing and database or spreadsheet management, the power of your hardware is usually not critical. By contrast, because desktop publishing makes extensive use of graphics, the hardware you use will determine to a certain extent how well your desktop system works.

The Computer

Publish It! and Publish It Lite! are designed to run on IBM PC, XT, AT, or PS/2 computers or compatibles. (A Macintosh version is also available.) Publish It! version 2.0 requires a minimum of 640K RAM, one 5 1/4- or 3 1/2-inch floppy drive, and one hard disk. Publish It Lite! and earlier versions of Publish It! require 512K RAM (with 640K recommended) and either two floppy drives or one floppy drive and one hard disk.

The Monitor

Most of the standard monitors that are being used for word processing and other applications programs do a less than brilliant job of displaying detailed graphics. Screen resolution is measured in *pixels,* or dots per inch, and the number of pixels per square inch on a particular monitor may be inadequate to provide a meaningful presentation of documents created in the desktop publishing environment. The quality of your screen resolution is largely dependent on the graphics adapter (see the next section, "The Graphics Adapter").

In addition, monitors usually display only a small portion of the page that is being worked on, making it difficult to get a clear idea of what the final result is going to look like. This is not to say that such monitors cannot be used for desktop publishing. It just makes it a bit more difficult. Some monitors can display entire pages in their actual size and even two facing pages at once. These are expensive, however, so it is up to the individual user to determine whether such an investment is justified. (The illustrations in this book that display screen images are taken from a standard color monitor.)

The Graphics Adapter

A *graphics adapter,* or *graphics card,* is a plug-in circuit board that allows a computer to produce and display graphics. Graphics adapters currently on the market cover a wide range of prices and performance. Some are monochrome and others are color adapters. Their quality is largely based on the number of pixels per square inch–the more the better. Which one you choose depends on how much money you want to spend and what degree of sophistication you expect in the documents you produce using desktop publishing techniques.

Basically, graphics adapters are divided into CGA, EGA, VGA, and Hercules cards. CGA is an adequate but not exceptional color graphics adapter. When it is used, all work done with Publish It! and Publish It Lite! appears on the screen in black and white. EGA and VGA cards are higher quality color graphics adapters that display the Publish It! screen in a variety of colors. While this is not particularly necessary, it does result in a display that is easier to read. Hercules is a monochrome adapter; it does not create multicolor displays. Publish It! is able to work with almost all makes and models of popular graphics adapters.

The Printer

Virtually all desktop publishing involves producing camera-ready material that is subsequently copied and multiplied using offset printing or similar techniques. The quality of your original printed desktop publishing document is of overriding importance, which means your printer must be capable of producing high-quality hard copies.

Printers fall into five categories: daisy wheel, dot matrix, laser, ink jet, and PostScript. For desktop publishing, *daisy wheel printers* can be immediately eliminated. They are incapable of printing graphics or the fonts produced by desktop publishing software.

Dot-matrix printers come in 9-pin and 24-pin models. The 9-pin models produce fairly crude graphics; the 24-pin models do a pretty good job. One advantage of dot-matrix printers is their speed. Printing speeds of up to 300 characters per second (cps) are not unusual. Dot-matrix printers are reasonably priced and are manufactured by many companies.

Laser printers produce the highest quality hard copies, ideal for use as camera-ready copy. They are expensive, although the prices have been coming down. These printers use ink contained in cartridges that can generally print about 4000 pages, depending on the amount of ink used per page. Replacement or recharging of these cartridges is also expensive, although with the increasing popularity of laser printers and the associated competition, these prices are also beginning to come down.

Ink jet printers are a fairly recent addition. They are less expensive than laser printers and can do a comparable job. They sometimes require the use of special paper, which adds to the cost if paper is used in great quantity. Ink jet printers are manufactured as black-and-white and color printers.

PostScript printers differ somewhat from the others mentioned here. Publish It! 2.0 can work with a PostScript printer if such a printer has been selected using the INSTALL and FONTWID programs. In that case one of the advantages is that the printer uses the Adobe 35 set of fonts. Earlier versions of Publish It! (except Publish It Lite!) can produce files for PostScript-compatible printers but the PostScript output must be captured in a disk file that can then be taken to a professional print shop or service bureau for actual typeset quality output.

The Input Device

An input device is any means by which you communicate with your computer. Your keyboard is one type of input device. A mouse is another, and throughout this book it is assumed that a mouse is part of the computer system that you are using. All versions of Publish It! as well as Publish It Lite! can be operated without a mouse; however, if no input device other than a keyboard is available, accessing functions and executing commands in Publish It! or Publish It Lite! becomes unnecessarily tedious. Therefore, a mouse or similar input device such as one of the new trackball systems is definitely recommended.

The Software

Publish It!, like all desktop publishing software, is designed to be used in conjunction with a wide assortment of other software to produce or provide the material comprising your documents. You use word-processing software to produce your text, and there are many types of spreadsheet and database software that you may already be using in your business. The results obtained with these programs can be imported into Publish It! and integrated into your printed documents. There are also paint programs that you can use to produce your original graphics designs, logos, and other images. You can use programs that specialize in producing business graphics such as graphs, pie charts, and bar and line charts. Computer-aided-design (CAD) programs, depending on their sophistication, often can produce two-dimensional and three-dimensional scientific and architectural designs. Other programs let you produce freehand illustrations.

Clip-art collections are graphic images that can be imported by other programs and used in all kinds of documents. There are literally hundreds of such programs, some offering general subjects and others concentrating on technical graphics, such as electrical symbols, architectural symbols, and symbols dealing with plumbing, chemistry, mathematics, medicine and anatomy, and zoology. Some collections include pictures of every conceivable animal; maps of the U.S., the 50 states, and the world and individual countries; flags; banners; vehicles; road signs; and much more. The diversity of the available clip art boggles the mind.

Not all clip-art collections can be used with all desktop publishing programs. However, you can usually identify which clip art is compatible with your desktop publishing program by the filename extensions. For instance, clip-art files with .IMG and .PCX extensions can be used by Publish It! and Publish It Lite!. Some collections use the .PCC extension, representing a format that in some but not all instances is identical to .PCX and can be used without prior conversion or renaming. Some files with the .PIC extension, such as the ones generated by Lotus 1-2-3, Quattro, and Quattro Pro, are vector graphics and are compatible with Publish It!, whereas certain others are bit-mapped and may not work. Chapter 4, "The Menus," gives detailed information on clip-art filename extensions that are accepted by Publish It!.

Font libraries are software programs that offer huge varieties in font styles and sizes. Some can be used in conjunction with Publish It!, but many cannot. Also, not all are compatible with all printers. Great care should be taken in making certain that the font source you purchase works with your desktop publishing program and printer. Chapter 5, "The Publish It! Libraries," covers fonts and how to use them.

Programs that generate scientific symbols, when used with word processing programs, let you use the keyboard to generate symbols used in scientific and mathematical equations. Some of these programs produce the symbols in graphics formats that are stored with the .PCX extension. They are printed automatically when a document produced by a word processor is sent to the printer.

Unless you are blessed with unlimited funds, try not to become a software junkie. Make sure that you know exactly what you really need, and then try to find the best program to fill that need. Chapter 9, "Using External Files," discusses the use of external programs in conjunction with Publish It!.

2

A Trial Run

This chapter is for readers who would like a quick hands-on tour of Publish It! or Publish It Lite!. By following the series of steps presented here, you will create the simple one-page document shown in Figure 2-1 using the EXAMPLE text file included in both software packages. (At any time during the exercise, you can save your work, quit, and then return to it later. Steps 60 and 61 save your document, and step 62 tells you how to reactivate the program after a shutdown.)

The illustrations in this chapter may differ slightly from the results you obtain, depending on which type of video display and printer are installed with your system. Also, if you are not using a mouse, be sure to review the section in the Publish It! or Publish It Lite! manual on using the program with the keyboard only. In addition, users of earlier versions of Publish It! and Publish It Lite! who do not have a hard disk may find that some of the steps involved may be different.

1. Start Publish It! or Publish It Lite! by typing **PUBLISH** or **LITE** at the root directory prompt of your disk drive (C:\ >, for example) and pressing ENTER.

Figure 2-1. *The document used in this chapter*

Desktop Publishing

Another First From Timeworks

Timeworks Inc. of Northbrook, Illinois, announces a professional-quality Desktop Publishing package for the IBM PC. The program, called Publish It!, is a full featured, fully integrated desktop publisher for the IBM PC, PS/2 and compatible computers.

Breakthrough

Publish It! is a very exciting breakthrough in performence and ease of use with a feature list that rivals that of Ventura or PageMaker, but is especially designed to get the user up and running in less than one hour.

It's Packed With Features!

Only Publish It! gives you all the DTP features you want, including fully integrated word processing, page layout, and graphics:

- Frame-based page layout
- Five zoom modes
- Style sheets
- Wide range of fonts supplied
- Multiple text styles
- Direct text input and editing
- Styled text imported from Word Writer, 1st Word Plus, Word Perfect, Wordstar, Microsoft Word, and MS-Works
- ASCII text imported from other word processors
- Automatic justification
- Automatic hyphenation
- Text block cut, paste, copy, and restyle
- Drawn, painted, and scanned picture import
- Picture scaling and cropping
- Automatic text runaround
- Image editing mode
- Graphics drawing mode
- Wide range of printers supported
- Fonts, Point Sizes, and Text Styles

A huge range of different faces is available for use with Publish It! For example, many different faces can be generated using Serif and Sans fonts alone!

Here are just a few examples:

- 20 point Drury Lane
- 20 point Sans
- 20 point Courier bold
- 16 point Serif light

- 24 point Madison underline
- 20 point Sans italic
- 14 point Sans italic superscript
- 20 point Serif italic
- 18 point Ravinia
- 10 point Sans
- 7 point Serif
- 36 point Serif

2. After a brief pause, the Publish It! or Publish It Lite! title page appears and then is replaced by the initial working screen shown in Figure 2-2.

At this point you have several options. You can import text immediately, in which case the text remains in memory until you decide where to put it. You can create a page layout and then import text directly into a selected portion of that page. If the document to be created consists of more than one page, you can create a master page, the layout of which is used automatically by all pages in the document.

Master pages are not available with Publish It Lite!.

Since the document you create in this chapter is only one page, start by importing the text. (If you are using Publish It Lite!, some of the screen displays shown here may appear slightly different. For details of these differences, see Chapter 4, "The Menus.")

Figure 2-2. *The initial working screen*

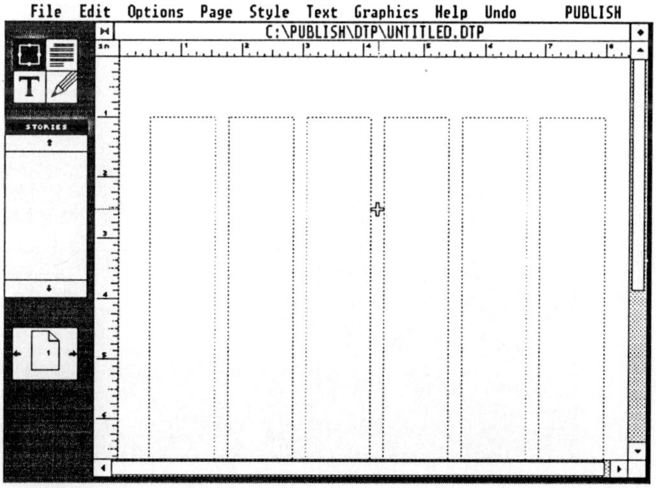

Figure 2-3. *The File menu with <Import text> selected*

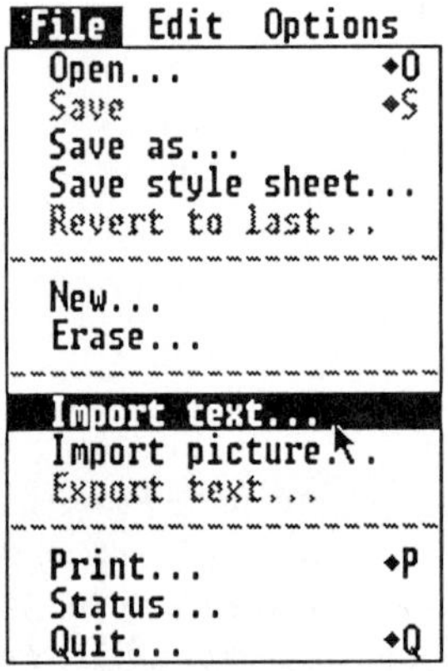

3. Select the File menu and click on <Import text>, as shown in Figure 2-3.
4. A dialog box appears displaying the different types of text you can import directly (see Figure 2-4). Since the EXAMPLE text file was

Figure 2-4. *The Import Text dialog box*

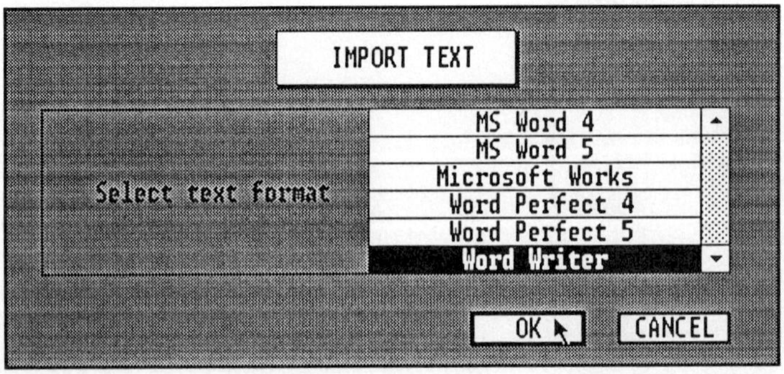

created in Publish It! version 2.0 using Word Writer PRO, highlight Word Writer and click on <OK> or press (ENTER). If the desired text file format is not shown, click on the up or down indicators to scroll through the 12 available file formats.

5. A new Item Selector box appears showing the options <EXAMPLE> and <PARTY.ASC>. Highlight <EXAMPLE> and click on <OK> (see Figure 2-5).
6. After a few moments the word "EXAMPLE" appears in the Library window, which is titled STORIES, as illustrated in Figure 2-6.

You have imported a file of text, but so far there is no place to put it. The next few steps involve designing the page.

7. Open the Page menu, highlight <Size to fit>, and click on it to select it, as shown in Figure 2-7.
8. The screen changes to show the full page on the left half, represented by six dotted rectangles. The rectangles are guides that simplify the creation of frames that will contain text and graphics.

Figure 2-5. *The Item Selector box displaying filenames*

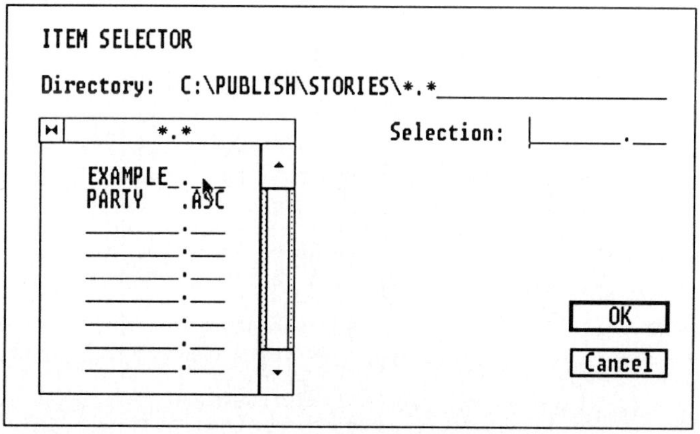

Figure 2-6. *The selected filename displayed in the Library window*

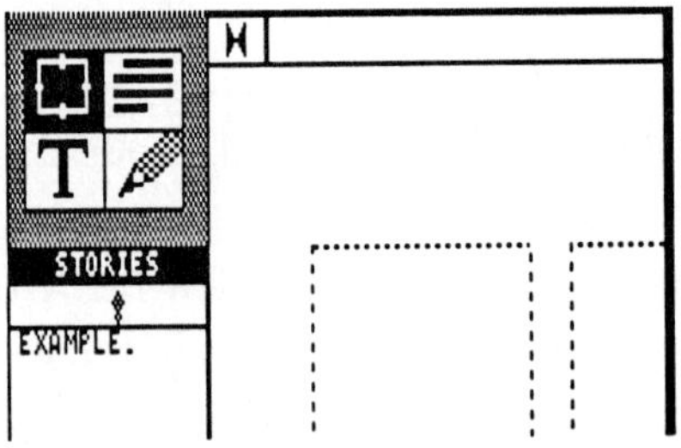

The pointer is an open cross, and the <FRAME> icon in the toolbox is highlighted, which indicates that you are in the <FRAME> mode, as shown in Figure 2-8. Move the pointer to the upper-left corner of the left rectangle, press the mouse button, and hold it down while dragging the mouse down to the lower-right corner of the second dotted rectangle. Release the mouse button. You now have a frame

Figure 2-7. *The Page menu*

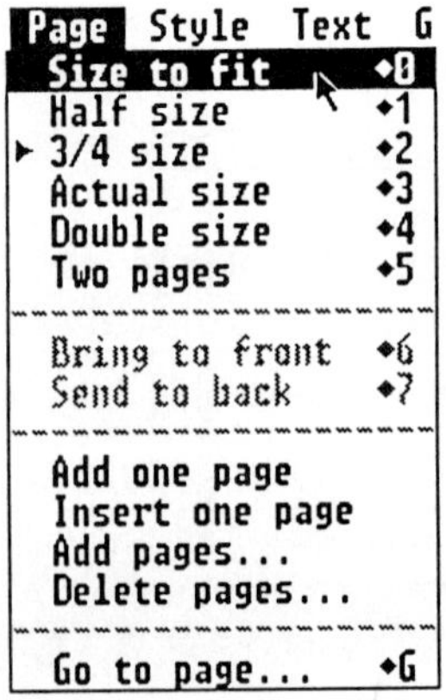

Figure 2-8. *A full page displayed in <FRAME> mode*

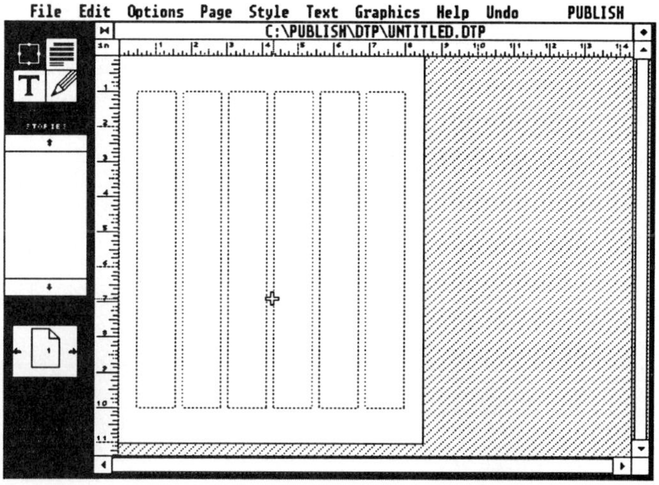

encompassing the two left rectangles. The frame has little boxes, known as *handles,* on the corners and the sides. These handles indicate that the frame is currently selected, as shown in Figure 2-9.

9. Repeat step 8, this time starting at the upper-left corner of the third rectangle and dragging the mouse to the lower-right corner of the far right rectangle, thus creating a new frame twice as wide as the one produced previously. The handles will move from the periphery of the first frame to the second frame, as shown in Figure 2-10.
10. Move the pointer to a position anywhere inside the first frame and click the mouse button to select it. Note that the handles reappear around the first frame.
11. Move the pointer to EXAMPLE in the Library window to the left and click on it. After a moment the left frame is filled either with very small and probably illegible type, as shown in Figure 2-11, or with gray lines representing the actual text (this is called *greeked format*).

Figure 2-9. *The first frame occupying two column guides*

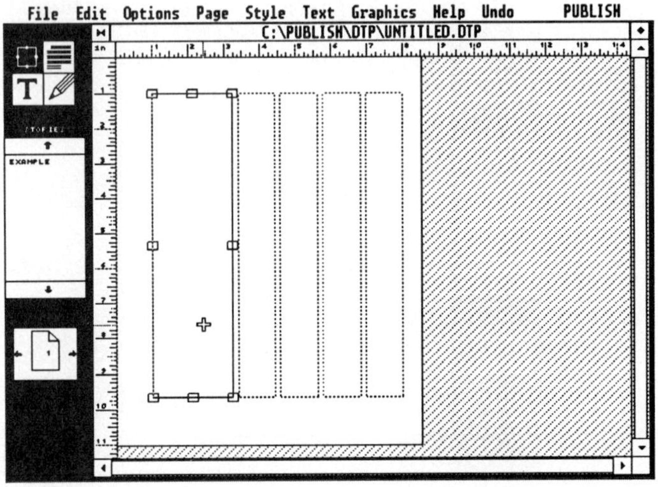

Figure 2-10. *A second frame occupying four column guides*

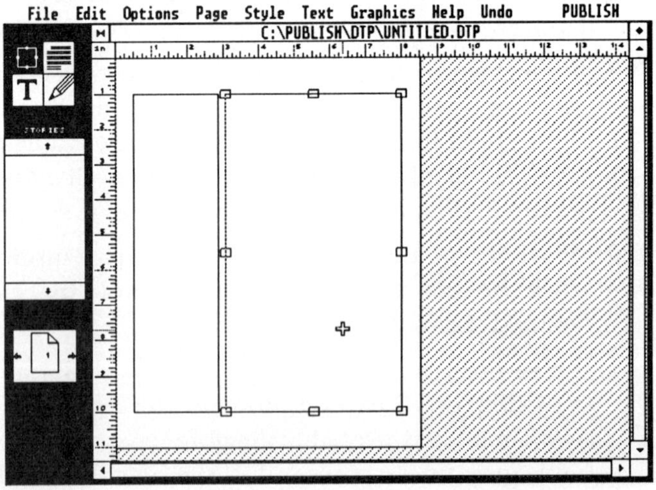

2

Figure 2-11. *Text poured into the selected frame*

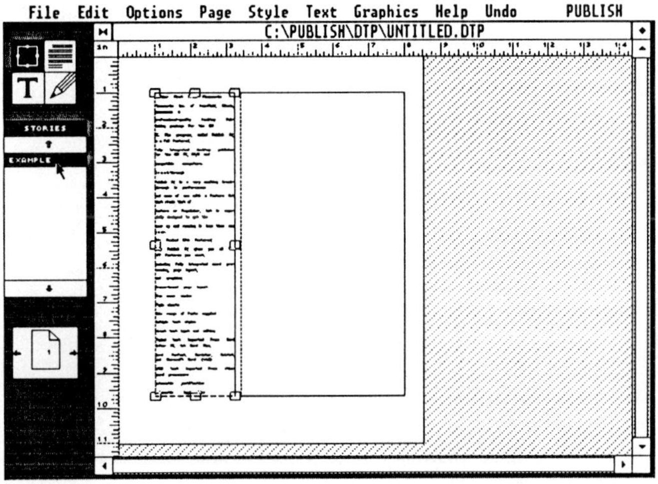

12. Move the pointer anywhere inside the second frame and click the mouse button to select that frame.
13. Once again click on EXAMPLE. Figure 2-12 shows how the rest of the text is imported into the second frame.

The text representing the EXAMPLE document has been "poured" into the two frames. The following steps show how to format the text to produce an attractive final result. To begin, you might want to read the actual text.

14. Click on the left frame to select it, and then open up the Page menu and click on <Double size>. After a few moments the text is displayed on the screen in the readable size shown in Figure 2-13. You can move around the page by placing the pointer on the scroll bars at the lower and right edges, holding down the mouse button, and moving the bars.

Publish It Lite! users skip to step 15L. Publish It! users continue with step 15.

Figure 2-12. *Balance of text poured into the second frame*

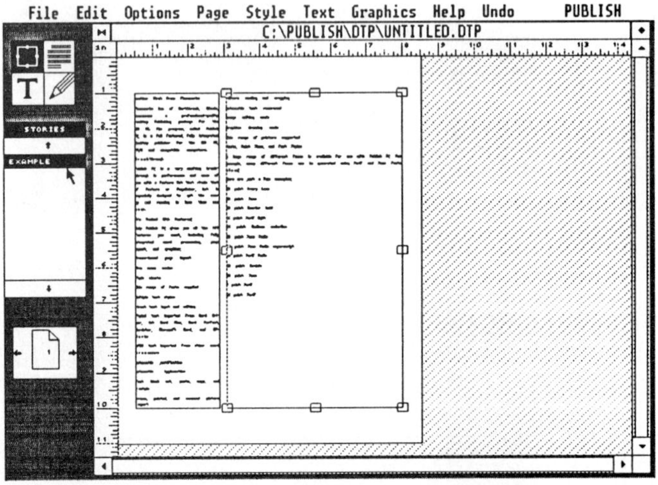

Figure 2-13. *Text displayed in double size*

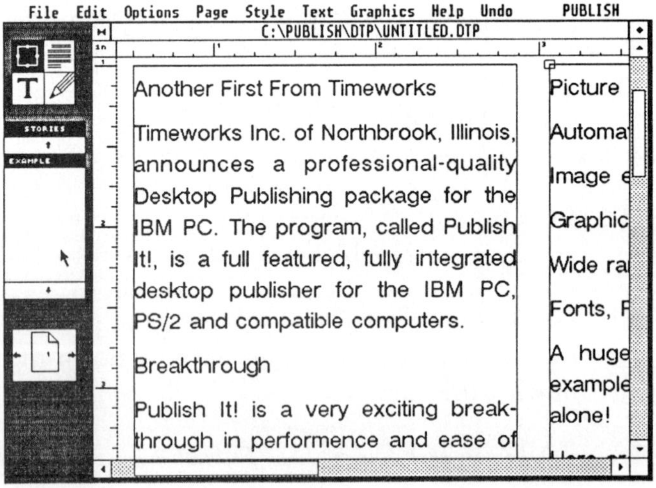

15. To produce the final document, you first create a distinctive headline. Place the pointer on the <PARAGRAPH> icon in the toolbox (the upper-right square) and click on it. The icon is now highlighted, and a number of options are listed in the Library window, as shown in Figure 2-14.
16. As you move the pointer into the work space, notice that the pointer has changed to the paragraph symbol, illustrated in Figure 2-15.
17. Move the pointer onto the first word, "Another," and click on it. The entire paragraph, which represents the headline, is highlighted. As Figure 2-16 shows, BODY TEXT is also highlighted in the Library window for the paragraph style.
18. Move the pointer to the HEADLINE selection in the Library window and click on it. The highlighted paragraph is reformatted to huge letters, making the headline too large to be seen in its entirety. Figure 2-17 shows the result.

Publish It! users skip to step 19. Publish It Lite! users continue with step 15L.

Figure 2-14. *<PARAGRAPH> mode accessed*

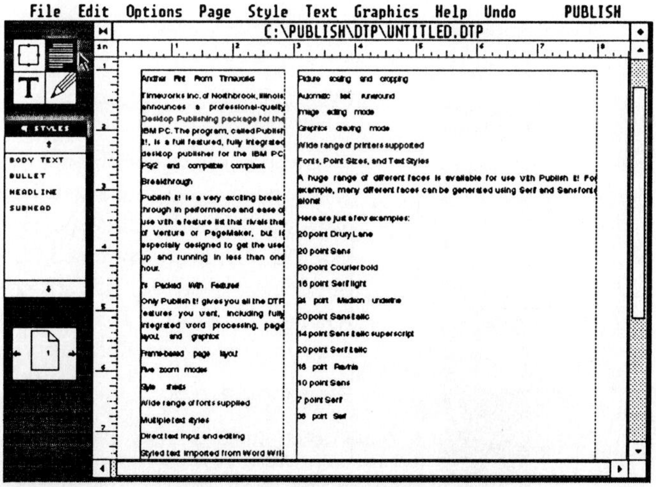

Figure 2-15. *Pointer in the shape of a paragraph symbol*

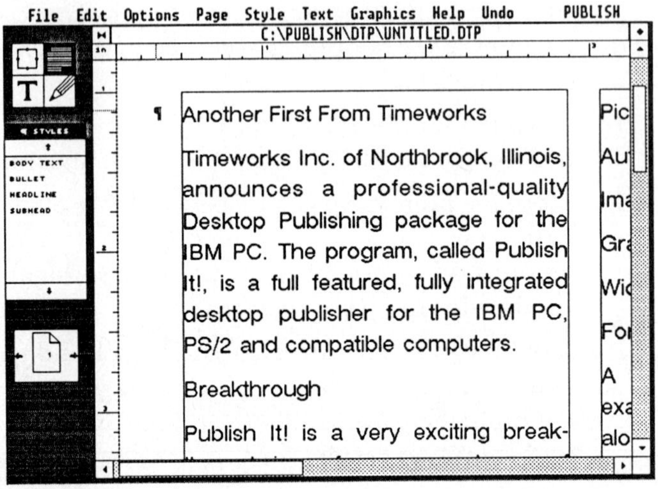

Figure 2-16. *First paragraph selected, with BODY TEXT selected as paragraph style*

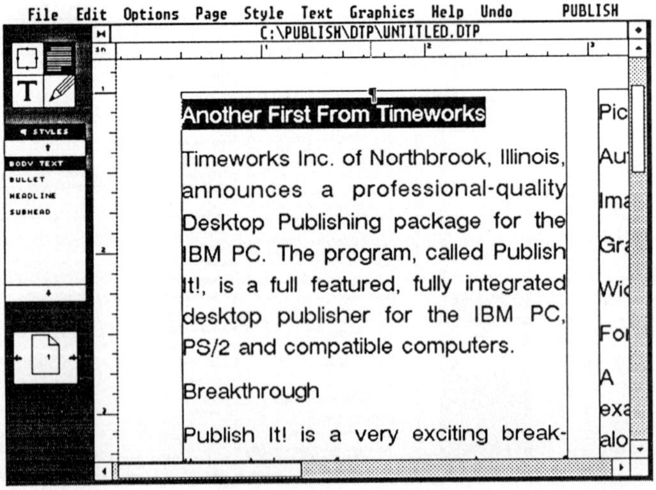

Figure 2-17. *Headline style selected*

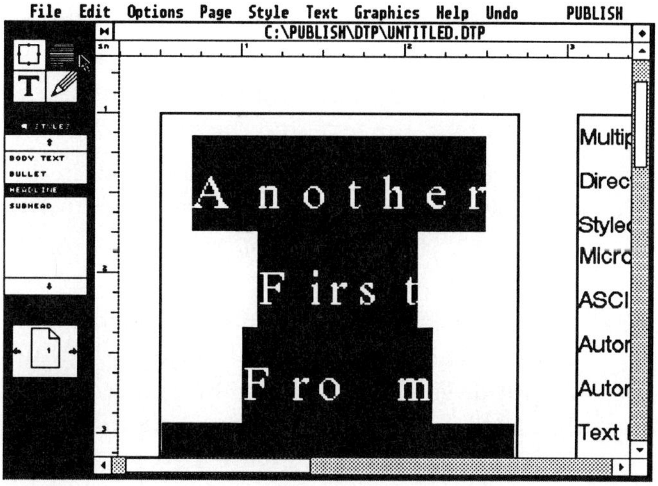

15L. One of the first steps in producing the final document is creating a distinctive headline. Place the pointer on the <TEXT> icon in the lower-left portion of the toolbox, and click on it. The icon is now highlighted.

16L. As you move the pointer into the work space, notice that the pointer has changed to the I-beam shape.

17L. Move the pointer to the beginning of the first word, "Another," hold down the mouse button, and drag the mouse until the entire line, "Another First From Timeworks," is highlighted, as shown in Figure 2-16.

18L. Select <Font/size> from the Style menu and click on <DUTCH>, <36>, and <OK>. The highlighted paragraph is reformatted to appear in huge letters, making the headline too large to be seen in its entirety, as illustrated in Figure 2-17.

Both Publish It! and Publish It Lite! users continue with step 19.

19. Open the Page menu and click on <Actual size>. After a moment the display is reformatted to show a portion of the page in actual size, as seen in Figure 2-18. Obviously there is something wrong. That leftover "s" cannot be left hanging on a line of its own.
20. Open the Page menu and click on <Size to fit>. The full page with both frames, the text, and the enlarged headline is shown.
21. Move the pointer to the <FRAME> icon in the toolbox and click on it. Now move the pointer to anywhere inside the right frame and click on it. The handles reappear, indicating that the frame has been selected.
22. Move the pointer to the center-left handle and hold down the mouse button. The pointer changes to a hand with a pointing finger, as shown in Figure 2-19. Drag the pointer to the right until the frame has been reduced to half its width and release the mouse button. The result is shown in Figure 2-20.
23. Move the pointer to anywhere inside the left frame; click to select it. Now move the pointer to the center-right handle on the left frame.

Figure 2-18. *Actual size display of headline*

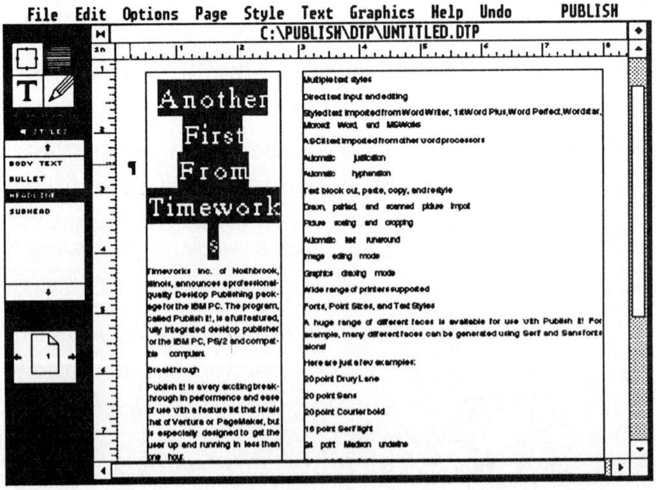

Figure 2-19. *The right frame selected with the pointer in the shape of a hand*

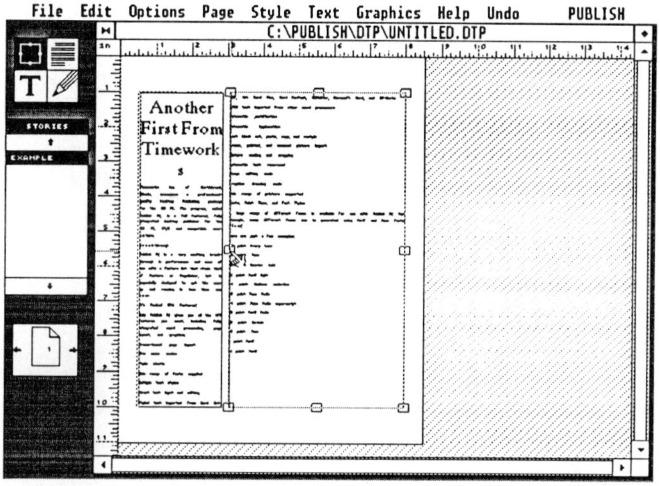

Figure 2-20. *The right frame narrowed*

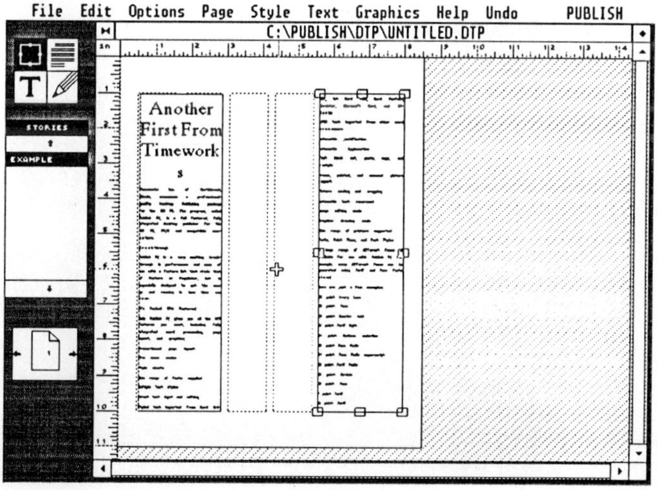

Click and hold down the mouse button while dragging the mouse to the right. The width of the frame is increased to twice its original size. Let go of the mouse button. You now have a wide frame on the left and a narrow one on the right, as shown in Figure 2-21. Note that the leftover "s" has moved into its correct position and the rest of the text has been reformatted to fit into the new frame sizes.

In the next few steps you will create subheads in a character format that differentiates them from the body text. After that, you can set off the items in the second half of the document by placing a bullet in front of each.

Publish It Lite! users skip to step 24L. Publish It! users continue here.

24. In the Page menu, click on <Actual size>. Move the pointer to the toolbox and highlight the <PARAGRAPH> icon by clicking on it.
25. Place the pointer anywhere on the word "Breakthrough" in the text and click on it. The word is now highlighted.

Figure 2-21. *The left frame widened*

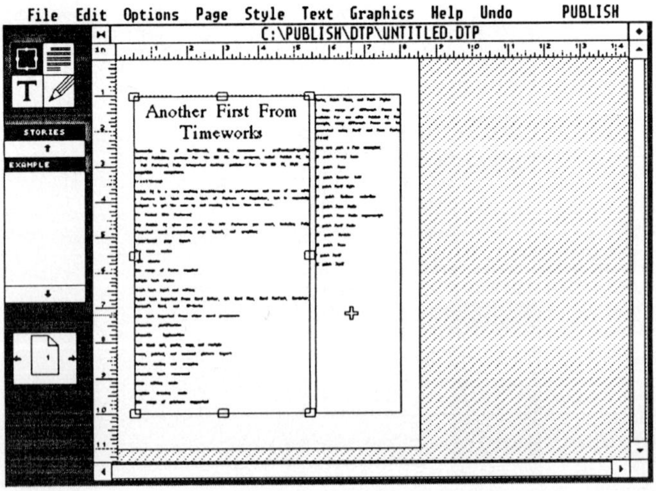

26. Move the pointer to the option SUBHEAD in the Library window and click on it. The highlighted word "Breakthrough" now appears in the larger type, as shown in Figure 2-22.
27. Move the pointer anywhere on the subhead "It's Packed With Features!," and click on it to highlight it. If the phrase is not visible on the screen, use the scroll bars to make it appear, and then change the paragraph style.
28. Repeat step 26.
29. Now place the pointer anywhere on the line "Frame-based page layout," and click on it to highlight that line.
30. Move the pointer into the Library window and highlight BULLET. Click on it to insert a bullet and move the line of text to the right. Figure 2-23 shows the result.
31. Repeat steps 29 and 30 for the next 17 items. A bullet is placed in front of each line or group of lines until the line "Fonts, Point Sizes, and Text Styles" has been changed.
32. Skip the paragraph starting with "A huge range" and the line "Here are just a few examples:," and then change each of the following lines

Figure 2-22. *The headline and subhead displayed*

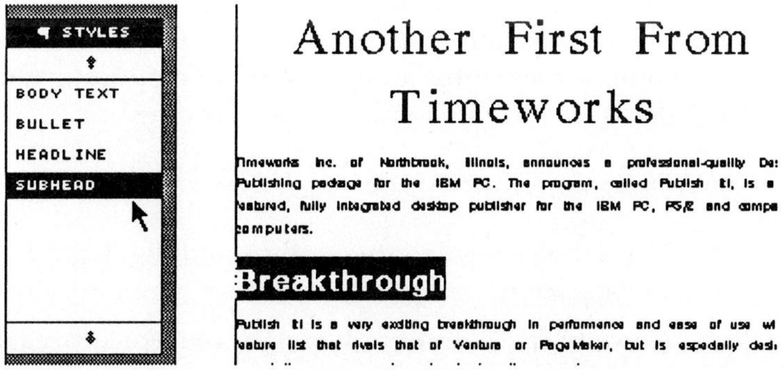

Figure 2-23. *A bullet placed to the left of indented text*

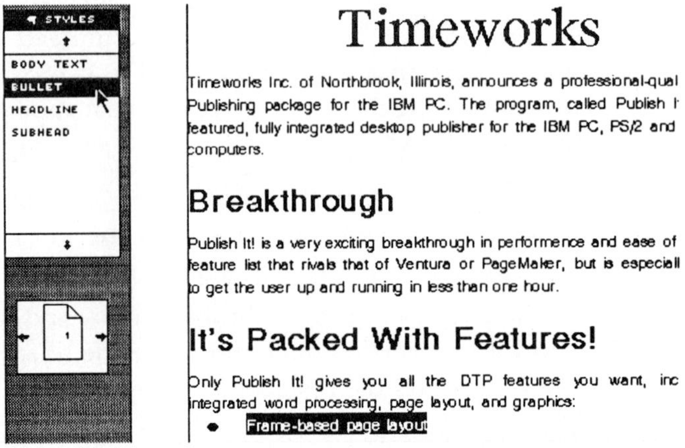

into the bullet paragraph style. Figure 2-24 illustrates that you now have a fairly unattractive page. It also shows that when bullets are added to multiple-line items, the second and subsequent lines are indented.

At this point, just to play it safe, you may want to save your work. Access the File menu and click on <Save as>. In the resulting Item Selector box, remove UNTITLED.DTP by pressing (ESC). Then type **EXAMPLE1** and click on <OK>. Publish It! automatically adds the .DTP extension. Now if there is a power failure or any other unexpected interruption, your work is saved as EXAMPLE1.DTP and can be recalled at any time.

Publish It! users skip to step 33. Publish It Lite! users continue here.

24L. Move the pointer to the toolbox and highlight the <TEXT> icon by clicking on it.

25L. Now use the pointer to highlight the word "Breakthrough."

Figure 2-24. *The text as it would now be printed*

Another First From Timeworks

Timeworks Inc. of Northbrook, Illinois, announces a professional-quality Desktop Publishing package for the IBM PC. The program, called Publish It!, is a full featured, fully integrated desktop publisher for the IBM PC, PS/2 and compatible computers.

Breakthrough

Publish It! is a very exciting breakthrough in performence and ease of use with a feature list that rivals that of Ventura or PageMaker, but is especially designed to get the user up and running in less than one hour.

It's Packed With Features!

Only Publish It! gives you all the DTP features you want, including fully integrated word processing, page layout, and graphics:

- Frame-based page layout
- Five zoom modes
- Style sheets
- Wide range of fonts supplied
- Multiple text styles
- Direct text input and editing
- Styled text imported from Word Writer, 1st Word Plus, Word Perfect, Wordstar, Microsoft Word, and MS-Works
- ASCII text imported from other word processors
- Automatic justification
- Automatic hyphenation
- Text block cut, paste, copy, and restyle
- Drawn, painted, and scanned picture import
- Picture scaling and cropping
- Automatic text runaround
- Image editing mode
- Graphics drawing mode
- Wide range of printers supported
- Fonts, Point Sizes, and Text Styles

A huge range of different faces is available for use with Publish It! For example, many different faces can be generated using Serif and Sans fonts alone!

Here are just a few examples:

- 20 point Drury Lane
- 20 point Sans
- 20 point Courier bold
- 16 point Serif light
- 24 point Madison underline
- 20 point Sans italic
- 14 point Sans italic super-script
- 20 point Serif italic
- 18 point Ravinia
- 10 point Sans
- 7 point Serif
- 36 point Serif

26L. Click on <Font/size> in the Style menu and on <20> and <OK> to make the font style and size used for the section heading 20-point Swiss.

27L. Now click on BOLD in the Library window. The highlighted word, "Breakthrough," appears in the larger type, as shown in Figure 2-22.

28L. Repeat the above steps with the subhead "It's Packed With Features!"

29L. Highlight the line "Frame-based page layout."

30L. Click on <Bullet justified> in the Paragraph menu to insert a bullet and move the line of text to the right, as shown in Figure 2-23.

31L. Repeat steps 29L and 30L for the next 17 items to place a bullet in front of each line or group of lines.

32L. Skip down the text past the paragraph starting with "A huge range..." and the line "Here are just a few examples:." Place bullets in front of the remaining lines. You now have the fairly unattractive page shown in Figure 2-24.

Publish It! and Publish It Lite! users, continue from here.

In the steps that follow you will import a picture, place it on the page, add a headline to the top of the page, and then adjust the size of the imported picture until the copy in the right-hand column goes to the bottom of the page. Like text, graphics must be poured into a frame. Even though it is possible to import a picture before placing a frame for it in the document, this time you'll do it the other way around.

33. Move the pointer into the toolbox area and click on the <FRAME> icon. Move the pointer back into the work area. Note that it has changed back to an open cross. If you are not in <Actual size>, open the Page menu and select it by clicking on it.

34. Place the pointer to the right of the word "performance" in the line below "Breakthrough" and hold down the mouse button while dragging the mouse down about two inches and to the right of the right frame. This creates a new frame. Figure 2-25 shows that the handles on the frame indicate it is selected. At this point the size of the new frame is unimportant.

Figure 2-25. *A new frame created*

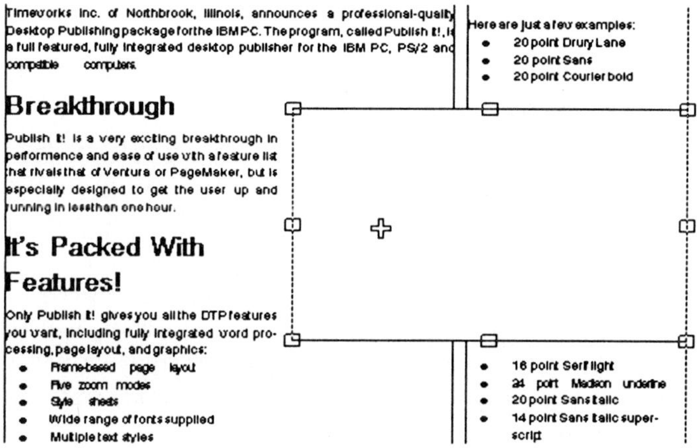

35. Open the Page menu and click on <Half size> so you can see most of the page but still recognize some of the larger text.

Publish It Lite! users, click on <Size to fit>. You will see the page in its entirety.

36. If the handles are no longer displayed around the new frame, select the frame by placing the pointer anywhere inside it and clicking on it. The handles will reappear. If the right edge of the selected frame does not extend to the right edge of the right text frame, place the pointer on the right-center handle and hold the mouse button down while dragging the mouse to the right until the right edge of the frame is at the right edge of the right column. Let go of the mouse button. To center your new frame vertically on your screen, you may use the right scroll bar to move it down a bit.
37. Place the pointer on the center handle at the bottom of the frame and adjust the bottom edge, as in step 36. Finally, move the pointer to the left-center handle until you have an approximately square

frame. Figure 2-26 shows that the text is moved around the new frame each time its dimensions are changed.

38. Open the File menu and click on <Import picture> to select that option, as in Figure 2-27.
39. A dialog box appears asking you to identify the type of graphics file you want to import. Move the pointer to <GEM Paint (.IMG)> to highlight it and click on <OK>, as shown in Figure 2-28.
40. An Item Selector box appears, indicating the active subdirectory is PICTURES. Two files, MONALISA.IMG and TIGER.IMG are displayed. You may choose either of these, but for this trial run, one of the other available clip-art files is selected. It was saved in the subdirectory ARTWORK. Click on the Directory: line shown in Figure 2-29 and, using the (LEFT ARROW) key, move the cursor past the backslash (\). Then erase PICTURES and type **ARTWORK**. The selection of available graphics files appears.

Figure 2-26. *The new frame enlarged*

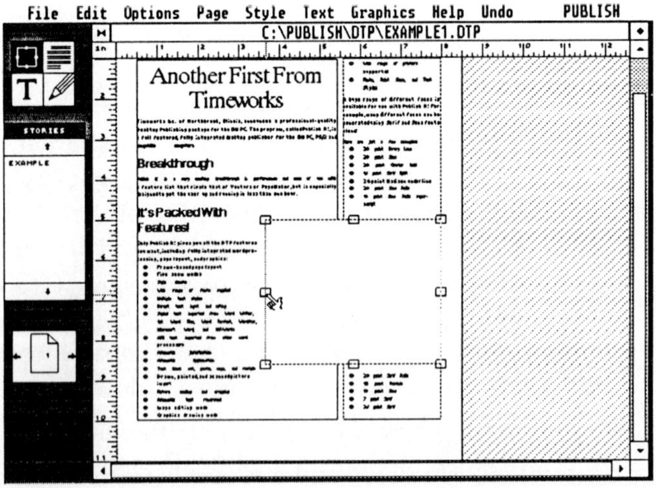

Figure 2-27. *The File menu with <Import picture> selected*

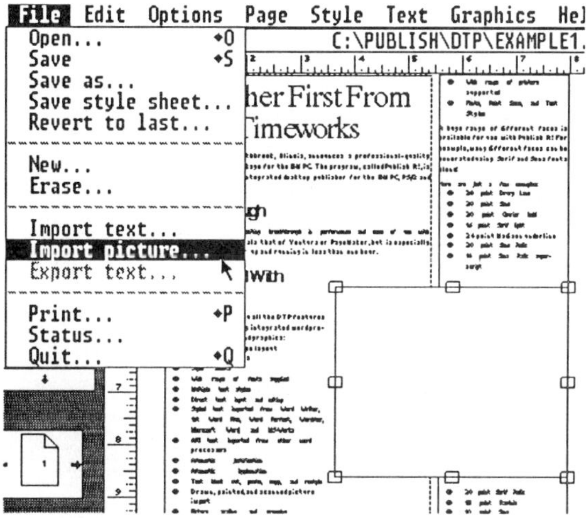

Figure 2-28. *The Import Picture dialog box*

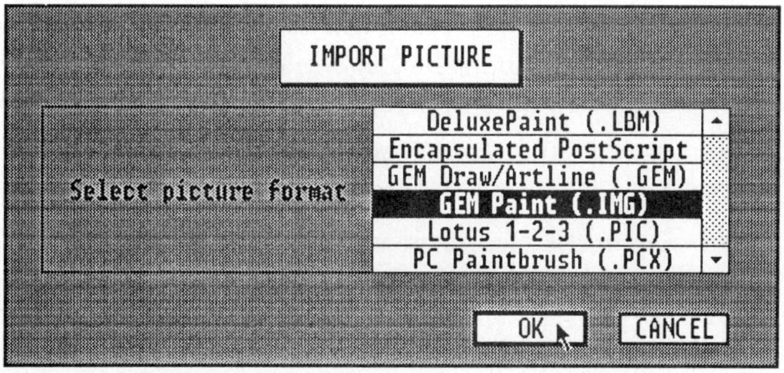

Figure 2-29. *The Item Selector box displaying available directories*

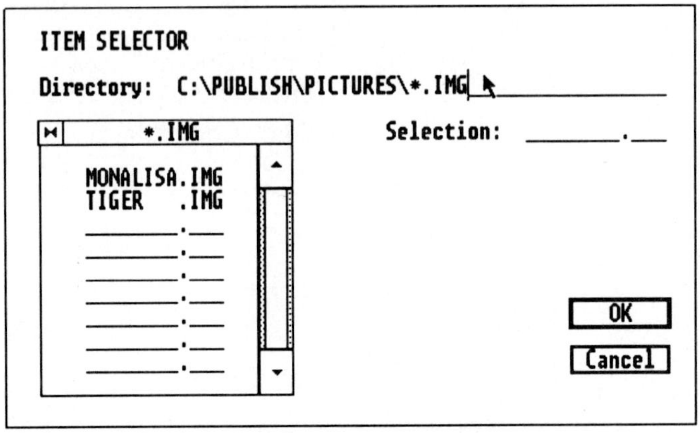

41. Use the scroll bar to display SKYLINE.IMG. Highlight it, and click on <OK> as shown in Figure 2-30. Other versions of Publish It! may display just a list of the available directories. In that case, highlight the one you want and click on <OK>.
42. The picture does not look right in the frame, as Figure 2-31 shows. Therefore the picture will have to be cropped or moved into a better position. Open the Page menu and select <Actual size>. Then use the scroll bars to place the picture frame fully onto the screen.
43. Be sure the handles are showing. If not, click anywhere inside the frame to select the frame.
44. Open the Graphics menu, shown in Figure 2-32, and select <Crop picture> by clicking on it.
45. Figure 2-33 shows that the pointer has changed to the shape of a pair of scissors.
46. Position the pointer over the upper-left corner of the skyline image. Hold down the mouse button, drag the mouse diagonally down and

Figure 2-30. *The ARTWORK directory listing graphics filenames*

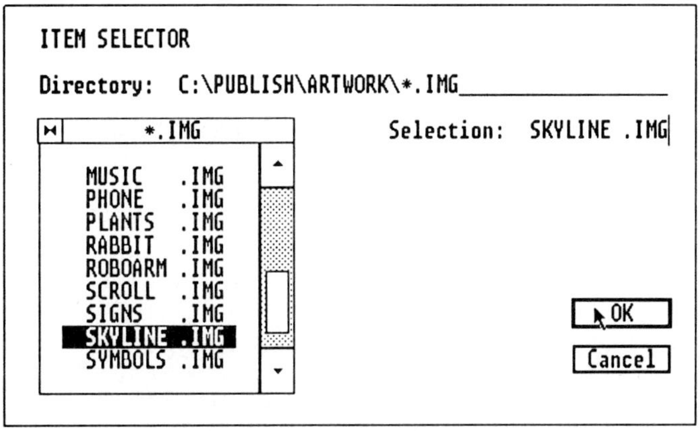

Figure 2-31. *The picture poured into the selected frame*

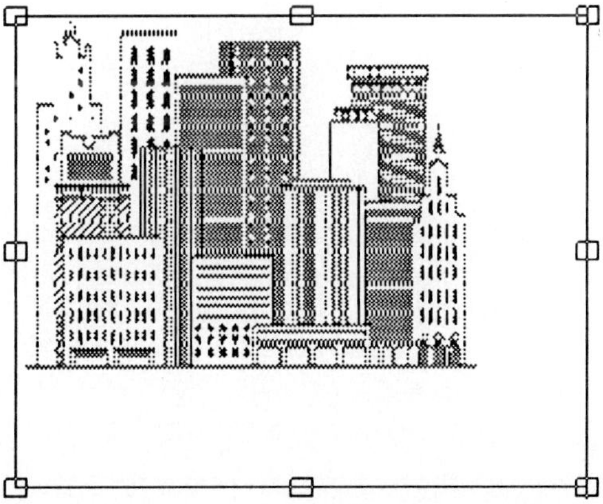

Figure 2-32. *The Graphics menu with <Crop picture> selected*

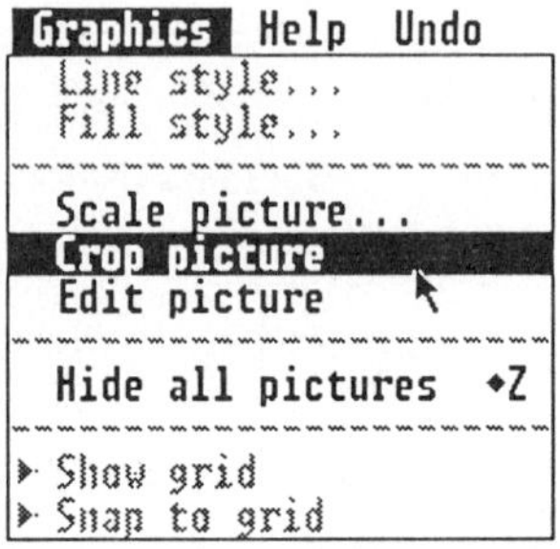

across to the lower-right corner of the actual image. A dotted line appears to show how the picture will be cropped. Let go of the mouse button. Figure 2-34 depicts the cropped picture in its new dimensions in the frame.

Figure 2-33. *Pointer in the shape of scissors*

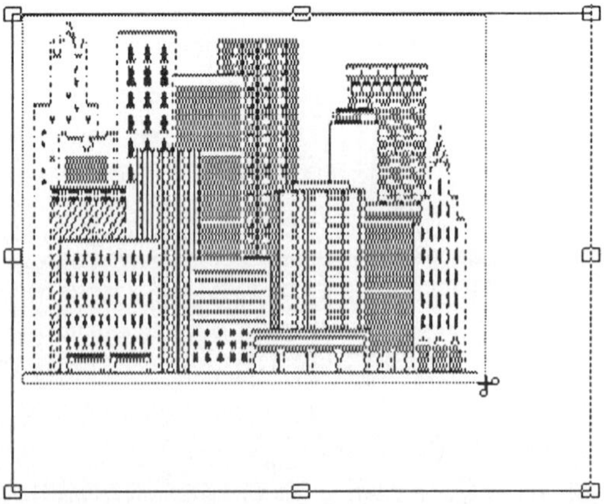

For the moment don't worry about what the text looks like. It can be adjusted later, after you add a headline.

47. Open the Page menu and select <Half size>. Check the scroll bar on the right to make sure you are looking at the top of the page.

<Half size> is not available in Publish It Lite!. Use <Actual size> instead.

48. If the rulers are not already displayed, open the Options menu and select <Show rulers>, as shown in Figure 2-35. This option will simplify the task of creating the correct size of frame by displaying the rulers.
49. Place the pointer on the upper-left corner of the left column, which represents a spot one inch down from the top. Hold down the mouse button and drag the pointer down approximately one inch and all the way across to the right edge of the right column. This creates the narrow frame, shown in Figure 2-36, that covers the width of the entire page.

Figure 2-34. *The picture after cropping*

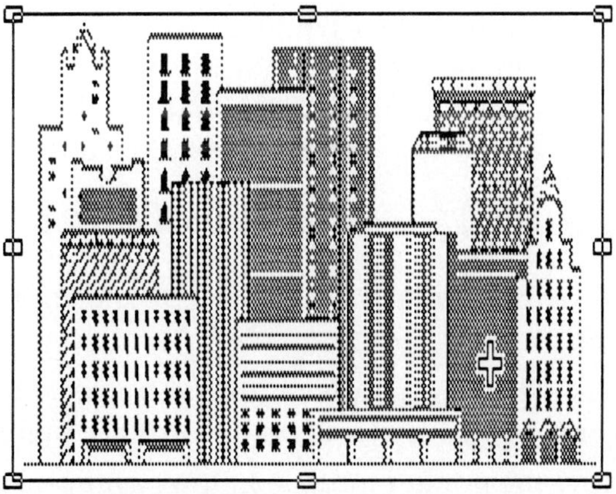

Figure 2-35. *The Options menu with <Show rulers> selected*

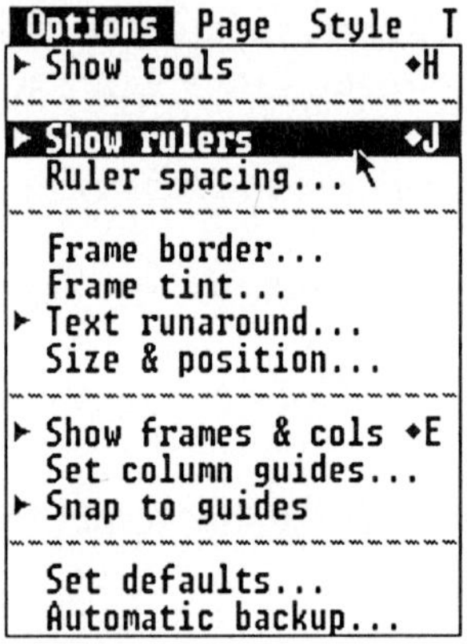

50. Once again, in the Page menu click on <Actual size>. Next move the pointer onto the <TEXT> icon in the toolbox and click on it. The pointer changes into the I-beam shape shown in Figure 2-37.
51. Place the pointer anywhere inside the selected frame and click. A narrow vertical line, the text cursor, appears at the upper-left corner of the frame. Now type the words **Desktop Publishing**; they will appear in the upper-left portion of the new frame as you type them. You might click on <Double size> in the Page menu to get a better look at what you have typed, as shown in Figure 2-38.

Publish It Lite! users skip to step 52L. Publish It! users continue with step 52.

52. Move the pointer into the toolbox and click on the <PARAGRAPH> icon.
53. Move the new pointer into the frame and click anywhere on the words you have typed; both words are highlighted.
54. Move the pointer into the Library window and click on HEADLINE. Your new headline will appear in large type, centered in the frame.

2

Figure 2-36. *A one-inch frame placed across the page*

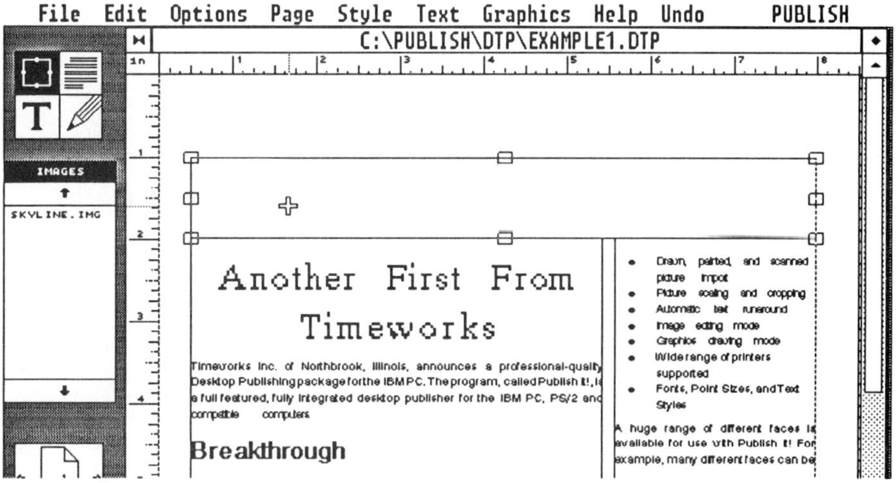

Figure 2-37. *The pointer in the shape of an I-beam*

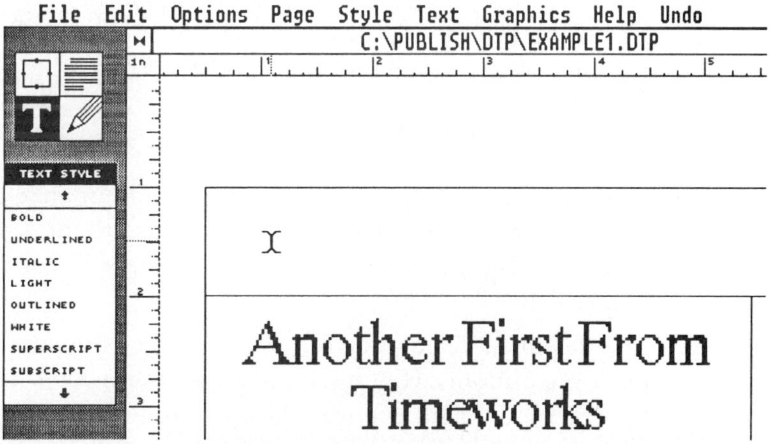

Figure 2-38. *The text cursor as a vertical line*

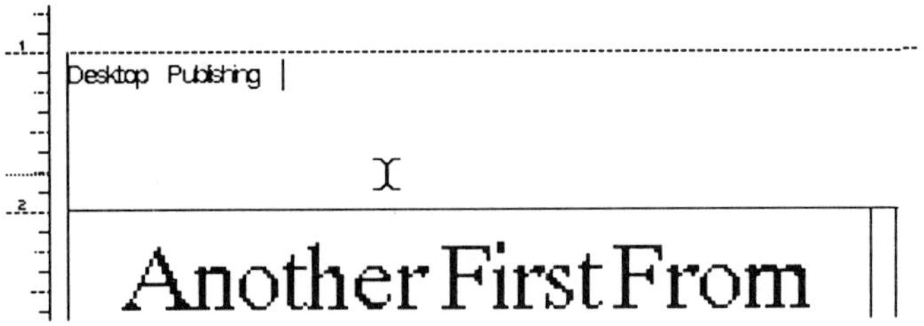

In the Page menu click on <Size to fit> to see the overall effect shown in Figure 2-39.

Publish It! users skip to step 55. Publish It Lite! users continue here.

52L. Highlight the entire headline that you typed.

53L. Select <Font/size> from the Style menu. Click on <DUTCH>, on <36>, and on <OK>.

54L. Click on <Centered> in the Paragraph menu. Your new headline appears in large type, centered in the frame. In the Page menu click on <Size to fit> to see the overall effect shown in Figure 2-39.

Both Publish It! and Publish It Lite! users continue with step 55.

55. A border around the new headline would enhance the final document. Click on the <FRAME> icon to return to the <FRAME> mode. Open the Options menu and select <Frame border>, as shown in Figure 2-40.

56. The displayed dialog box offers a number of border styles and line position options. Highlight the double border one up from the bottom on the right. Figure 2-41 shows how this automatically selects <All around> by highlighting it. Click on <OK>. After a moment a

Figure 2-39. *Text in the top frame displayed as a headline*

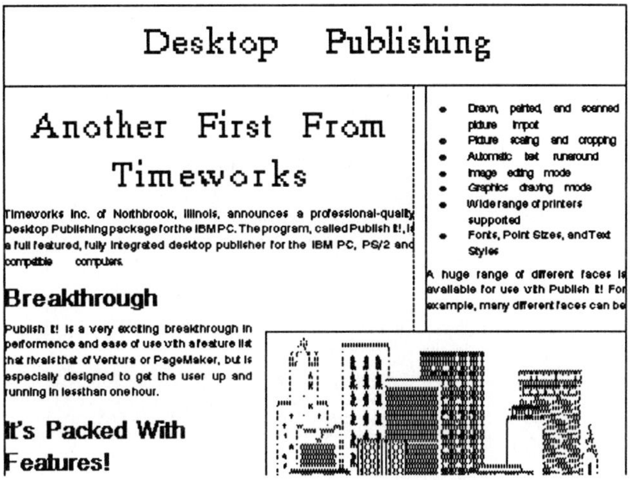

Figure 2-40. *The Options menu with <Frame border> selected*

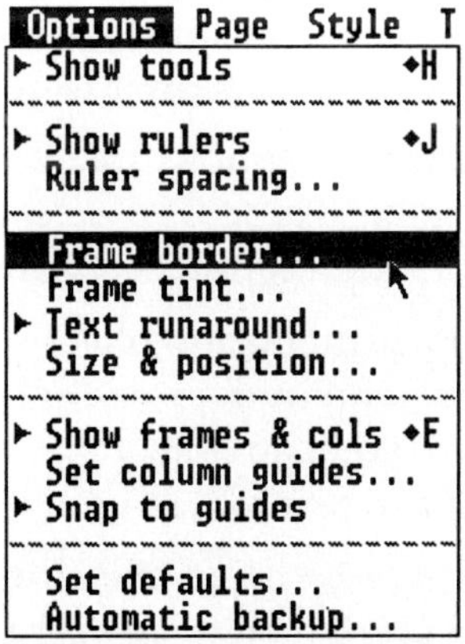

Figure 2-41. *The Frame Border dialog box*

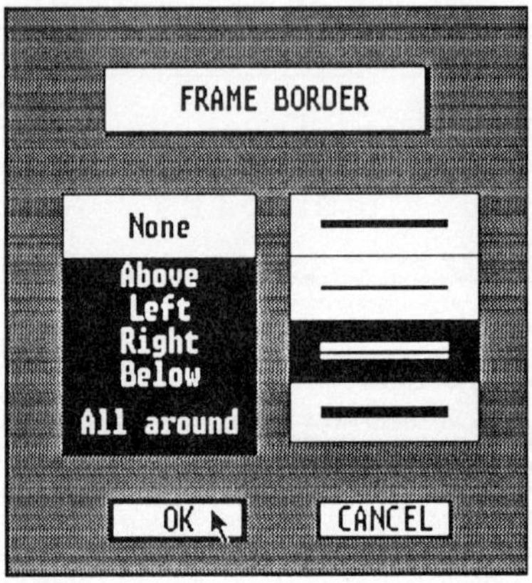

double frame appears around the headline, as shown in Figure 2-42. If the text is not vertically centered to your satisfaction, you can adjust the width of the border and the frame by placing the pointer on the center handle and dragging the mouse up or down.

57. It is also a good idea to place a border around the picture. Use the scroll bars to bring the picture into view. Place the pointer anywhere in the frame, and click on it to select it.

58. Again, open the Options menu and select <Frame border>. From the subsequent dialog box, select the thin line one down from the upper-right, and then select <All around>. Click on <OK>.

59. Open the Page menu and select <Size to fit>. If the text at the bottom of the right column does not end at the same line as the text in the left column, you can adjust the size of the graphic image until the position of the text looks right.

60. When you are satisfied that the text and picture are attractively positioned on the page, open the File menu and click on the <Save as> option, as shown in Figure 2-43.

Figure 2-42. *Double border placed around the headline*

61. An Item Selector box appears asking that you type in a filename. Press (ESC) to erase UNTITLED.DTP on the filename line, and type a name of your choice, such as **FIRSTTRY.DTP**. Click on <OK>, as shown in Figure 2-44.
62. Your work is being saved as a file called FIRSTTRY. The file can be called at any time by opening the File menu, selecting the <Open> option shown in Figure 2-45, highlighting the .DTP file by the name you gave it, and clicking on <OK>, as illustrated in Figure 2-46.

Figure 2-43. *The File menu with <Save as> selected*

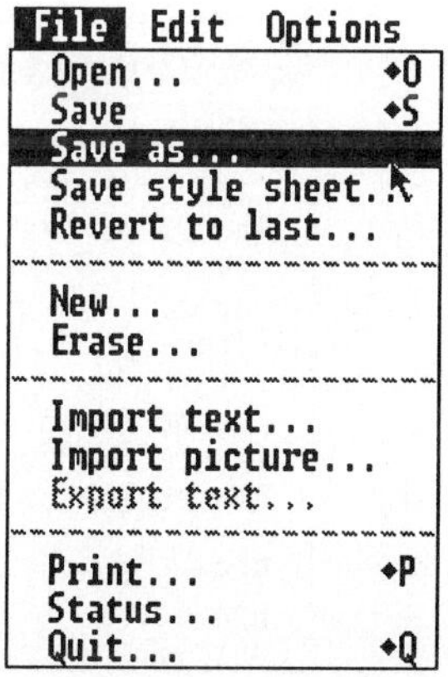

Figure 2-44. *The filename entered on the selection line*

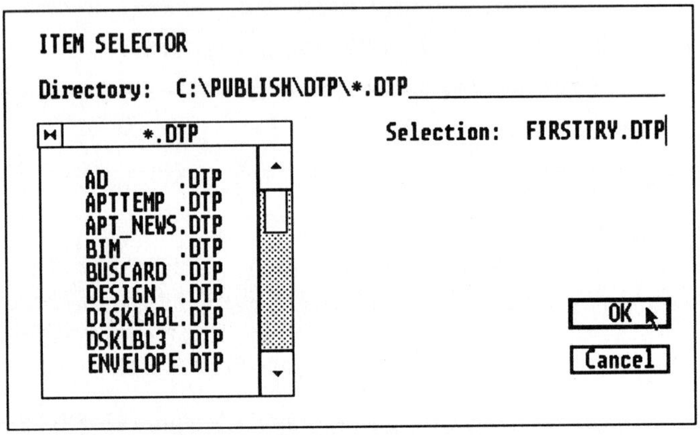

Figure 2-45. *The File menu with <Open> selected*

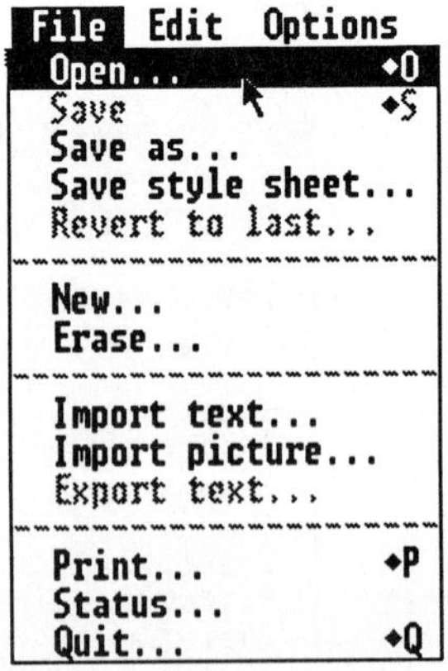

63. Finally, it is time to print your work. Open the File menu and select <Print>. The Print Document dialog box appears, as shown in Figure 2-47. Click on <OK> and wait. A second screen appears, showing in the window under PRINTING what is taking place at any given moment, such as "Sending page data to printer," as shown in Figure 2-48. It is likely to take quite a while, but eventually you will have a printed page like the one shown in Figure 2-49.

This ends the quick run-through using the major features offered by Publish It! and Publish It Lite!.

64. Open the File menu and click on <Quit>. You are returned to the DOS prompt and the root directory (C:\). The PUBLISH directory now contains the new file you created.

By using the basic steps you have learned in this chapter, you can import any text from a word processor or text editor to create simple documents. You can also use any illustrations included with the Publish It! and Publish It

Figure 2-46. *An Item Selector box dislaying available filenames*

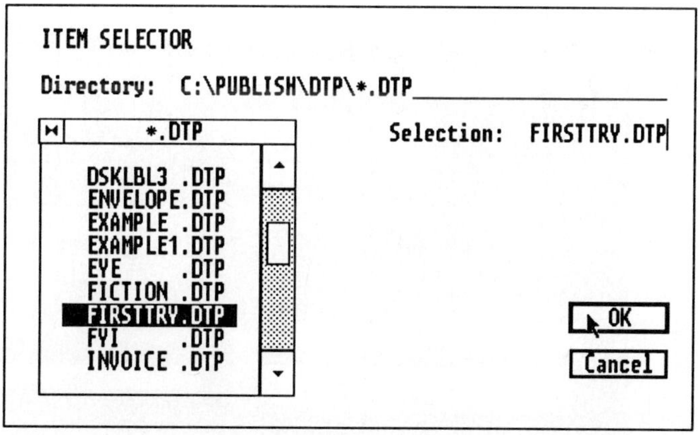

Figure 2-47. *The Print Document dialog box*

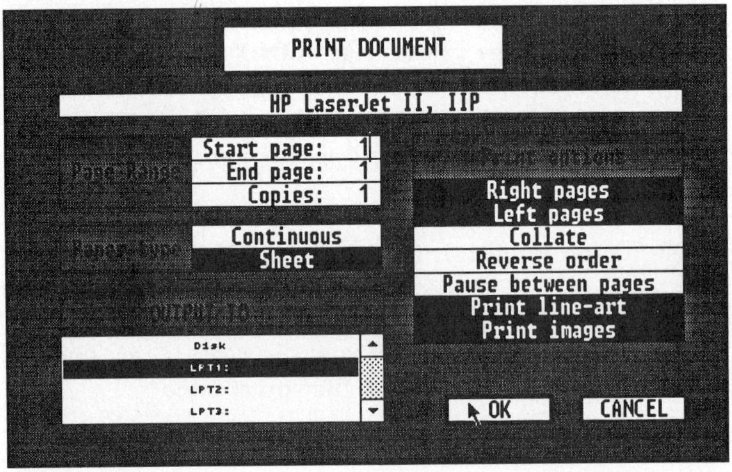

Figure 2-48. *The Printing dialog box*

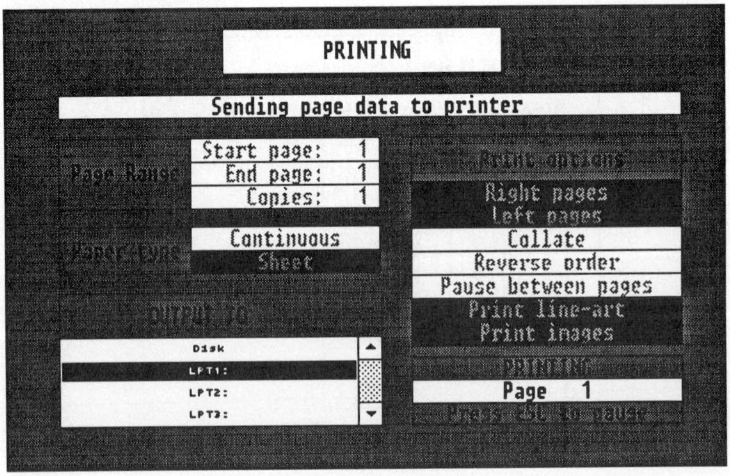

Figure 2-49. *The final document*

Desktop Publishing

Another First From Timeworks

Timeworks Inc. of Northbrook, Illinois, announces a professional-quality Desktop Publishing package for the IBM PC. The program, called Publish It!, is a full featured, fully integrated desktop publisher for the IBM PC, PS/2 and compatible computers.

Breakthrough

Publish It! is a very exciting breakthrough in performence and ease of use with a feature list that rivals that of Ventura or PageMaker, but is especially designed to get the user up and running in less than one hour.

It's Packed With Features!

Only Publish It! gives you all the DTP features you want, including fully integrated word processing, page layout, and graphics:

- Frame-based page layout
- Five zoom modes
- Style sheets
- Wide range of fonts supplied
- Multiple text styles
- Direct text input and editing
- Styled text imported from Word Writer, 1st Word Plus, Word Perfect, Wordstar, Microsoft Word, and MS-Works
- ASCII text imported from other word processors
- Automatic justification
- Automatic hyphenation
- Text block cut, paste, copy, and restyle
- Drawn, painted, and scanned picture import
- Picture scaling and cropping
- Automatic text runaround
- Image editing mode
- Graphics drawing mode
- Wide range of printers supported
- Fonts, Point Sizes, and Text Styles

A huge range of different faces is available for use with Publish It! For example, many different faces can be generated using Serif and Sans fonts alone!

Here are just a few examples:

- 20 point Drury Lane
- 20 point Sans
- 20 point Courier bold
- 16 point Serif light

- 24 point Madison underline
- 20 point Sans italic
- 14 point Sans italic superscript
- 20 point Serif italic
- 18 point Ravinia
- 10 point Sans
- 7 point Serif
- 36 point Serif

Lite! packages (see Chapter 5, "The Publish It! Libraries"), or you can import graphics from another program (see Chapter 9, "Using External Files").

This chapter has demonstrated how, in about an hour, you can create simple documents using either Publish It! or Publish It Lite!. But if you are serious about producing truly outstanding documents, you should study the individual features and functions described in the following chapters as well as try the hands-on examples in Chapter 8, "Hands-on Practice," and Chapter 9, "Using External Files."

II

Program Elements

3

The Screen Displays

The screens produced by the various versions of Publish It! differ from those that are created using Publish It Lite!. The screens shown in the first portion of this chapter are those created using Publish It! version 2.0. The screens produced by earlier versions of Publish It! differ only slightly from these. The second portion of this chapter deals with the Publish It Lite! screens.

The Publish It! Screen

The Publish It! screen is the area in which all work is performed. It consists of a work area surrounded by a menu bar and a title bar, scroll bars, a toolbox, and a number of other features that display available choices or perform certain functions. Figure 3-1 is the screen that appears when Publish It! is started. This chapter explains each of the features and functions in detail.

Figure 3-1. *The opening Publish It! screen*

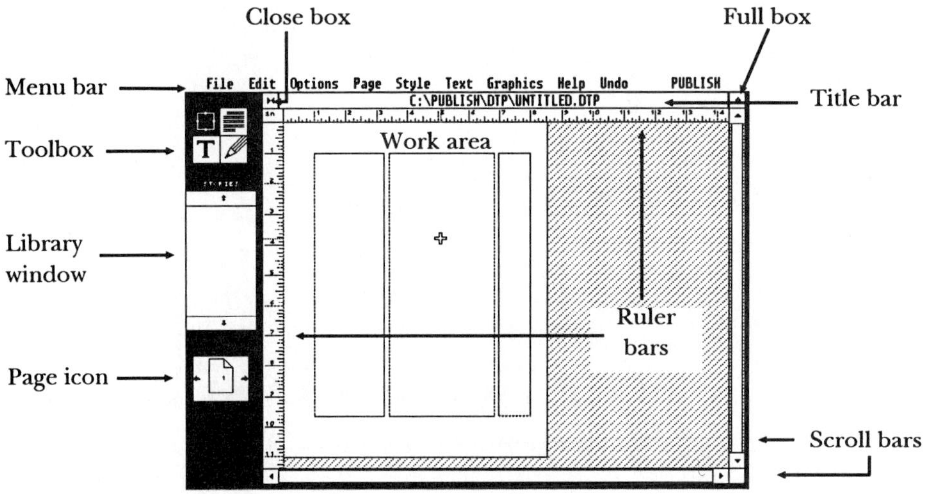

The Menu Bar

Across the top of the screen is the *menu bar,* as shown here:

`File  Edit  Options  Page  Style  Text  Graphics  Help  Undo        PUBLISH`

The menu bar displays nine pull-down menus—eight contain all the options you'll use to create and enhance your documents, and one, the Help menu, gives you information anytime you need it. At the far right of the menu bar is the name of the currently active program.

To access each of the menus, move the arrow-shaped pointer onto the name, either by dragging the mouse or by using the arrow keys. As soon as the pointer touches the name of a menu, that menu drops down. When you move the pointer along the items in the menu, each item becomes highlighted as the pointer touches it. You can select a highlighted item either by clicking the mouse button on it or by pressing the (HOME) key.

Some of the menu selections may be light gray, which indicates they are not available in the currently active mode. For example, if you access the Page menu with no frame selected, the options <Bring to front> and <Send to back> appear gray because there is nothing selected. The term *mode,* as used throughout this book, refers to the type of procedure you are doing, such as working on your copy in the <TEXT> mode, or on pictures in the <GRAPHICS> mode, and so on.

The Title Bar

Beneath the menu bar is the title bar, as shown here:

The title bar displays the title of the work on which you are currently working, as well as the disk/directory on which the files will be or have been saved. When you are working on a new document that has not yet been saved to disk, the title bar reads C:\PUBLISH\DTP\UNTITLED.DTP. (In earlier versions, the title bar appears without the DTP subdirectory.) That filename indicates the active disk drive is C, the active directory is PUBLISH, and the temporary filename is UNTITLED; the DTP extension is added automatically by the program indicating that the file is a Publish It! file. The title bar shows the drive and path used on your system. Floppy drive users would see A:\UNTITLED.DTP. After you have saved a document to disk under a unique filename, that filename will replace UNTITLED.DTP in the title bar. For example, it might read C:\PUBLISH\FIRSTTRY.DTP if FIRSTTRY is the name of the file.

The Full Box

To the far right of the title bar is a diamond-shaped mark in a square box, referred to as the *full box.* To select the full box, place the pointer on it and click on it. The full box removes the items around the periphery of the work area so the work area fills the entire screen. With the full box active, you can see 7 1/2 inches of the full 8 1/2-inch width of a page in the actual size page view. The full box is a toggle, which simply means that the same action turns an option on and off. Clicking on the full box again returns the screen to its previous display, which includes the items around the screen's periphery.

The Close Box

At the left of the title bar is another box, referred to as the *close box.* Clicking on the close box cancels any editing without saving it. To avoid annoying mistakes, when you click on the close box a dialog box will be displayed asking whether you want to save the work before exiting, abandon the work, or cancel the command altogether, which returns you to the condition that existed before you clicked on the close box.

The Toolbox

On the left side of the screen near the top is the toolbox. The toolbox contains the four options shown in Figure 3-2. Each of the options, displayed as icons, represents one of the modes in which Publish It! functions. The upper-left portion of the toolbox contains a square; clicking on the square activates the <FRAME> mode. You use the <FRAME> mode to create new frames into which you can import text or graphics, or to select previously created frames that may or may not contain text or graphics. In this mode you can also resize or move frames, copy frames, or cut and paste frames. Note that the pointer is an open cross in the <FRAME> mode.

Figure 3-2. *The Publish It! toolbox with four options*

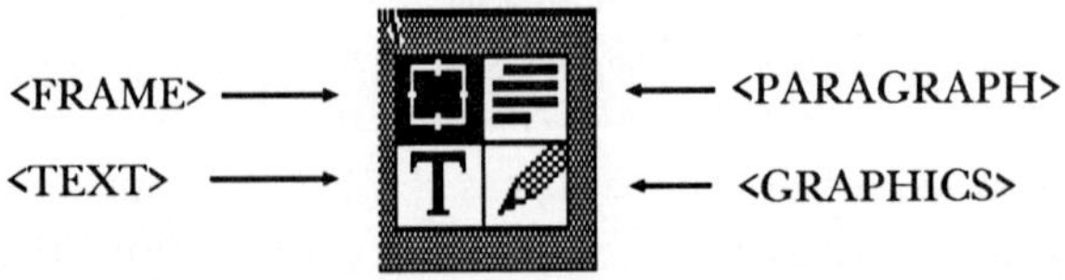

The <FRAME> mode is the default mode. It is available when you activate the program, because nothing can be achieved until frames have either been created or selected.

In the upper-right portion of the toolbox is the icon that represents the <PARAGRAPH> mode. You use the <PARAGRAPH> mode to select text paragraphs in order to change their character style or size or to create your own paragraph styles. When this mode is activated, the available character styles, such as HEADLINE and SUBHEAD, are displayed. The pointer is a paragraph symbol in this mode.

In the lower-left area of the toolbox is the square that activates the <TEXT> mode. When you select that square, you can type new text or edit text that was imported from other sources. In this mode the pointer is an I-beam.

When you place the pointer into an empty frame and click the mouse button or press the HOME key, the text cursor—a single vertical line—appears in the upper-left corner of the frame. If the pointer is clicked within existing text, the text cursor appears at that location. Once the text cursor has been placed in a frame, text can be entered or edited at the cursor position. In the <TEXT> mode, the available character styles, such as UNDERLINE and ITALIC, are displayed in the Library window.

In the lower-right portion of the toolbox is the square that represents the <GRAPHICS> mode. You can use it to create original graphics with the drawing options displayed in the Library window, as illustrated in Figure 3-3. The diagonal line icon (upper left) draws straight lines. You use the arrow tool in the upper right much like the frame tool to select and move objects created by the other graphics tools. The square icon draws rectangles with sharp corners. The icon to its right draws rectangles with rounded corners. The round icon draws circles. The oval icon draws ovals. You use the Z-shaped icon to draw a series of connected straight lines. The squiggle icon in the lower right produces freestyle lines. In each of these drawing modes, the graphics cursor appears as a small hairline cross.

The Library Window

Below the toolbox is the Library window, shown in Figure 3-4. In the <FRAME> mode the Library window displays text and graphics files being

Figure 3-3. *The <GRAPHICS> mode Library window*

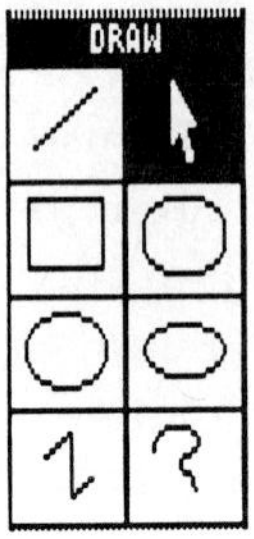

used. In the <PARAGRAPH> mode the window displays the available character styles. In the <TEXT> mode it displays the available text styles, and in the <GRAPHICS> mode it displays the graphics icons previously described. In any mode a displayed item can be selected by clicking on it. For example, when you select a paragraph of text in the <PARAGRAPH> mode and click the pointer on a paragraph style name, such as SUBHEAD or HEADLINE, the text that represents the selected paragraph changes to the font chosen for that particular paragraph style.

Figure 3-4. *The Library window*

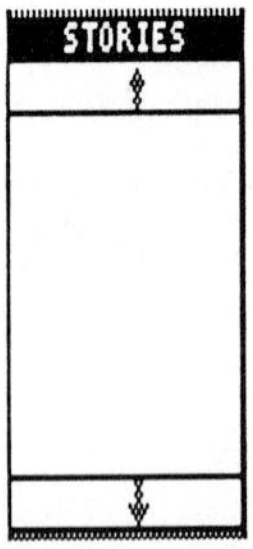

The <PAGE> Icon

Below the Library window is the <PAGE> icon, shown in Figure 3-5. This icon displays the number of the displayed page (it is possible to display two pages at a time, but only one page number is listed in the <PAGE> icon). By clicking on the left or right arrow, you can access the preceding or following page. A folded corner is displayed on the left for left (even-numbered) pages and on the right for right (odd-numbered) pages.

The Work Area

The work area is the space where documents are created and displayed. Earlier versions of Publish It! were able to display material in actual size, double size, or half size. Publish It! version 2.0 adds three-quarters size; when the program is activated this is the default display. The <Size to fit> option displays the entire page, and <Two pages> displays two pages at once. In any option other than <Size to fit> or <Two pages>, the area can be scrolled horizontally and vertically to display different portions of the document.

When the program is activated, the work area displays a group of dotted-line rectangles, as shown in Figure 3-6. These are guides to help you create frames. The default number of frame guides is six, but you can change that number to a minimum of one or a maximum of nine.

Figure 3-5. *The <PAGE> icon*

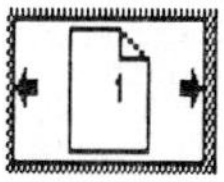

Figure 3-6. *Frame guides*

The Scroll Bars

Along the bottom and right edges of the screen are the scroll bars, shown here:

The bar at the bottom of the screen is used to scroll the displayed area horizontally; the bar at the screen's right edge scrolls the display up and down. You can place the pointer on the bars and drag them to another position, or you can click on the tiny triangles at the ends of the scroll bar locations to move the bars by small increments with each click. When you click anywhere in the space between the bar and the arrow at the end, the bar jumps toward that end.

The Program Pointers and Cursors

The program pointers and the cursors take on any one of ten different shapes, depending on the currently active mode.

The Standard Pointer The standard black arrowhead pointer, shown in Figure 3-7, appears whenever the pointer is outside the actual work area. It is used to select menus, toolbox icons, and other options.

The Open Cross Pointer An open cross pointer, shown in Figure 3-8, appears when the <FRAME> mode is active and the pointer is in the work area. It is used to create new frames and select existing frames. To create a new frame, place the cursor on the upper-left corner of the frame to be created. Hold down the mouse button and drag it to the lower-right corner of that frame. When you release the mouse button, the new frame is displayed and selected.

To select an existing frame, place the pointer anywhere inside the frame to be selected and click on it. The handles will be on the edges and corners of the frame, indicating that the frame has been selected.

The Grabber Pointer An open hand pointer, known as the *grabber,* is used to move selected frames. The grabber pointer appears in the <FRAME> mode when you place the pointer anywhere inside a selected frame and hold down the mouse button while dragging the mouse in the desired direction. A dotted line representing the new frame position appears, as illustrated in Figure 3-9. When you release the mouse button, the selected frame appears in its new location.

The Pointing Hand Pointer A hand with a pointing finger is used to resize selected frames. To call up the pointing hand pointer in the <FRAME> mode,

Figure 3-7. *The arrowhead pointer used when outside work area*

Figure 3-8. *The open cross pointer in <FRAME> mode*

place the pointer on one of the handles of a selected frame. Hold down the mouse button and drag the mouse in the desired direction. A dotted rectangular line indicates the changing shape of the frame, as shown in Figure 3-10. When you release the mouse button, the selected frame changes to its new dimensions.

The Paragraph Pointer The paragraph pointer, shown in Figure 3-11, appears when you use the <PARAGRAPH> mode. It is used to select individual paragraphs from within the displayed text. To select a paragraph, place the pointer anywhere within the paragraph to be selected and click the mouse button. The selected paragraph will appear in reverse video.

The I-beam Pointer When you are in <TEXT> mode, the pointer is the I-beam shape shown in Figure 3-12. Click it inside a frame containing text at the position where you want to edit text. That places the text cursor—a vertical

Figure 3-9. *The grabber pointer appears when moving a frame*

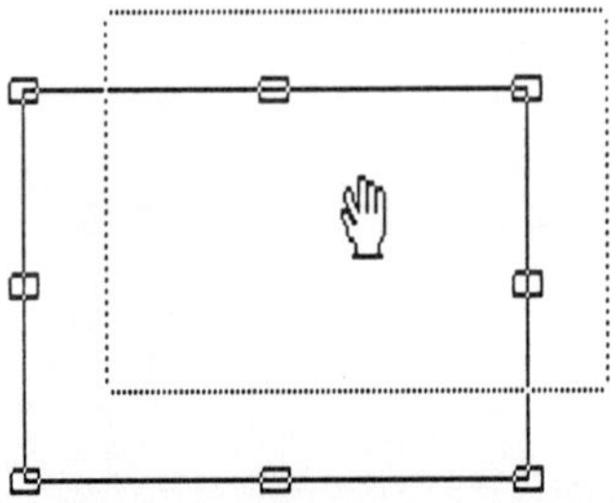

Figure 3-10. *The pointing hand pointer appears when changing size or proportion of frame*

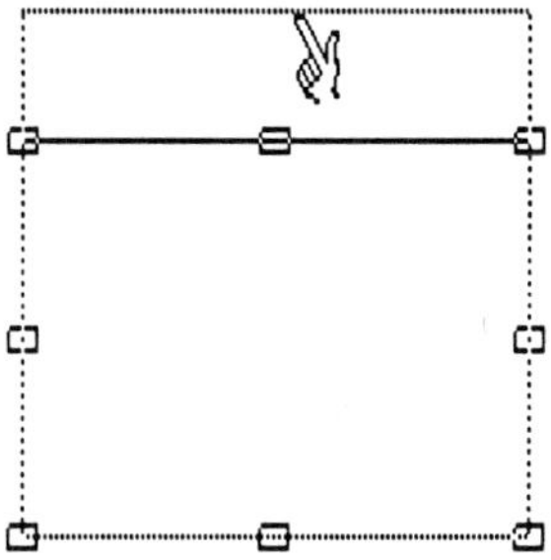

line—on a selected place. Click it inside an empty frame to position the text cursor at the upper-left corner of the frame.

The Outline Pointer Figure 3-13 shows the empty outline pointer that is used when you are in the <GRAPHICS> mode and no drawing icon is selected.

The Cross Hair Cursor When you select a drawing icon, the pointer becomes the cross hair-shaped graphics cursor shown in Figure 3-14. To produce one of the drawing shapes, place the cursor anywhere in a frame in the work area. Hold down the mouse button and drag the mouse to a new location.

Figure 3-11. *The <PARAGRAPH> mode pointer*

Figure 3-12. *The I-beam pointer in <TEXT> mode*

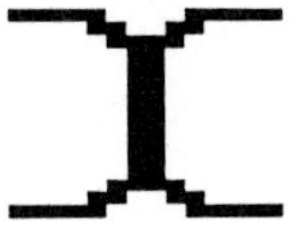

The Scissors Pointer When you select the <Crop picture> option from within <GRAPHICS> mode in order to eliminate unwanted portions of a picture, the open scissors pointer shown in Figure 3-15 appears. Place that pointer on the upper-left corner of the portion of the graphic image that is to be cropped. Then hold down the mouse button and drag the mouse to the lower-right corner of the portion of the graphic image you want to retain. This produces a dotted line around the cropped area. When you release the mouse button, the cropped portion of the image is redrawn into the existing frame.

The Rotating Ball The rotating ball icon shown in Figure 3-16 replaces the hourglass used in earlier versions to indicate that the computer is busy

Figure 3-13. *The open arrowhead pointer in <GRAPHICS> mode*

Figure 3-14. *The cross hair <GRAPHICS> cursor*

working. While the rotating ball is displayed, the program cannot accept additional commands. The rotating ball can change into a floppy-disk shape when the computer is busy accessing the disk drive.

The Publish It Lite! Screen

The Publish It Lite! screen, shown in Figure 3-17, is somewhat different from the Publish It! screen. For one thing, the Publish It Lite! screen has rulers calibrated in inches permanently installed along the top and the left side. Other differences are discussed in the following sections.

Figure 3-15. *The scissors pointer used to crop in <GRAPHICS> mode*

Figure 3-16. *The rotating ball shown when the computer is busy*

The Menu Bar

The Publish It Lite! menu bar appears across the top of the screen, as shown here:

`File  Edit  Options  Page  Style  Paragraph  Graphics  Help        LITE`

It contains seven menus, plus the Help menu. Instead of the Text menu used in the Publish It! version there is a Paragraph menu. The options offered by

Figure 3-17. *The opening Publish It Lite! screen*

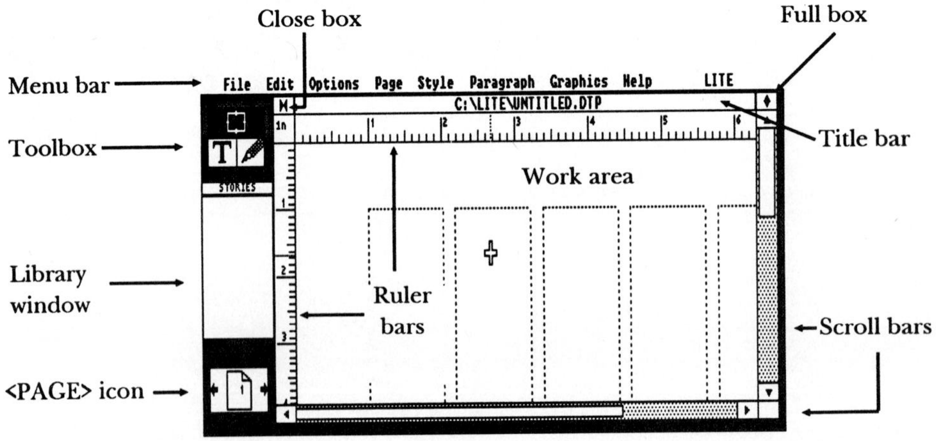

the individual menus are somewhat more limited than those available with Publish It!.

The Title Bar

The title bar shown is similar to the one described for the Publish It! version:

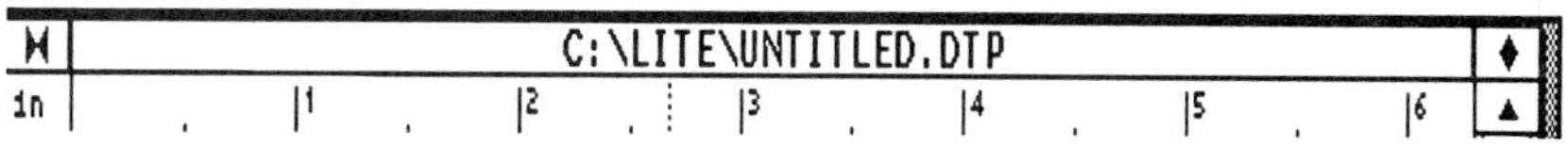

It includes the disk drive, directory, and filename information. It also contains the full box to the right and the close box at the far left.

The Toolbox

The Publish It Lite! toolbox offers the three options shown in Figure 3-18. They are the <FRAME> icon across the top and the <TEXT> and <GRAPHICS> icons at the bottom.

Figure 3-18. *The Publish It Lite! toolbox with three options*

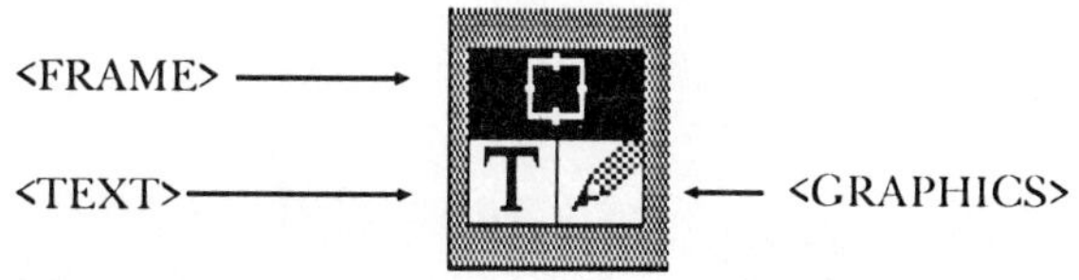

The <GRAPHICS> Mode

In the <GRAPHICS> mode the available options shown in the Library window are limited to a straight line, a rectangle that can be changed to a square, and an oval that can be changed into a circle by resizing the frame.

The rest of the Publish It Lite! screen is identical to the Publish It! screen, as are the methods of accessing the menus and other options.

4

The Menus

Publish It! and Publish It Lite! are menu-driven programs, which means they include a number of menus, each consisting of a group of related commands that can be selected and executed by clicking on them. The menu names are displayed across the top of the screen on the menu bar. You select menus by placing the pointer on the menu name without clicking on it. The menu drops down into the work area, displaying the available options.

This chapter covers each of those menus and explains each of the options and commands. Associated with some of the displayed commands on the menus, you will notice a diamond-plus-letter or -digit combination. These represent *quick keys.* You can access the command by simultaneously pressing the (ALT) key and the letter or digit key instead of pulling down a menu and clicking with the mouse. For details about the available quick keys, see Appendix D, "Quick Keys."

The Publish It! Menus

When Publish It! is activated, it displays ten menu titles in the menu bar across the top of the screen. Virtually everything you do with Publish It! is accomplished using one of the options from a menu. The more familiar you are with each menu and its options, the more efficient your work with Publish It! will be.

The File Menu

The File menu displayed in Figure 4-1 is the first menu choice on the left end of the menu bar. When you select it you see 13 command options.

- *<Open>* Selecting <Open> opens an existing file that was created at an earlier session and saved on disk. When you select this option, the Item Selector box shown in Figure 4-2 is displayed. To select one of the displayed titles, simply click on it. To display other filenames, use the vertical scroll bar. The text cursor is located at the end of the Selection line. Press ESC or BACKSPACE to erase UNTITLED .DTP. Then type in any new filename.

Figure 4-1. *The Publish It! File menu*

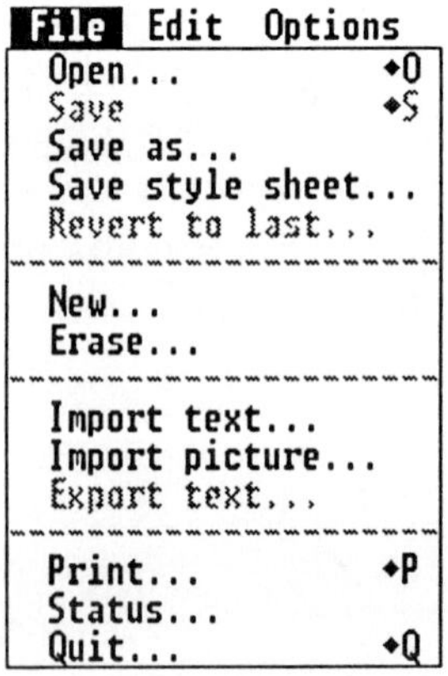

Figure 4-2. *The .DTP filenames Item Selector box*

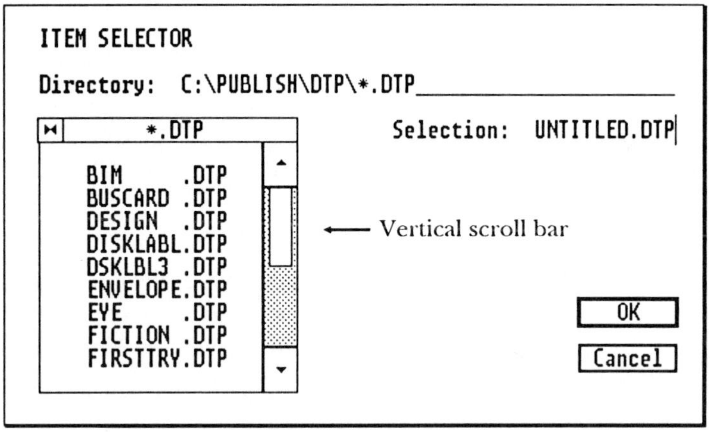

To display files on other disks or directories, click on the directory line. The text cursor moves to that line. Press (ESC) or use (BACKSPACE) to erase the displayed data. Then type the disk, directory, and file information that you are interested in. For instance, if you delete the line and then type **B:*.***, all files on the disk in drive B will be displayed in the Item Selector box.

- *<Save>* You cannot select <Save> when Publish It! is first activated, which is why it is light gray. It becomes available only after a document has been saved previously with the <Save as> option. <Save> saves the document with the same filename with which it was saved originally. To avoid errors, the dialog box in Figure 4-3 appears, asking whether the original file is to be overwritten and giving you the opportunity to change your mind.
- *<Save as>* You use <Save as> to save the document with a new filename. This may be a new document or one that you previously saved under a different filename. An Item Selector box like the one shown in Figure 4-2 is displayed. The text cursor is at the end of the selection line, waiting for you to type the new filename.

Figure 4-3. *The <Save> warning box*

- *<Save style sheet>* You use <Save style sheet> to save a new and unique paper style and size. You also use this option to save all attributes, including paragraph styles, margin details, and other data for your current document. Selecting this option displays another Item Selector box, shown in Figure 4-4, that asks you to key in a filename. The .STY extension is supplied automatically by the program.

Figure 4-4. *The .STY filenames Item Selector box*

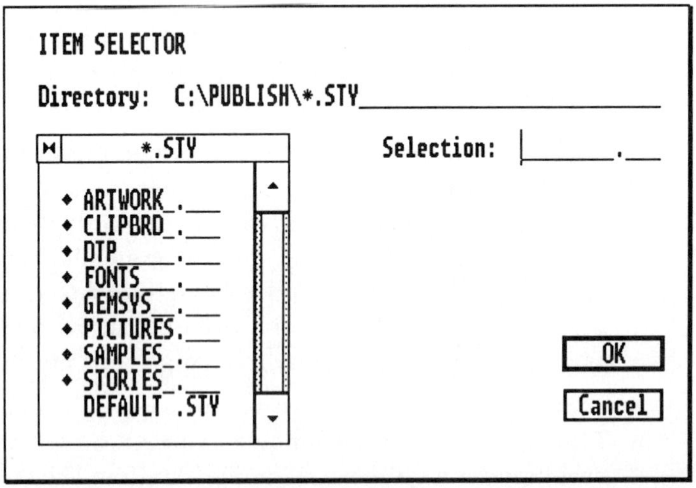

Figure 4-5. *The <Revert to last> warning box*

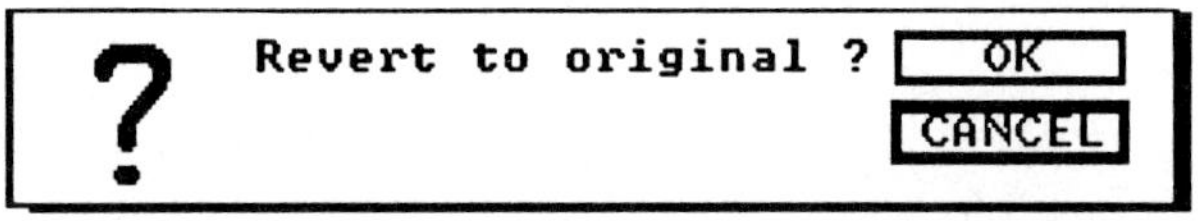

- *<Revert to last>* Selecting <Revert to last> erases any editing that you did during the current session. To avoid errors, the dialog box shown in Figure 4-5 is displayed, offering you the opportunity to change your mind. When you click on <OK>, the currently displayed document is replaced by the one that was last saved on disk.
- *<New>* Using <New> displays the dialog box in Figure 4-6, asking whether or not you want to load a style sheet. Clicking on <YES> produces the Item Selector box shown in Figure 4-4, which displays the available style sheets. If you choose not to load a style sheet, Publish It! displays the dialog box in Figure 4-7. It displays the available options in terms of page dimensions and orientation. It also includes a <Custom size> option (available only with Publish It! version 2.0). Selecting it permits you to change the height and width data in the <Custom size in inches> block. In Figure 4-8 these have been changed to 8.50 and 3.65, which results in the page size shown in Figure 4-9.

Figure 4-6. *The <New> warning box*

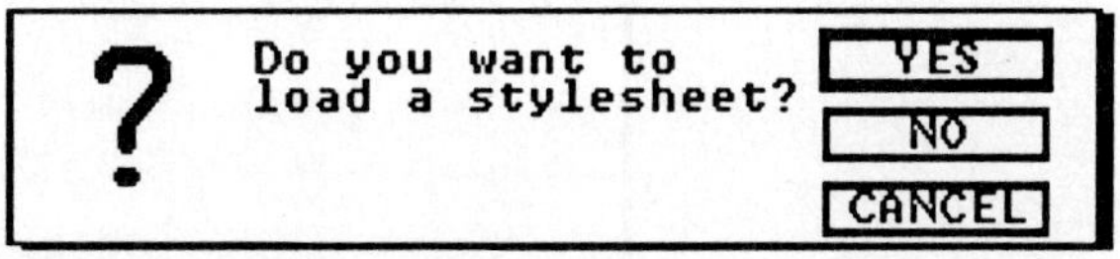

Figure 4-7. *The Page Format dialog box with <Custom size> highlighted*

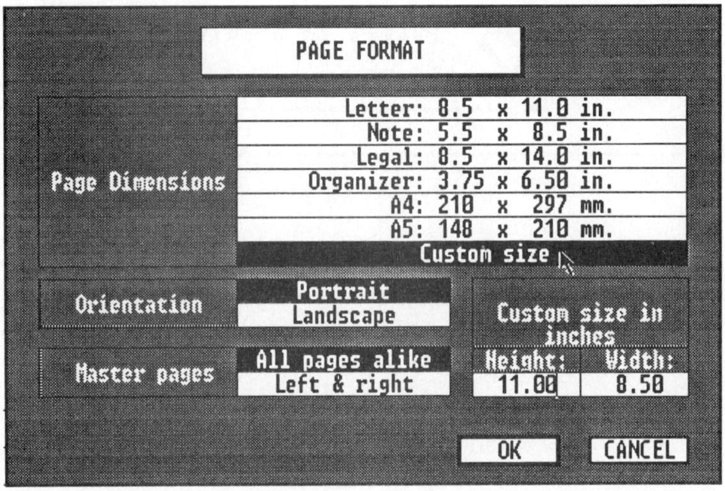

Figure 4-8. *New page dimensions (8.50 x 3.65) entered in the <Custom size in inches> box*

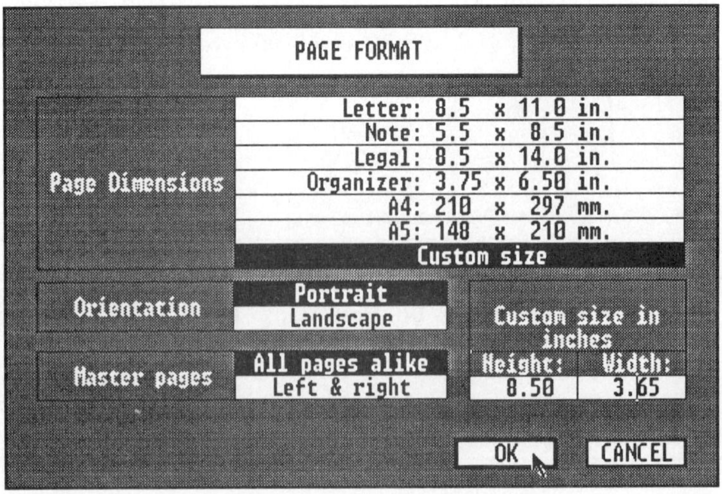

- *<Erase>* Selecting <Erase> produces an Item Selector box that displays all files on the currently active directory. The Item Selector box asks you to enter the name of the file to be deleted from that directory. Its primary purpose is to free up disk space without exiting Publish It!. In general, you should use this option only to delete files you created yourself: either documents with the .DTP extension, style sheets with the .STY extension, or the backup files with the .BAK and .ATB extensions, created by Publish It! version 2.0.
- *<Import text>* Selecting <Import text> displays a dialog box that asks you to click on the type of text file that you want to import. The 12 types of text files that Publish It! version 2.0 supports can be displayed by scrolling through the file types. Figure 4-10 shows all 12. (Earlier versions of Publish It! supported only 8 file types, eliminating the scroll option.) Once a file type has been selected, an Item Selector box displays the text files available in the C:\PUBLISH\STORIES directory, as shown in Figure 4-11.
- *<Import picture>* Selecting <Import picture> displays a dialog box. By scrolling it up or down you see the eight file types supported by

Figure 4-9. *The new custom-sized page is displayed*

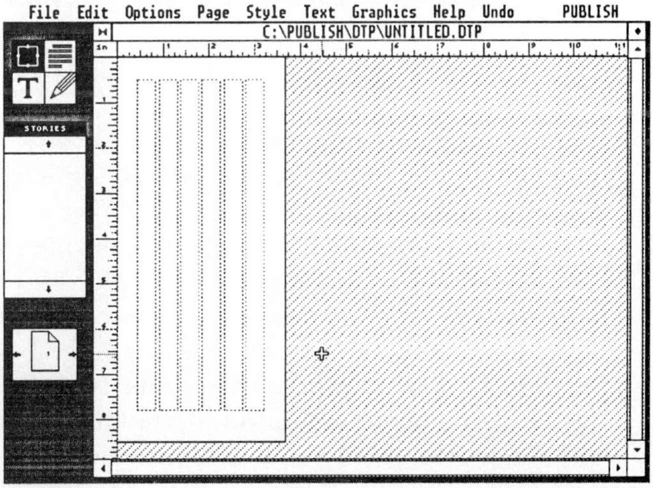

Figure 4-10. *The 12 word processor options displayed upon clicking on <Import text> in the File menu with Publish It! version 2.0*

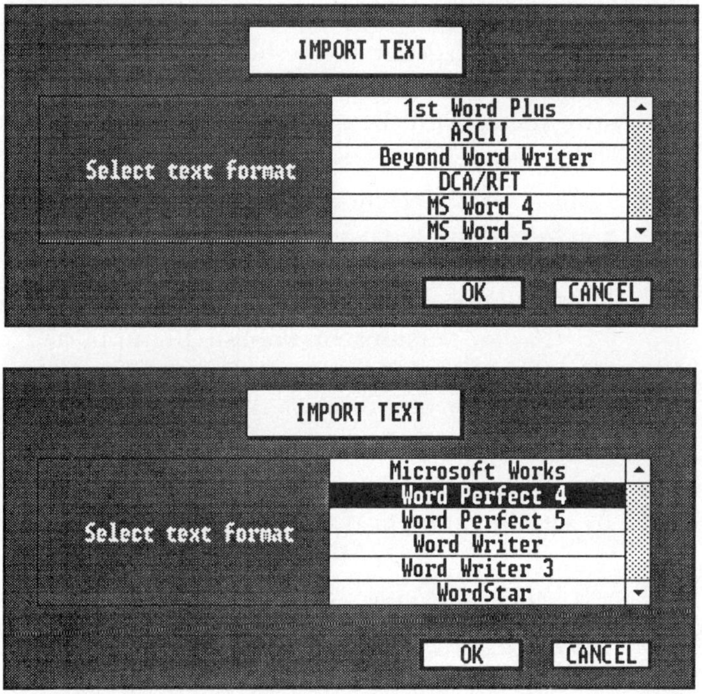

Publish It! version 2.0, as shown in Figure 4-12. (Earlier versions of Publish It! supported only four graphics file types and eliminated the scroll option.) Click on the type of picture file to be imported. Files with the .GEM extension are usually files from GEM Draw or any other program that can create graphic files in this format. Files with the .IMG extension are either the result of using GEM Paint or are created by some external graphics program. Files with the .PIC extension are those produced by Lotus 1-2-3, Quattro, Quattro Pro, or compatible programs. Be aware that certain other graphics programs produce files with .PIC extensions that are not necessarily compatible. The .PCX files are created using PC Paintbrush or are

Figure 4-11. *The text files available in the C:\PUBLISH\STORIES directory*

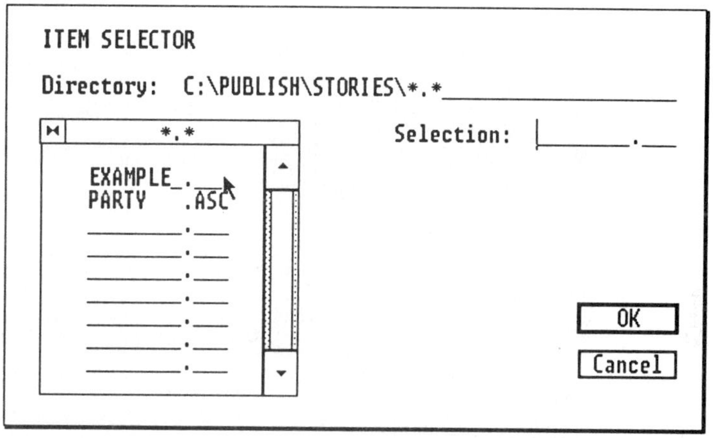

clip-art files available from a wide selection of manufacturers. Certain clip-art collections consist of files with the .PCC extension. Some of them are identical to .PCX files and can be used without being converted or renamed. Once a selection has been made, another Item Selector box is displayed. It contains the files with the selected extension, if any.

- *<Export text>* The <Export text> selection is available only with Publish It! version 2.0. Its purpose is to convert text typed using the Publish It! <TEXT> mode into ASCII format and to save it on disk under a filename with an .ASC extension that is provided automatically. Before this option can be used, the text in question must be given a name. To name the text, go to the <FRAME> mode and select the frame in which the text is located. Access the Text menu and select <Name text>, as in Figure 4-13. A dialog box is displayed, as shown in Figure 4-14. Type a name for this text (do not type the extension) and click on <OK>. The new name appears in the Stories Library window with the extension added automatically. With the frame that holds the text to be exported still selected, access the File menu again and click on <Export text>. An Item Selector box

Figure 4-12. *The eight graphics file types displayed when <Import picture> is selected with Publish It! version 2.0*

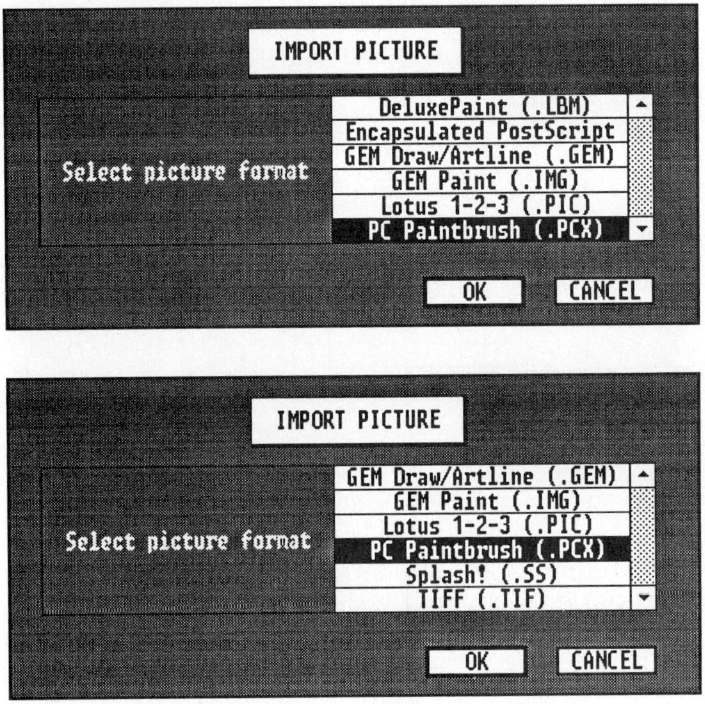

appears, as shown in Figure 4-15. Click on <OK> and the new file can now be found in the C:\PUBLISH\STORIES directory, as shown in Figure 4-16. Selecting it and clicking <OK> imports it into the work area.

- *<Print>* You use this to print your document. The <Print> option displays the dialog box shown in Figure 4-17. It contains options that you can either accept or reject and change. When you click on <OK> the currently active document is printed.

Figure 4-13. *Selecting <Name text> from the Text menu*

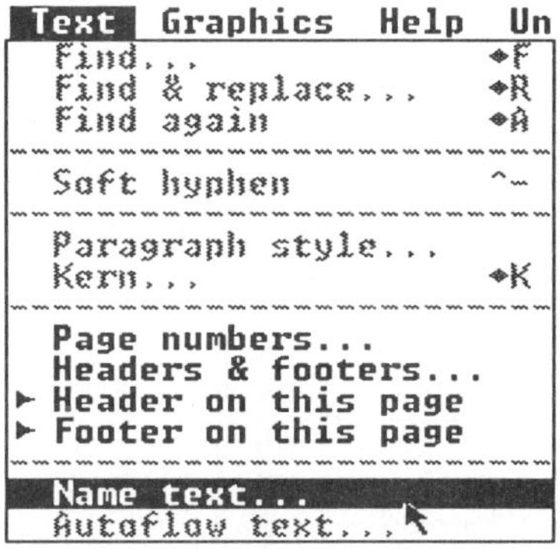

4

- *<Status>* Selecting <Status> displays a box that indicates the current status of the document on which you are working, as shown in Figure 4-18.

Figure 4-14. *The new name (NEWSTORY) in the Name Text dialog box. Publish It! provides the .ASC extension*

Figure 4-15. *Clicking on <OK> in the Item Selector box enters the new file into the STORIES subdirectory*

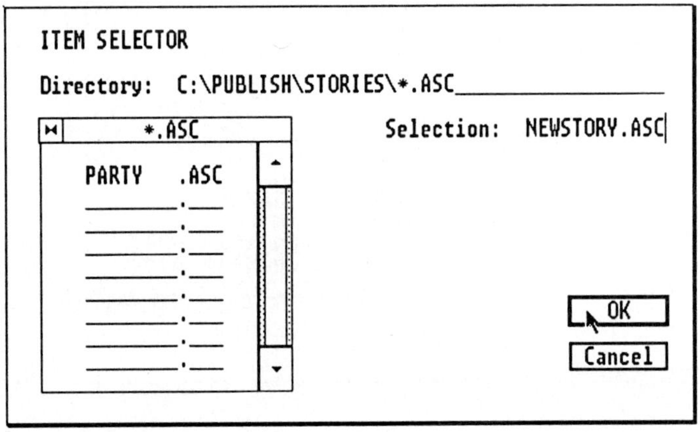

- *<Quit>* Use <Quit> to exit Publish It!. It displays the warning box shown in Figure 4-19. It asks whether you want to save or abandon

Figure 4-16. *The Item Selector box now displays the new file*

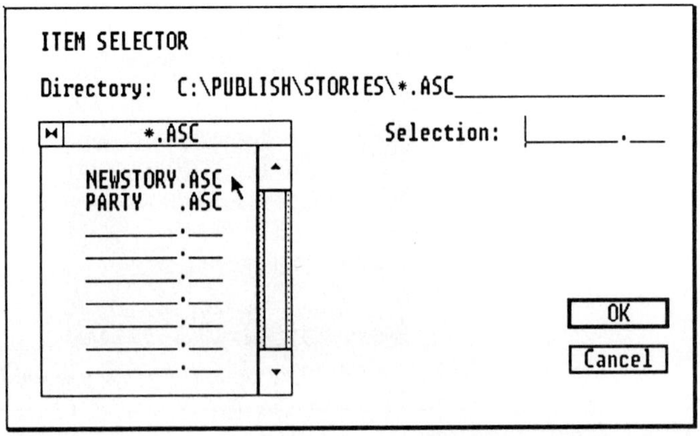

Figure 4-17. *The Print Document dialog box*

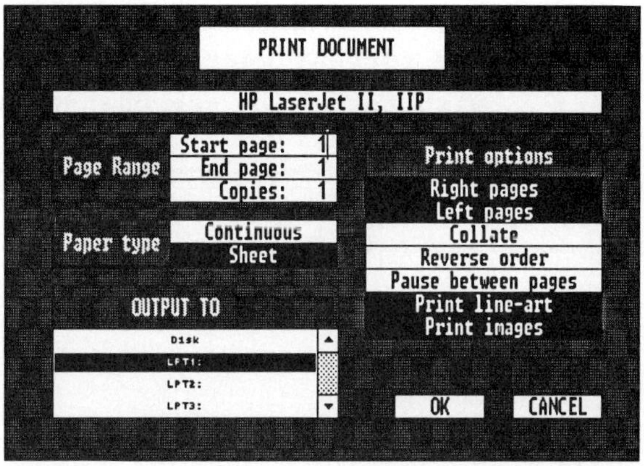

the current document. Alternatively you can click on <CANCEL>, which cancels the <Quit> command altogether.

Figure 4-18. *The Status dialog box*

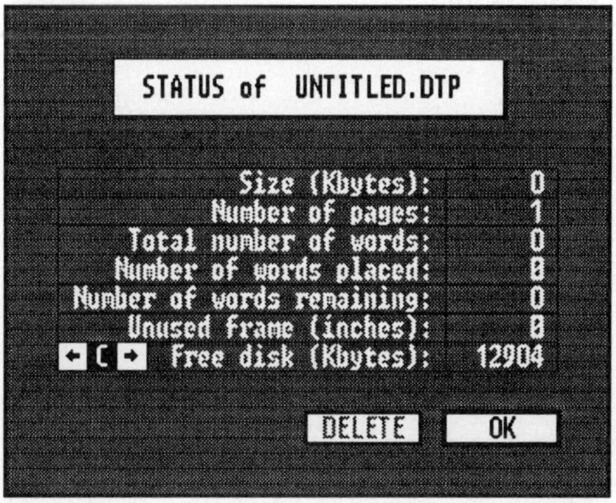

Figure 4-19. *The <Quit> warning box*

The Edit Menu

The Edit menu, shown in Figure 4-20, is used to move blocks of text or graphics from one place in a document to another or to copy material to another place in the current document or another document. The Edit commands are available only when you are actually working on a document and there is something available to be cut or copied and pasted.

- *<Cut>* Use <Cut> to remove the selected frame, block of text, or graphic from the display and hold it in a memory buffer for subsequent recall. Publish It! establishes three discrete and separate buffer areas in RAM for frames, text, and graphics. Thus, cutting a frame after having cut something other then a frame will not affect it. But only one item of each type can be retained in a memory buffer at one time.

Figure 4-20. *The Publish It! Edit menu*

- *<Copy>* Use <Copy> to place the material to be copied into a memory buffer. That material remains on display in its current location and is available to be copied to another area in the current document or to a different document.
- *<Paste>* Use <Paste> to place the cut or copied material back into the currently active or other document. In the <FRAME> mode the frame is superimposed over the original frame, slightly offset, if you continue to work on the same page. If, after using <Cut> or <Copy> you move to another page before clicking on <Paste>, the frame appears on the same position on that new page. Anything contained within the frame, text, or graphics, is cut, copied, and pasted along with the frame, as are frame borders and frame tints. The newly pasted frame remains selected and can be moved using the grabber function, the open hand that appears if you hold down the mouse button inside a selected frame, as described in Chapter 3, "The Screen Displays."

  If you want to cut or copy several frames at once, hold down the SHIFT key and click on the frames to be selected, or hold down the mouse button and drag the mouse across the desired frames. All frames selected in this manner are enclosed on the screen, as shown in Figure 4-21, and can now be cut, copied, or pasted as a group.
- *<Select all>* If you want all frames on the active page to be selected simultaneously, click on <Select all> as in Figure 4-22, and all frames on the page are instantly enclosed as shown in Figure 4-23, and can now be cut, copied, or pasted at will.

The Options Menu

The options in the Options menu, shown in Figure 4-24, represent a variety of functions affecting the screen display and selected frames. Most of the options available from the Options menu are toggles: when you click on one for the first time the option is selected, and when you click on it again the option is canceled.

Figure 4-21. *Two frames selected simultaneously*

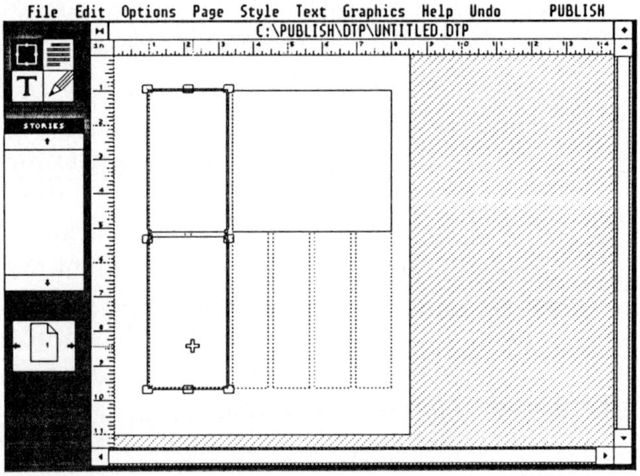

Figure 4-22. *Clicking on <Select all> selects all frames on the page*

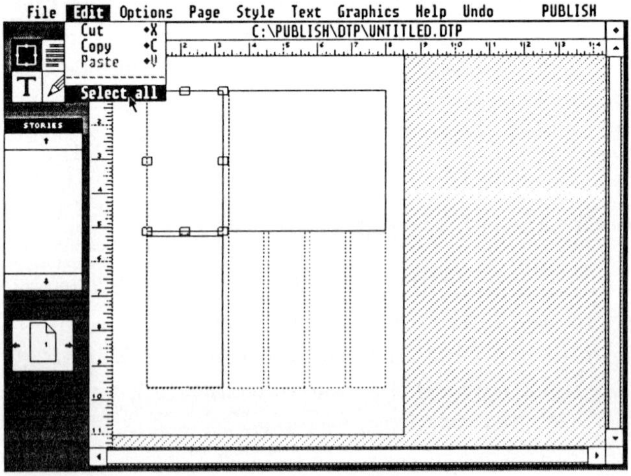

Figure 4-23. *All frames on the page are selected*

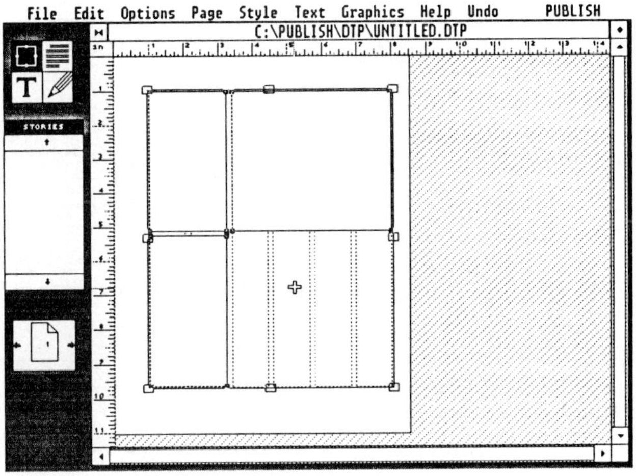

- *<Show tools>* You use <Show tools> to expand the document screen to cover the entire screen area, hiding the toolbox icons as well as

Figure 4-24. *The Publish It! Options menu*

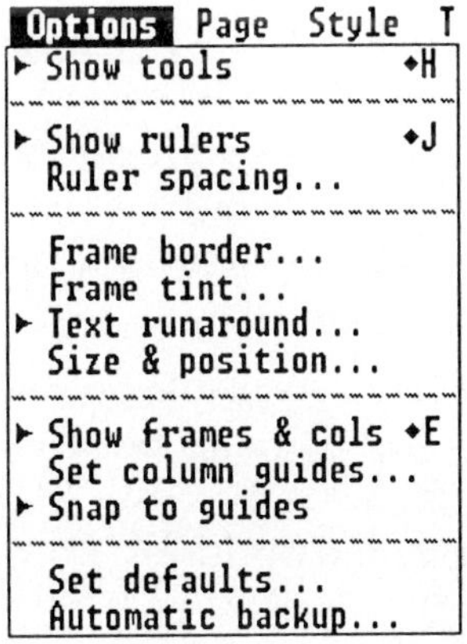

Figure 4-25. *The Ruler Spacing dialog box*

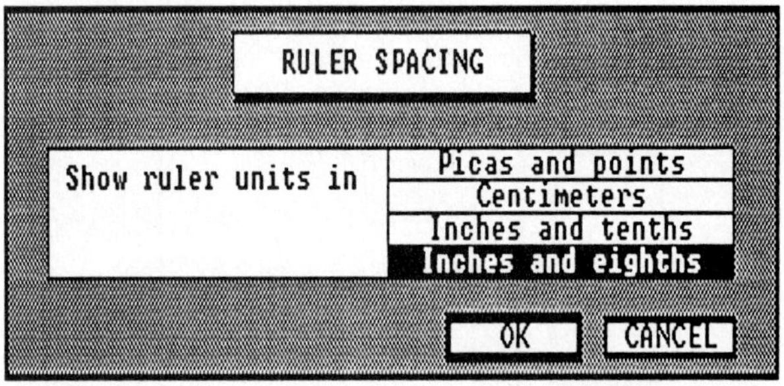

the Library window and the <PAGE> icon. The effect is identical to that obtained by clicking on the full box. When the toolbox is hidden, the tool selection can be changed by using the ALT-M quick key.

- <*Show rulers*> Use <Show rulers> to toggle rulers on or off along the top and left edge of the document screen. When you move the pointer inside the work area, fine lines move along in the rulers to indicate the exact X and Y positions of the pointer. Unless otherwise programmed, the rulers are calibrated in inches and eighths of an inch.
- <*Ruler spacing*> Use <Ruler spacing> to change the calibration, which by default is inches and eighths of an inch. You can select <Inches and eighths>, <Inches and tenths>, <Picas and points>, or <Centimeters> by using the dialog box shown in Figure 4-25. Whatever measurement you choose affects all measurement-related data used in dialog boxes.
- <*Frame border*> Available only when there is a selected frame in the work area, the <Frame border> option produces the dialog box shown in Figure 4-26, from which you can select different frame border styles and positions. Borders created in this manner are tied

Figure 4-26. *The Frame Border dialog box*

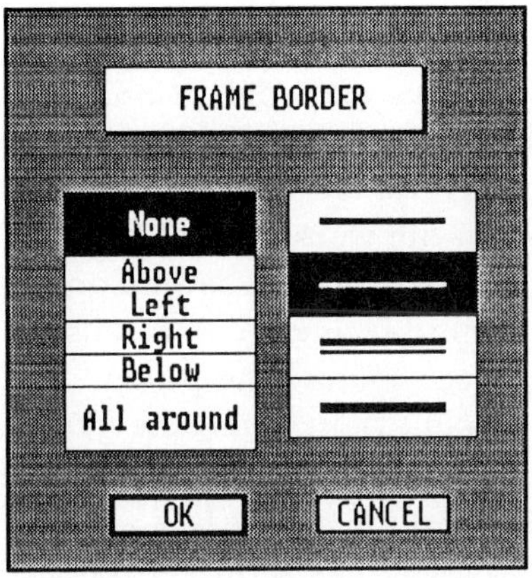

to the frames with which they are associated. If the frame dimensions are changed, the borders change accordingly.

- <*Frame tint*> Available only when a frame is selected, the <Frame tint> option produces the dialog box shown in Figure 4-27, from

Figure 4-27. *The Frame Tint dialog box*

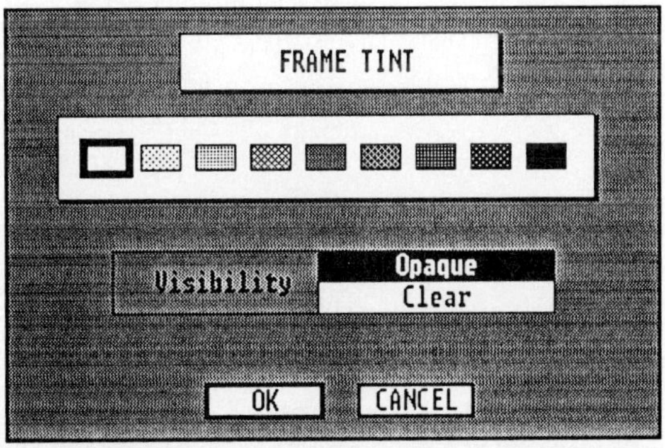

which you can select tint styles ranging from pure white to solid black. When you select the <Clear> option for a frame placed in front of another, the one in the back shows through.

- *<Text runaround>* You use <Text runaround> to control the manner in which text is positioned around a frame that is placed onto one or several text frames. It is available only when there are active frames in the work area. When you select it, the dialog box shown in Figure 4-28 displays several options. By default, text automatically runs around frames. You can use this box to specify the amount of blank space around the frame.

  You might want to use the <Text runaround> option to have text flow smoothly around a graphic like the one shown in Figure 4-29. Then, when the dialog box appears, click on <Define> in the <Left border> block, as shown in Figure 4-30. This produces a hairline cross cursor that controls a thin dashed line anchored to the top and bottom center handles. As you move the cursor, it produces a new left frame border that can be anchored in as many as 29 spots by clicking the mouse button. When the left border is complete, double-click to return to the dialog box. Click on <Define> in the

Figure 4-28. *The Text Runaround dialog box*

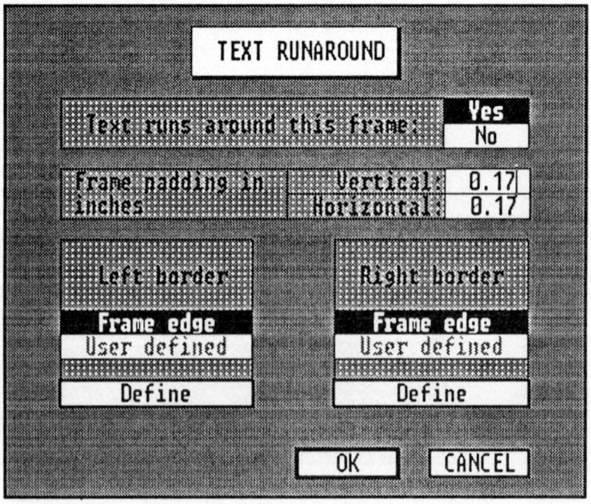

Figure 4-29. *After importing a graphic, <Text runaround> is selected in the Options menu*

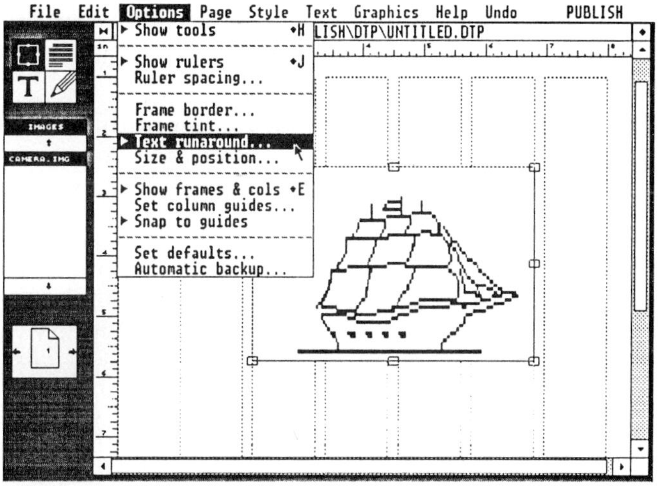

Figure 4-30. *Clicking on <Define> activates the option that produces odd-shaped frames*

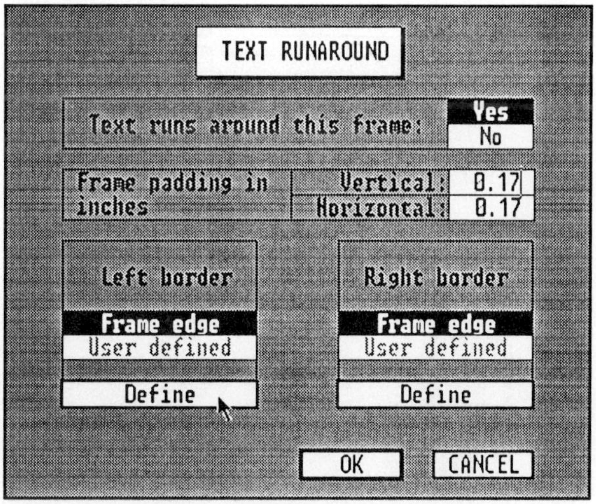

<Right border> block and repeat the procedure for the right border, as shown in Figure 4-31. When you're finished (see Figure 4-32), double-click, and the original rectangular frame becomes transparent while the new free-form frame remains visible (Figure 4-33). If this frame is included in a block of text, the text will flow neatly around the free-form outline.

You can use the same routine with an empty frame to create a frame of any shape (see an example in Figure 4-34). You can now either import text from an external text file into this user-defined frame, or you can access the <TEXT> mode and type text directly into it. To produce Figure 4-35, in the <Frame tint> option in the Option menu, black was selected and in the <TEXT> mode <White> was selected by clicking on it in the Library window. Then the text was typed directly into the diamond-shaped frame.

- *<Size & position>* <Size & position> is available only when there are selected frames in the work area. When you select it, the dialog box

Figure 4-31. *The new frame can be anchored on up to 29 spots*

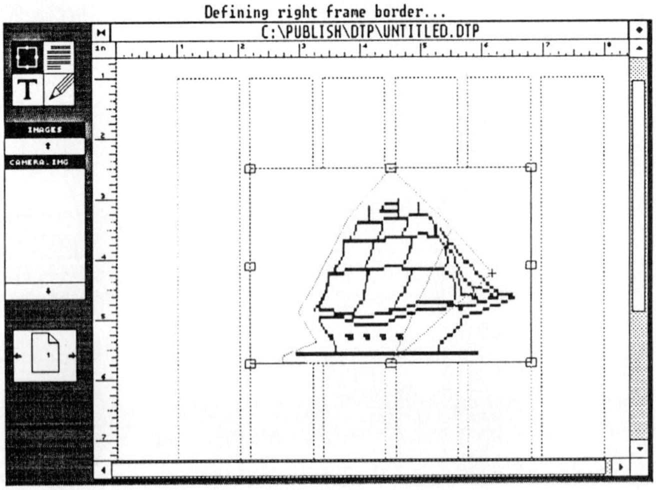

Figure 4-32. *A new frame is drawn around the graphic*

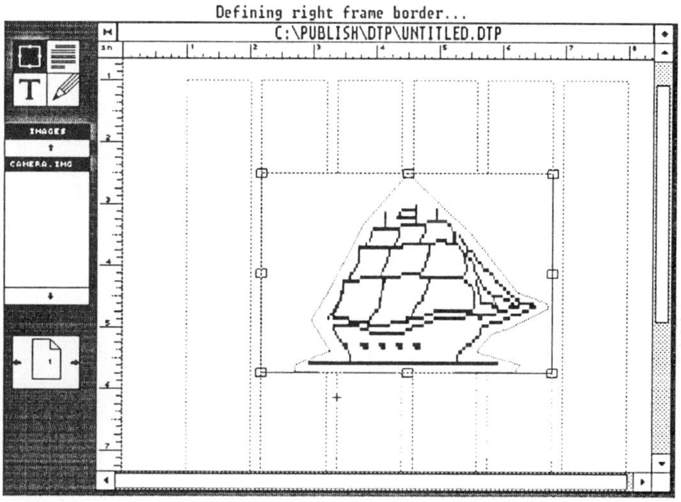

Figure 4-33. *Finally, the rectangular frame becomes transparent while the new frame remains visible*

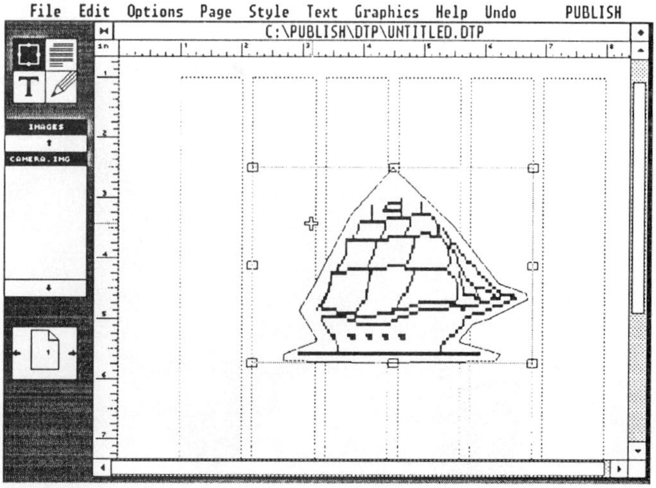

4

Figure 4-34. *Empty frames can take on any shape*

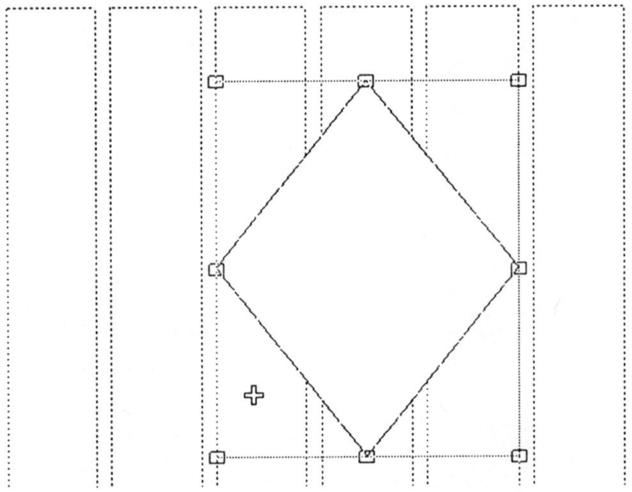

Figure 4-35. *A printout with white text on black in a diamond-shaped frame*

shown in Figure 4-36 is displayed. It shows the X and Y (horizontal and vertical) positions and the width and height of the selected frame. It uses the measurements that you selected from the <Ruler spacing> option or the default measurements.

- *<Show frames and columns>* You use <Show frames and columns> to choose to hide or show the dotted column guides and the outlines of frames. What remains on the screen is the material that will be printed. You will find that this option often helps you visualize what the final printed page will look like.
- *<Set column guides>* Use <Set column guides> to display the dialog box shown in Figure 4-37. You can use this to set up a group of specifications. You can specify the top, bottom, inner, and outer margins on each page. You can specify the number of column guides on each page (the default is 6, the minimum is 1, and the maximum is 9). You can specify the amount of white space between columns. And you can control the print offset that is printer dependent.

  Different printers may print data in a somewhat different position from that shown on the screen. To determine how your printer handles this problem, follow these steps:

1. Select <Open> from the File menu, and if necessary change the directory line to show the files in the SAMPLES subdirectory on

Figure 4-36. *The Size and Position dialog box*

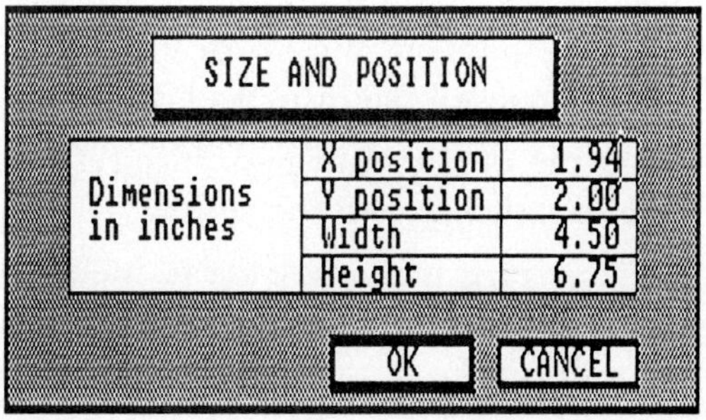

Figure 4-37. *The Set Column Guides dialog box*

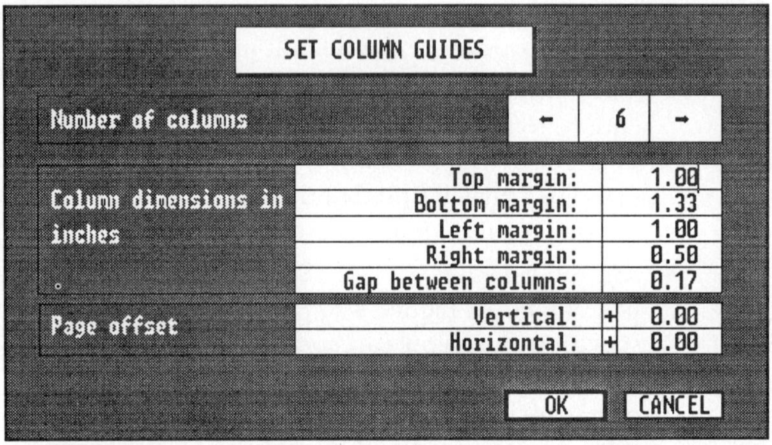

the hard drive. Select <TESTCARD.DTP> from the Item Selector box.

2. Select <Show rulers> in the Options menu.
3. Select <Print> in the File menu to print the TESTCARD.DTP file.
4. Use a ruler or measuring tape to measure how far up and to the left the print position should be moved in order to match the display on the screen.
5. Select <Set column guides> in the Options menu. Enter those measurements in the Vertical Page offset and Horizontal Page offset boxes in the displayed dialog box.
6. Print the document again. If necessary repeat the process until you're satisfied with the result.

At this stage it is advisable to modify the default style sheet in order to make sure that all subsequent documents use the corrected print position. To do so, follow these steps:

1. Select <New> in the File menu.
2. Click on <No> in the dialog box that asks whether or not you want to load a style sheet.
3. Select <Set column guides> from the Options menu and enter the position adjustment measurements into the two Page offset fields.
4. Select <Save style sheet> from the File menu and save the new version of DEFAULT.STY to disk.

All subsequently produced documents with the .DTP extension will be printed in the correct position on the page. Documents you have already created and saved will have their page offset changed before you print them again.

- *<Snap to guides>* Using <Snap to guides> attaches frames automatically to the dotted column guides horizontally and to the dots vertically. This simplifies the task of having all frames correctly aligned. It is the default condition. You can deactivate it by clicking on it if you want frames to be placed near but not on the column guides.
- *<Set defaults>* <Set defaults> is available only with Publish It! version 2.0. Clicking on <Set defaults> results in a dialog box that displays all currently used default conditions, as shown in Figure 4-38. You can click on any one of the options and then replace it with another option that then becomes the default condition from then on. Here the <Use EMS (LIM)> or <Use XMS> options, if available, are used to control how Publish It! makes use of any available expanded or extended memory.
- *<Automatic backup>* <Automatic backup> is available only with Publish It! version 2.0. Selecting it displays the dialog box shown in Figure 4-39. It lets you activate the <Automatic backup> option, determine at what interval you want your work saved, whether to simply sound a warning beep or to perform an actual save, and if the latter, what file extension you want to give the backup files.

Figure 4-38. *The Set Defaults dialog box*

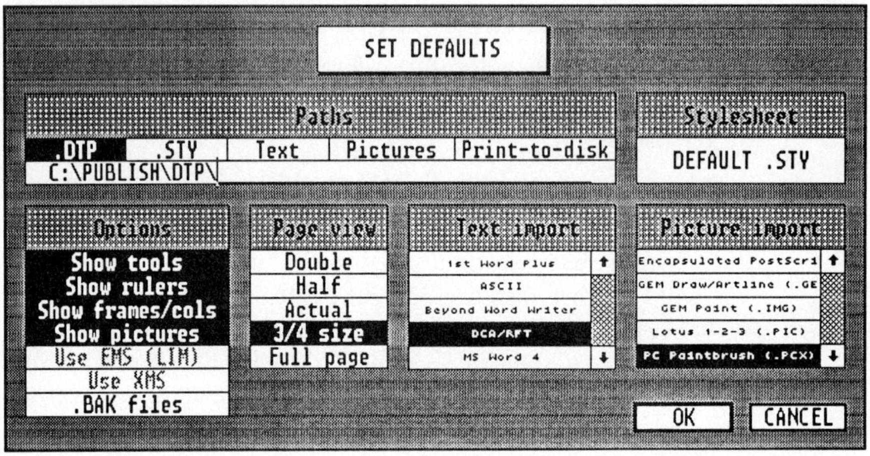

Figure 4-39. *The Automatic Timed Backup dialog box*

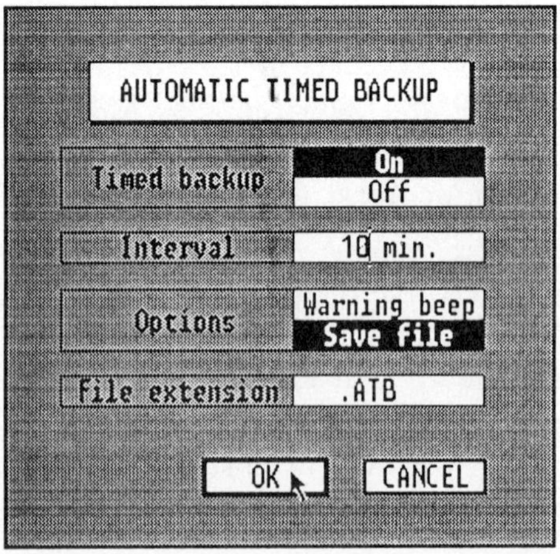

The Page Menu

The Page menu, shown in Figure 4-40, consists of two groups of commands for pages and one group for overlapping frames, which is available only when there are active frames to work with. The commands in the Page menu let you insert or delete pages, move to specified pages quickly, and provide different views of the document screen.

- *<Size to fit>* Using <Size to fit> displays the entire page. In this option the text appears greeked, which means that text is replaced by squiggly lines. This size is especially useful to determine whether or not the overall layout is pleasing to the eye.
- *<Half size>* Use <Half size> to display the document half its actual size. This feature is useful when you want to get a better idea of the layout of your page.
- *<3/4 size>* Available only with Publish It! 2.0, <3/4 size> displays the current page in a size that shows much of the page but retains legible text.
- *<Actual size>* The default condition when Publish It! is first started, <Actual size> displays a portion of the document in actual size–the size in which it will eventually appear on the printed page. Depend-

Figure 4-40. *The Publish It! Page menu*

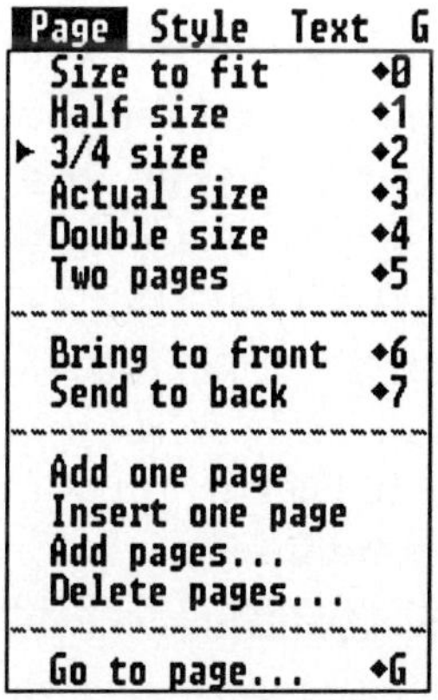

ing on the resolution of your monitor, small text may be a bit difficult to read in this view.

- *<Double size>* Use <Double size> to display a portion of the document twice the actual size. In this view even small text is clearly readable, making this option the best one to effect formatting changes and do detail work on graphics and text.
- *<Two pages>* Using <Two pages> displays two pages in the same size as <Size to fit>. When a document consists of multiple pages, this option is useful in determining whether the appearance of two facing pages in relation to one another is satisfactory. Odd-numbered pages are always displayed on the right and even-numbered on the left.
- *<Bring to front>* Used when the document includes overlapping frames, <Bring to front> displays the hidden portion of the selected frame and hides a portion of the other frame. If the frame in front is transparent (see the <Clear> option from the <Frame tint> selection in the Options menu), the contents of the frame in the back will show through.
- *<Send to back>* Also used when the document includes overlapping frames, <Send to back> causes the frame in front to be moved to the back. Portions of this frame will be hidden. If the frame that is now in front is transparent (see the <Clear> option from the <Frame tint> selection in the Options menu), the contents of the frame in the back will show through. <Text runaround> from the Options menu will also have an effect on frame overlapping.
- *<Add one page>* Use <Add one page> to insert a blank page after the currently active page. If a master page was created for this document, clicking on <Add one page> creates a copy of the master page and inserts it after the current page.
- *<Insert one page>* Use <Insert one page> to insert a blank page before the currently active page. If a master page was created for this document, clicking on <Insert one page> creates a copy of the master page and inserts it before the current page.
- *<Add pages>* Available only with Publish It! version 2.0, <Add pages> is used to insert any number of pages between the currently

Figure 4-41. *The Add Pages dialog box*

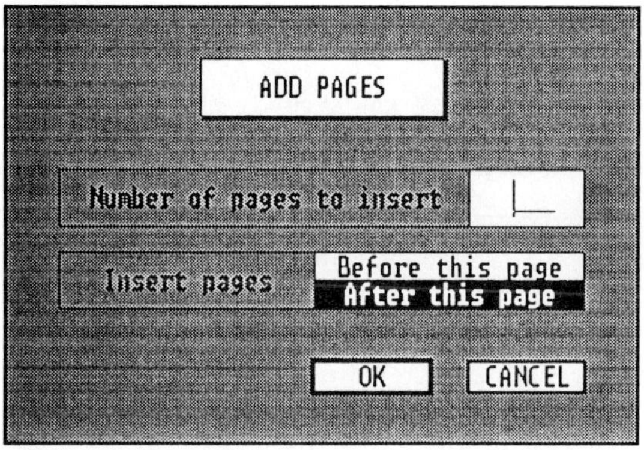

active page and the next numbered page, or before the currently active page, using the dialog box in Figure 4-41.

- *<Delete pages>* Available only in Publish It! 2.0, the <Delete pages> option displays the dialog box in Figure 4-42. It asks that you specify

Figure 4-42. *The Delete Pages dialog box*

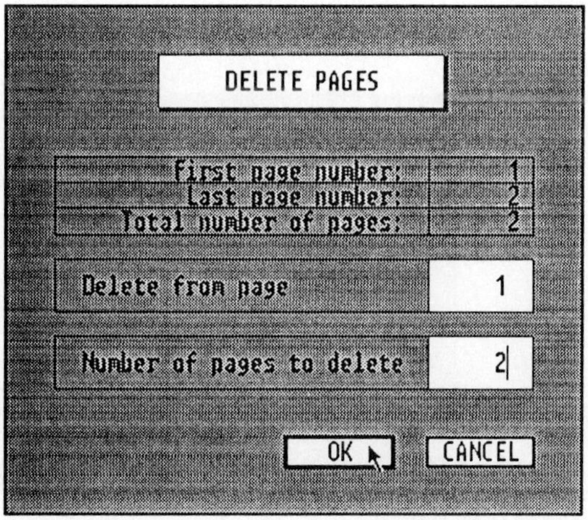

Figure 4-43. *The warning box that appears before pages are deleted*

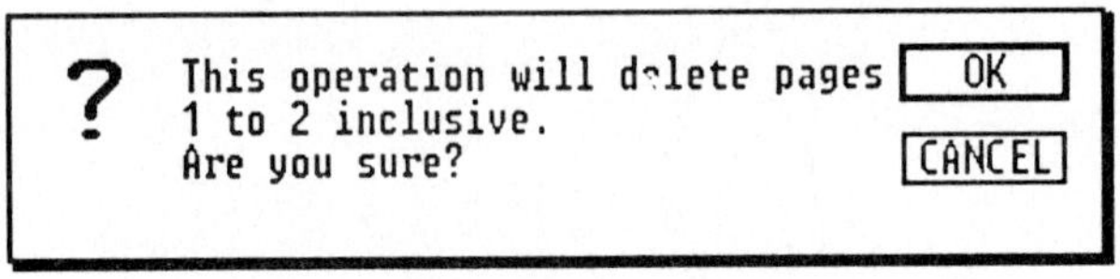

which pages you want to delete, resulting in a warning box, as shown in Figure 4-43, that makes sure that the selected number of pages is actually to be deleted. (Earlier versions included a <Delete page> option that resulted in a warning box.)

- *<Go to page>* Using <Go to page> sends the computer directly to a specified page or to the master page, if one was prepared for the document. It displays the dialog box shown in Figure 4-44, from which one of the available choices can be selected by entering a page number or clicking on the check mark.

Figure 4-44. *The Go to Page dialog box*

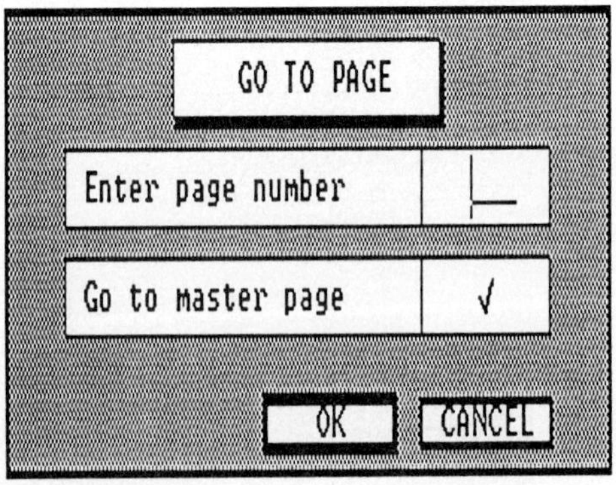

The Style Menu

The Style menu, shown in Figure 4-45, offers a group of options that control the style and size of text being typed or of entire paragraphs of text. In the <TEXT> mode this menu contains a group of commands that affect the text style, font, and point size of newly typed text or of marked text. Text is marked by dragging the I-beam pointer across the portion of text that is to be affected. If no text is marked, only text that is typed subsequently is affected. In the <PARAGRAPH> mode it affects previously marked paragraphs and all paragraphs that use the same label as the marked paragraph. (For a discussion of labels, see Chapter 6, "Importing and Manipulating Text.") Attributes selected in the <TEXT> mode override those selected in the <PARAGRAPH> mode.

- *<Font/size>* Selecting <Font/size> displays the dialog box shown in Figure 4-46, which shows the available font styles and sizes. The displayed sizes vary when different font styles are selected, because not all styles are available in all sizes. You might consider preparing a text document that uses all styles in different sizes. Print it in order to find out how your printer handles the different text attributes.

Figure 4-45. *The Publish It! Style menu*

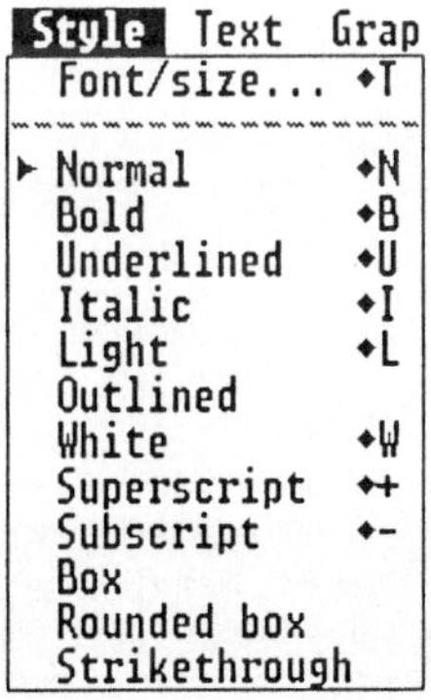

The <Bullets> option produces a number of art symbols. These symbols, known as dingbats in typesetting circles, can be used to emphasize items in lists or to accentuate short phrases. While these bullets could be produced by typing the lowercase letters "a" through "o" in version 1.1, in all versions later than 1.2, bullets are inserted one at a time using the bulleted paragraph style.

- *<Normal>* Using <Normal> resets marked text or paragraphs to the font style and size that was used before the last <Font/size> command.

The following options are toggle commands, meaning that clicking on one activates the option for the selected text or paragraph. Clicking on it a second time returns the text or paragraph to its previous state.

- *<Bold>* Using <Bold> causes the selected text or paragraph to be printed in bold type.
- *<Underlined>* Use <Underlined> to underline the selected text or paragraph.
- *<Italic>* Use <Italic> to change the selected text or paragraph to italic in the active typeface.

Figure 4-46. *The Font & Size dialog box*

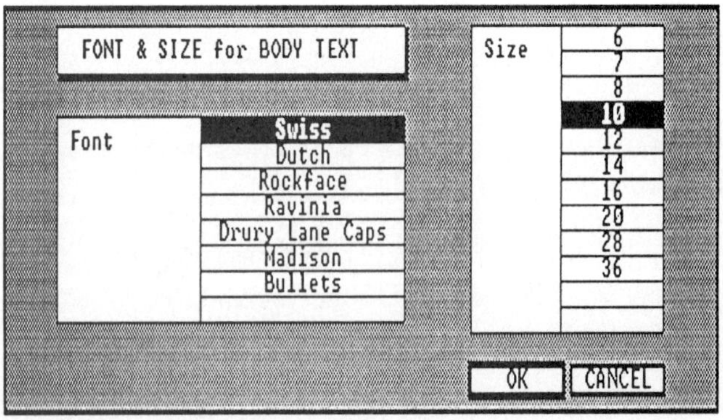

- *<Light>* Use <Light> to print text in a lighter shade.
- *<White>* Use <White> to print text in white on a dark background. You can produce dark or black background colors using the <Frame tint> option in the Options menu.
- *<Superscript>* Using <Superscript> places typed characters a half line width up.
- *<Subscript>* Using <Subscript> places typed characters a half line width down.
- *<Box>* Available only with Publish It! version 2.0, <Box> places a rectangular box around selected text.
- *<Rounded box>* Available only with Publish It! version 2.0, <Rounded box> places a rectangular box with rounded corners around selected text.
- *<Strikethrough>* Available only with Publish It! version 2.0, <Strikethrough> draws a line through selected text. Figure 4-47 shows the results of these last three options.

Figure 4-47. *Using the <Box>, <Rounded box>, and <Strikethrough> options*

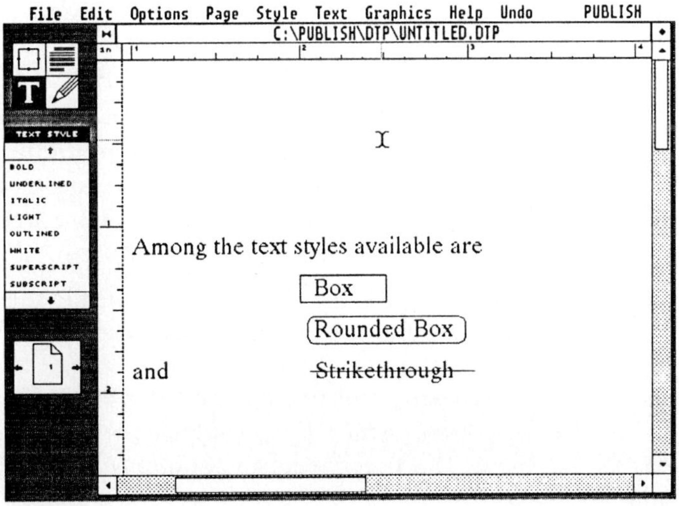

Figure 4-48. *The Publish It! Text menu*

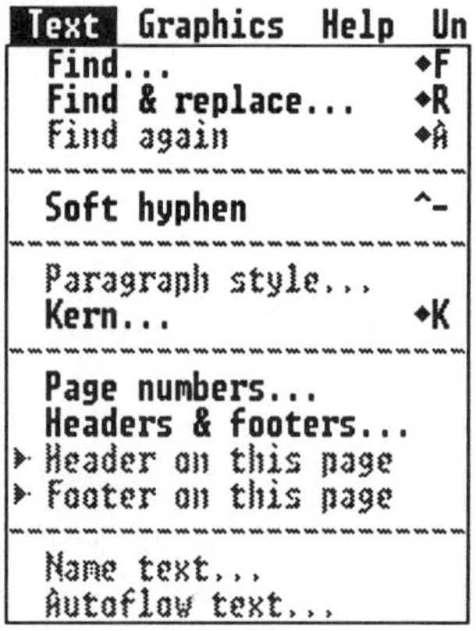

The Text Menu

The Text menu, shown in Figure 4-48, is used to find and replace words or phrases, to include typographic and hyphenation options, and to produce headers and footers.

- *<Find>* Using <Find> displays the dialog box shown in Figure 4-49. You key in the word or phrase you are looking for. It also includes the option to either match or ignore upper- or lowercase.
- *<Find & replace>* Using <Find & replace> displays the dialog box shown in Figure 4-50, in which you type the word or phrase to be replaced and the replacement text. The upper- or lowercase option is included, as is an option to replace all occurrences of the word or phrase, some of them, or only one of them.
- *<Find again>* Use <Find again> to continue the <Find> or the <Find & Replace> options selected previously.

<Find>, <Find & replace>, and <Find again> are available only when you are in the <TEXT> mode. These options affect text from the cursor position forward to the end of the document. Text from the cursor position back to the front of the document remains unaffected.

Figure 4-49. *The Find dialog box*

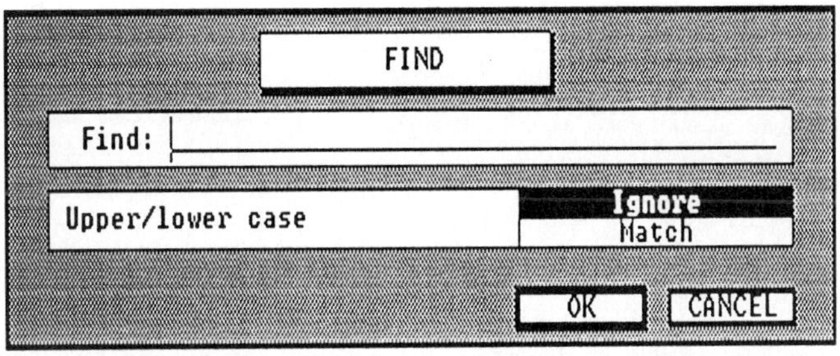

Figure 4-50. *The Find and Replace dialog box*

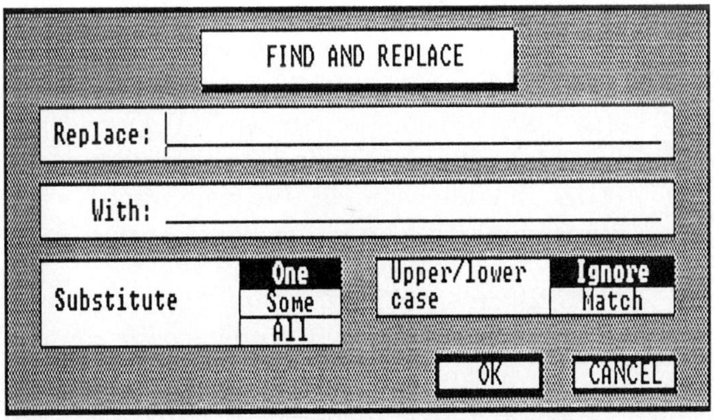

Figure 4-51. *A Paragraph Style dialog box*

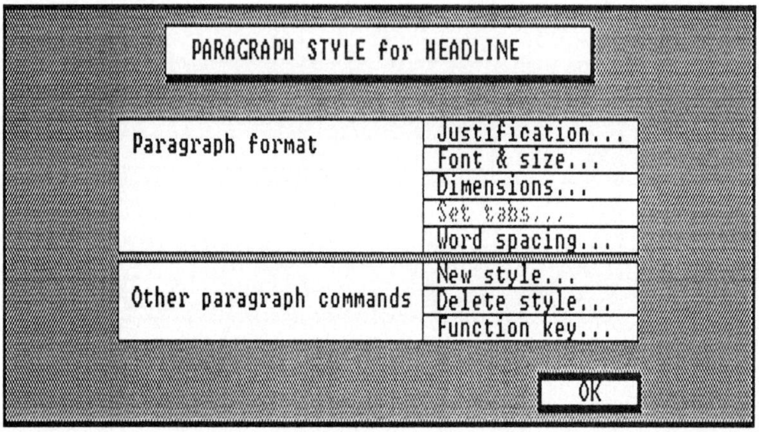

- *<Soft hyphen>* Use <Soft hyphen> to enter your own hyphenation of a given word instead of the one added automatically by Publish It!. The hyphen is inserted at the text cursor position and takes preference over the hyphens added by the program. Placing a soft hyphen at the start of a word prevents it from being hyphenated at all.
- *<Paragraph style>* Available in the <PARAGRAPH> mode, the Paragraph Style dialog box, shown in Figure 4-51, contains options that produce secondary dialog boxes that show the current paragraph styles. In this example, the paragraph is entitled "Headline," as shown in the title box. The options are as follows:

  Click on <Justification> and the dialog box shown in Figure 4-52 appears. This is used to determine the justification format for the currently selected paragraph. The options are <Flushed left>, <Flushed right>, <Justified>, <Centered>, and <Table>. The currently selected option, <Centered>, is highlighted. It can be

Figure 4-52. *The Paragraph Options dialog box*

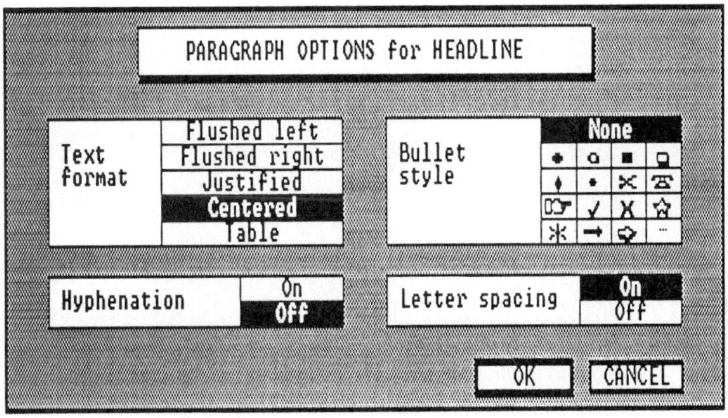

changed by clicking on one of the other options displayed. Also included in the Paragraph Options secondary dialog box is the <Hyphenation> option that controls automatic hyphenation; the <Letter spacing> option, which determines the spaces between letters in individual words when <Justified> is selected; and the <Bullet style> selection box, in which you can click on the bullet symbol you wish to use.

Click on <Font & size> to produce the dialog box shown in Figure 4-53. That dialog box displays the available font styles and sizes. This dialog box is identical to the one that appears when you click on <Font/size> in the Style menu.

Click on <Dimensions> to display the dialog box shown in Figure 4-54. You can use it to determine the amount of white space above the paragraph, the size of any first-line indent, the sizes of the left and right paragraph indents, and the amount of space between the lines of text.

Figure 4-53. *The Font & Size dialog box*

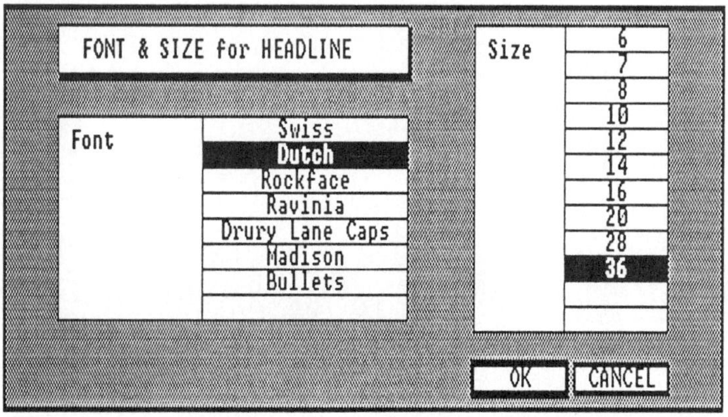

Figure 4-54. *The Paragraph Dimensions dialog box*

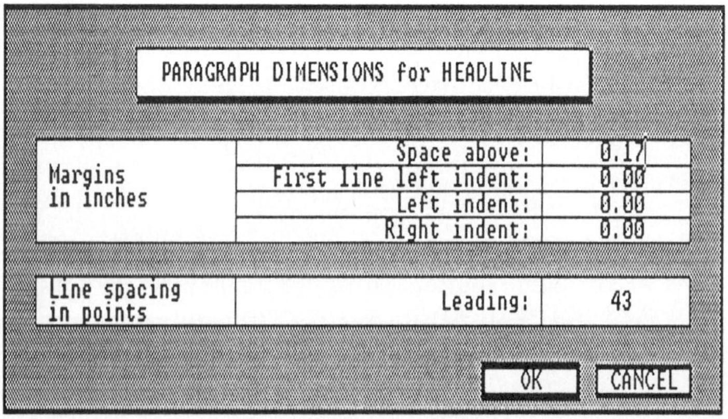

Click on <Word spacing> to display the dialog box shown in Figure 4-55. You use it to set the maximum and minimum space between words and the size of an acceptable hyphenation zone that can result from the justification option.

Click on <New style> and the dialog box shown in Figure 4-56 displays the current style with the text cursor to its right. Press BACKSPACE or ESC to erase the displayed style and replace it with another. You can assign the new choice to one of the function keys. Function keys that are already assigned to a particular style are dimmed or pale gray and not available.

If you select <Delete style> you receive the warning shown in Figure 4-57. Remember that Body Text can never be deleted.

The <Function key> option displays a dialog box like the one shown in Figure 4-56. You can use it to assign styles to function keys.

In the earlier versions of Publish It! you are able to select <Set tabs> only if the Table style is selected by clicking on <Justifica-

Figure 4-55. *The Word Spacing dialog box*

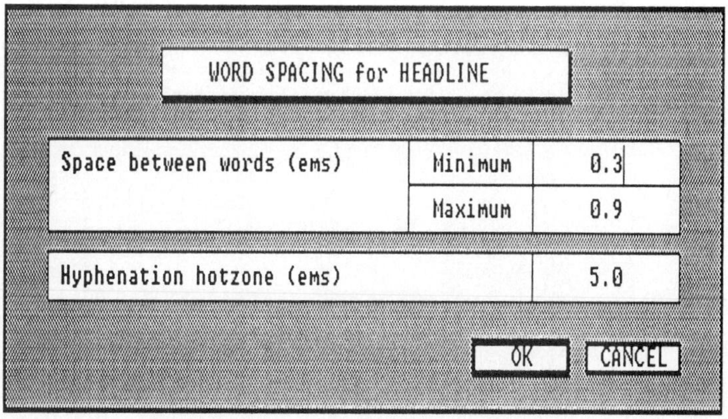

Figure 4-56. *The Paragraph Style Name dialog box*

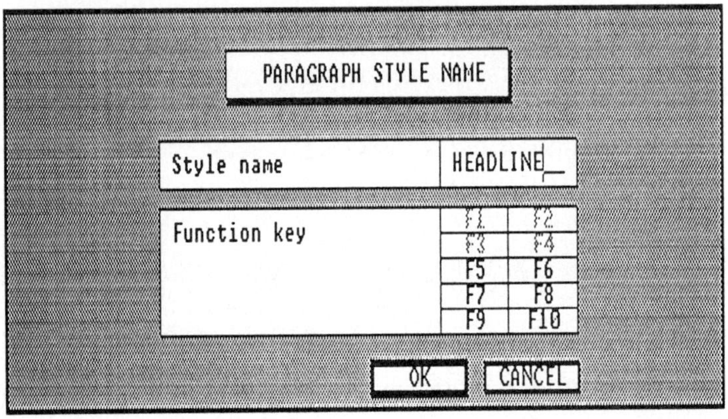

Figure 4-57. *The warning box that appears when <Delete style> is selected*

Figure 4-58. *The Set Tab Points dialog box*

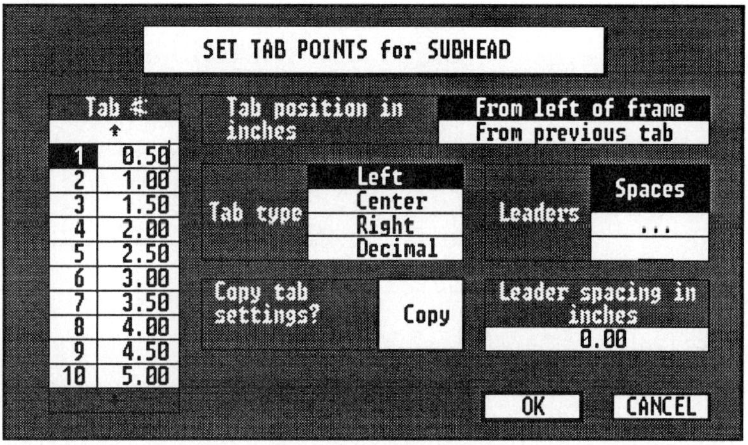

tion> and selecting <Table> from the displayed options. In the Paragraph Style dialog box shown in Figure 4-53, the <Set tabs> option is grayed to indicate that it is not available at that stage. The <Set tabs> option displays the dialog box shown in Figure 4-58. You can use it to determine the kind of tab stop: left, center, right, or decimal. This determination must be made before tab positions are entered. Up to 14 tab positions (9 in earlier versions) can be entered. Publish It! version 2.0 has simplified the task, using a <Copy tab settings> option. Say, for example, you want to space all your tabs .75 apart and have the space between the tabbed items filled with leaders. You set Tab #1 at .75 and select leaders. You then click on the <Copy> button and all other tabs share those identical parameters.

- *<Kern>* <Kern> moves individual characters closer together or farther apart. It displays a dialog box, shown in Figure 4-59, that asks you to key in the kerning amount in points and specify either + (farther apart) or – (closer together). It is possible to use the quick key ALT-K to move characters closer together by a half point rather than display the dialog box.

Figure 4-59. *The Kern dialog box*

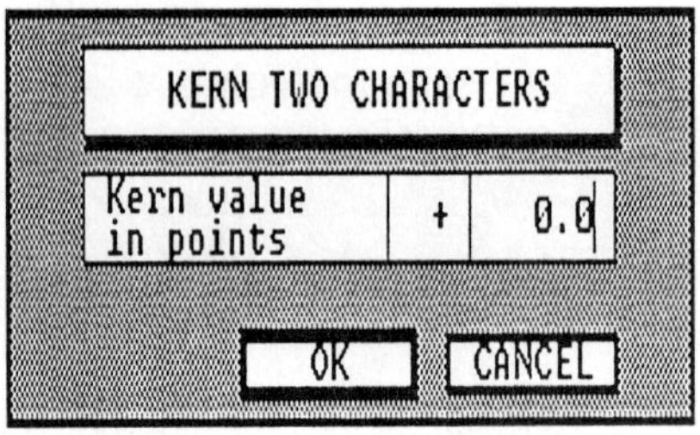

- *<Page numbers>* <Page numbers> is available only with Publish It! version 2.0. Clicking on <Page numbers> gives you the dialog box shown in Figure 4-60. It displays the different formats available for page numbering.
- *<Headers & footers>* Use <Headers & footers> to display the dialog box shown in Figure 4-61. Each header and footer can have up to three sections: one left aligned, one centered, and one right aligned. The headers and footers can appear exclusively on left pages, right

Figure 4-60. *The Page Number Format dialog box*

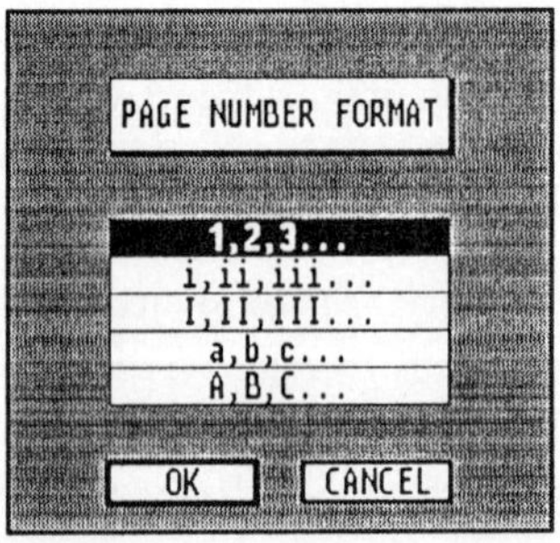

Figure 4-61. *The Headers and Footers dialog box*

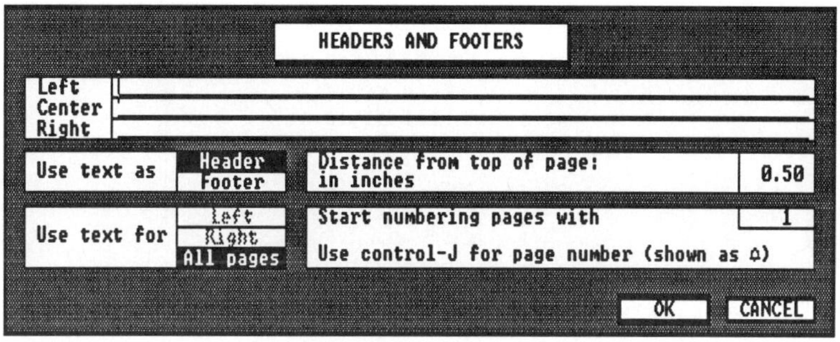

pages, or on all pages. This dialog box also is used to set distances from the tops of pages for headers and the bottoms of pages for footers. If the key combination CTRL-J is typed into a header or footer, it is replaced automatically by the current page number. In Publish It! version 2.0 you can automatically generate "Page X of X" information using the percent sign (%) where you want the total number of pages to appear.

- *<Header on this page>* Using <Header on this page> turns the header off for the current page.
- *<Footer on this page>* Using <Footer on this page> turns the footer off for the current page.
- *<Name text>* See the <Export text> discussion under "The File Menu" earlier in this chapter.
- *<Autoflow text>* See Appendix F, "Publish It! Version 2.0," for a discussion of this option.

The Graphics Menu

The Graphics menu, shown in Figure 4-62, performs a variety of functions, such as determining the style of lines to be drawn and the type of designs with which frames can be filled, as well as scaling, cropping, or editing graphic

Figure 4-62. *The Publish It! Graphics menu*

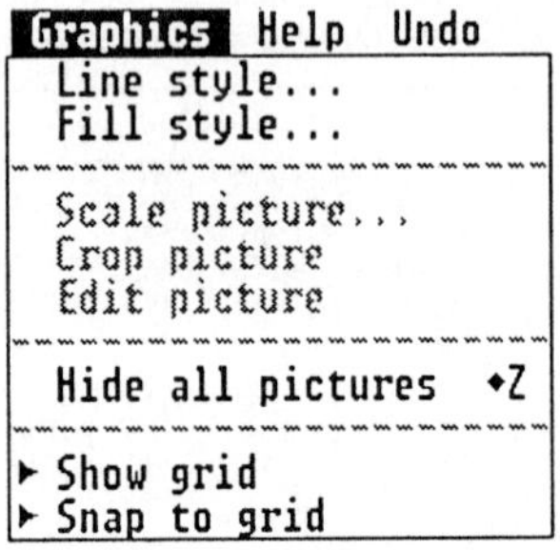

images. When no picture has been imported, the three center commands are not available and are pale gray.

- *<Line style>* Using <Line style> displays the dialog box shown in Figure 4-63, which lets you determine the color of the line (black or white), the hairline style (dotted, dot-dashed, dashed, or solid), and the rule style (very narrow, narrow, medium, or wide). You can also choose to place arrow heads at the beginning, end, or both ends of hairlines or rules. If a currently existing line has been selected, the style applies to it. If not, it applies to the next line(s) to be drawn.
- *<Fill style>* Using <Fill style> displays the dialog box shown in Figure 4-64, which lets you determine the type of design with which an area is to be covered and the color to be used, either black or white. You can choose whether the fill pattern is to be clear to let other objects show through, or opaque to hide other objects. You can also decide whether or not the outer edge of the object is to be displayed.
- *<Hide all pictures>* The <Hide all pictures> option replaces the graphic images with two diagonal lines running through all graphic frames. Since drawing and redrawing graphic images can take a fair amount of time, this is an important time-saver when working with, manipulating, or reformatting text pages that include graphics.

Figure 4-63. *The Line Style dialog box*

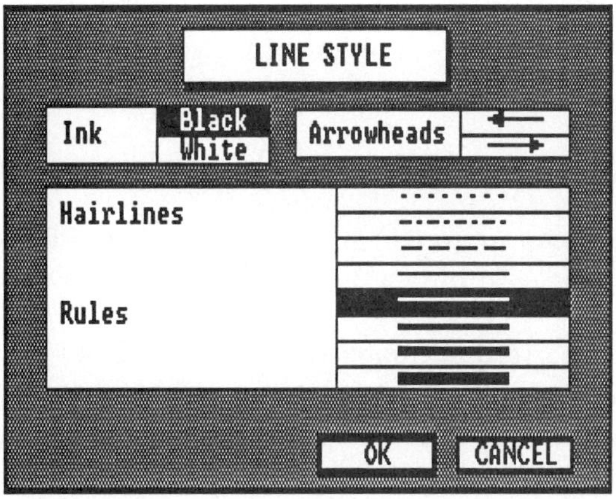

Figure 4-64. *The Fill Style dialog box*

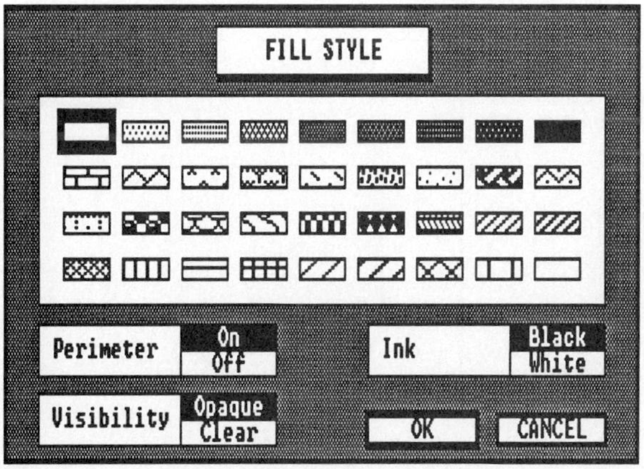

In earlier versions of Publish It! this option is on the Options menu.

- *<Show grid>* A toggle command, <Show grid> lets you either display or hide the graphics grid. Figure 4-65 shows a rounded rectangle in a frame containing the grid lines.

Depending on your video monitor, these grid lines may be hard to see.

- *<Snap to grid>* When used in the <GRAPHICS> mode, <Snap to grid> simplifies the task of aligning different graphic items.

When a graphic image is present and has been selected, the Graphics menu shown in Figure 4-64 changes. The three grayed commands become active, and the four previously active commands are now no longer available.

- *<Scale picture>* Using <Scale picture> displays the dialog box shown in Figure 4-66, which lets you adjust the proportion in terms of depth and width of an image. If the <Aspect ratio> is <Ignore>, the picture is stretched automatically to fill the selected frame. The <Preserve> option maintains the correct aspect ratio. <Whole pixel scaling>

Figure 4-65. *The grid lines in a frame with a rounded rectangle graphic*

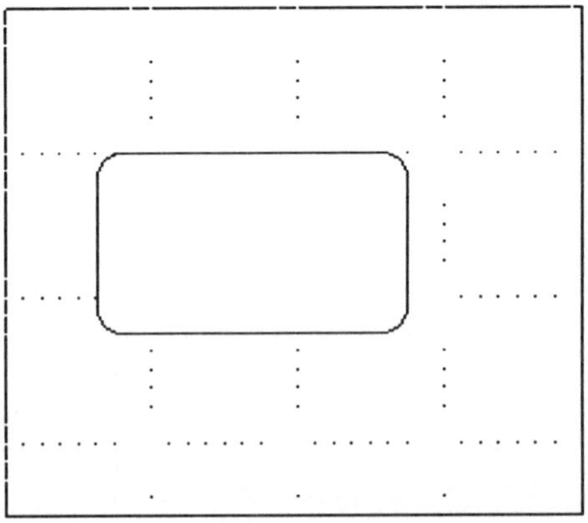

Figure 4-66. *The Scale Picture dialog box*

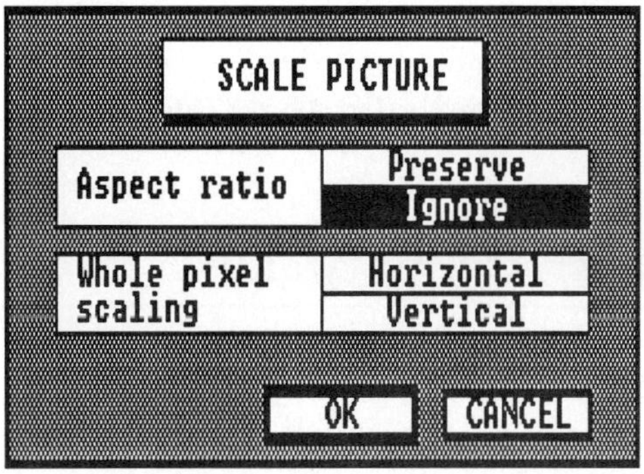

prohibits the strange pattern that tends to occur when an image is enlarged or reduced by a fractional amount.

- *<Crop picture>* The <Crop picture> option turns the pointer into a pair of scissors. When you place the pointer onto the upper-left corner of the portion of the image to be retained and drag the mouse to the lower-right corner, a dotted line appears to indicate where the image is going to be cropped. Release the mouse button when you are satisfied with the cropping indication and the cropped portion of the image is redrawn in the selected frame.
- *<Edit picture>* The <Edit picture> option places a huge enlargement (four times the actual size) of a small portion of the picture on the screen. In this mode you can edit the picture by adding or deleting individual pixels. Clicking on a blank spot adds a pixel. Clicking on an existing pixel deletes it. To exit this mode, click on the Close box. The displayed warning box asks whether to save or abandon the editing changes that were made. Either way, the original image file on disk is not affected. If the edited image has been flowed into more than one frame, each frame is affected.

The Undo Menu

The Undo menu, available only with Publish It! versions 1.2 and 2.0 and shown in Figure 4-67, includes four options, determining what type of material is involved with the steps that you want undone.

The Publish It Lite! Menus

When Publish It Lite! is activated, it displays eight menu titles in the menu bar across the top of the screen. Virtually everything you do with Publish It Lite! is accomplished using one of the options from a menu. Obviously, the more familiar you are with each menu and its options, the more efficient your work with Publish It Lite! will be.

The File Menu

The File menu, shown in Figure 4-68, offers ten command options: <Open>, <Save>, <Save as>, <New>, <Erase>, <Import text>, <Import picture>, <Print>, <Status> and <Quit>. These are used in exactly the same manner as

Figure 4-67. *The Publish It! Undo menu*

Figure 4-68. *The Publish It Lite! File menu*

with Publish It!. (In a recently released version of Publish It Lite!, the <Beyond Words> option in the Import Text dialog box has been replaced with <Word Writer PRO>. This option can be used to import text created using Beyond Word Writer, Word Writer 3, and Word Writer PRO.) The differences in File menu options between the two programs are that in Publish It Lite! the options <Save style sheet>, <Revert to last>, and <Export text> are not available, and the <Import text> and <Import picture> commands produce dialog boxes with fewer options, as shown in Figures 4-69 and 4-70.

The Edit Menu

The Edit menu, shown in Figure 4-71, includes seven command options. The <Cut>, <Copy>, and <Paste> command options are identical to the commands in the Publish It! Edit menu. <Find>, <Replace>, <Kern>, and <Soft hyphen> function in the same manner as the similar commands in the Text menu in Publish It!.

Figure 4-69. *The Publish It Lite! Import Text dialog box*

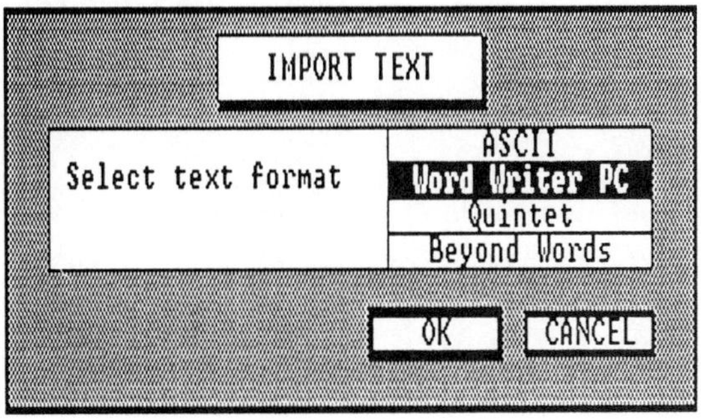

Figure 4-70. *The Publish It Lite! Import Picture dialog box*

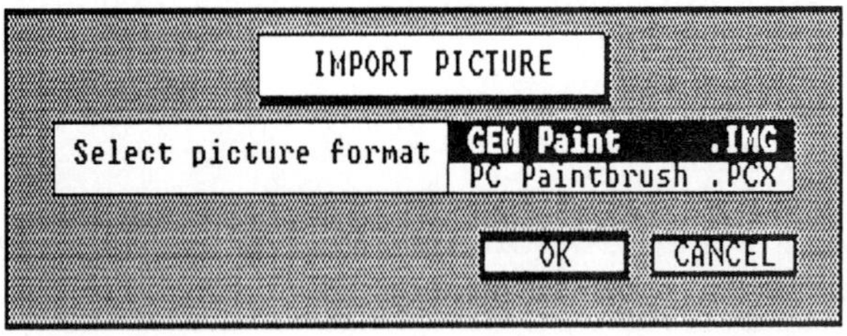

Figure 4-71. *The Publish It Lite! Edit menu*

The Options Menu

The Options menu, shown in Figure 4-72, is limited to five options. <Frame border>, <Size & position>, and <Set column guides> are identical to those commands in Publish It!, except <Frame border> produces a dialog box with fewer options, as shown in Figure 4-73. The <Bring to front> and <Send to back> commands function the same as the Publish It! Page menu commands of the same name.

The Page Menu

The Page menu, shown in Figure 4-74, offers seven options, all of which are also available in the Publish It! Page menu. They function in the same manner, except that <Go to page> produces a dialog box with fewer options, as shown in Figure 4-75.

Figure 4-72. *The Publish It Lite! Options menu*

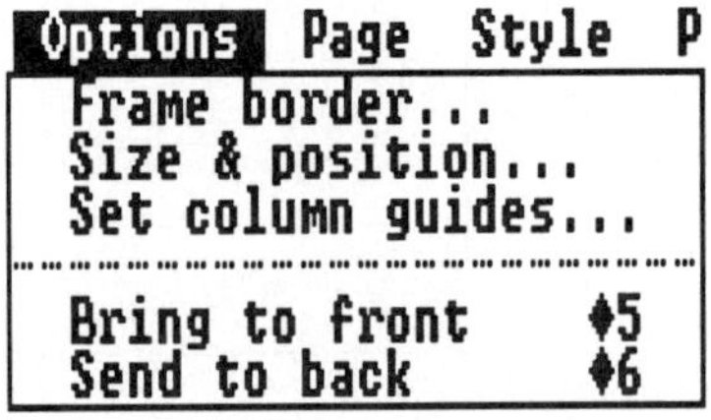

Figure 4-73. *The Publish It Lite! Frame Border dialog box*

Figure 4-74. *The Publish It Lite! Page menu*

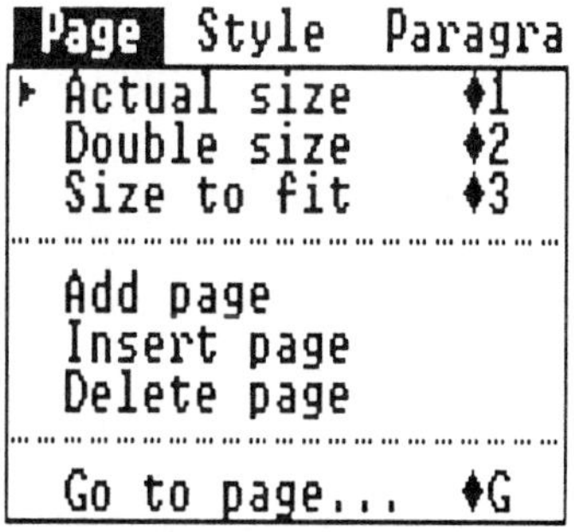

Figure 4-75. *The Publish It Lite! Go to Page dialog box*

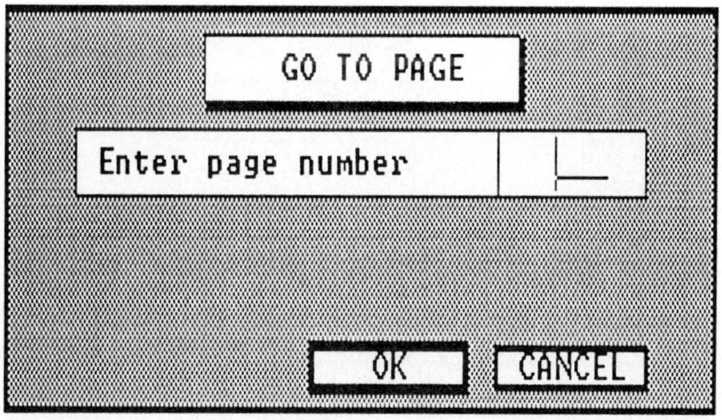

The Style Menu

The Style menu is identical to that for Publish It!, shown in Figure 4-47. When <Font/size> is selected, however, the resulting dialog box offers considerably fewer selections, as shown in Figure 4-76.

The Paragraph Menu

The PARAGRAPH menu, shown in Figure 4-77, is entirely new, and its command options are in different menus than in the Publish It! version.

- *<Left>* Using <Left> means left-justifying or producing ragged copy that starts at the left edge of the paper and extends as far to the right as is possible without unacceptable hyphenation. Pressing (TAB) in this mode indents the text 3/4 of an inch to the right.

Figure 4-76. *The Publish It Lite! Font & Size dialog box*

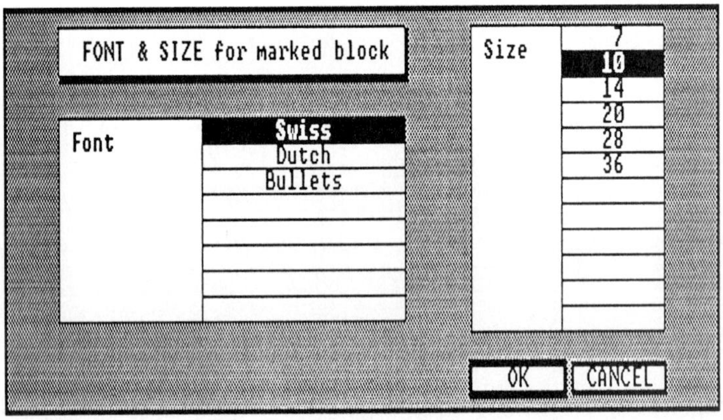

Figure 4-77. *The Publish It Lite! Paragraph menu*

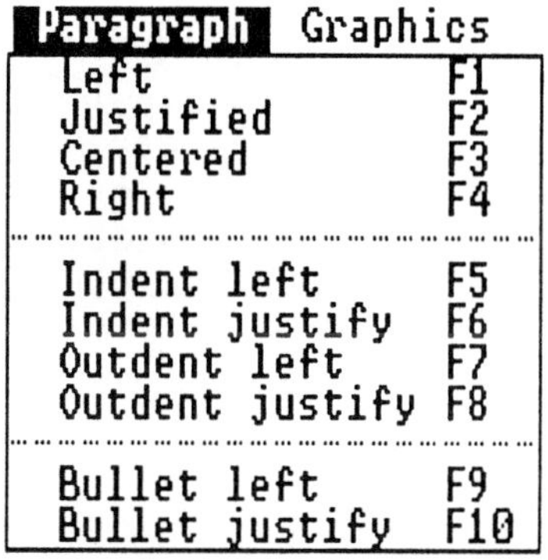

- *<Justified>* Using <Justified> causes both the left and right sides of the text to be justified, resulting in varying spaces between words.
- *<Centered>* Using <Centered> causes text to be centered, with even amounts of blank space to the left and right. This option centers the text in the selected frame, not on the page.
- *<Right>* Using <Right> gives you the same results as <Left>, except the right edge is aligned and the left one is ragged.
- *<Indent left>* Using <Indent left> indents the first line in the selected paragraph 3/4 of an inch.
- *<Indent justify>* Using <Indent justify> indents the first line in the same manner as <Indent left>, but the rest of the paragraph is left and right justified.
- *<Outdent left> and <Outdent justify>* These two options cause the first line to start farther left than the rest of the paragraph. Otherwise they operate in the same manner as the indent options.
- *<Bullet left> and <Bullet justify>* These two options place a bullet at the left and indent the rest of the paragraph, which then appears either ragged at the right or justified on both sides.

Figure 4-78. *The Publish It Lite! Graphics menu*

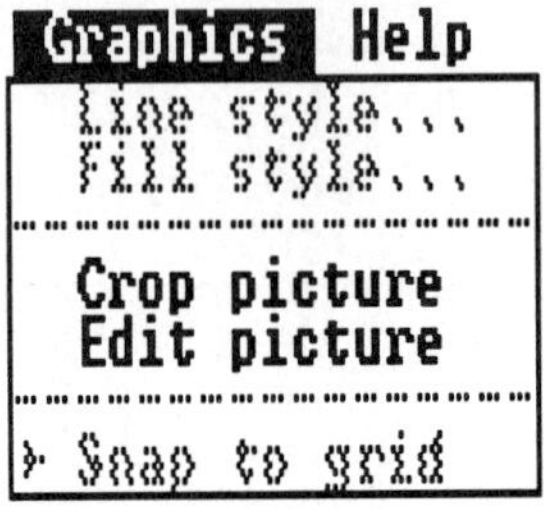

The Graphics Menu

The Graphics menu, shown in Figure 4-78, offers five command options that operate identically to the comparable five options in the Publish It! Graphics menu.

Figure 4-79. *The Publish It! and Publish It Lite! Help menu*

Figure 4-80. *A typical page from the Help menu*

4

The Help Menu

The Help menu, shown in Figure 4-79, is the same in both versions of the program. It calls up helpful information on a number of different subjects listed on the menu. When one of the displayed subjects is selected, a text page like the one in Figure 4-80 appears. In most instances it is the first of a series of such text pages. The Help menu and its options are available at all times, regardless of the currently active mode of operation.

It takes a while to become familiar with all the options offered by Publish It! and Publish It Lite!. Each feature and function is listed in the index of this book to help you find out how to access an option when you need it.

5

The Publish It! Libraries

Publish It Lite! and all three versions of Publish It! each include a Font library, an Art library, and a Document library. The Font library consists of the typefaces available with the selected printer. Publish It! version 2.0 also includes the complete Typografica fonts package, which is described in greater detail later in this chapter and in Appendix A, "Installation." The Art library consists of pages of clip art. Each page contains a selection of images representing related themes. Again, Publish It! version 2.0 also includes two large libraries of high-resolution graphics described later in this chapter. The Document library contains a selection of sample documents that can serve as useful guides in the creation of similar original documents.

The Font Library

Both Publish It! and Publish It Lite! include a variety of font styles and sizes. The available selection depends on the printer that is currently installed with the program. Publish It! supports an enormous number of printer makes and models. During the installation procedure, described in detail in Appendix A, "Installation," you are asked to identify the printer(s) that you intend to use for your desktop publishing work. You are then asked to run a program called FONTWID that is provided as part of the Publish It! program package. It lists the printer(s) that you selected during the installation, and asks that you select the one specific printer that you will be using. It then installs the font styles and sizes that your printer can use into Publish It!, where they are displayed when the <Font/size> option is selected from the Style menu.

The Publish It! Font Library

The font styles and sizes available in Publish It!, assuming a Hewlett-Packard or compatible laser printer or one of the popular Epson LQ dot-matrix or similar printers, are illustrated in Figure 5-1 and outlined here. In Publish It! version 2.0 the *Dutch* and *Swiss* fonts are called simply *Serif* and *Sans* respectively to conform with the Typografica font library.

Swiss (called *Sans* in version 2.0) is a clean-cut sans serif typeface that is ideal for headings, technical instruction booklets, business documents, certificates, licenses, and similar types of documents. The font sizes available with Swiss depend on the printer installed with Publish It!.

Dutch (called *Serif* in version 2.0) is an elegant, fairly classic serif typeface that is ideal for body text. The font sizes available with Dutch are the same as those available with Swiss.

Drury Lane is a somewhat arty typeface consisting only of uppercase letters, digits, and some symbols, including & and $. Drury Lane is available in two font sizes that depend on the printer that was installed with Publish It!. Drury Lane is available only in uppercase, so be careful to avoid changing lowercase letters into this typeface.

Madison is similar to Drury Lane but less fancy. It includes both uppercase and lowercase characters. The font sizes available with Madison depend on the printer that was installed with Publish It!.

Figure 5-1. *Some typical font styles and sizes. The bullets (four lines, bottom right) are not available for typing in Publish It! versions 1.2 and 2.0*

5

Rockface is a strong, emphatic typeface with slab serifs. It could be used with either Swiss or Dutch to lend emphasis to a word or phrase. The font sizes available with Rockface depend on the printer that was installed with Publish It!.

Ravinia is a fairly pretentious typeface that claims to be especially elegant. The font sizes available with Ravinia depend on the printer that was installed with Publish It!.

The Publish It Lite! Font Library

The font styles available with Publish It Lite! are limited to Swiss and Dutch. The sizes available with each font style are more limited and depend on the printer installed with Publish It Lite!.

Special Characters

In addition to its fonts, Publish It! lets you use many characters that are not available directly from the keyboard. The *GEM International Character Set* comprises 90 special characters you can print by pressing the (ALT) key in combination with a number from 128 to 217 on the numeric keypad. Figure 5-2 lists all the key combinations and the characters that result. Pressing (ALT)-142, for instance, prints the character Ä.

These 90 characters are available in the Swiss and Dutch font styles and sizes; they are not available in most of the other font styles and sizes. If pressing an (ALT)-*number* combination produces a question mark (?), the desired character is not available in that character style or size.

External Font Libraries

Publish It! can also accommodate fonts in the Bitstream Fontware font libraries. To use them, follow the instructions provided by Bitstream.

The Bitstream library option is not available with Publish It Lite!.

Figure 5-2. *The GEM International Character Set*

Ç	ALT-128	á	ALT-160
ü	ALT-129	í	ALT-161
é	ALT-130	ó	ALT-162
â	ALT-131	ú	ALT-163
ä	ALT-132	ñ	ALT-164
à	ALT-133	Ñ	ALT-165
å	ALT-134	ª	ALT-166
ç	ALT-135	º	ALT-167
ê	ALT-136	¿	ALT-168
ë	ALT-137	“	ALT-169
è	ALT-138	”	ALT-170
ï	ALT-139	‹	ALT-171
î	ALT-140	›	ALT-172
ì	ALT-141	¡	ALT-173
Ä	ALT-142	«	ALT-174
Å	ALT-143	»	ALT-175
É	ALT-144	ã	ALT-176
æ	ALT-145	õ	ALT-177
Æ	ALT-146	¥	ALT-178
ô	ALT-147	¢	ALT-179
ö	ALT-148	œ	ALT-180
ò	ALT-149	Œ	ALT-181
û	ALT-150	À	ALT-182
ù	ALT-151	Ã	ALT-183
ÿ	ALT-152	Õ	ALT-184
Ö	ALT-153	§	ALT-185
Ü	ALT-154	‡	ALT-186
ø	ALT-155	†	ALT-187
£	ALT-156	¶	ALT-188
Ø	ALT-157	©	ALT-189
¤	ALT-158	®	ALT-190
ƒ	ALT-159	™	ALT-191

5

Figure 5-2. *The GEM International Character Set* (continued)

”	ALT-192	Í	ALT-205
...	ALT-193	Î	ALT-206
‰	ALT-194	Ï	ALT-207
•	ALT-195	Ò	ALT-208
–	ALT-196	Ó	ALT-209
—	ALT-197	Ô	ALT-210
°	ALT-198	Š	ALT-211
Á	ALT-199	š	ALT-212
Â	ALT-200	Ù	ALT-213
È	ALT-201	Ú	ALT-214
Ê	ALT-202	Û	ALT-215
Ë	ALT-203	Ÿ	ALT-216
Ì	ALT-204	ß	ALT-217

Other font packages compatible with the GEM operating system generally work with Publish It! as well.

You can also create drop caps using external graphics programs and importing them as graphics files. If you have access to a scanner, you can scan fonts from printed documents and import them into Publish It!. For more information on this, see Chapter 9, "Using External Files."

The Art Library

The Art libraries available with Publish It! vary with the version of the program. Versions 1.1 and 1.2 as well as Publish It Lite! include some 25 .IMG files representing some 200-plus images and one .GEM file depicting a personal computer. Publish It! version 2.0 includes, in addition to these, 13 .GEM files, 16 .PCX files, and 2 .EPS files. The procedures for loading these

Figure 5-3. *The clip art in the Art library*

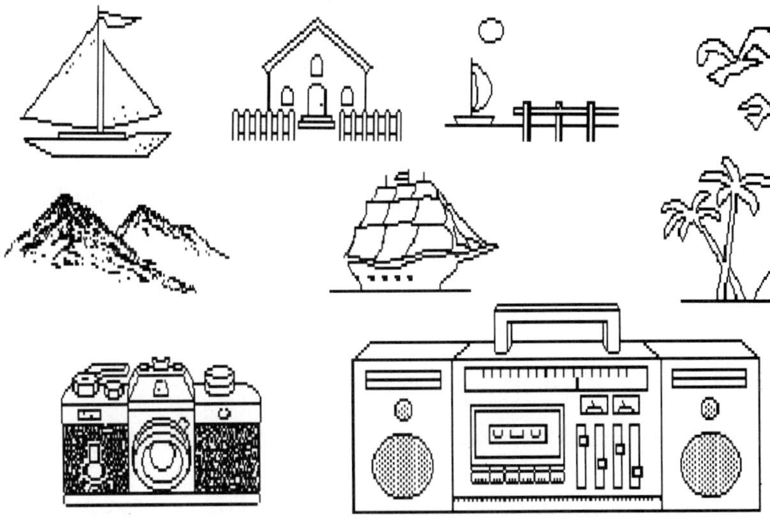

different files into the appropriate directories are discussed in detail in Appendix A, "Installation."

Most of the .IMG files contain a collection of more or less related images. By using the <Crop picture> option from the Graphics menu, you can extract an image and then enlarge or otherwise manipulate it. To work with the images in the .IMG Art library, follow these steps:

1. Click on <Size to fit> in the Page menu.
2. In the <FRAME> mode, create a frame that is the width of the entire vertical page, occupying the top half of the page.
3. Click on <Import picture> in the File menu. From the dialog box, click on <GEM Paint .IMG>.
4. From the Item Selector box, click on <CAMERA.IMG>; if necessary, first change to the appropriate drive and directory and then click on <OK>. The frame is filled with the images that make up that file, as shown in Figure 5-3.

5

5. Click on <Actual Size> in the Page menu. Place the house with the picket fence into the display; if necessary, use the scroll bars.
6. With the cursor inside the frame, click to select the frame.
7. Click on <Crop picture> in the Graphics menu. The pointer changes to scissors.
8. Start at the top left of the house image and drag the cursor to the bottom right. That will place a rectangular dotted line around the image. Release the mouse button. The picture is instantly redrawn to fill the entire frame with the house.
9. To see the entire frame, click on <Half size> in the Page menu.

Use <Size to fit> with Publish It Lite!.

10. If you are not already in the <FRAME> mode, click on the <FRAME> icon in the toolbox. Select the frame and place the cursor on the lower-right handle of the frame. Hold down the mouse key and drag the mouse diagonally up and to the left until the frame is approximately 1/4 of its original size.
11. Click on <Actual size> in the Page menu. Repeat step 10 until the frame is approximately the size of a large postage stamp.
12. If you like, you can now use the image as a small illustration on a sample letterhead, such as the one in Figure 5-4.

The 26 art files in the Art library are as follows:

ADS.IMG	HOUSE.IMG
BALLOONS.IMG	KEY.IMG
BORDER.IMG	LABELS.IMG
CAMERA.IMG	MEMO.IMG
FLAGS1.IMG	MONALISA.IMG
FLAGS2.IMG	MUSIC.IMG
FLAGS3.IMG	PC.GEM
HANDS.IMG	PHONE.IMG

PLANTS.IMG	SKYLINE.IMG
RABBIT.IMG	SYMBOLS.IMG
ROBOARM.IMG	TIGER.IMG
SCROLL.IMG	TIME.IMG
SIGNS.IMG	XMAS.IMG

Depending on when your Publish It! or Publish It Lite! software was shipped, your filenames may be slightly different.

In addition to the files listed previously, Publish It! version 2.0 includes two high-resolution graphics collections, the Image Club collection in the .GEM format and the Metro Image Base collection with .PCX and .EPS extensions (the latter being available only when a PostScript printer is installed).

Figure 5-4. *Sample letterhead*

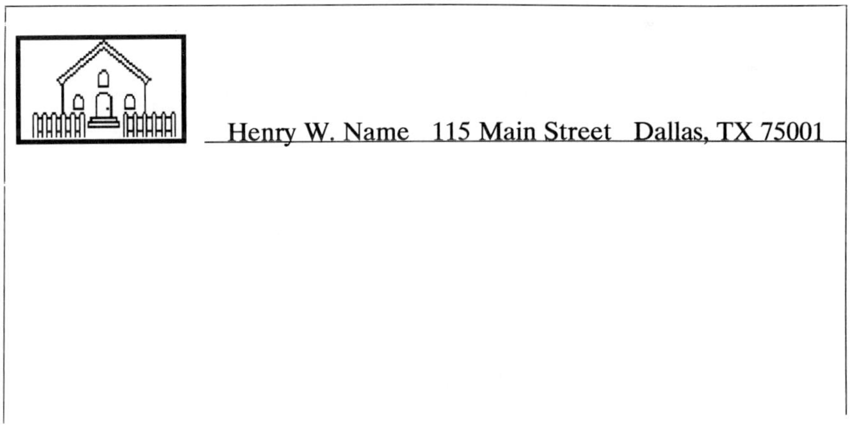

To work with the .GEM library, use a series of steps similar to those described earlier. With .GEM files, the <Scale picture> and <Preserve> options from the Graphics menu are inoperative. It is up to you to dimension the individual graphics frames in such a way that the picture appears in fairly realistic proportions. The .GEM file names are

1040TIME.GEM	MEGAPHON.GEM
35MMSTRP.GEM	MICROPHO.GEM
CARDS.GEM	NEWSPAPR.GEM
DIAMOND.GEM	SODAPOP.GEM
DOG_C.GEM	THE_END.GEM
FORGET.GEM	TIME_FLY.GEM
LIGHTBLT.GEM	

When working with the .PCX files the steps are the same. With these files, always use <Scale picture> and <Preserve> from the Graphics menu because many of these files contain realistic images that should not be distorted, and these options are once more available with .PCX files. The file names are

AD070X2.PCX	NF089X2.PCX
BB060X2.PCX	NM085X2.PCX
BG080X2.PCX	PE020X2.PCX
CT086X2.PCX	RE065X2.PCX
EF031X2.PCX	RM033X2.PCX
FO027X2.PCX	TR009X2.PCX
FS033X2.PCX	TS004X2.PCX
HC064X2.PCX	WS057X2.PCX

If the clip-art images available with your version of Publish It! are insufficient for your specific needs, you can import large numbers of special clip-art files from other libraries. There are many such libraries on the market, designed to serve almost any conceivable need for illustration.

The Document Library

The Document library consists of eight sample documents in Publish It! and seven in Publish It Lite!.

AD.DTP	A sample display advertisement
APT-NEWS.DTP	A sample newsletter page
FYI.DTP	A sample four-page newsletter (not included with Publish It Lite!)
INVOICE.DTP	A sample invoice format
LETTER.DTP	A sample letter
LETTERHD.DTP	A sample letterhead
REPORT.DTP	The main page for a typical report
RESUME.DTP	A sample resume

The sample documents are included as examples of different document types. Although you can alter them to fit your needs, it may be more trouble than it is worth. You're better advised to create similar but original documents, using your own text and graphics files. The more you experiment, the more types of useful functions and features will occur to you and the better the final results of your work will be.

If you do, however, want to use the sample documents for experimentation, you can move the individual components in each document around, enlarge or reduce portions, change typefaces and sizes, and so on. After you load a sample document using the <Open> command in the File menu, use the <Save as> command to save the file under a different name. In that way you can keep the sample document in its original format for future use.

Chapter 11, "Special Tricks and Techniques," describes a simple procedure that you can use to transform any of these sample documents into templates to be utilized for future documents serving other purposes.

III

Text and Graphics

6

Importing and Manipulating Text

As you produce documents with Publish It!, working with text is likely to be your most important activity—whether importing files or manipulating text on the page.

Importing Text

Importing text that was produced using some other program, such as a word processor or text editor, generally is the first step in the creation of a new document. Publish It! can directly import text produced in any of the following formats:

1st Word Plus	
ASCII	
Beyond Word Writer	
DCA/RFT	Available only with Publish It! version 2.0

Microsoft Word 4	
Microsoft Word 5	Available only with Publish It! version 2.0
Microsoft Works	Available only with Publish It! version 2.0
WordPerfect 4	
WordPerfect 5	Available only with Publish It! versions 1.2 and 2.0
Word Writer	
Word Writer 3	Available only with Publish It! version 2.0
Word Writer PRO	Available only with Publish It! version 2.0
WordStar	

Text files produced by any other word processors should first be converted to one of these formats using one of the many available text file conversion programs.

Publish It Lite! can import only those files created in

ASCII
WordWriter PC
Quintet
Beyond Words

This means that files produced by any other program, including the three most popular ones, WordPerfect, Microsoft Word, and WordStar, must be converted using the FILE EXCHANGE program described later in this chapter or converted to ASCII files. None of them is capable of converting to any of the other listed formats.

ASCII Files

ASCII text files were either originally created in the ASCII format using one of the many text editors, or written elsewhere on a word processor not compatible with yours. In the latter case files are converted to the ASCII format to provide you with a file format that you can use. Figure 6-1 shows a list that was produced in this manner. There are a number of ways in which ASCII files can be utilized with Publish It!. The one thing that you cannot do is simply import the ASCII file into Publish It! because Publish It! ignores all

Figure 6-1. *The original ASCII document*

SOFTWARE	MFR.	TYPE
3D Drafting	Generic Software	3-D design program
Actor	Whitewater Group	windows 3.0 programming
AutoSketch	AutoDesk, Inc.	computer-aided design
Beyond Word Writer	TimeWorks, Inc.	word processor
Byline	Ashton-Tate	desktop publ.
CADD Level 3	Generic Software	computer-aided design
CalndarMaker PC	CE Software, Inc.	windows 3.0 calendar pgm.
Camera Ready	Straight Forward	desktop publ
CATReader	OCR Software	scan text reader
CorelDraw	Corel	2-D design program
Correct Grammar	Lifetree	grammar & style checker
Creative Music System	Creative Labs	music synthesizer
dBASE III Plus, IV	Ashton-Tate	database
Design CAD 3-D	American Small Bus.Comp.	3-D design program
Designer	Micrografx	graphics
Diagraph	Computer Support Corp.	graphics
DrawPerfect	WordPerfect	graphics program
Echo PC +	Street Electronics	speech synthesizer
EnerGraphics	Enertronics	graphics
Exact	Technical Support Softw.	scientific symbol generator
Express Publisher 2.0	PowerUp	desktop publishing
Exsys	Exsys, Inc.	expert system
Finesse	Logitech, Inc.	desktop publishing
First Publisher 2.0 3.0	Software Publishing	desktop publ
Font Effects	Softcraft, Inc.	graphics
Fontgen IV+, V	VS Software	graphics
FoxPro 2.0	Fox Software	database program
GEM/3	Digital Research	desktop publ
Graph Plus	Micrografx, Inc.	graphics
Halo DPE	Media Cybernetics	desktop publ
IBM BASIC BASICA	IBM	language
Insight2+	Level 5 Research	expert system
Instrument Flight Trainer	Flight Deck Software	aircraft simulator
KnowledgePro	Knowledge Garden, Inc.	windows 3.0 programming
Laser Fonts for WordPerfect	Softcraft, Inc.	fonts
Lotus 1-2-3, version 2.2	Lotus Development	spreadsheet program
Magic Mirror	SoftLogic	utility
Microsoft C version 5	Microsoft	language
Microsoft Windows 2.04 3.0	Microsoft	operating environment
MoneyCounts 6.0	Parson's Technology	account organizer
Mouse Programmer's Toolkit	Logitech	programming aid
Mouse Programmer's Toolkit	Microsoft	programming aid
Near Laser Nice Print	Spies Laboratories	font/script generator
PageMaker	Aldus Corp.	desktop publ
Paintbrush	Microsoft	graphics program
PaintShow/Plus	Logitech	graphics
PCGlobe	Comwell Systems	177-country database
Personal Consultant Easy	Texas Instruments	expert system
Picture Perfect	Computer Support Corp.	graphics
Pizazz Plus	Application Techniques	screen capture program
Power BASIC	Spectra Publishing	language
PowerBASIC	Spectra Publishing	BASIC language/compiler
Publish It!, 1.1, 1.2, 2.0	Timeworks, Inc.	desktop publishing
Publish It Lite!	TimeWorks, Inc.	desktop publishing
Publisher	Logitech	desktop publ
Publisher's PicturePak	Marketing Graphics, Inc.	graphics
Quattro, Quattro Pro	Borland Int'l.	spreadsheet
RightWriter	RightSoft, Inc.	Grammar and style checker
RTLink/Plus	Pocket Soft, Inc.	linking program
Sage Professional Editor	Sage Software	program editor

single carriage returns, resulting in the entire text being converted to a truly dreadful block of text, as shown in Figure 6-2.

One rather primitive method of overcoming this problem is to place double carriage returns ((ENTER) (ENTER)) at the end of each line or paragraph. That would result in Publish It! recognizing these carriage returns. This method is tedious at best. A much better idea is for you to simply import the ASCII file into your word processor and save it in your word processor's native format. When you then import it into Publish It! the line or paragraph breaks are recognized and maintained. What is not recognized are the tab stops that

Figure 6-2. *The ASCII document transferred unchanged into Publish It!*

SOFTWARE MFR. TYPE --3D Drafting Generic Software 3-D design program Actor Whitewater Group windows 3.0 programming AutoSketch AutoDesk, Inc. computer-aided design Beyond Word Writer TimeWorks, Inc. word processor Byline Ashton-Tate desktop publ. CADD Level 3 Generic Software computer-aided design CalndarMaker PC CE Software, Inc. windows 3.0 calendar pgm. Camera Ready Straight Forward desktop publ CATReader OCR Software scan text reader CorelDraw Corel 2-D design program Correct Grammar Lifetree grammar & style checker Creative Music System Creative Labs music synthesizer dBASE III Plus, IV Ashton-Tate database Design CAD 3-D American Small Bus.Comp. 3-D design program Designer Micrografx graphics Diagraph Computer Support Corp. graphics DrawPerfect WordPerfect graphics program Echo PC + Street Electronics speech synthesizer EnerGraphics Enertronics graphics Exact Technical Support Softw. scientific symbol generator Express Publisher 2.0 PowerUp desktop publishing Exsys Exsys, Inc. expert system Finesse Logitech, Inc. desktop publishing First Publisher 2.0 3.0 Software Publishing desktop publ Font Effects Softcraft, Inc. graphics Fontgen IV+, V VS Software graphics FoxPro 2.0 Fox Software database program GEM/3 Digital Research desktop publ Graph Plus Micrografx, Inc. graphics Halo DPE Media Cybernetics desktop publ IBM BASIC BASICA IBM language Insight2+ Level 5 Research expert system Instrument Flight Trainer Flight Deck Software aircraft simulator KnowledgePro Knowledge Garden, Inc. windows 3.0 programming Laser Fonts for WordPerfect Softcraft, Inc. fonts Lotus 1-2-3, version 2.2 Lotus Development spreadsheet program Magic Mirror SoftLogic utility Microsoft C version 5 Microsoft language Microsoft Windows 2.04 3.0 Microsoft operating environment MoneyCounts 6.0 Parson's Technology account organizer Mouse Programmer's Toolkit Logitech programming aid Mouse Programmer's Toolkit Microsoft programming aid Near Laser Nice Print Spies Laboratories font/script generator PageMaker Aldus Corp. desktop publ Paintbrush Microsoft graphics program PaintShow/Plus Logitech graphics PCGlobe Comwell Systems 177-country database Personal Consultant Easy Texas Instruments expert system Picture Perfect Computer Support Corp. graphics Pizazz Plus Application Techniques screen capture program Power BASIC Spectra Publishing language PowerBASIC Spectra Publishing BASIC language/compiler Publish It!, 1.1, 1.2, 2.0 Timeworks, Inc. desktop publishing Publish It Lite! TimeWorks, Inc. desktop publishing Publisher Logitech desktop publ Publisher's PicturePak Marketing Graphics, Inc. graphics Quattro, Quattro Pro Borland Int'l. spreadsheet RightWriter RightSoft, Inc. Grammar and style checker RTLink/Plus Pocket Soft, Inc. linking program Sage Professional Editor Sage Software program editor Sidekick 2.0 Borland Int. RAM resident Sidekick 1.0 Borland Int'l. RAM resident Sidekick Plus Borland Int'l. RAM resident Sled VS Software graphics Software Carousel SoftLogic utility Spellbinder Lexisoft desktop publ Springboard Publisher Springboard Softw.,Inc. desktop publishing/word processor Symphony Lotus Development database/spreadsheet Tracon II (ATC) Wesson International simulator Tracon (Air Traffic Control) Wesson International simulator Turbo BASIC Borland Int'l. language Turbo C version 1.5 Borland Int'l. language Turbo Expert Thinking Software expert system Turbo Pascal version 3.0 Borland Int'l. language Turbo Pascal for Windows 3.0 Borland Int'l. language Turbo Pascal Toolboxes Borland Int'l. Pascal utilities Turbo Pascal version 4.0 Borland Int'l. language Turbo Prolog version 2.0 Borland Int'l. language Turbo Prolog version 1.0 Borland Int'l. language Ventura Publisher 2.0 Xerox desktop publ VP Graphics Paperback Software graphics VP-Expert Paperback Software expert system Windows 3.0 Microsoft operating environment Windows Draw Micrografx graphics Windows Graph Micrografx graphics Word for Windows Microsoft wordprocessor WordPerfect Library WordPerfect Corp. utility pgms. WordPerfect 5.0, 5.1 WordPerfect Corp. wordprocessor WordStar version 4.0, 6.0 WordStar Int'l. wordprocessor WordStar 2000 Release 3 MicroPro Int'l. wordprocessor were used in the original document, as shown in Figure 6-3. Follow these steps to fix this:

1. Access the <PARAGRAPH> mode and highlight the first line.
2. Select the <Paragraph style> option in the Text menu.
3. In the resulting dialog box, click on <Set tabs>.
4. In the Set Tab Points dialog box, enter the appropriate tab settings for the second and third columns, as shown in Figure 6-4. Click on <OK> and again on <OK> in the next dialog box. When you see your document again, the tab settings will have been reestablished as shown in Figure 6-5.

This method of converting ASCII files into your word processor's file format works not only with lists but with any type of text.

Word Processor Files

6

The different versions of Publish It! can accept files from a number of word processors, as described earlier in this chapter. If you are planning to use Publish It! often, then by all means acquire one that your version of Publish It! can deal with. If, for one reason or another, that is not feasible, there are several text file conversion programs such as Word for Word available that you can use to convert your text files into a compatible format before importing them into Publish It!.

Assuming that you are using a word processor that can be used by Publish It! without conversion, the next step is to determine which features are successfully imported and which are not. Try to produce a document that includes all the formatting commands that you are likely to use. Import that document into Publish It! and observe the differences between your original and the version displayed on the Publish It! screen. Figures 6-6 and 6-7 are extreme examples of such a transfer set. Figure 6-6 is a file called PRINTER.TST that is provided by WordPerfect 5.1 to determine which of the features available with that version can actually be used by the active printer (an Epson LQ-850 in this example). Figure 6-7 is a printout of this document imported into Publish It! version 2.0. The only formatting codes

Figure 6-3. *After the ASCII file is converted to WordPerfect it is imported into Publish It!*

SOFTWARE MFR. TYPE ---

3D Drafting Generic Software 3-D design program

Actor Whitewater Group windows 3.0 programming

AutoSketch AutoDesk, Inc. computer-aided design

Beyond Word Writer TimeWorks, Inc. word processor

Byline Ashton-Tate desktop publ.

CADD Level 3 Generic Software computer-aided design

CalndarMaker PC CE Software, Inc. windows 3.0 calendar pgm.

Camera Ready Straight Forward desktop publ

CATReader OCR Software scan text reader

CorelDraw Corel 2-D design program

Correct Grammar Lifetree grammar & style checker

Creative Music System Creative Labs music synthesizer

dBASE III Plus, IV Ashton-Tate database

Design CAD 3-D American Small Bus.Comp. 3-D design program

Designer Micrografx graphics

Diagraph Computer Support Corp. graphics

DrawPerfect WordPerfect graphics program

Echo PC + Street Electronics speech synthesizer

EnerGraphics Enertronics graphics

Exact Technical Support Softw. scientific symbol generator

Express Publisher 2.0 PowerUp desktop publishing

Exsys Exsys, Inc. expert system

Finesse Logitech, Inc. desktop publishing

First Publisher 2.0 3.0 Software Publishing desktop publ

Font Effects Softcraft, Inc. graphics

Fontgen IV+, V VS Software graphics

FoxPro 2.0 Fox Software database program

GEM/3 Digital Research desktop publ

Graph Plus Micrografx, Inc. graphics

Halo DPE Media Cybernetics desktop publ

IBM BASIC BASICA IBM language

Insight2+ Level 5 Research expert system

Instrument Flight Trainer Flight Deck Software aircraft simulator

Figure 6-4. *The Set Tab Points dialog box*

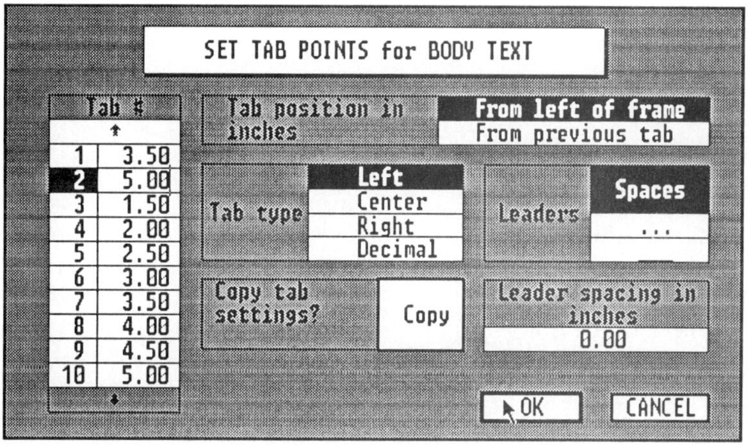

that managed to remain active in this example were bold, italic, single underlining, superscript, subscript, and the copyright symbol. All other features would have to be re-created using the options available in the Publish It! <Paragraph style> selection in the Text menu and elsewhere.

The <TEXT> mode

You can enter text directly into selected frames using the <TEXT> mode of Publish It! and Publish It Lite!. It is a slow process and not recommended for anything other than headlines and very short blocks of text, picture captions, and the like. Each letter is really a graphic image that must be created by the program, and that takes time. If you try to type as fast as you are able to on a word processor or text editor, the program may be incapable of keeping up and may actually end up skipping some letters.

Figure 6-5. *The document with the tab settings restored*

SOFTWARE	MFR.	TYPE
3D Drafting	Generic Software	3-D design program
Actor	Whitewater Group	windows 3.0 programming
AutoSketch	AutoDesk, Inc.	computer-aided design
Beyond Word Writer	TimeWorks, Inc.	word processor
Byline	Ashton-Tate	desktop publ.
CADD Level 3	Generic Software	computer-aided design
CalndarMaker PC	CE Software, Inc.	windows 3.0 calendar pgm.
Camera Ready	Straight Forward	desktop publ
CATReader	OCR Software	scan text reader
CorelDraw	Corel	2-D design program
Correct Grammar	Lifetree	grammar & style checker
Creative Music System	Creative Labs	music synthesizer
dBASE III Plus, IV	Ashton-Tate	database
Design CAD 3-D	American Small Bus.Comp.	3-D design program
Designer	Micrografx	graphics
Diagraph	Computer Support Corp.	graphics
DrawPerfect	WordPerfect	graphics program
Echo PC +	Street Electronics	speech synthesizer
EnerGraphics	Enertronics	graphics
Exact	Technical Support Softw.	scientific symbol generator
Express Publisher 2.0	PowerUp	desktop publishing
Exsys	Exsys, Inc.	expert system
Finesse	Logitech, Inc.	desktop publishing
First Publisher 2.0 3.0	Software Publishing	desktop publ
Font Effects	Softcraft, Inc.	graphics
Fontgen IV+, V	VS Software	graphics
FoxPro 2.0	Fox Software	database program
GEM/3	Digital Research	desktop publ
Graph Plus	Micrografx, Inc.	graphics
Halo DPE	Media Cybernetics	desktop publ

Figure 6-6. *The WordPerfect 5.1 PRINTER.TST file*

WordPerfect 5.1 Printer Test

WordPerfect 5.1 has many new features such as labels, spreadsheet imports, tab sets relative to margins, pull-down menus, mouse support, and more advanced macro and merge functions. WordPerfect 5.1 also supplements your printer's available characters by graphically printing over 1,500 international, legal, math, scientific, and typographical characters.

Japanese   Copyright ©   Hand ☛   Greek Δ

Equations can be created using WordPerfect's Equation feature.

$$\int_0^\infty x^{n-1}e^{-x}dx = \int_0^1\left(\log\frac{1}{x}\right)dx = \frac{1}{n}\prod_{m=1}^{\infty}\frac{\left(1+\frac{1}{m}\right)}{1+\frac{n}{m}} = \Gamma(n),\ n\neq 0,-1,-2,-3,\ldots$$

The Tables feature in WordPerfect 5.1 creates, formats, and edits tables easily. The Tables Options[1] can be used to improve the appearance of the table.

Print Attributes	567,845.56	Centered	Right Aligned
	67,887.47	Shadow	SMALL CAPS
	635,733.03	Redline	~~Strikeout~~

Fine, Small, Normal, **Large, Very Large, Extra Large**, Superscript, and Subscript are some of the printing features that have made **WordPerfect the world's number one word processor.**

You can create ruled and numbered paper by using User Boxes with numbers and graphic lines as borders. Text **size** and ***appearance*** may be changed without affecting the numbers or lines.

Integrating Text and Graphics

Graphic images can be scaled, rotated, and moved. You can indicate the style of the border and include a caption.

MOUSE

The graphic image can be placed anywhere on the page, inserted in a line, tied to a paragraph, or included in a header or footer.

[1] Although only double and single lines are used in this table, many other border styles are available including dashed lines, dotted lines, thick lines, extra thick lines, and no lines at all.

This document printed in WordPerfect 5.1 - June 10, 1991 10:07 am.

Figure 6-7. *The result when PRINTER.TST is imported into Publish It! version 2.0*

WordPerfect 5.1 Printer Test

WordPerfect 5.1 has many new features such as labels, spreadsheet imports, tab sets relative to margins, pull-down menus, mouse support, and more advanced macro and merge functions. WordPerfect 5.1 also supplements your printer's available characters by graphically printing over 1,500 international, legal, math, scientific, and typographical characters.

Japanese ?Copyright ©Hand ?Greek ?

Equations can be created using WordPerfect's Equation feature.

The Tables feature in WordPerfect 5.1 creates, formats, and edits tables easily. The Tables Options[1]

----

[1]Although only double and single lines are used in this table, many other border styles are available including dashed lines, dotted lines, thick lines, extra thick lines, and no lines at all.

----

can be used to improve the appearance of the table.

Print

Attributes

567,845.56CenteredRight Aligned67,887.47ShadowSmall Caps635,733.03RedlineStrikeout

Fine, Small, Normal, Large, Very Large, Extra Large, ^{Super}script, and $_{Sub}$script are some of the printing features that have made **WordPerfect the world's number one word processor.**

You can create ruled and numbered paper by using User Boxes with numbers and graphic lines as borders. Text size and ***appearance*** may be changed without affecting the numbers or lines.

Integrating Text and Graphics

Graphic images can be scaled, rotated, and moved. You can indicate the style of the border and include a caption.

The graphic image can be placed anywhere on the page, inserted in a line, tied to a paragraph, or included in a header or footer.

Manipulating Text

Once you have imported text from external files or have entered text directly in the <TEXT> mode, the next step is manipulating it to make it fit into your document. Publish It! includes many ways in which text can be adjusted. Among other options, it lets you change font styles and sizes and the type of justification from paragraph to paragraph.

Style Sheets

The Publish It! package includes a file called DEFAULT.STY, which is a style sheet that determines the size and orientation of the page that you expect to be working on. DEFAULT.STY produces a standard 8.5 x 11 inch page in vertical (portrait) orientation. Each page will appear with six column guides, which is the default number. In order to change the number of column guides, click on the <Set column guides> command in the Options menu, and click on either the right or the left arrow in the top box to increase or decrease the displayed number by one per click. The maximum number is nine and the minimum is one. Once the appropriate number of column guides has been reached, click on <OK> and then select the <Save style sheet> option from the File menu. When the Item Selector box appears, enter a filename, such as NINE.STY for a style sheet with nine column guides. (The .STY extension is provided automatically, so you don't need to type it.)

Style sheets also can be used to select different paper sizes. The available sizes are the default letter size of 8.5 x 11 inches, the standard notepaper size of 5.5 x 8.5 inches, the legal size of 8.5 x 14 inches, and the European letter size of 210 x 297 millimeters. (Version 2.0 of Publish It! offers a maximum page size of 22.5 x 22.5 inches in the portrait and landscape orientations. In addition, page dimensions created with the <Custom size> option in the Page Format dialog box can be saved as style sheets for later use.) Each can be selected in the portrait or landscape orientation, and each can be used with from one to nine column guides. Publish It! does not print in landscape orientation on 9-pin dot-matrix printers (IBM ProPrinter, IBM/Epson high-resolution printers, and compatibles), so ignore that option with those printers.

Once your selection has been made, save it as a .STY file, assuming that you will use this configuration in the future. Then, when you click on <New> in the File menu and you are asked "Load a style sheet?," click on <Yes>. An Item Selector box displays the available .STY files. Click on the one you want to use, and the proper page style and orientation are loaded automatically and remain associated with that file for as long as that file exists.

When you have produced a document, use the <Save style sheet> option in the File menu to produce a file that contains all the attributes of the document. This includes the page size and orientation, all font styles and sizes, all paragraph formatting commands, and so on. When such a style sheet is loaded, all that information is automatically loaded again. The text labels that were used are displayed in the Library window.

Style sheets cannot be printed. In order to see what a given style sheet looks like, click on <New> in the File menu and, when asked whether a style sheet is to be loaded, click on <Yes>. From the Item Selector box, click on the .STY file that you are interested in, and then click on <OK>. Once the document screen has been restored, click on <Size to fit> in the Page menu. If necessary, click on <Show column guides> in the Options menu to see the configuration and orientation represented by the style sheet. You can use the displayed rulers to verify the actual dimensions. You then see displayed a blank page formatted as the document with which the style sheet was saved. Click on the <PARAGRAPH> icon. The Library window title changes to STYLES and the paragraph style labels are displayed. Click on the <FRAME> icon. As you click on the Library window title, it rotates among STORIES, LINE ART, and IMAGES. Each is blank until some item is added to the page in view.

Master Pages

Master pages are a means of making sure that all pages in a multipage document are identical. In documents with left and right pages, the master page assures that all left-hand pages are identical and all right-hand pages are identical. Master pages are saved automatically with the document. If additional pages are subsequently added to the file, they also match. This does not mean that you cannot add special features to pages. You can always add frames for graphics or other special material. The master page simply controls the initial layout of each page, such as the number of columns per page, the width of the individual columns, their placement on the page, and headers and footers that are to appear on each page. Master pages are not printed.

To create a master page, follow these steps:

1. Open Publish It! in the usual manner.
2. Access the Page menu and click on <Go to page>.

3. The dialog box shown in Figure 6-8 appears, asking that you identify the type or number of the page you are looking for. Click on the check mark in <Go to master page>.
4. Notice that the legend in the <PAGE> icon has changed to MASTER, as shown in Figure 6-9.
5. Access the Page menu and click on <Size to fit>.
6. You should be in the <FRAME> mode. (If you are not, click on the <FRAME> icon in the toolbox.) Create the basic page layout by producing the frames that represent the columns that you might want repeated on every page.
7. When you are satisfied with your layout, as shown in Figure 6-10, open the Page menu and click on <Go to page>.
8. The Go to Page dialog box appears again. Notice that the text cursor is in the Enter Page Number box. Type **1** and click on <OK>, as shown in Figure 6-11. The legend in the <PAGE> icon at the left bottom corner changes to 1.

You have created the master page for your multipage document. Now whenever you access this document to add or edit pages, the basic page layout always remains the same. You can add frames for graphics, or you can change a frame size on the particular page you are working on, but the initial layout for all other pages remains unaffected.

Figure 6-8. *The Go to Page dialog box*

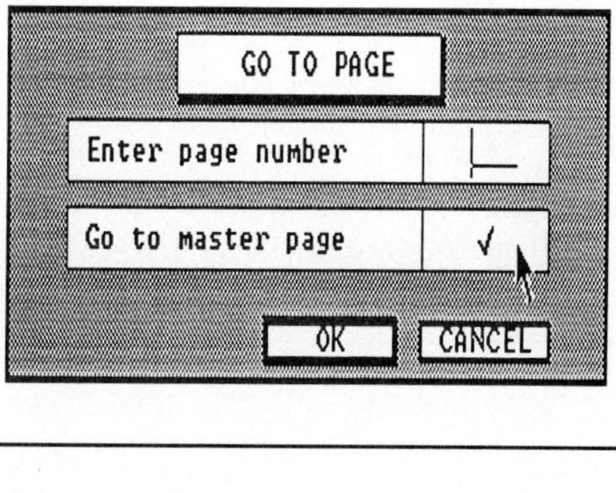

Figure 6-9. *The <PAGE> icon indicating a master page*

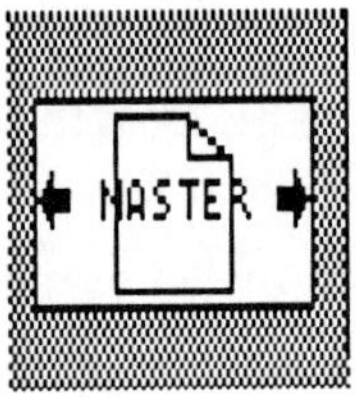

If you want different layouts for the left and right pages in a multipage document, start by taking these steps:

1. From the File menu click on <New>. In the dialog box dealing with style sheets, click on <No>.

Figure 6-10. *A typical master page for document with identical pages*

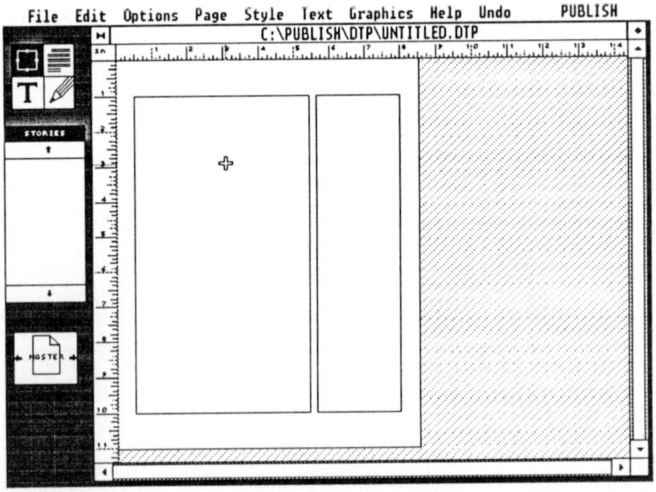

Figure 6-11. *The Go to Page dialog box used to go to page 1*

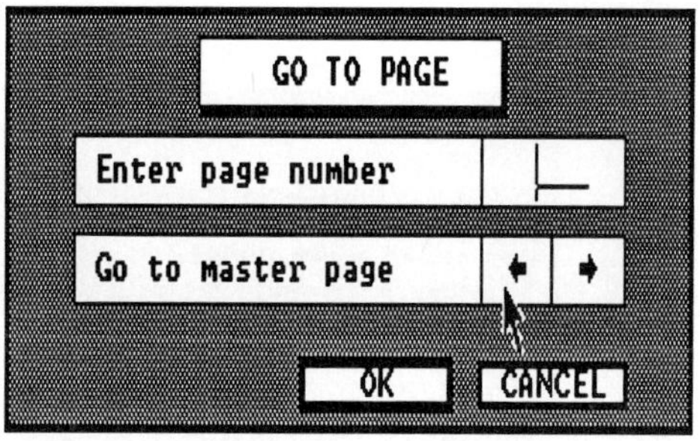

2. A dialog box appears describing the default page size and type. Click on <Left & Right Pages> and <OK>.
3. Follow steps 2 and 3 in the previous process. When the Go to Page dialog box appears, it displays two arrows associated with the <Go to master page> option, as shown in Figure 6-12. Click on the left arrow and follow the previous steps to create the layout for left pages.
4. Return to the Page menu and again click on <Go to page>. In the resulting dialog box, click on the right arrow, and repeat the remaining steps to create the page layout for the right page.

The master pages for left and right pages are shown in Figure 6-13. In each case each master page is automatically saved with the document. If in the future you want to refresh your memory, you can click on <Go to page> in the Page menu and then click on the <Go to master page> option in the dialog box. The master page is displayed.

If halfway through a document you want to change the page layout for the remainder of the document, the routine is simple. Insert a new copy of the master page *after* the current page by clicking on <Add pages> (<Add a page> in earlier versions) in the Page menu and then clicking on <Go to page>.

Figure 6-12. *The Go to Page dialog box used to select master page options for left and right pages*

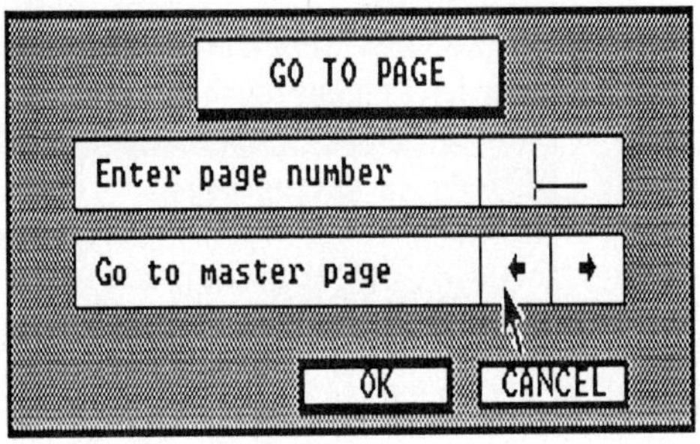

Figure 6-13. *The master pages for documents with left and right pages*

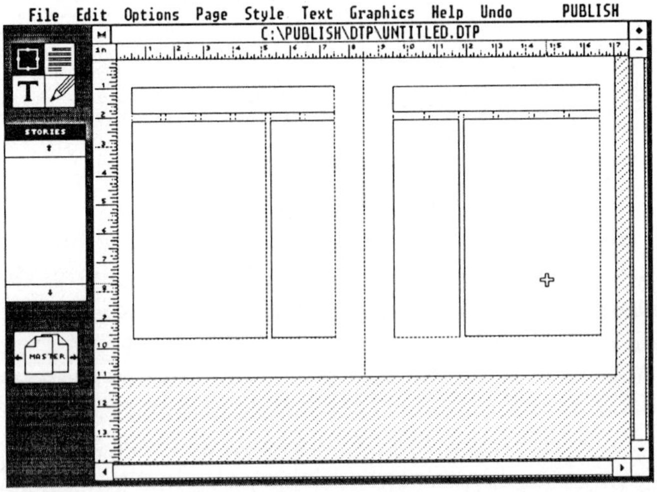

You continue with step 3 of the previously described steps. To place the new copy of the master page *ahead* of the current page, click on <Insert one page> (<Insert a page> in earlier versions) in the Page menu and then continue in the same manner.

The <Add pages> and <Insert one page> options are not available if you are in the <Two page> view format.

If a page already contains a frame when the master page is created, that page does not change to the master page format but remains untouched. If you want the first page(s) in your document to be different from the master page, lay them out before going to the master page for the first time. This is useful for creating a title page and then having the rest of the document follow a standard format.

Layout Considerations

As previously mentioned, the maximum number of columns available is nine. Obviously those columns will be quite narrow, and such narrow columns should not be used for text because it tends to create havoc with long words. In Figure 6-14 some example text was squeezed into one column in the nine-column format. The program managed to intelligently hyphenate most words, but the result is less than attractive.

By contrast, using columns that are excessively wide tends to produce unattractive and hard-to-read clumps of text or excessive amounts of white space, as illustrated in Figure 6-15.

To control the number of column guides displayed on the page, click on <Set column guides> in the Options menu to display the dialog box shown in Figure 6-16. It offers a number of options. You can change the number of column guides on the page. The column dimensions can be adjusted by changing the top, bottom, left, and right margins of the page and the gap that is to exist between the columns. You can also add a page offset, either horizontally, vertically, or both.

The column guides, when used in conjunction with the default <Snap to guides> option in the Options menu, ensure that the frames being created end up on comparable horizontal and vertical locations. In this mode, whenever

Figure 6-14. *Text in a column that is too narrow*

Another First
From Time-
works

Timeworks Inc.
of Northbrook,
I l l i n o i s ,
announces a
professional-
quality Desktop
Publishing pack-
age for the IBM
PC. The pro-
gram, called
Publish It!, is a
full featured, fully
integrated desk-
top publisher for
the IBM PC, PS/2
and compatible
computers.

Breakthrough

Publish It! is a
very exciting
breakthrough in
performence and
ease of use with
a feature list that
rivals that of
Ventura or Page-
Maker, but is
especially desig-
ned to get the
user up and run-
ning in less than
one hour.

It's Packed With
Features!

Only Publish It!
gives you all the
DTP features you
want, including
fully integrated
word processing,

Figure 6-15. *Text in a column that is too wide*

Another First From Timeworks

Timeworks Inc. of Northbrook, Illinois, announces a professional-quality Desktop Publishing package for the IBM PC. The program, called Publish It!, is a full featured, fully integrated desktop publisher for the IBM PC, PS/2 and compatible computers.

Breakthrough

Publish It! is a very exciting breakthrough in performence and ease of use with a feature list that rivals that of Ventura or PageMaker, but is especially designed to get the user up and running in less than one hour.

It's Packed With Features!

Only Publish It! gives you all the DTP features you want, including fully integrated word processing, page layout, and graphics:

l Frame-based page layout
l Five zoom modes
l Style sheets
l Wide range of fonts supplied
l Multiple text styles
l Direct text input and editing
l Styled text imported from Word Writer, 1st Word Plus, Word Perfect, Wordstar, Microsoft Word, and MS-Works
l ASCII text imported from other word processors
l Automatic justification
l Automatic hyphenation
l Text block cut, paste, copy, and restyle
l Drawn, painted, and scanned picture import
l Picture scaling and cropping
l Automatic text runaround
l Image editing mode
l Graphics drawing mode
l Wide range of printers supported
l Fonts, Point Sizes, and Text Styles

A huge range of different faces is available for use with Publish It! For example, many different faces can be generated using Serif and Sans fonts alone!

Here are just a few examples:

l 20 point Drury Lane
l 20 point Sans
l 20 point Courier bold
l 16 point Serif light
l 24 point Madison underline
l 20 point Sans italic
l 14 point Sans italic superscript
l 20 point Serif italic
l 18 point Ravinia
l 10 point Sans
l 7 point Serif
l 36 point Serif

6

Figure 6-16. *The Set Column Guides dialog box*

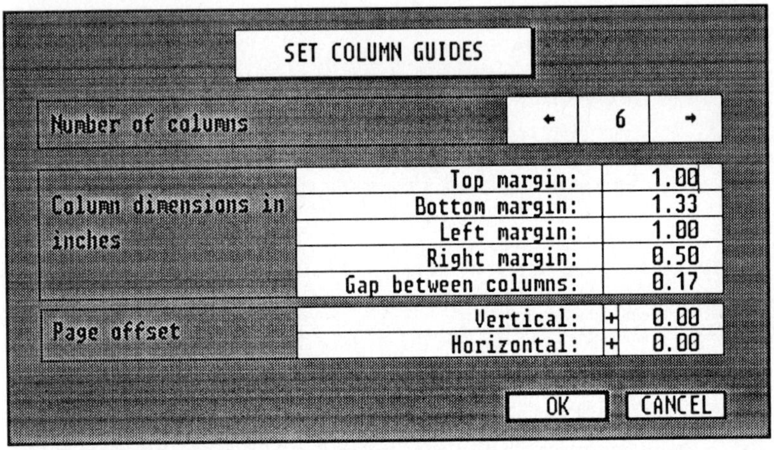

a frame ends up somewhere near one of the column guides, it automatically aligns itself with it. This option can be disabled by clicking on it.

When it is important that a frame is an exact distance from the top, bottom, left, or right edge of the page, click on <Show rulers> from the Options menu. It places rulers along the upper and left sides of the page. The default calibration for these rulers is inches and eighths of an inch. To change the calibration click on <Ruler spacing> in the Options menu. The dialog box shown in Figure 6-17 is displayed. In it the calibration can be changed to picas and points, centimeters and millimeters, or inches and tenths of an inch.

When the rulers are displayed, the actual calibration changes with the currently active view. In the <Actual size> view, an inch is actually an inch. In the <Double size> view option, an inch is two inches on the screen. Conversely, in the smaller view options, an inch is proportionately smaller on the screen than an actual inch.

With the rulers displayed, as the pointer is moved around in the work area, two hairlines, one in each ruler, move along, always indicating the exact horizontal and vertical positions of the pointer at any given moment (the X and Y positions, where X stands for horizontal and Y for vertical). Using these hairline indications, you can position the pointer a precise distance from the

Figure 6-17. *The Ruler Spacing dialog box*

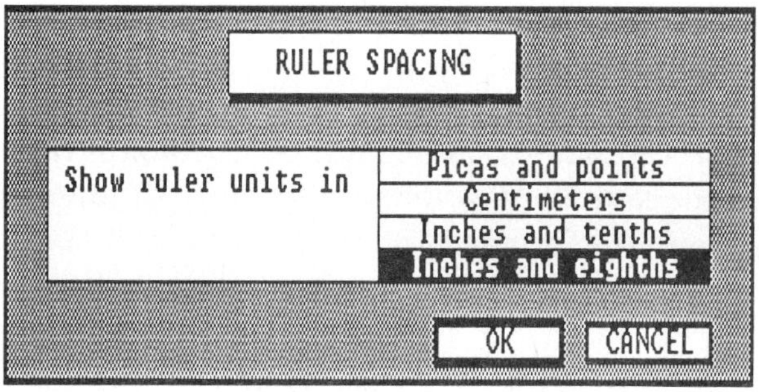

top and side of the page and drag it to another precise position, creating a frame in the desired location on the page.

Once a frame has been created, either directly or as the result of an existing master page, it can easily be changed or even moved to a new location. To change the dimension of a frame, make sure that it is selected. If it is not, place the pointer inside the frame to be redimensioned and click. The eight handles appear around the sides and at the corners of the frame, indicating that it has been selected. To stretch the frame horizontally, place the pointer on the center handle on the side to which it is to be stretched and hold down the mouse button. The pointer changes to a hand with a pointing finger. Hold the mouse button down, and drag the pointer in the direction in which the frame is to be stretched. When the right dimension has been reached, release the mouse button. The frame will be redrawn in the new dimension.

Shrink a frame using the same method, except hold down the mouse button and drag the pointer toward the *inside* of the frame; release the button when the new dimension has been achieved.

To redimension a frame vertically and horizontally at the same time, place the pointer on a corner handle and, again holding down the mouse button, drag it diagonally either toward the inside of the frame to shrink it or away from the inside of the frame to enlarge it. A bit of practice and experimentation is sure to turn you into an expert in minutes.

Position frames with mathematical precision by first selecting the frame with the <FRAME> tool. Then select the <Size & position> option from the Options menu. You now have the opportunity to choose an exact height and width for the frame and the precise position of the frame on the page.

Frames need not be empty to be redrawn. You can stretch or shrink frames that contain text and graphics. The text is reformatted automatically to accommodate the new dimension. If the frame is reduced in size, some text is eliminated from it. If a frame is enlarged, more of the text in the file is added. Graphics are redrawn from scratch to fit into the new frame.

Headers and Footers

At any time while you are working on a document, you can add header or footer lines. Access the Text menu and click on <Headers & Footers>. The dialog box shown in Figure 6-18 is displayed. Tell the program whether you want to create a header or footer by clicking in the appropriate <Use text as> box. The <Use text for> option offers three choices. Clicking on <Left> adds the header or footer only on left (even-numbered) pages. Clicking on <Right> does the same for right (odd-numbered) pages. The default, <All pages>, is self-explanatory. The <Left> and <Right> options make it possible to have different headers and/or footers added to the odd- and even-numbered

Figure 6-18. *The Headers and Footers dialog box*

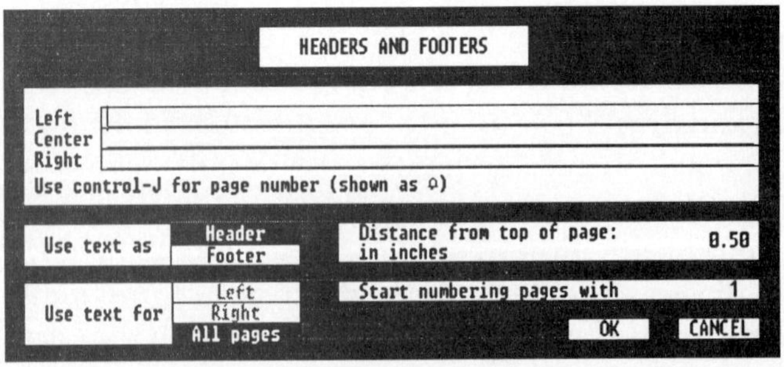

pages. Remember, if your document is set up with one master page for all pages of the document, headers and footers will be identical on all pages.

It is possible to prevent a header or footer from appearing on a specific page by clicking on the <Header on this page> or <Footer on this page> option from the Text menu. Both are toggle commands that are turned on and off by repeatedly clicking on them. For obvious reasons, these options are not available in the <Two pages> view mode.

Once you have determined whether a header or footer is to be added, type the text into one of the three text lines at the top of the dialog box. Text typed in the <Left> line will start at the left edge. Text typed in the <Center> line is centered on the page. Text typed in the <Right> line is right justified. The length of the headers and footers is limited to the length of the window in the dialog box, meaning that they cannot contain more than one line of text.

After you enter the text, click on <OK> and the typed copy is shown at the top or bottom of the active page. Once created, headers and footers act like paragraph styles. Font, spacing, and other information about the headers and footers can be changed through the paragraph tagging procedure, just like regular text.

Tagging Paragraphs

Unless codes are entered into a document to identify different portions of text as stand-alone sections, all body copy is treated the same with respect to font styles and sizes. To make it possible to treat different paragraphs differently, take these steps:

1. To cause the headline to be treated as a headline, type **<headline>** immediately before the headline text: **<headline>DOUBLE YOUR MONEY** (note that there should be no space between the code and the text).
2. To identify the basic body text as such, precede each paragraph with **<body text>**.
3. For any subheads, type **<subhead>** immediately before the subhead copy.

4. For any text that you want to be treated differently from any of the standard parameters automatically available in Publish It!, type **<one>** immediately before the text to be treated differently.

Here the <one> in brackets can be any instruction other than body text, bullet, headline, or subhead, which are the paragraph styles always available in Publish It!. In this manner you can identify as many paragraphs as you like with different words in brackets. Then, when the document is imported into Publish It!, all the identification words that you used are listed alphabetically in the Library window, as shown in Figure 6-19.

In the <PARAGRAPH> mode, a tagged paragraph is highlighted by clicking on it, and the code that is identified with that paragraph is highlighted in the Library window. You can then click on any of the options in the list of paragraph styles in the Library window. The selected paragraph is reformatted to the selected style. If you know that you always want to display two or more paragraphs in the same style and size, then tag those paragraphs with identical code names. Figure 6-20 is a short document in which the type styles of individual paragraphs were changed using this method.

Figure 6-19. *Paragraph style labels in the Library window*

Figure 6-20. *Text formatted for a number of font styles and sizes*

DOUBLE YOUR MONEY

Every once in a while it would be kind of fun to know roughly how long it would take to double a given amount of investment, based on currently available annual interest rates and applicable compounding periods.

The simplest method involves something that we might refer to as a "magic number," which must be divided by the interest rate in order to produce the time period in terms of years and decimal fractions of years that will be involved in doubling the investment. For instance, if the compounding period is daily then the "magic number" is **69**. Assuming the available interest rate is **7.75%** then the equation would be:

69 / 7.75 = 8.9

which means that it would take eight years and approximately 11 months to double the initial amount.

The magic numbers are:

69 if the interest is anywhere from **5%** to **19.9%** and the compounding period is **daily.**

70 if the interest is anywhere from **5%** to **19.9%** and the compounding periods are **monthly** or **quarterly.**

71 if the interest is anywhere from **5%** to **19.9%** and the compounding period is **semi-annually.**

72 if the interest is anywhere from **5%** to **9.9%** and the compounding period is **annually.**

73 if the interest is anywhere from **10%** to **14.9%** and the compounding period is **annually.**

75 if the interest is anywhere from **15%** to **19.9%** and the compounding period is **annually.**

Performing the calculations is a simple matter with any hand-held calculator or you can write a simple computer program that will produce the desired results in a matter of seconds. The one shown here is written in Turbo BASIC but with only very few modifications it can be adjusted to any other dialect of BASIC or Pascal and C programmers can use the algorithm, consisting of the line

PT = Z / I

in producing the program in those languages. The variables used are **PV** for **present value**

I for **interest rate**

CP$ for **compounding period**

Z for the **magic number**

PT for the **time period in years**

with **X**, **X$** and **YN$** being convenience variables that are self-explanatory.

The program, as written, uses the Turbo BASIC COLOR function in order to produce a pleasant display, assuming that a color monitor is available.

Another way to manipulate type styles for individual paragraphs is to double-click on the paragraph tag in the Library window. For example, when you double-click on EDIT, the dialog box shown in Figure 6-21 is displayed. It offers two groups of commands that can be used to manipulate the style of any paragraphs labeled <edit>. To create the desired attributes for the paragraphs tagged as <edit>, your options are

- Click on <Justification> and the dialog box shown in Figure 6-22 appears. It displays options for justification, hyphenation, and letter spacing, and lets you use a bullet to set off a paragraph.
- Click on <Font & size> to display the dialog box in Figure 6-23. It lists the available font styles and sizes with the parameter that was used originally with the paragraph tagged <edit> highlighted.

- Click on <Dimensions> to display the dialog box in Figure 6-24, which lets you adjust margins and line spacing.
- Click on <Word spacing> to display the dialog box shown in Figure 6-25. It is used to set the minimum and maximum space between words and an acceptable hyphenation zone.
- Click on the <New style> or <Function key> option. Both result in the dialog box shown in Figure 6-26. In it you can assign selected styles and sizes to a function key. Later, when adding text in the <TEXT> mode, pressing the function key activates the style assigned to it without making you exit the <TEXT> mode.

The <New style> option allows you to create new paragraph styles. Many documents contain a dozen or more styles, usually created with this option. When you click on <New style>, you get a dialog box like the one shown in Figure 6-26. You must then give the new style a name or assign a function key to it. When first created, the new style has all the same attributes, justification, font and size dimensions, and so on as the style that you selected when you went to <New style>. After creating and naming the new style, make any changes you want to the existing attributes. You can then return to the document and tag paragraphs with this new style.

You can use <New style> when you want to have a section of text that is centered, while the text surrounding it remains fully justified. Start by

Figure 6-21. *The Paragraph Style dialog box*

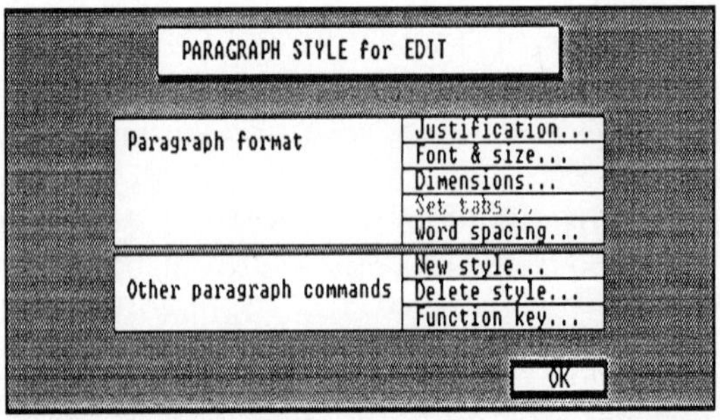

Figure 6-22. *The Paragraph Options dialog box*

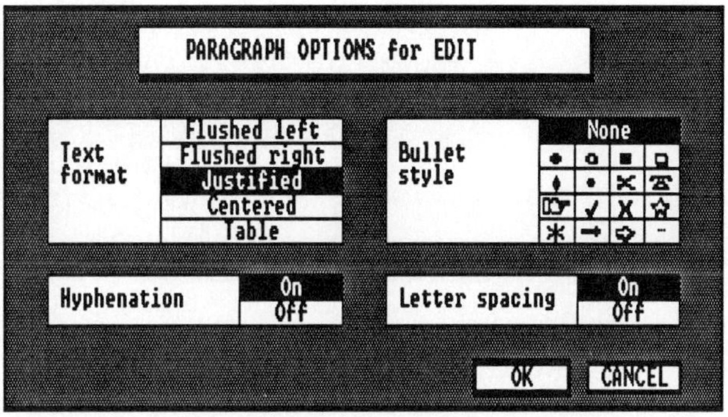

selecting the <PARAGRAPH> icon, and then double-click on the BODY TEXT style name. Once paragraph styles for the BODY TEXT come up, pick the <New style> option. Name the new style BODY CENTER and click on <OK>. Change the justification for BODY CENTER to <Centered>, and then return to your document. You can tag any paragraphs you want to have

Figure 6-23. *The Font & Size dialog box*

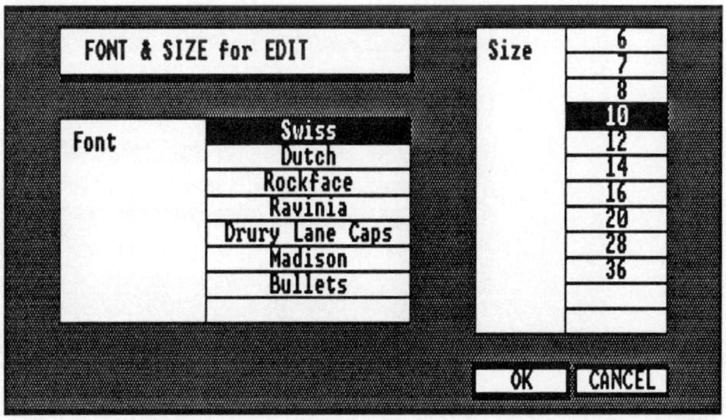

Figure 6-24. *The Paragraph Dimensions dialog box*

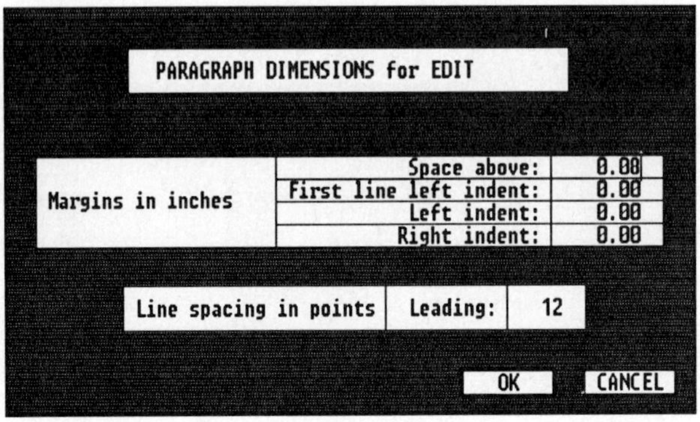

centered with this new style, while leaving your regularly justified paragraphs untouched.

When the <Set tabs> option is selected, the dialog box shown in Figure 6-27 appears. From it you can choose <Left>, <Center>, or <Right> tabs. If

Figure 6-25. *The Word Spacing dialog box*

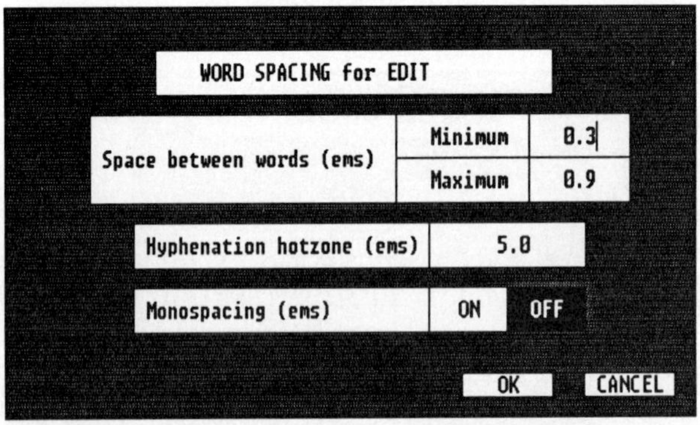

Figure 6-26. *The Paragraph Style Name dialog box*

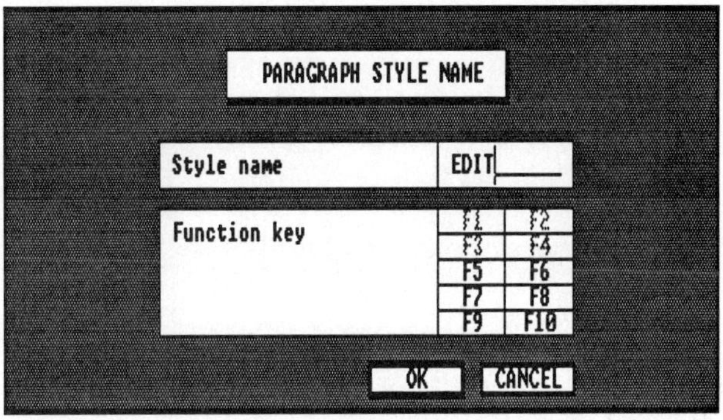

<Left> or <Right> is selected, the word typed after the (TAB) key is pressed is left or right aligned. If you select <Center>, the word typed after pressing (TAB) is centered on the line. The <Decimal> option is used only for entering numbers. It causes numbers to be aligned at the decimal point.

The tab options can be used in conjunction with leaders. Clicking either on <....> or <___> in the Leaders portion of the dialog box results in something like

Item One...........$66.43

or

Item Two__________$125.07

For multiple tabs to work properly, the lower number tabs must be closer to the left edge of the page than the higher number tabs.

Selecting <Delete style> displays the warning box shown in Figure 6-28, giving you an opportunity to change your mind.

Figure 6-27. *The Set Tab Points dialog box*

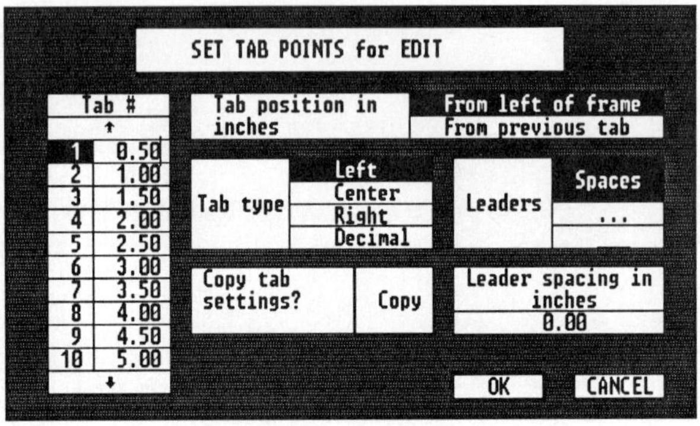

Editing Text

You can edit copy at any time, regardless of the style and size of the text that requires editing. You must be in the <Actual size> or <Double size> view mode. Simply click on the <TEXT> icon in the toolbox, place the pointer

Figure 6-28. *The paragraph style deletion warning box*

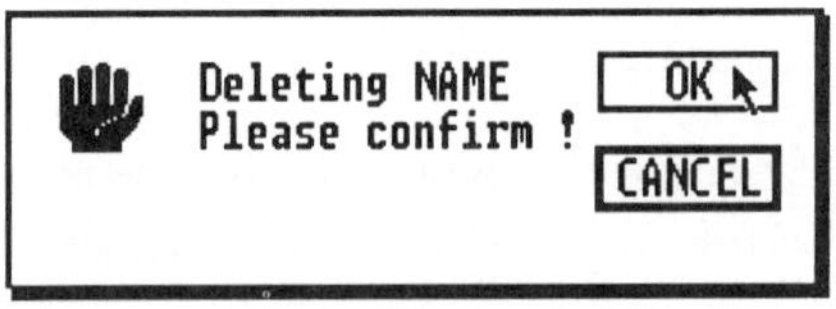

somewhere on the word that you want to edit, and click on it. The editing cursor, the vertical line, appears at that position. You can reposition it using the arrow keys, and you can delete the letter to the right of the cursor by pressing the DEL key. Delete the character to the left of the cursor by pressing the BACKSPACE key. You can insert characters or whole words or phrases starting at the cursor position by typing the text. (Do not type too fast. Each letter is a graphic symbol that must be created as you type.) If styles are assigned to function keys, you can press the appropriate function key while in the <TEXT> mode to change the paragraph in which the text cursor is located to the appropriate paragraph style.

You can also delete entire blocks of copy by highlighting the block and then pressing DEL. To highlight a block of text in the <TEXT> mode, place the I-beam pointer at the beginning of the block of text to be deleted and drag it to the end of that block. The entire block of text is then highlighted in reverse video. Pressing DEL or ALT-X deletes the entire block of text.

To type new text directly into Publish It!, create the frame into which the text is to be written. Click on the <TEXT> icon in the toolbox, place the I-beam pointer anywhere inside the empty frame, and click on it. The editing cursor appears in the upper-left corner of the frame. You can start typing, or you can move the cursor using the spacebar to move it to the right, or press ENTER to drop it down one line.

The style and size of text typed directly in this manner can be manipulated in the same way as any imported text. Simply highlight the portion of the text to be affected. Then select a style or size either from those displayed in the Library window or from those available from the Style menu.

6

Kerning

Kerning is the term used by typesetters to refer to adjusting the space between individual letters in a word. For instance, in normal spacing, the letters "i" and "l" are given just as much space as the letters "m" and "w." Also, the letter spacing in a word like "willow" looks better if the letters are pulled closer together (see Figure 6-29.)

Figure 6-29. *Kerning makes the word "Willow" more attractive and readable*

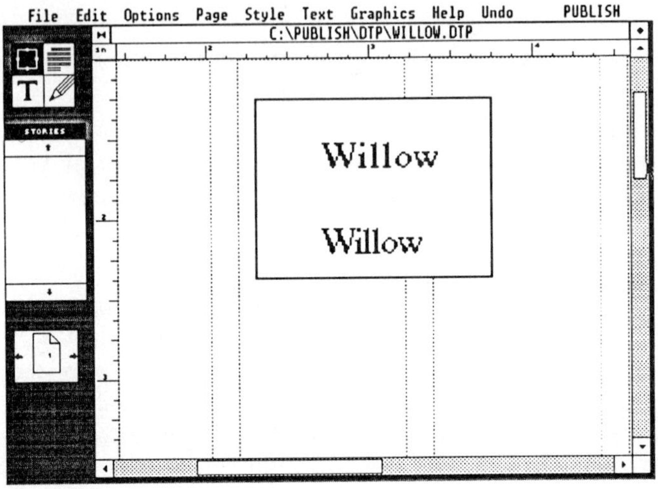

In Publish It! there are two ways to kern. One way is to place the text cursor between the two letters to be pulled closer together and press ALT-K as many times as necessary to produce the desired result.

Figure 6-30. *The Kern Two Characters dialog box*

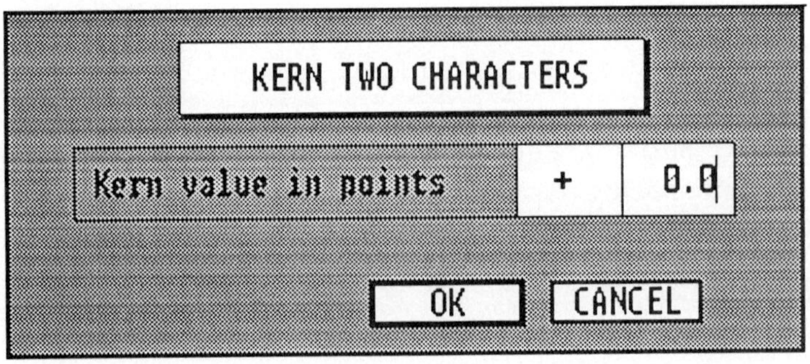

For the other method you use the <Kern> option from the Text menu. Place the text cursor between the two letters to be kerned and click on <Kern> in the Text menu. The dialog box shown in Figure 6-30 appears. It allows you to either add or subtract points or fractions of points of space between the two characters. When you click on the + or – sign itself, the sign changes to the opposite. The + sign means that space will be added and the – sign means that space will be narrowed by the amount you enter in the box containing 0.0, where the text cursor is automatically displayed.

Hyphenation

Publish It! has a system of automatic hyphenation that nearly always hyphenates words correctly. This automatic hyphenation can be disabled by selecting <Paragraph style> from the Text menu and clicking on <Hyphenation OFF>. Automatic hyphenation can be overridden by simply entering a soft hyphen at the place in the word where you would like it to be hyphenated, as shown in Figure 6-31. If you are not sure where the word to be hyphenated will hit the right edge of the text area or column, enter multiple hyphens in the appropriate places; one will be used and the others will be ignored.

Publish It! uses a dictionary for words that do not follow the normal rules of hyphenation. This dictionary is a list of words stored in an ASCII text file called PUBLISH.HYP stored on the PUBLISH subdirectory. As long as you

Figure 6-31. *Using soft hyphens where you want a word to be hyphenated*

You can influence the hy-
phenation by placing a soft
hyphen at the place where
your word is to be hyphena-
ted

keep the list in alphabetical order, you can add your own words to it with a text editor, putting hyphens where they belong.

Fixed Spaces

If you have words or digits that should not be split between lines when they happen to fall at the end of a line, insert a fixed space between the words or digits by placing the text cursor between them and pressing CTRL-SPACEBAR. This creates a space of one character width that will not be affected in any way by justification.

Status Information

At times it may be useful to know the status of a document—information such as how much of the document has been imported into frames and how much is being held in abeyance, waiting to be poured into additional frames. To obtain this information double-click on the name of the document in the

Figure 6-32. *The Status dialog box*

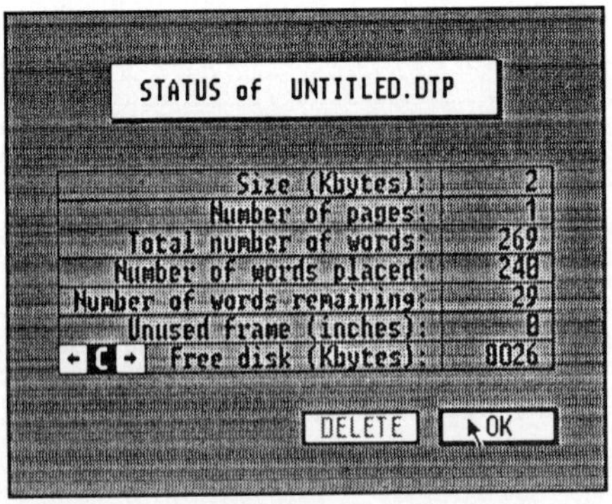

Library window. The dialog box shown in Figure 6-32 appears and it displays the size of the document in kilobytes, the number of pages used, the total number of words, the number of words already placed and the number waiting to be entered into frames, and the amount of unused space in existing frames measured in inches.

The text cursor is displayed at the end of the filename. If you like, you can rename the file by backspacing or pressing (ESC) and typing a new name for the document.

The Status dialog box can also be called up by clicking on <Status> in the File menu. This gives you the status of the whole document and lets you know the total word count as well as how much free disk space remains for your document.

Runaround Text

You can place a new, empty frame anywhere on top of one or several existing frames and reshape such a new frame any way you like after it is created. All text in the existing frames automatically wraps around the periphery of the new frame and keeps adjusting itself whenever the shape of that new frame is changed. You can then import a graphic image or another text file to be poured into that new frame, as in Figure 6-33. Even after that has been done, the size and shape of the frame can be changed and the entire frame, including its contents, can be moved to a new position on the page.

Two considerations should be kept in mind when such frames are superimposed over text frames. One is the amount of space that remains between the edge of the new frame and the edge of the page or frame either right or left. If the remaining space is too narrow, it produces text in a hard-to-read and rather unpleasant format. It is preferable, therefore, to either leave ample space or to extend the new frame all the way to the edge of the preceding one.

The other consideration is the amount of white space in the imported graphic. If the graphic image that is poured into the new frame has a lot of white space surrounding it, then it is a good idea to use the <Frame border> option from the Options menu and place a border around the image, as in Figure 6-34.

Figure 6-33. *A graphic added to a text document*

DOUBLE YOUR MONEY

Every once in a while it would be kind of fun to know roughly how long it would take to double a given amount of investment, based on currently available annual interest rates and applicable compounding periods.

The simplest method involves something that we might refer to as a "magic number," which must be divided by the interest rate in order to produce the time period in terms of years and decimal fractions of years that will be involved in doubling the investment. For instance, if the compounding period is daily then the "magic number" is **69**. Assuming the available interest rate is **7.75%** then the equation would be:

69 / 7.75 = 8.9

which means that it would take eight years and approximately 11 months to double the initial amount.

The magic numbers are:

69 if the interest is anywhere from **5%** to **19.9%** and the compounding period is **daily.**

70 if the interest is anywhere from **5%** to **19.9%** and the compounding periods are **monthly** or **quarterly.**

71 if the interest is anywhere from **5%** to **19.9%** and the compounding period is **semi-annually.**

72 if the interest is anywhere from **5%** to **9.9%** and the compounding period is **annually.**

73 if the interest is anywhere from **10%** to **14.9%** and the compounding period is **annually.**

75 if the interest is anywhere from **15%** to **19.9%** and the compounding period is **annually.**

Performing the calculations is a simple matter with any hand-held calculator or you can write a simple computer program that will produce the desired results in a matter of seconds. The one shown here is written in Turbo BASIC but with only very few modifications it can be adjusted to any other dialect of BASIC or Pascal and C programmers can use the algorithm, consisting of the line

PT = Z / I

in producing the program in those languages. The variables used are **PV** for **present value**

I for **interest rate**

CP$ for **compounding period**

Z for the **magic number**

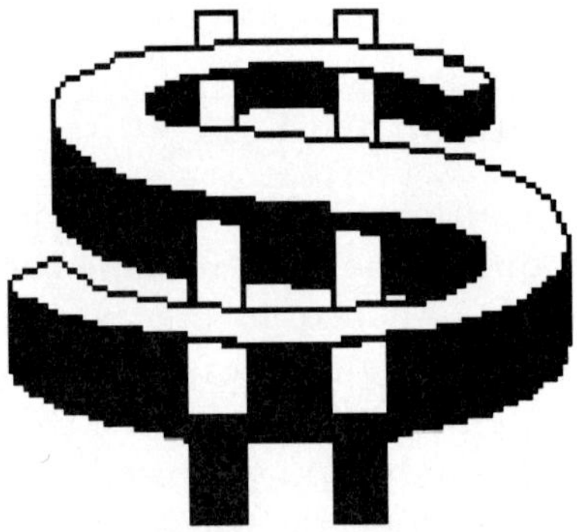

PT for the **time period in years**

with **X, X$** and **YN$** being convenience variables that are self-explanatory.

The program, as written, uses the Turbo BASIC COLOR function in order to produce a pleasant display, assuming that a color monitor is available.

Similarly, if you want to include a box with explanatory text, then create a border around the frame. Otherwise the division between the individual

Figure 6-34. *A border drawn to set off the graphic image*

DOUBLE YOUR MONEY

Every once in a while it would be kind of fun to know roughly how long it would take to double a given amount of investment, based on currently available annual interest rates and applicable compounding periods.

The simplest method involves something that we might refer to as a "magic number," which must be divided by the interest rate in order to produce the time period in terms of years and decimal fractions of years that will be involved in doubling the investment. For instance, if the compounding period is daily then the "magic number" is **69**. Assuming the available interest rate is **7.75%** then the equation would be:

69 / 7.75 = 8.9

which means that it would take eight years and approximately 11 months to double the initial amount.

The magic numbers are:

69 if the interest is anywhere from **5%** to **19.9%** and the compounding period is **daily.**

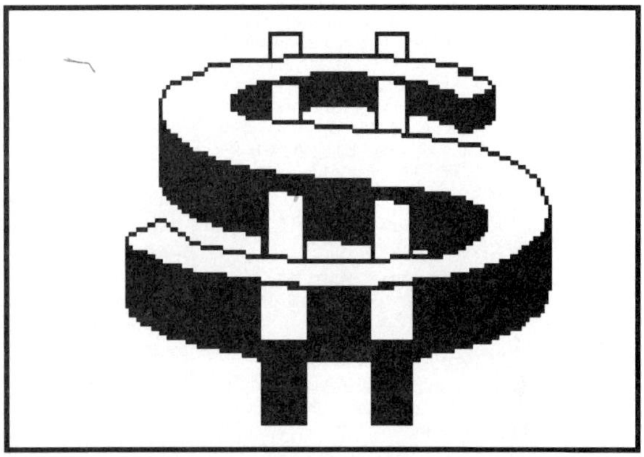

70 if the interest is anywhere from **5%** to **19.9%** and the compounding periods are **monthly** or **quarterly.**

71 if the interest is anywhere from **5%** to **19.9%** and the compounding period is **semi-annually.**

72 if the interest is anywhere from **5%** to **9.9%** and the compounding period is **annually.**

73 if the interest is anywhere from **10%** to **14.9%** and the compounding period is **annually.**

75 if the interest is anywhere from **15%** to **19.9%** and the compounding period is **annually.**

Performing the calculations is a simple matter with any hand-held calculator or you can write a simple computer program that will produce the desired results in a matter of seconds. The one shown here is written in Turbo BASIC but with only very few modifications it can be adjusted to any other dialect of BASIC or Pascal and C programmers can use the algorithm, consisting of the line

PT = Z / I

in producing the program in those languages. The variables used are **PV** for **present value**

I for **interest rate**

CP$ for **compounding period**

Z for the **magic number**

PT for the **time period in years**

with **X, X$** and **YN$** being convenience variables that are self-explanatory.

The program, as written, uses the Turbo BASIC COLOR function in order to produce a pleasant display, assuming that a color monitor is available.

items will become blurred even if different text styles and sizes are used, as in Figure 6-35. You might also put a background color into such a box to set it off from the rest of the material on the page, as in Figure 6-36.

Figure 6-35. *A box of text added and set off with a double border*

DOUBLE YOUR MONEY

Every once in a while it would be kind of fun to know roughly how long it would take to double a given amount of investment, based on currently available annual interest rates and applicable compounding periods.

The simplest method involves something that we might refer to as a "magic number," which must be divided by the interest rate in order to produce the time period in terms of years and decimal fractions of years that will be involved in doubling the investment. For instance, if the compounding period is daily then the "magic number" is **69**. Assuming the available interest rate is **7.75%** then the equation would be:

69 / 7.75 = 8.9

which means that it would take eight years and approximately 11 months to double the initial amount.

The magic numbers are:

69 if the interest is anywhere from **5%** to **19.9%** and the compounding period is **daily.**

70 if the interest is anywhere from **5%** to **19.9%** and the compounding periods are **monthly** or **quarterly.**

71 if the interest is anywhere from **5%** to **19.9%** and the compounding period is **semi-annually.**

72 if the interest is anywhere from **5%** to **9.9%** and the compounding period is **annually.**

73 if the interest is anywhere from **10%** to **14.9%** and the compounding period is **annually.**

75 if the interest is anywhere from **15%** to **19.9%** and the compounding period is **annually.**

Performing the calculations is a simple matter with any hand-held calculator or you can write a simple computer program that will produce the desired results in a matter of seconds. The one shown here is written in Turbo BASIC but with only very few modifications it can be adjusted to any other dialect of BASIC or Pascal and C programmers can use the algorithm, consisting of the line

PT = Z / I

in producing the program in those languages. The variables used are **PV** for **present value**

I for **interest rate**

CP$ for **compounding period**

Z for the **magic number**

PT for the **time period in years**

with **X, X$** and **YN$** being convenience variables that are self-explanatory.

```
100:CLS:FOR X = 1 to 10:PRINT:NEXT X:COLOR 13
PRINT "This program determines how long it takes to double a given"
PRINT "amount of money, by interest rates and compounding periods"
PRINT:PRINT "Interest rates may be between 5% and 19.9%"
PRINT "The results are rounded-off approximations"
PRINT:COLOR 7:INPUT "Press ENTER to go on",X$
CLS:FOR X = 1 TO 10:PRINT:NEXT X:COLOR 14
INPUT "Enter present value $",PV:INPUT "Annual rate of interest? %",I
PRINT "Select the compounding period:":PRINT "D = daily"
PRINT "M=monthly":PRINT "Q = quarterly":PRINT "S = semi-annually"
PRINT "A = annually":PRINT:INPUT "Type the appropriate letter ",CP$
IF I>=5 AND I<20 AND CP$="D" THEN Z=69:IF I>=5 AND I<20 AND CP$ = "M" THEN Z=70
IF I >= 5 AND I < 20 AND CP$ = "Q" THEN Z = 70:IF I >=5 AND I< 20 AND CP$ = "S" THEN Z=71
IF I >= 5 AND I < 10 AND CP$ = "A" THEN Z = 72:IF I >= 10 AND I<15 AND CP$="A" THEN Z=73
IF I >= 15 AND I < 20 AND CP$ = "A" THEN Z = 75:PT = Z / I
CLS:FOR X = 1 TO 10:PRINT:NEXT X:COLOR 11:PRINT USING "In ##.##";PT;
PRINT "years $";PV;" will have doubled to $";PV * 2:PRINT:COLOR 7
INPUT "Run another calculation? (Y/N)",YN$:<xx>IF YN$ = "Y" THEN 100 ELSE:CLS:END
```

The program, as written, uses the Turbo BASIC COLOR function in order to produce a pleasant display, assuming that a color monitor is available.

Figure 6-36. *Shading added to the box*

DOUBLE YOUR MONEY

Every once in a while it would be kind of fun to know roughly how long it would take to double a given amount of investment, based on currently available annual interest rates and applicable compounding periods.

The simplest method involves something that we might refer to as a "magic number," which must be divided by the interest rate in order to produce the time period in terms of years and decimal fractions of years that will be involved in doubling the investment. For instance, if the compounding period is daily then the "magic number" is **69**. Assuming the available interest rate is **7.75%** then the equation would be:

69 / 7.75 = 8.9

which means that it would take eight years and approximately 11 months to double the initial amount.

The magic numbers are:

69 if the interest is anywhere from **5%** to **19.9%** and the compounding period is **daily.**

70 if the interest is anywhere from **5%** to **19.9%** and the compounding periods are **monthly** or **quarterly.**

71 if the interest is anywhere from **5%** to **19.9%** and the compounding period is **semi-annually.**

72 if the interest is anywhere from **5%** to **9.9%** and the compounding period is **annually.**

73 if the interest is anywhere from **10%** to **14.9%** and the compounding period is **annually.**

75 if the interest is anywhere from **15%** to **19.9%** and the compounding period is **annually.**

Performing the calculations is a simple matter with an hand-held calculator or you can write a simple compute program that will produce the desired results in a matte of seconds. The one shown here is written in Turb BASIC but with only very few modifications it can be adjusted to any other dialect of BASIC or Pascal and C programmers can use the algorithm, consisting of the line

PT = Z / I

in producing the program in those languages. The variables used are **PV** for **present value**

I for **interest rate**

CP$ for **compounding period**

Z for the **magic number**

PT for the **time period** in **years**

with **X**, **X$** and **YN$** being convenience variables that are self-explanatory.

```
100:CLS:FOR X = 1 to 10:PRINT:NEXT X:COLOR 13
PRINT "This program determines how long it takes to double a given"
PRINT "amount of money, by interest rates and compounding periods"
PRINT:PRINT "Interest rates may be between 5% and 19.9%"
PRINT "The results are rounded-off approximations"
PRINT:COLOR 7:INPUT "Press ENTER to go on",X$
CLS:FOR X = 1 TO 10:PRINT:NEXT X:COLOR 14
INPUT "Enter present value $",PV:INPUT "Annual rate of interest? %",I
PRINT "Select the compounding period:":PRINT "D = daily"
PRINT "M=monthly":PRINT "Q = quarterly":PRINT "S = semi-annually"
PRINT "A = annually":PRINT:INPUT "Type the appropriate letter ",CP$
IF I>=5 AND I<20 AND CP$="D" THEN Z=69:IF I>=5 AND I<20 AND CP$ = "M" THEN Z=70
IF I >= 5 AND I < 20 AND CP$ = "Q" THEN Z = 70:IF I >=5 AND I< 20 AND CP$ = "S" THEN Z=71
IF I >= 5 AND I < 10 AND CP$ = "A" THEN Z = 72:IF I >= 10 AND I<15 AND CP$="A" THEN Z=73
IF I >= 15 AND I < 20 AND CP$ = "A" THEN Z = 75:PT = Z / I
CLS:FOR X = 1 TO 10:PRINT:NEXT X:COLOR 11:PRINT USING "In ##.##";PT;
PRINT "years $";PV;" will have doubled to $";PV * 2:PRINT:COLOR 7
INPUT "Run another calculation? (Y/N)",YN$:<xx>IF YN$ = "Y" THEN 100 ELSE:CLS:END
```

The program, as written, uses the Turbo BASIC COLOR function in order to produce a pleasant display, assuming that a color monitor is available.

6

Figure 6-37. *Text wrapped around a graphic image*

The different versions of Publish It! can accept files from a number of different word processors as described earlier in this chapter. If you are planning to use Publish It! with any degree of frequency, then by all means, acquire one that your version of Publish It! can deal with. In case, for one reason or another, that is not feasible, there are several text-file-conversion programs such as Word for Word available that you can use to convert your text files into a compatible format before importing it into Publish It!.

Assuming that you are using a word processor that can be used by Publish It! without conversion, the next step is to determine which features are successfully imported and which are not. Try to produce a document that includes all the formatting commands that you are likely to use. Import that document into Publish It! and observe the differences between your original and the version displayed on the Publish It! screen. Figures 6-6 and 6-7 are extreme examples of such a transfer test. Figure 6-6 is a file called PRINTER.TST that is provided by Wordperfect 5.1 to determine which of the features available with that version can actually be used by the active printer (Epson LQ-850 in this example). Figure 6-7 is a printout of this document imported into Publish It! 2.0. The only formatting codes that managed to remain active were **bold,** *italic*, single underlining, Superscript, Subscript and the copyright symbol. All other features would have to be recreated using the options available in the Publish It! <Paragraph style> selection in the Text menu and elsewhere.

Running Text Around a Graphic Image

With Publish It! 2.0 it is now also possible to cause text to flow smoothly around a graphic shape. Figure 6-37 shows an example. The steps involved to produce it follow.

1. Create an empty frame of any size and select it.
2. Use the <Import picture> option from the File menu. In the dialog box select the file format of the graphic to be imported (in this example, .IMG).
3. If necessary, change the disk\directory line to the one containing the graphic file and click on the filename in the Item Selector box (in this example FLAGS1.IMG).
4. Use the <Crop picture> option in the Graphics menu to separate the image you want from the others, as in Figure 6-38. The selected image fills the frame. Use the <Scale picture> and <Preserve> options to correct any distortions, resulting in the image shown in Figure 6-39.
5. Select <Text runaround> in the Options menu. In the resulting dialog box, click on <Define> in the Left border box, as shown in Figure 6-40.

6

Figure 6-38. *Cropping one image from the .IMG clip-art file*

Figure 6-39. *The selected image in its correct proportions*

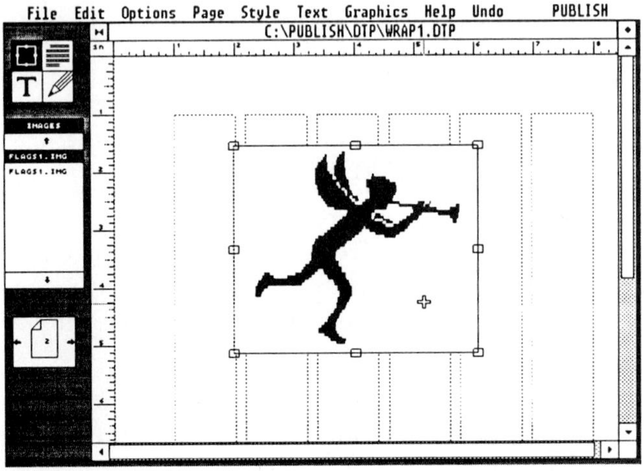

6. Use the routine described in Chapter 4, "The Menus," to place a border around the graphic image. Figure 6-41 shows this action in progress. When you are finished with the left border, double-click

Figure 6-40. *The Text Runaround dialog box*

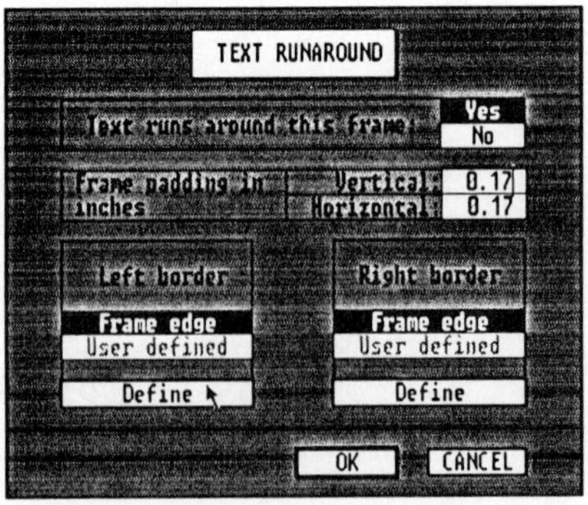

Figure 6-41. *The process of defining the left border*

to return to the Text Runaround dialog box and repeat the process for the right border. Then double-click and click on <OK>, which displays the final result shown in Figure 6-42.

7. Select <Size to fit> in the Page menu and reduce the size of the graphic frame to a more manageable size, as in Figure 6-43.
8. Draw a larger frame for the text to be imported around the graphic frame. Select <Send to back> in the Page menu to see both frames as shown in Figure 6-44.
9. Click on <Import text> in the File menu and on the appropriate file format in the resulting dialog box.
10. In the Item Selector box you may need to change the disk\directory line to the disk or directory containing the text to be imported. Then click on the appropriate filename and on <OK>. Figure 6-45 shows the result.
11. Using the grabber hand pointer you can now move the graphic frame around the text frame and watch the effect as the text keeps wrapping itself around the graphic.

6

Figure 6-42. *The left and right borders are defined*

Figure 6-43. *The frame is reduced in size*

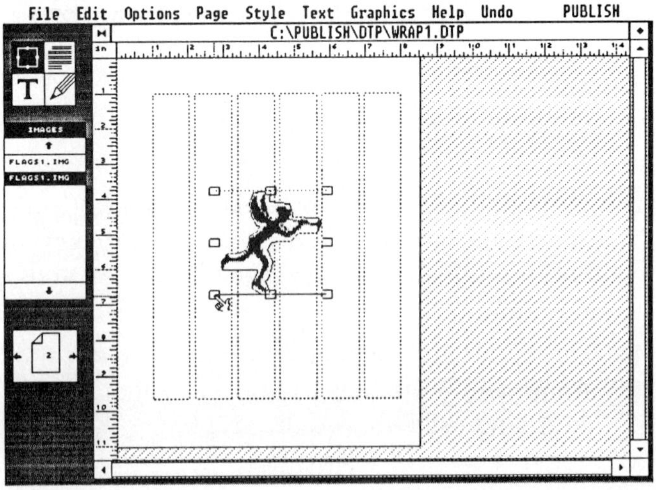

Figure 6-44. *Viewing both frames*

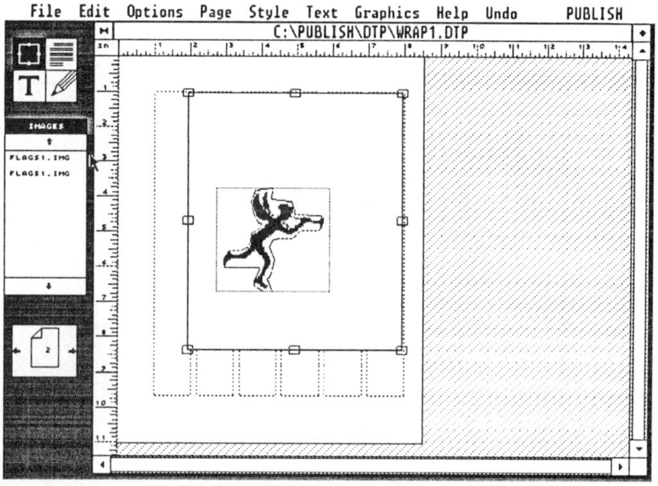

Figure 6-45. *Text is imported into the text frame*

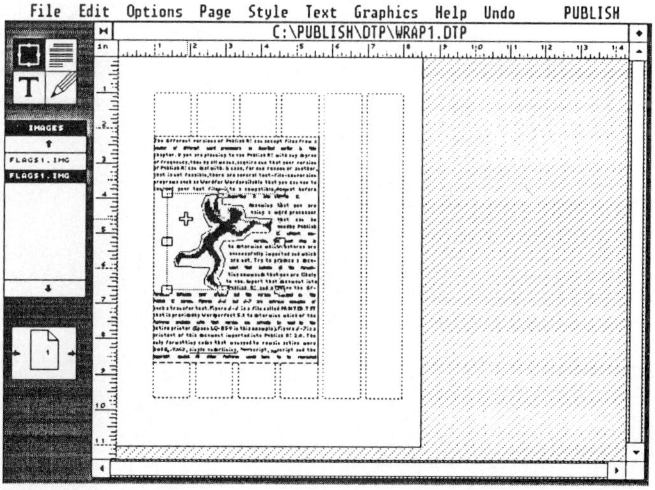

Placing Text into Shaped Areas

In Figure 6-46 a diamond-shaped box is created and text is imported into it. Then special effects are added. Follow these steps:

1. Use the <Text runaround> option in the Options menu to create the diamond shape (or any shape you like).
2. Click on <Frame tint> in the Options menu and select a tint dark enough to set off white lettering.
3. Click on <Import text> in the File menu and select the text file to be imported. The text is poured in black lettering into your shaped frame.

Figure 6-46. *Text imported into a diamond shape with tints added*

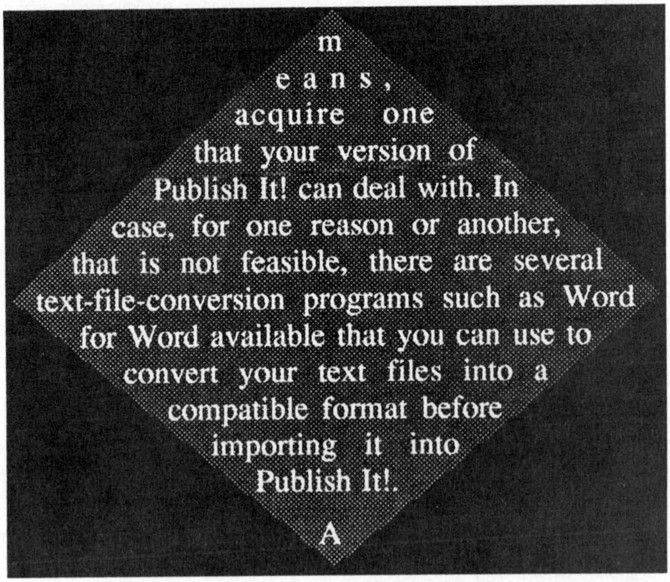

4. Click on the <TEXT> icon in the toolbox. Then drag the I-beam pointer from the upper-left corner of the square frame to its bottom-right corner to select and highlight all the text.
5. Click on <White> in the Library window, and the lettering turns from black to white.
6. Create a new frame the exact same size and proportion of your original rectangular frame. Your shaped frame with its text disappears.
7. Click on <Frame tint> in the Options menu and select <Black>. Click on <OK>. The new frame turns solid black.
8. Click on <Send to back> in the Page menu. Your shaped frame with the text reappears, as in Figure 6-46.

Notice the "m" at the very top of the frame. To avoid such bad breaks the shape of the frame may have to be adjusted or you can use the <TEXT> mode to make whatever changes in the text necessary to avoid such bad breaks.

Odd Shapes

Figure 6-47 is an example in which the <Text runaround> option was used to produce the cut corners on the image of a 3 1/2-inch disk. (The rest of the image was created simply with tints and overlapping frames.)

If you are tempted to use this function to create circles, ellipses, or similar shapes, you will find that it takes considerable patience together with skillful use of your input device to create such shapes. If at all possible, you're probably better off sticking to various geometric designs or to free-form shapes that do not require perfectly smooth curves. Figures 6-48 and 6-49 are some additional examples. As shown in Figure 6-49, you can use the <Cut>, <Copy>, and <Paste> commands in the Edit menu with these free-form frames as with any others. You can then add different tints to each copy.

If smooth circles or curves are required, you can use the <GRAPHICS> mode as in Figures 6-50 and 6-51, but note before trying this that combining such shapes with text is not always easy.

Figure 6-47. *Using the <Text runaround> option on a non-text object*

Figure 6-48. *Text imported into a special shape*

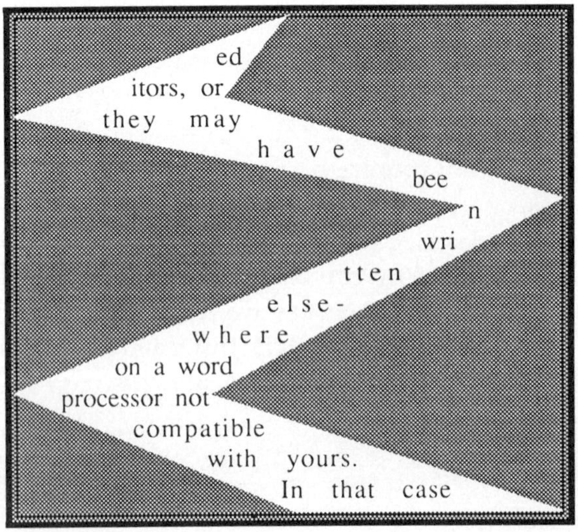

Figure 6-49. *The <Copy> and <Paste> options used with a free-form shape*

Figure 6-50. *Smooth curves created using the <GRAPHICS> mode*

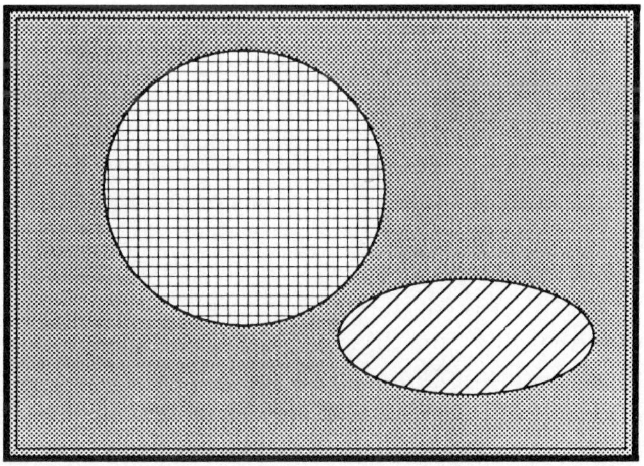

Figure 6-51. *Text was added to shapes produced in the <GRAPHICS> mode*

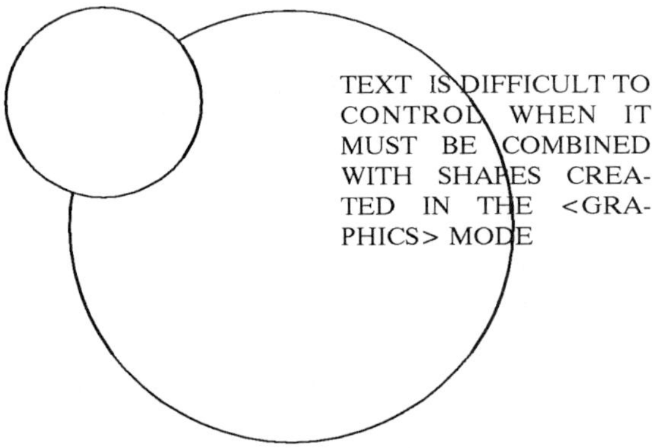

Blocks of Text

You can mark any block of text and copy it either to another place in the active document or to another document. You can also remove a block of text from the current document and replace it in a different location or a different document.

Click on the <TEXT> icon in the toolbox to enter the <TEXT> mode, and drag the I-beam pointer across the block of text to be manipulated by holding down the mouse button. The block of text will be highlighted in reverse video. Now access the Edit menu and click on <Cut> if you want to delete the block from its current position. Alternatively, you can click on <Copy>, which leaves the block of text in its current location undisturbed. Either way the block of text is placed into a memory buffer, replacing anything of the same type (text, graphic, frame) that might have been cut or copied before. You can now move the text cursor to another position in the active document, or you can activate a different document, and click on <Paste> in the Edit menu. The block of text will be inserted at the pointer position. Pressing the (INS) key or (ALT)-(V) accomplishes the same thing.

Since the cut or copied block of text remains in the memory buffer either until it is replaced by another or Publish It! is exited, the block of text can be pasted into as many locations and documents as you might like.

The <Cut>, <Copy>, and <Paste> options also can be used for frames. Select a frame and click on <Cut> to remove it from the screen and place it into the memory buffer. Clicking on <Copy> does the same thing without removing the frame from the screen. Click on <Paste> to place the frame into any selected location.

Memory Buffers

Publish It! establishes separate memory buffers for frames, text, and graphics. Thus, cutting or copying a frame does not affect text or graphics that may currently be held in memory. Remember what is being held in memory to avoid erasing it accidentally.

7

Importing and Manipulating Graphics

The most important feature of desktop publishing software, in contrast to word processing programs, is the manner in which graphics can be integrated into documents. Publish It! and Publish It Lite! include a limited number of graphic files. Both also offer a <GRAPHICS> mode in which simple graphic images can be drawn from scratch. The real power of these programs is their ability to use and manipulate graphics produced by external means.

Earlier versions of Publish It!, as well as Publish It Lite!, include 23 pages of clip art, while Publish It! version 2.0 includes an additional 31 clip-art files, any of which can be imported into your documents. Publish It! version 2.0 has expanded its graphics capabilities to include the following:

.IMG Files created using GEM Paint and a number of other graphics programs

.PCX Files created with PC Paintbrush and used by a large number of other graphics programs and clip-art libraries

.PIC	Files created using Lotus 1-2-3, Quattro, Quattro Pro, and others
.TIF	Files produced primarily by the various scanning hardware systems; available only with Publish It! versions 1.2 and 2.0
.EPS	Encapsulated PostScript files; available only with Publish It! versions 1.2 and 2.0
.GEM	Files created by GEM Draw and Artline programs
.LBM	DeLuxePaint files; available only with Publish It! versions 1.2 and 2.0
.SS	Splash! files; available only with Publish It! versions 1.2 and 2.0

For more information on using material from external files, see Chapter 9, "Using External Files."

Importing Publish It! Clip-Art Files

The easiest way to incorporate graphics into your document is by using selected images from the clip art that is included in the Publish It! and Publish It Lite! software packages.

Access the File menu and click on <Import picture>. The resulting dialog box asks that you identify the source from which you want to import. The selections are shown in Figure 7-1. The clip-art files available with Publish It! version 2.0 include .IMG, .GEM, and .EPS files (earlier versions include only .IMG files and one .GEM file). Click on the appropriate file format to see the available files in that format displayed in the Item Selector box, as shown in Figure 7-2, assuming that they are on the active disk and directory. If they are not, then click on the Directory line. Press (ESC) to erase the directory information and type in the name of the disk/directory in which the files are located.

Whenever a graphic is needed for your document, try to select it from the graphics files available with the Publish It! or Publish It Lite! package

Figure 7-1. *The Import Picture dialog box displaying available graphics file types*

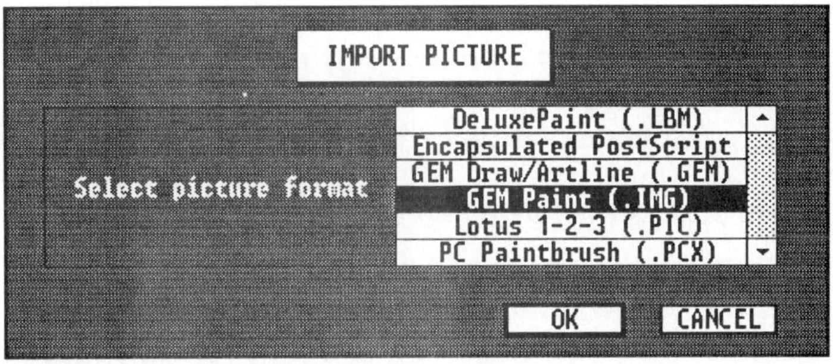

before resorting to files that must be imported from external program sources.

For demonstration purposes import the clip-art page with the filename FLAGS1.IMG, which is located in the ARTWORK directory. Since the page

Figure 7-2. *The Item Selector box displaying .IMG files in the PUBLISH\ PICTURES directory*

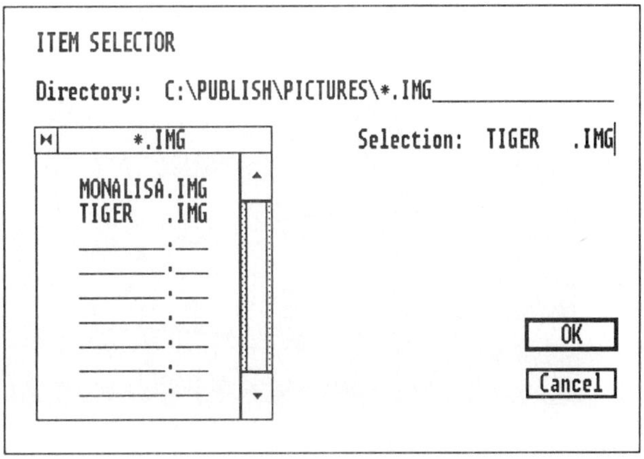

is horizontal, you may be tempted to use landscape orientation by going to <New> and choosing <Landscape> from the Paper Size Options dialog box. There is nothing wrong with that except you cannot subsequently use any of the figures in a document in the portrait (vertical) orientation; you must save the selected figure, exit the document, and start over. For that reason it is better to remain in the portrait (default) orientation and to import the clip-art file into a frame that occupies approximately half a page. Follow these steps.

1. Access the File menu and click on <Import picture>.
2. With the dialog box on display, click on <GEM Paint (.IMG)> and <OK>, as shown in Figure 7-3.
3. From the Item Selector box click on <FLAGS1.IMG> and <OK>, as shown in Figure 7-4. After a moment FLAGS1.IMG appears in the Library window.
4. While in <FRAME> mode click on <Size to fit> in the Page menu and create a horizontal frame covering the top half of the page, as illustrated in Figure 7-5.
5. Be sure the frame is selected and the handles are showing. Click on FLAGS1.IMG in the Library window, and the clip-art page should appear in the frame as shown in Figure 7-6.

Figure 7-3. *The .IMG format selected from the Import Picture dialog box*

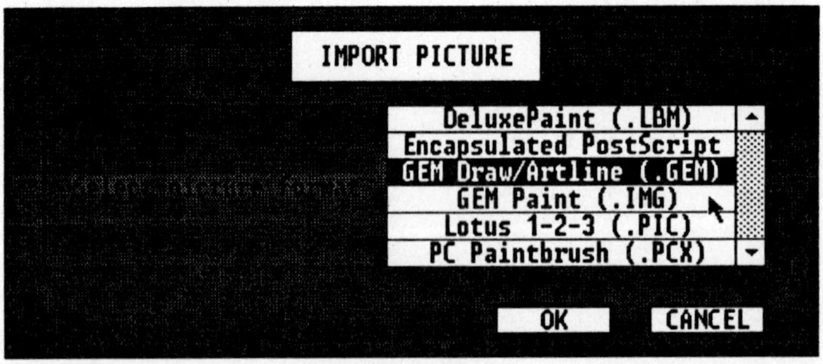

Figure 7-4. *FLAGS1.IMG selected from the Item Selector box*

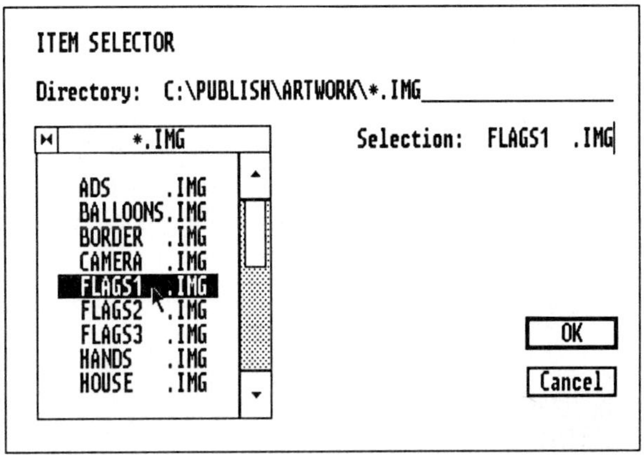

6. Click on <Double size> in the Page menu. A small portion of the page is displayed. To select the trumpeting angel, access the Graphics menu and click on <Crop picture>, as shown in Figure 7-7.
7. As the pointer changes to scissors, drag it across the figure of the trumpeting angel from the top left to the bottom right, creating a dotted frame that encompasses the entire figure. The moment you let go of the mouse button, the picture is redrawn with the figure filling the entire screen.
8. Click on <Half size> in the Page menu, and the complete frame is displayed, displaying the figure in the unpleasantly distorted manner shown in Figure 7-8.
9. Place the cursor on the bottom-center handle and, holding down the mouse button, drag the frame down until the figure looks more like the one in Figure 7-9.
10. You do not want to use the figure in such a large size. Place the pointer on the lower-right corner handle, hold down the mouse button, and drag it diagonally toward the upper-left corner to reduce the size of the image to the one shown in Figure 7-10.

Figure 7-5. *A horizontal frame drawn to receive clip art*

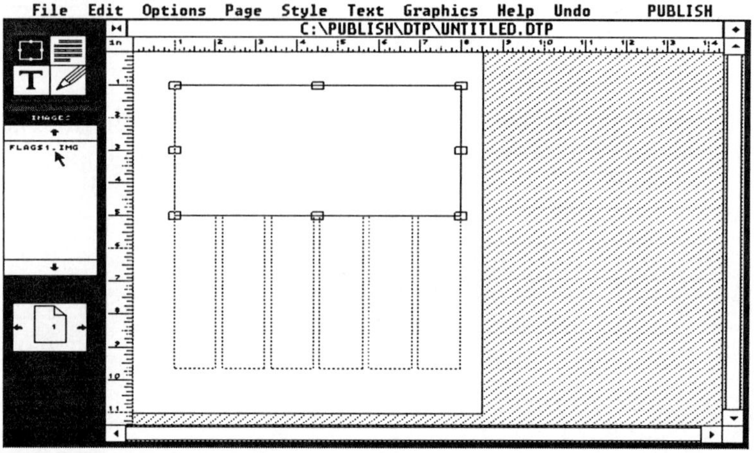

Figure 7-6. *The FLAGS1.IMG file imported into the frame*

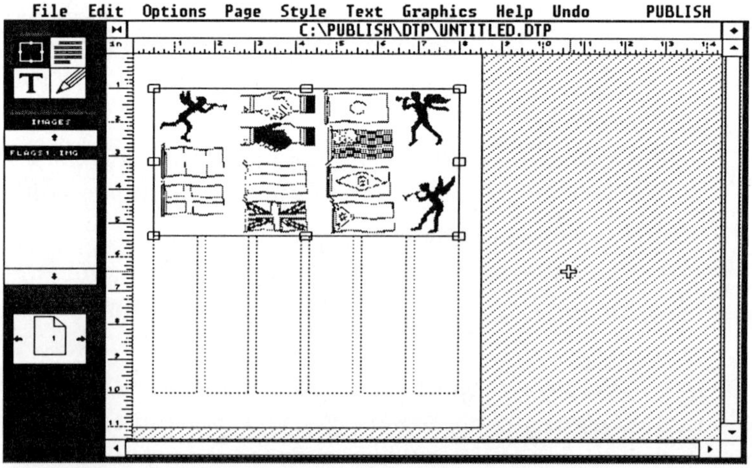

Figure 7-7. *<Crop picture> selected from the Graphics menu in <Double size> view*

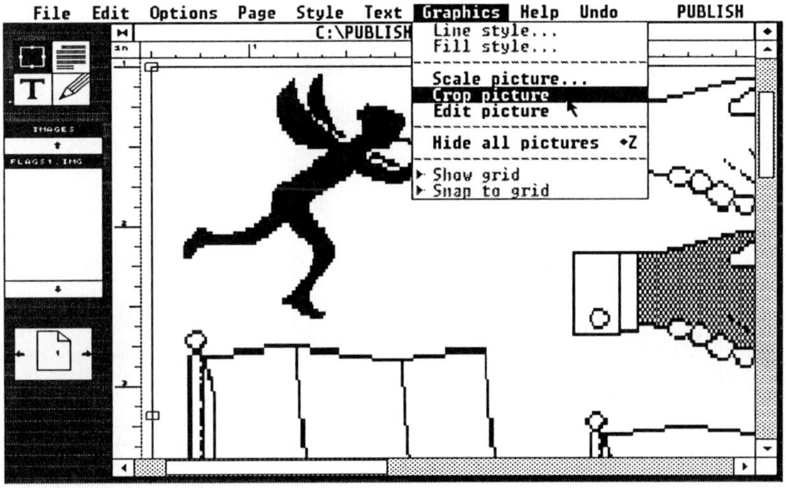

11. For the moment it will simplify matters to get the picture out of the way while you are getting ready to import the text. Make sure that the frame is still selected with the handles showing. Access the Edit menu and click on <Cut>. The frame with its picture disappears from view but is kept in a memory buffer.

7

Figure 7-8. *The cropped portion filling the frame*

Figure 7-9. *Frame redrawn to produce better proportions*

12. Click on <Size to fit> in the Page menu and create frames that will be used to hold the text you intend to import.
13. From the File menu click on <Import text> and, from the displayed dialog box, identify the type of text to be imported from the selection shown in Figure 7-11 by clicking on your choice and then on <OK>.
14. From the Item Selector box, click on the text file displayed in Figure 7-12 and on <OK>.
15. The imported text fills the selected frame. By selecting additional frames and clicking on the filename in the Library window, the rest of the text is poured into those frames.
16. You should still be in the <FRAME> mode. Place the cursor inside one of the frames with the text and create a new, empty frame. The text automatically wraps around that empty frame.
17. Access the Edit menu and click on <Paste>. The picture of the trumpeting angel appears in the upper-left corner of the page, causing some havoc with the text.
18. Place the cursor inside the frame with the picture and click on it to select it. When the handles are in view, place the cursor inside the frame, hold down the mouse button, and drag the entire frame into the empty frame area. Let go of the mouse button and the picture

Figure 7-10. *Frame reduced to a more useful size*

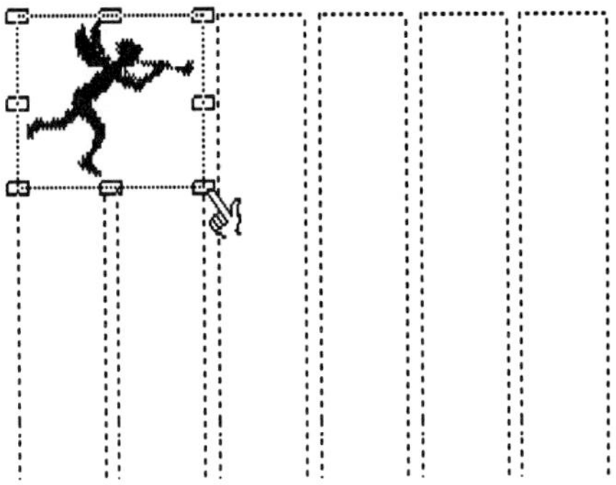

is now in the empty frame while the dislodged text has been replaced.

It is not necessary to create an empty frame before using the <Paste> option. You can simply drag the graphic with its own frame to any place on the page and the text wraps around it.

7

Figure 7-11. *WordStar format selected in the Import Text dialog box*

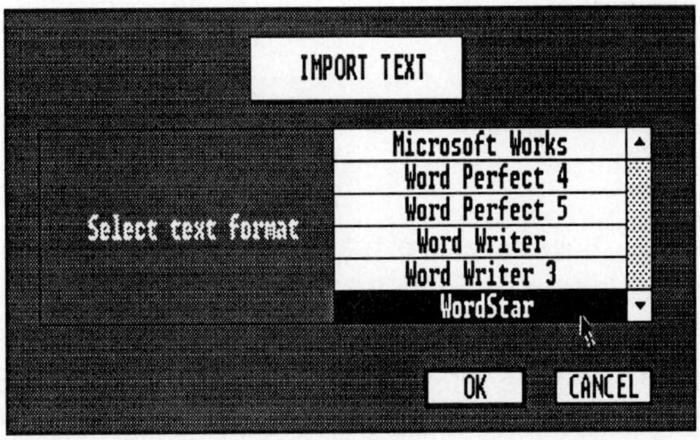

Figure 7-12. *DOUBLE.DOC selected in the Item Selector box*

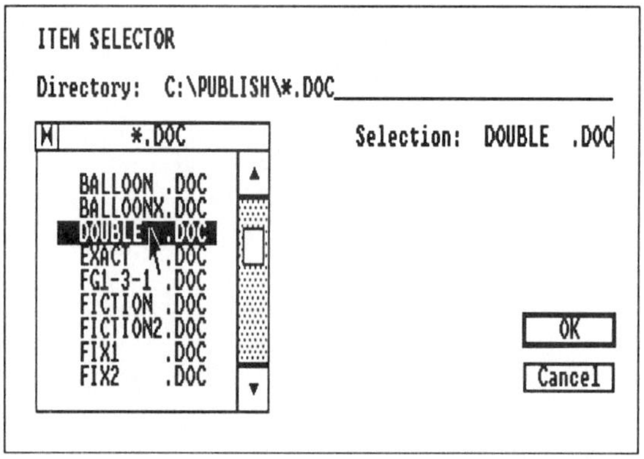

19. You may have to do some resizing to make the picture fit into its space, as shown in Figure 7-13. You can still make changes in the size and position of the picture without hurting either the graphic or the text. When you are satisfied, click on <Save as> in the File menu. In the Item Selector box, press (ESC) to erase UNTITLED .DTP and replace it with a filename of your choice.

Editing Graphics

Publish It! includes a graphics editing function that enables you to add or eliminate individual pixels. (The term *pixel* refers to the individual dots that make up a graphic image.) It is accessed by clicking on <Edit picture> in the Graphics menu. This produces an enlarged portion of the currently selected graphic image that fills the entire screen, as shown in Figure 7-14.

Clicking the mouse button with the point of the arrow pointer in a white area causes a single pixel, a small black rectangle, to appear at that position. Clicking the mouse button with the point of the arrow pointer in a black area removes a pixel and replaces it with a small white rectangle.

Figure 7-13. *The graphics frame combined with several frames of wrapping text*

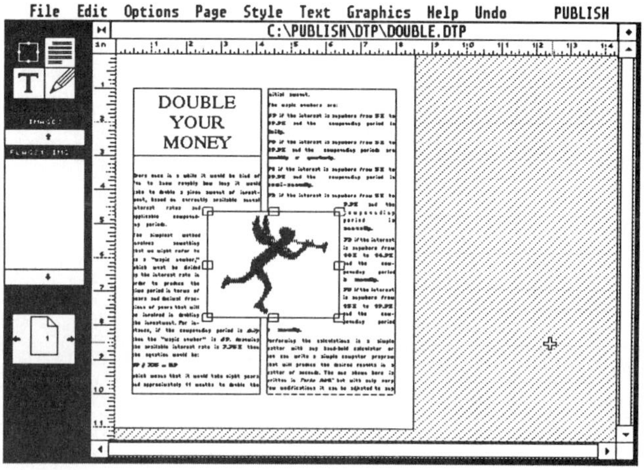

Figure 7-14. *In <Edit picture>, a portion of the picture fills the entire work area*

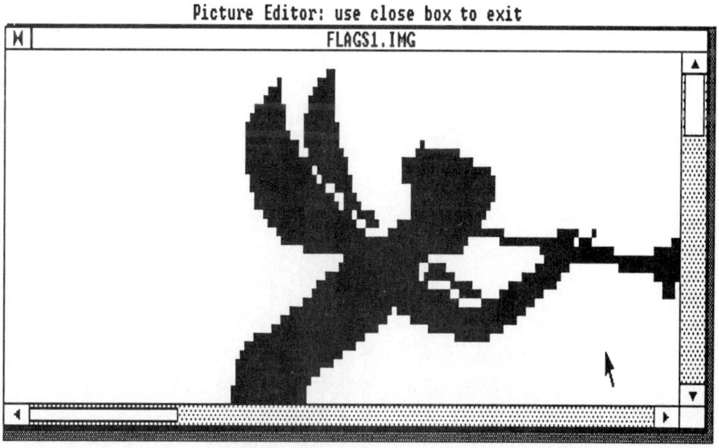

7

This editing option can be used to smooth out rough edges or to effect minor changes in the graphic image itself. It is a tedious process that requires considerable patience, so it is not recommended except when absolutely necessary.

To exit the editing screen, click on the close box in the upper-left corner. You return to the screen configuration that was last used.

Scaling a Graphic Image

Through the Graphics menu you also can adjust the proportion of a graphic image. Often the frame you created to contain a specific graphic image is not the appropriate length or width.

Figure 7-15 shows a frame that is too long and narrow; consequently, the tiger appears to have a rather long face. Access the Graphics menu, and click on <Scale picture>, as shown in Figure 7-16. The Scale Picture dialog box shown in Figure 7-17 is displayed. In the Aspect Ratio box, the <Preserve> option reformats the image to its original proportions regardless of the dimensions of the frame. <Ignore>, the default setting, causes the graphic image to fill the frame completely. Click on <Preserve> and on <OK>, and the head of the tiger is reformatted immediately to its original and correct

Figure 7-15. *The imported picture filling the frame*

Figure 7-16. *The <Scale picture> option selected to change the proportion of the image*

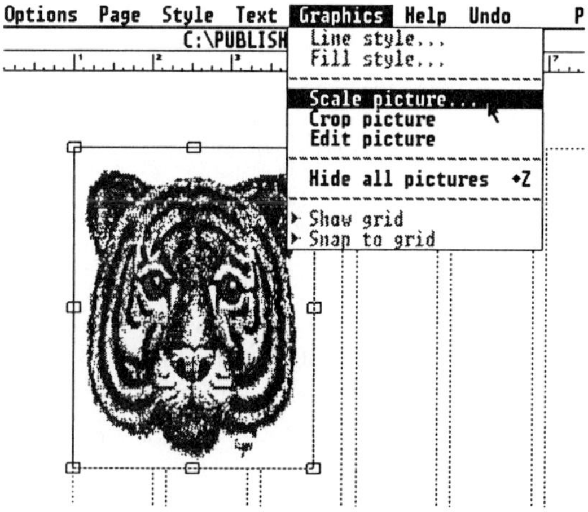

Figure 7-17. *The Scale Picture dialog box*

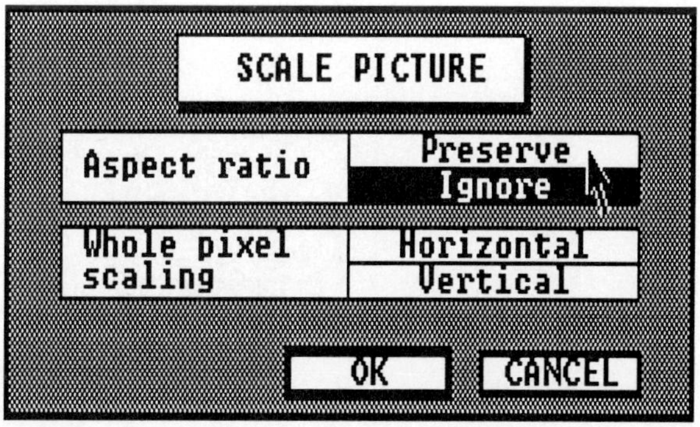

proportions, as shown in Figure 7-18. When you select the <Preserve> aspect ratio option, the image no longer fills the entire frame. It is sized to fit the narrower frame dimensions, leaving white space in the wider dimension.

The options in the Whole Pixel Scaling box serve a special purpose. They can be used when a file is enlarged or reduced by a fractional amount to avoid the so-called "tartan" effect that sometimes occurs.

Using the Graphics Drawing Function

Publish It! and Publish It Lite! offer a number of functions used to produce original freehand drawings. Click on the <GRAPHICS> icon in the lower-right area of the toolbox, and the Library window changes to display the tools shown in Figure 7-19 for Publish It! and in Figure 7-20 for Publish It Lite!.

The arrowhead tool (at the top right in Figures 7-19 and 7-20) is used to click on frames in order to select them and display the grid. It is also used to move and resize graphic elements that have already been drawn. It functions much like the <FRAME> tool in the main mode of Publish It!.

The line tool (top left) lets you draw a straight line. To draw a line, hold down the mouse button and drag the pointer from the place where the line

Figure 7-18. *The picture restored to the correct proportion in the active frame*

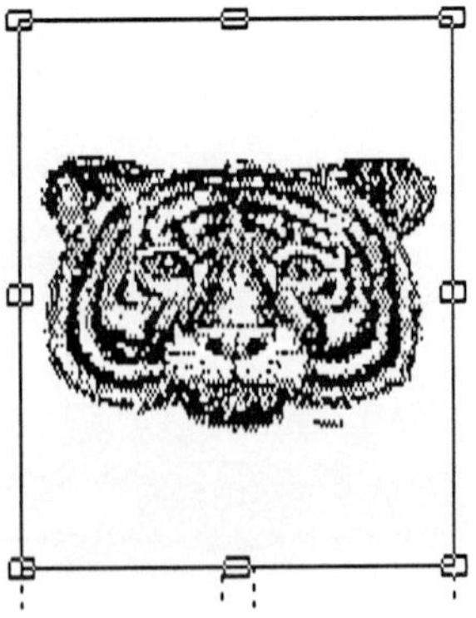

Figure 7-19. *The <GRAPHICS> mode options available with Publish It!*

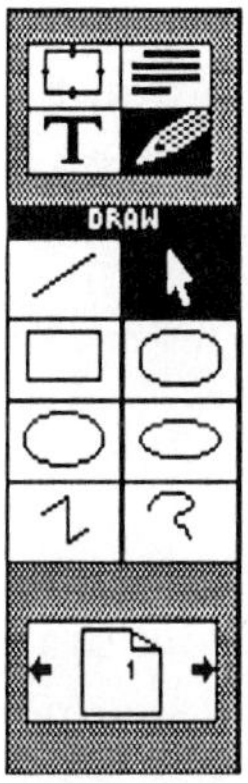

begins to where it ends. Let go of the mouse button and the line remains in place.

The box tool produces a rectangular box. Press the mouse button where one corner of the box is to be placed and then drag the pointer diagonally to the opposite corner.

Figure 7-20. *The <GRAPHICS> mode options available with Publish It Lite!*

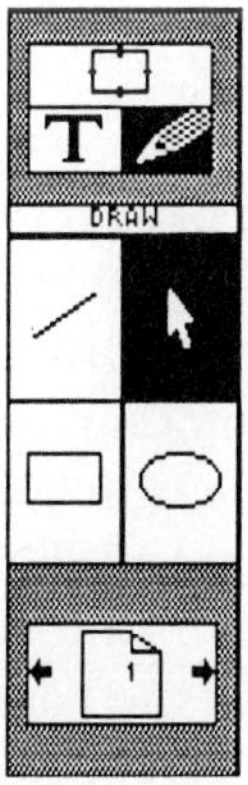

The circle tool (not available with Publish It Lite!) lets you draw circles of varying sizes depending on how far the pointer is dragged in a straight line. This tool requires some experimentation. It is difficult to know in advance exactly where that circle is going to appear. Use the arrow tool to resize and move the circle once it has been drawn.

The rounded rectangle tool (not available with Publish It Lite!) works just like the rectangle, but with rounded corners.

The ellipse tool works like the circle, except it produces an elliptical shape that can be adjusted by changing the dimensions of the frame into which it is drawn.

The polygon tool in the lower-left corner, shaped like a "Z," (not available with Publish It Lite!) lets you draw a series of connected straight lines. Draw a straight line in the usual manner. Anchor it by clicking the mouse button. Then continue with another straight line in a new direction. To quit, carefully double-click the mouse button.

The freehand tool, the squiggle in the lower-right corner (not available with Publish It Lite!) permits you to draw freehand. While holding the mouse button down, drag the pointer all over the place and draw any design you desire. It isn't easy. If freehand drawing is an important option to you, consider getting a graphic tablet with a stylus, which feels more like a pencil and makes drawing easier.

These tools are covered more thoroughly in Chapter 10, "Computer-Generated Artwork."

Adding Text

Drawings created with the drawing function can be combined with text in the same manner as imported graphics. With your drawing in its own frame anywhere on the active page, click on <Import text> in the File menu. From the Item Selector box, click on the filename of your choice and on <OK>. The filename is displayed in the Library window.

In the <FRAME> mode click on the frame holding the drawing, and then click on <Cut> in the Edit menu. The frame with the drawing disappears from the screen but is retained in a memory buffer.

Click on <Size to fit> in the Page menu (if you are not already there), and create the frames that you want to hold your text. Select the first frame and click on the filename in the Library window. The text is poured into the first frame. Repeat the procedure for the remaining frames.

Click on <Paste> in the Edit menu, and the frame with the drawing reappears in its original position, temporarily displacing the text. With the drawing frame selected, place the pointer inside the frame. Hold down the mouse button, and move the entire frame along with its drawing to its location in your document. Use the various handles to resize the drawing to fit your layout.

With the drawing frame still selected, click on <Frame border> in the Options menu. Click on the border style that appeals to you and then on <OK>. A border is drawn around your drawing.

To make the drawing stand out, you might want to add a tint. Click on <Frame tint> in the Options menu, and from the resulting dialog box select one of the tint options and click on <OK>. The tint is poured into the frame around your drawing, as illustrated in Figure 7-21.

If you want to add text that will appear across or inside your drawing, the best method is to first save your drawing as a file with a .DTP extension. Next, unless the text file to be used already exists, produce the text using your word processor or text editor.

Select <Open> from the File menu, and from the Item Selector box click on the filename that represents your previously saved drawing and then on <OK>. With the drawing on the screen, click on <Cut> in the Edit menu to temporarily get rid of it.

Click on <Import text> in the File menu, and from the Item Selector box click on the appropriate filename and on <OK>. The name of the file appears in the Library window. In the <FRAME> mode, create the frames that you want to use and then click on the filename in the Library window to pour the text into the respective frames.

Select one frame after another and click on <Frame tint> in the Options menu. Click on <Clear> and on <OK>, as shown in Figure 7-22. Now that each frame has received the <Clear> attribute, click on <Paste> in the Edit menu and the drawing reappears in its original place, covering the text area. Select the drawing frame and use the corner handles to adjust its size to the entire page or to whatever size appeals to you.

With the drawing frame still selected, click on <Send to back> in the Page menu. The text will reformat to fill the page as before and your drawing will show through, as illustrated in Figure 7-23.

Figure 7-21. *Text file with a picture, border, and tint*

Albuquerque Balloon Fiesta

The air is crisp. Not quite at the freezing level, but there's a distinct chill. Pickups, campers, station wagons with their trailers, their license plates identifying home as Michigan, New York, Washington State, Texas, Minnesota, Canada, Mexico and elsewhere are turning off Interstate 25, moving across the open field, their headlights painting bright patterns onto the clouds of dust raised by their wheels.

Predawn sharply outlines the jagged crest of the Sandia mountain range to the east. A few stubborn stars fight a losing battle against the slowly brightening light of morning.

Shadowy figures emerge from heated vehicle cabs, unloading and shouting greetings in a potpourri of dialects, east, south, north and west and over a dozen other languages. Steaming coffee warms cold-stiff hands as miles of colored fabric are stretched across the shrub-covered desert ground.

The eastern sky brightens sharply, its cold grey-blue mixing with yellow as the first rays of the sun struggle to conquer the two-mile-high mountain peak. Barely moving in the windless air, a helium-filled tethered blimp hangs forlorn in the sky, marking the site of ever more frantic activity. Then, just as a distinct touch of warmth announces the sun's inevitable victory, a shape, bulbous and huge, emerges from the flat of the desert, rising and taking shape slowly, silhouetted, like a monstrous teardrop refusing to fall and splatter.

Now the insistent ssshhhhh of gas-burning jets is heard all around. Fabric proudly displaying its brilliant colors in the brightening light of the day, swallows warmed air by the hundreds

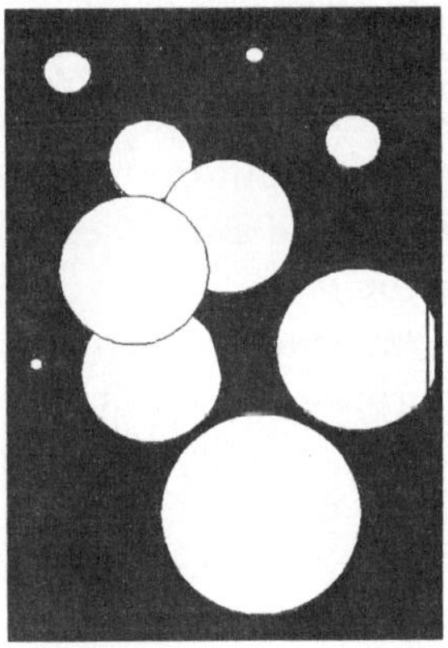

of cubic yards, jealously embracing and holding it while shedding the imprisoning effects of gravity, rising like so many impatient mushrooms, eager to fly.

Today is the third day of the nine designated officially as the Annual International Balloon Fiesta being held at Albuquerque, New Mexico each year starting at the first Saturday in October. Some 500 balloons (the number was chosen as the maximum allowable, after 605 balloons broke all previous records in 1988) representing over two dozen countries, are competing for recognition as the best in the world. Two-way radios coordinating the work of pilots and ground crews are spewing forth commands as lines are released and balloons rise skyward with deliberate majesty. One, two, five, twelve, twenty. The counting turns to guesswork as the turquoise sky fills, turning into a gay polka-dot tableau of color.

Slowly the spaces between the dots widen as the pilots, flying at different altitudes to take advantage of varying currents of air, drift silently into the distance. The captain of a TWA 747 could be excused for being somewhat stunned when being told by Albuquerque Tower: "Cleared to land; caution, balloons over the airport."

Hours pass and eventually spectators disband as the last of the balloonists is airborne. Ground crews, tied to one specific balloon by the invisible umbilical chord of radio communication search for the best among New Mexico's few and widely separate roads to maintain visual contact with their airborne partners. And the field, the site of so much pre-dawn activity, is now deserted. quietly resting to be ready again to produce another spurt of spectacular beauty at the dawn of the following day.

Figure 7-22. *The Frame Tint dialog box*

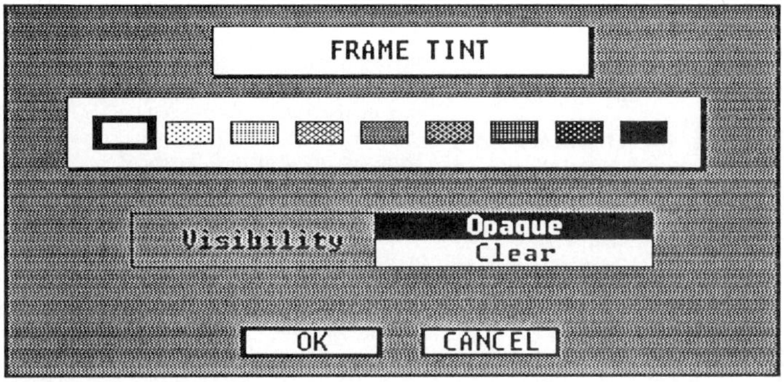

You can add a bit more tint to the drawing so it stands out better. Place the pointer into the space between the two text frames and click to select the drawing frame. Now click on <Frame tint> in the Options menu and select a fairly light tint, since you don't want to obscure the text. Click on <OK>, and the tint is poured into the drawing frame. Since the text frames are transparent, the picture shows through, as shown in Figure 7-24.

Open Versus Import Files

Images you create with the drawing options cannot be saved as graphics files (with .IMG, .GEM, or .PCX extensions), the kind that subsequently can be accessed using the <Import picture> option from the File menu. They can be saved as part of a Publish It! document, but the only way to retrieve them is to use <Open> again for the full document and perhaps edit or replace the text. Publish It! files with the .DTP extension cannot be combined. Therefore, the graphic image will always be part of the document it was created with. Drawings that are saved as .DTP files can only be combined with new or different text that is imported.

Figure 7-23. *The enlarged balloon picture showing through the text frames*

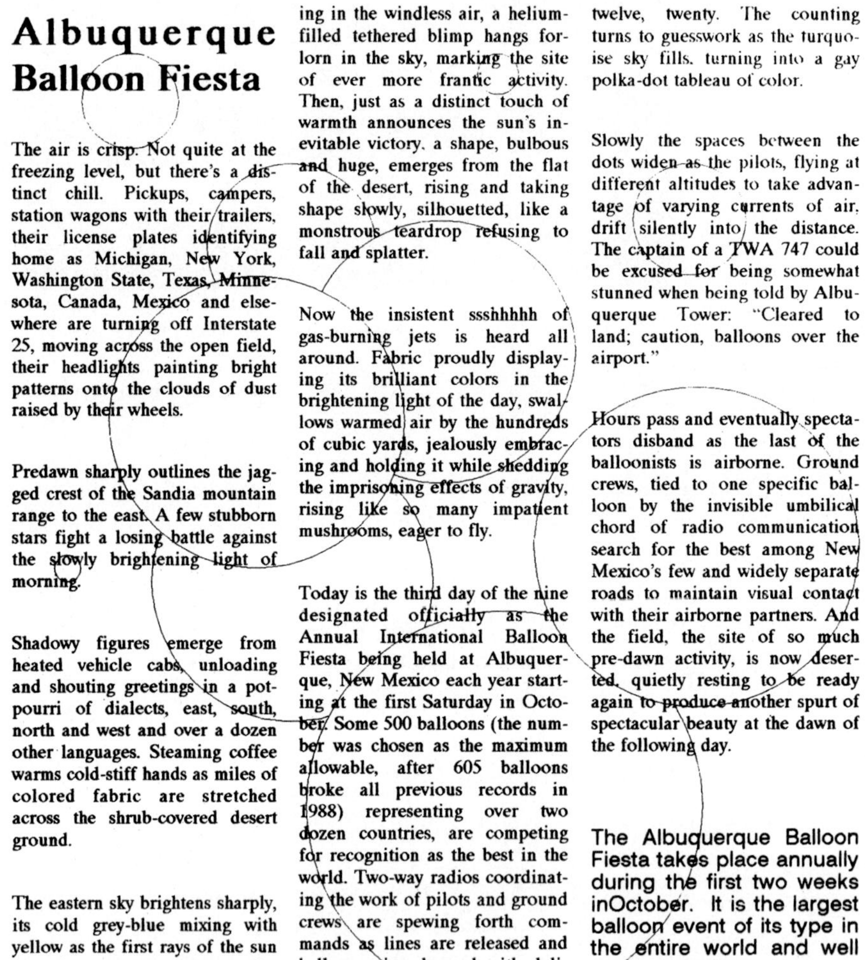

Albuquerque Balloon Fiesta

The air is crisp. Not quite at the freezing level, but there's a distinct chill. Pickups, campers, station wagons with their trailers, their license plates identifying home as Michigan, New York, Washington State, Texas, Minnesota, Canada, Mexico and elsewhere are turning off Interstate 25, moving across the open field, their headlights painting bright patterns onto the clouds of dust raised by their wheels.

Predawn sharply outlines the jagged crest of the Sandia mountain range to the east. A few stubborn stars fight a losing battle against the slowly brightening light of morning.

Shadowy figures emerge from heated vehicle cabs, unloading and shouting greetings in a potpourri of dialects, east, south, north and west and over a dozen other languages. Steaming coffee warms cold-stiff hands as miles of colored fabric are stretched across the shrub-covered desert ground.

The eastern sky brightens sharply, its cold grey-blue mixing with yellow as the first rays of the sun struggle to conquer the two-mile-high mountain peak. Barely moving in the windless air, a helium-filled tethered blimp hangs forlorn in the sky, marking the site of ever more frantic activity. Then, just as a distinct touch of warmth announces the sun's inevitable victory, a shape, bulbous and huge, emerges from the flat of the desert, rising and taking shape slowly, silhouetted, like a monstrous teardrop refusing to fall and splatter.

Now the insistent ssshhhhh of gas-burning jets is heard all around. Fabric proudly displaying its brilliant colors in the brightening light of the day, swallows warmed air by the hundreds of cubic yards, jealously embracing and holding it while shedding the imprisoning effects of gravity, rising like so many impatient mushrooms, eager to fly.

Today is the third day of the nine designated officially as the Annual International Balloon Fiesta being held at Albuquerque, New Mexico each year starting at the first Saturday in October. Some 500 balloons (the number was chosen as the maximum allowable, after 605 balloons broke all previous records in 1988) representing over two dozen countries, are competing for recognition as the best in the world. Two-way radios coordinating the work of pilots and ground crews are spewing forth commands as lines are released and balloons rise skyward with deliberate majesty. One, two, five, twelve, twenty. The counting turns to guesswork as the turquoise sky fills, turning into a gay polka-dot tableau of color.

Slowly the spaces between the dots widen as the pilots, flying at different altitudes to take advantage of varying currents of air, drift silently into the distance. The captain of a TWA 747 could be excused for being somewhat stunned when being told by Albuquerque Tower: "Cleared to land; caution, balloons over the airport."

Hours pass and eventually spectators disband as the last of the balloonists is airborne. Ground crews, tied to one specific balloon by the invisible umbilical chord of radio communication search for the best among New Mexico's few and widely separate roads to maintain visual contact with their airborne partners. And the field, the site of so much pre-dawn activity, is now deserted, quietly resting to be ready again to produce another spurt of spectacular beauty at the dawn of the following day.

The Albuquerque Balloon Fiesta takes place annually during the first two weeks inOctober. It is the largest balloon event of its type in the entire world and well worth attending.

Figure 7-24. *A tint added to the balloon frame*

Albuquerque Balloon Fiesta

The air is crisp. Not quite at the freezing level, but there's a distinct chill. Pickups, campers, station wagons with their trailers, their license plates identifying home as Michigan, New York, Washington State, Texas, Minnesota, Canada, Mexico and elsewhere are turning off Interstate 25, moving across the open field, their headlights painting bright patterns onto the clouds of dust raised by their wheels.

Predawn sharply outlines the jagged crest of the Sandia mountain range to the east. A few stubborn stars fight a losing battle against the slowly brightening light of morning.

Shadowy figures emerge from heated vehicle cabs, unloading and shouting greetings in a potpourri of dialects, east, south, north and west and over a dozen other languages. Steaming coffee warms cold-stiff hands as miles of colored fabric are stretched across the shrub-covered desert ground.

The eastern sky brightens sharply, its cold grey-blue mixing with yellow as the first rays of the sun struggle to conquer the two-mile-high mountain peak. Barely moving in the windless air, a helium-filled tethered blimp hangs forlorn in the sky, marking the site of ever more frantic activity. Then, just as a distinct touch of warmth announces the sun's inevitable victory, a shape, bulbous and huge, emerges from the flat of the desert, rising and taking shape slowly, silhouetted, like a monstrous teardrop refusing to fall and splatter.

Now the insistent sssshhhhh of gas-burning jets is heard all around. Fabric proudly displaying its brilliant colors in the brightening light of the day, swallows warmed air by the hundreds of cubic yards, jealously embracing and holding it while shedding the imprisoning effects of gravity, rising like so many impatient mushrooms, eager to fly.

Today is the third day of the nine designated officially as the Annual International Balloon Fiesta being held at Albuquerque, New Mexico each year starting at the first Saturday in October. Some 500 balloons (the number was chosen as the maximum allowable, after 605 balloons broke all previous records in 1988) representing over two dozen countries, are competing for recognition as the best in the world. Two-way radios coordinating the work of pilots and ground crews are spewing forth commands as lines are released and balloons rise skyward with deliberate majesty. One, two, five, twelve, twenty. The counting turns to guesswork as the turquoise sky fills, turning into a gay polka-dot tableau of color.

Slowly the spaces between the dots widen as the pilots, flying at different altitudes to take advantage of varying currents of air, drift silently into the distance. The captain of a TWA 747 could be excused for being somewhat stunned when being told by Albuquerque Tower: "Cleared to land; caution, balloons over the airport."

Hours pass and eventually spectators disband as the last of the balloonists is airborne. Ground crews, tied to one specific balloon by the invisible umbilical chord of radio communication search for the best among New Mexico's few and widely separate roads to maintain visual contact with their airborne partners. And the field, the site of so much pre-dawn activity, is now deserted, quietly resting to be ready again to produce another spurt of spectacular beauty at the dawn of the following day.

The Albuquerque Balloon Fiesta takes place annually during the first two weeks inOctober. It is the largest balloon event of its type in the entire world and well worth attending.

7

The only alternative is to create text in the <TEXT> mode and type it into a separate frame. That frame is then given the <Clear> attribute and moved over the drawing.

Drawing Letters or Digits

You might want to create specific letters, digits, or logos in a style or size that is not available in the font library. You can draw such letters, digits, and other symbols using the drawing options with <Snap to grid> active, as was done in creating the letter "A" shown in Figure 7-25. The larger such a symbol

Figure 7-25. *A huge letter drawn in <GRAPHICS> mode*

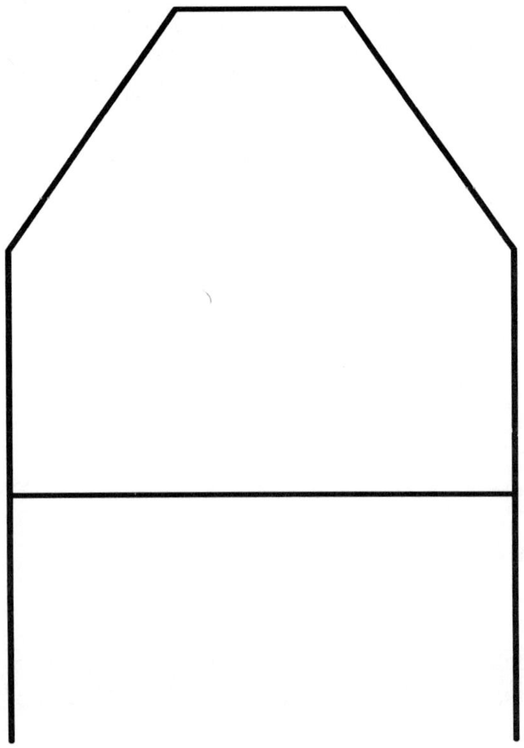

is drawn, the better it will look when reduced. Once such a letter or symbol has been created, it can be manipulated in many ways, some of which are illustrated in Figure 7-26.

Combining Text and Original Drawings

Since the exact placement of circles and ovals can present a problem, you can create them in separate frames and then superimpose them over a letter or symbol. For instance, to produce the copyright symbol, the letter "C" enclosed in a circle, in the <TEXT> mode select the type style and size you want to use and type the letter "C" into a frame. Using the spacebar and carriage returns, move the letter into the approximate center of your frame.

Next create another frame and go into the <GRAPHICS> mode. Click on the circle tool in the Library window. Place the graphics cursor into the new, empty frame and create a circle slightly larger than the "C."

You may want to click on the <Line style> option in the Graphics menu and, from the displayed dialog box, click on a line width that complements the "C."

Place the cursor inside the frame containing the "C" and click to select it. Click on <Frame tint> in the Options menu. In the dialog box click on <Clear> and <OK>.

Place the pointer into the frame with the "C" and, holding down the mouse button, drag it onto the frame with the circle until it is approximately centered. Release the mouse button. You may have to move the frame with the "C" several times until it is centered to your satisfaction. Then use the <Save as> option from the File menu to save the newly created copyright symbol, which is shown in Figure 7-27.

Of course, the copyright symbol is also available in some fonts using the GEM extended character set and pressing ALT-189 on the numeric keypad. The method just described, however, can produce equivalents of many of the GEM characters, even in the more decorative fonts where they would otherwise not be supported.

When combining text and graphics in this way, always make the frame containing the text transparent and place it in front of the frame containing the graphic, because the inside of a drawn circle, for instance, is never transparent.

Figure 7-26. *The letter manipulated in several ways*

Chapters 8, 9, and 10 are designed to help you gain hands-on experience in the use of Publish It!. In Chapter 8, "Hands-on Practice," you will produce several documents that combine text and graphics provided by Publish It!. Chapter 9, "Using External Files," explores the possibilities available when material from external programs is used. Chapter 10, "Computer-Generated Artwork," deals with computer-generated artwork and computer-aided design programs used in combination with Publish It!.

As you may have noticed, delving deeper into the features available with Publish It! reveals facets that were not obvious at the start. Do consider executing many of the steps described in the following chapters to learn still more about the available functions.

Figure 7-27. *Copyright symbol produced with <TEXT> mode "C" and <GRAPHICS> mode circle*

8

Hands-on Practice

This chapter describes in detail the process of producing a variety of different documents–some relatively simple, others more complicated. The purpose is twofold. First, performing the exercises will increase your familiarity with the different options that Publish It! offers. Second, every one of the individual documents created in the course of this chapter can be modified to fit your particular needs and taste. These models can readily serve your unique purposes if you replace the text and graphics files with your own.

Document design, layout, selection of font styles and sizes, and selection of graphics depend on both personal taste and the expediency of using material that is readily available from Publish It! or other sources.

This chapter uses graphic material available exclusively from Publish It!. Using material available from external sources is the subject of Chapter 9, "Using External Files."

Clip-Art Files

Publish It! version 2.0 includes three libraries of clip-art files. There are 23 files with the .IMG extension, 16 with the .PCX extension, 13 with the .GEM extension, and 2 with the .EPS extension. These files are contained in compressed form on one of the master disks and can be installed in uncompressed form on the C:\PUBLISH\ARTWORKS directory (or any other, if you prefer) by following the detailed installation instructions in Appendix A, "Installation." In addition, all versions of Publish It! include TIGER.IMG, MONALISA.IMG, and PC.GEM files that are installed on the C:\PUBLISH\PICTURES directory during the standard installation procedure. Earlier versions of Publish It! include only the 23 .IMG files in uncompressed form.

Certain early releases of Publish It! contained mislabeled clip-art files. If there seems to be a disparity between the names on the disk and the names shown for the graphics files in the clip-art pages in the manual, contact Timeworks for an updated list of names. Alternatively, your Publish It! package may include a document called "Additional Notes on Installation," which contains the correct list.

Since what follows makes use of some of the available clip-art images, you might want to create libraries of these files. To create a library containing the 23 .IMG files, pluse the TIGER.IMG and MONALISA.IMG files, take these steps:

1. Access the Page menu and click on <Go to page>.
2. A dialog box appears. Click on the check mark after <Go to master page>.
3. The document screen appears. Access the Options menu and click on <Show rulers>, which places calibrated rulers along the top and left sides of the document screen.
4. Access the Page menu and click on <Size to fit>.
5. In the <FRAME> mode, create a horizontal frame across the entire page but vertically extending only from the top of the frame guides down to the 4 3/4-inch mark.

6. With the new frame selected, access the Edit menu and click on <Copy>. Then access the Edit menu again and click on <Paste>. A new frame appears slightly offset from the original. Place the pointer inside it and, holding down the mouse button, drag it to the bottom half of the screen to a position starting at the 5-inch mark and extending to the 9 1/2-inch mark.
7. Between the top and bottom frames, produce a third frame a half inch high and as wide as the page.
8. With that new frame selected, access the Edit menu and click on <Copy>. Access that menu again and click on <Paste>. Place the pointer inside the offset frame and, holding down the mouse key, drag it to the bottom of the bottom page. You now have the master page, shown in Figure 8-1, with two large frames designed to hold the graphic images and two narrow frames designed to hold the filenames.

Figure 8-1. *The master page for the clip-art files*

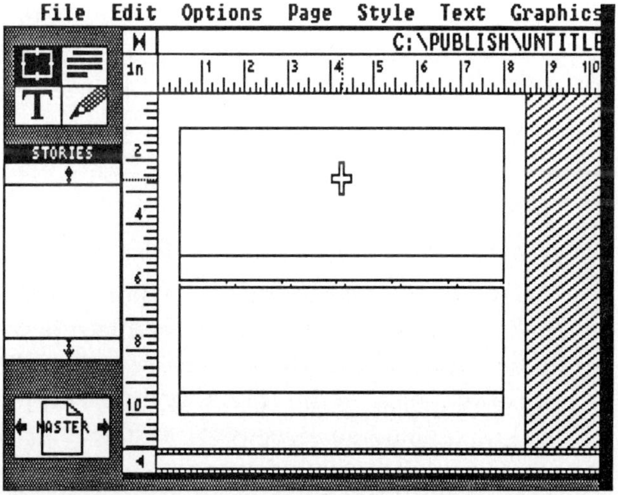

9. Access the Page menu and click on <Go to page> or use the ALT-G quick key. With the text cursor in the window to the right of <Go to page>, type **1** and click on <OK>, as shown in Figure 8-2, or simply press ENTER. Page 1 is displayed as an exact copy of the master page.

If you do not want to continue at this time, access the File menu, click on <Save as>, and enter a filename of your choice into the displayed Item Selector box. The .DTP extension is provided automatically by Publish It!. This saves the configuration of the master page, which is used whenever you're ready to go on.

When you want to resume work on your document, click on <Open> in the File menu, and from the Item Selector box click on the .DTP filename that you entered in the previous session and click on <OK>. Page 1 is displayed with the frames created for the master page.

10. In the <FRAME> mode click on the top frame to select it.
11. Access the File menu and click on <Import picture>.
12. From the dialog box click on <GEM Paint (.IMG)> and <OK>.
13. If you are using Publish It! version 2.0, the Directory line in the Item Selector box reads C:\PUBLISH\PICTURES*.IMG, and MONALISA.IMG and TIGER.IMG are displayed as available files.
    a. Click on the Directory line, and use LEFT ARROW to place the cursor to the left of the right backslash (\).
    b. Backspace to delete "PICTURES." Type **ARTWORK** and press ENTER, because the clip-art files were placed into that subdirectory during the installation.
    c. Click on ADS.IMG and on <OK>.

    If you are using an earlier version or Publish It Lite!, then from the Item Selector box click on the first file with an .IMG extension and on <OK>. (If the .IMG files are on the PICTURES directory or any other, click on the Directory line. This places the text cursor at the end of that line. Press ESC to delete the displayed line. Type in the desired disk/directory, for example, **B:*.IMG**, to list the .IMG files on that disk/directory.)

Figure 8-2. *The <Go to page> option used to go to page 1*

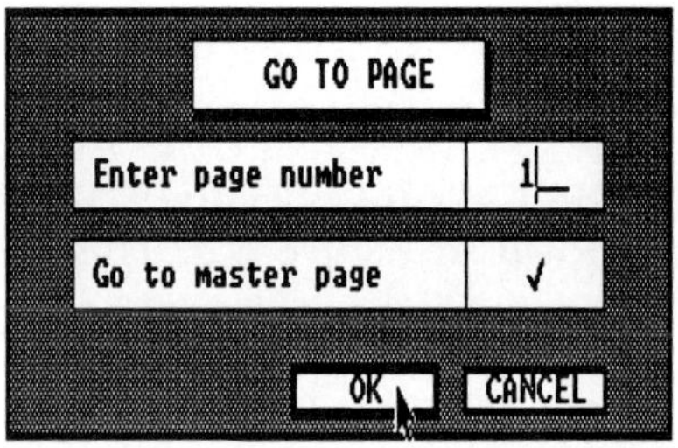

14. It takes some time for Publish It! to pour the graphic image into the top frame. When that has been accomplished, access the Graphics menu with Publish It! version 2.0 or the Options menu with earlier versions and click on <Hide all pictures> to replace the graphic image with two diagonal lines. This option is helpful because it increases the speed of all subsequent operations.
15. Click on the bottom large frame to select it. In the File menu click on <Import picture>, and from the dialog box click again on <OK>, since the previous .IMG file selection is still highlighted.
16. From the Item Selector box, click on the second of the displayed .IMG files and on <OK>. This time the importing of the picture is quite rapid because Publish It! does not actually have to draw the image.
17. In the Page menu click on <Double size>. Use the vertical scroll bar to move the first of the two narrow frames into view.
18. Click on the <TEXT> icon in the toolbox and, with the I-beam pointer inside the narrow frame, click on it. The text cursor appears at the upper-left corner of that narrow frame. Type the name of the first .IMG file.

8

19. Use the vertical scroll bar to display the bottom narrow frame. Place the I-beam pointer into it and click it. Type the name of the second .IMG file.
20. Click on the <FRAME> icon in the toolbox and click on <Size to fit> in the Page menu.
21. Place the pointer on the right arrow in the <PAGE> icon and click on it, as shown in Figure 8-3. The warning shown in Figure 8-4 is displayed, asking "Do you want to add a new page?". Click on <Yes>.
22. The page number in the <PAGE> icon has changed to 2. Repeat steps 10 through 21 until all .IMG files have been imported.

Throughout this process, maybe after every second or third page, click on <Save> in the File menu to ensure that all the work up to that point is safely recorded to disk. (If you did not save the master page as previously described, the first save must be made with the <Save as> option in order to provide a filename such as CLIPART.DTP.) Saving the file takes an increasingly long time as the file grows in size (you will probably end up with over 20 pages of .IMG files. The final file uses approximately 170,000 bytes, so make sure that there is sufficient space on the disk/directory to which your new .DTP file is being saved. Depending on the printer being used, printing the file will probably take an hour or more. Set it to print while you are busy with something else or before you leave for lunch.

If you do not have that much time to spare all at once, print only part of the file by going to the Print Options dialog box and changing the starting

Figure 8-3. *Adding a page with the <PAGE> icon*

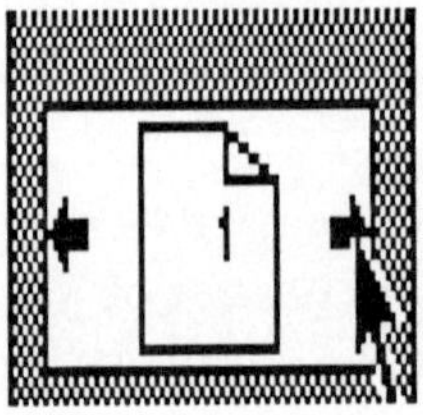

Figure 8-4. *The new page warning box*

and/or ending pages for the printout. To print only one page at a time, change both the starting and ending page numbers to the page you want to print.

Publish It! version 2.0 users can now follow the same routine to print the remaining clip-art files. The 13 .GEM files will take up seven pages. Look at the images as they are poured into the frames. You will probably want to narrow each frame horizontally to reduce the degree of distortion. The <Scale picture> option in the Graphics menu and its associated <Preserve> option are not operative with .GEM files. It is therefore up to you to establish acceptable proportions by adjusting the dimensions of the individual frames. Save this selection of images under a new filename.

When this has been done, you may want to do the same with the 16 .PCX files. Follow the steps described previously, this time selecting <PC Paintbrush (.PCX)> from the Import Picture dialog box. With .PCX files the <Scale picture> and <Preserve> options are operational. Use them after importing each image.

An Invitation to a Party

Invitations to parties are usually fairly casual and may be a good subject with which to start. For example, suppose you want to invite a few friends to a Christmas party and you need to prepare an invitation. One of the clip-art files called BORDER.IMG consists of a border of little Christmas trees, and a file called XMAS.IMG contains the words "MERRY CHRISTMAS" in fairly attractive lettering. A file called HOUSE.IMG includes a fir tree that could double as a Christmas tree. Follow these steps to produce a Christmas party invitation:

1. From the File menu click on <New> and in the resulting dialog box, click on <No> to indicate you do not want a style sheet. Next the Page Format dialog box is displayed. Click on <Note: 5.5 x 8.5 in.> and on <Landscape> and on <OK>, as shown in Figure 8-5. (If your printer cannot print in the landscape orientation, select <Portrait> instead.) You can now click on <Save style sheet> in the File menu to save that configuration for future use. In the resulting Item Selector box, type a filename of your choice and click on <OK>, as shown in Figure 8-6.
2. When the document screen appears, click on <Show rulers> in the Options menu to place the rules along the top and the left sides of the screen, shown in Figure 8-7. This makes subsequent placement of individual frames easier.
3. In the <FRAME> mode, create a single frame encompassing the entire document area, with the upper-left corner at the 1/1-inch X/Y position and the lower-right corner at the 4/8-inch X/Y position. (Remember that X represents the horizontal position and Y represents the vertical position.)
4. In the File menu click on <Import picture>, and in the dialog box click on <GEM Paint (.IMG)> and <OK>, or simply press ENTER.
5. If the .IMG files are not displayed in the Item Selector box, change the Directory line. Click on it to place the text cursor on the line. Press ESC to erase the line. Enter the new disk/directory information. Click on <BORDER.IMG> and <OK> (see Figure 8-8). The border is placed around the entire frame, as shown in Figure 8-9.
6. Now you need to create a place into which additional items can be imported. Click on <Add pages> (<Add a page> in earlier versions) in the Page menu. When the new page is being displayed, create a frame similar to the one that you created earlier for the first page. In the File menu click on <Import picture>, in the dialog box click on <OK>, and in the Item Selector box click on <HOUSE.IMG> and on <OK>.

Figure 8-5. *The Page Format dialog box*

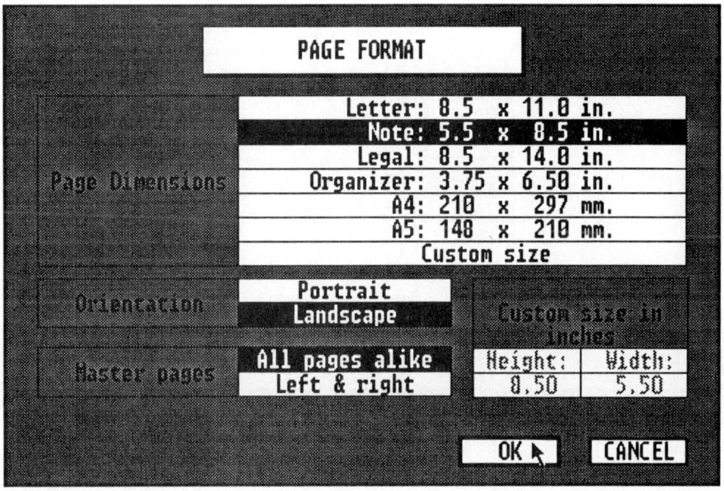

Figure 8-6. *The Item Selector box used to name the file*

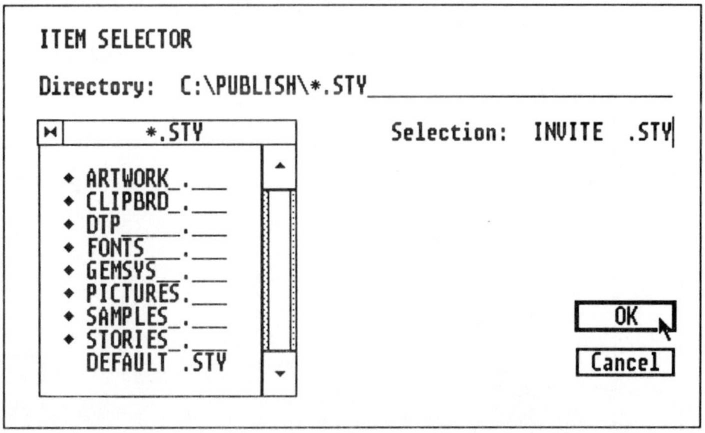

8

Figure 8-7. *The work area in landscape orientation with rulers showing*

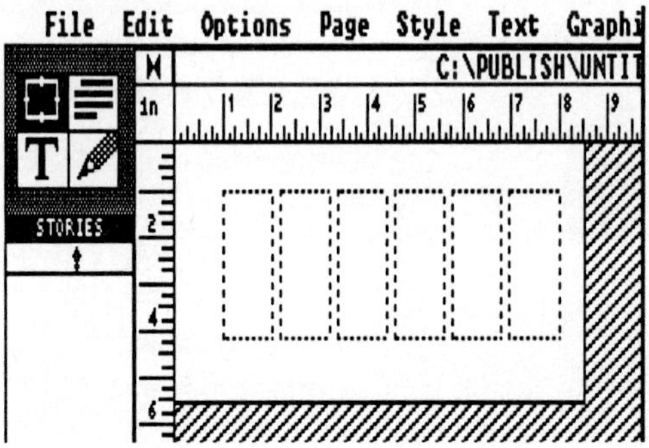

7. The complete group of images in the HOUSE.IMG file is imported. Click on <Crop picture> in the Graphics menu, and drag the scissors pointer from the top left to the bottom right of the fir tree at the

Figure 8-8. *The BORDER.IMG graphics file is imported*

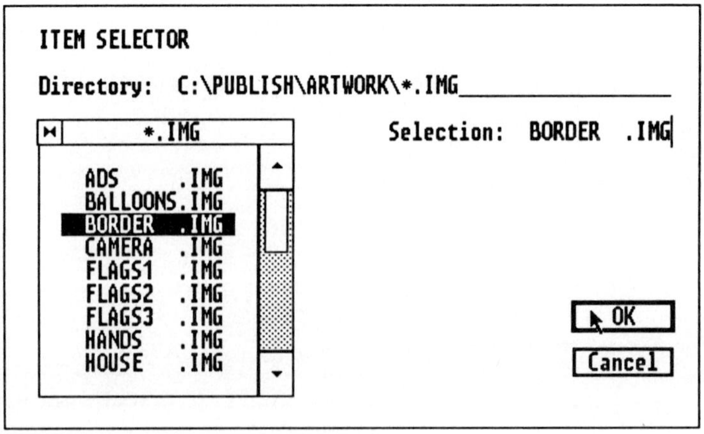

Figure 8-9. *The border poured into its frame*

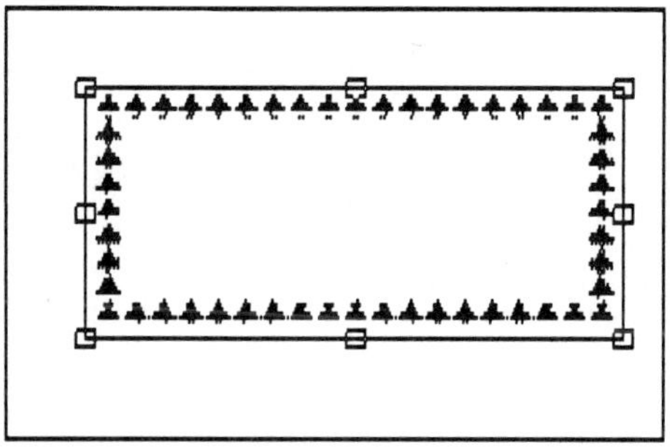

top right of the picture. Figure 8-10 shows the greatly distorted tree image that results.

8. Open the Graphics menu and click on <Scale picture>, as shown in Figure 8-11. In the dialog box displayed, click on <Preserve> and <OK>, as shown in Figure 8-12. The tree is rescaled to its original proportions, as shown in Figure 8-13.
9. Access the Edit menu, and click on <Cut> or use the ALT-X quick key. The frame and its picture disappear. In the <PAGE> icon, click on the left arrow to return to page 1. Access the Edit menu and click

8

Figure 8-10. *The distorted tree image*

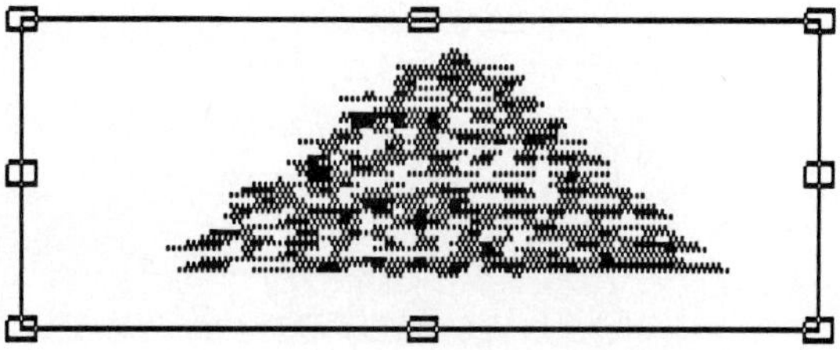

Figure 8-11. *The <Scale picture> option in the Graphics menu*

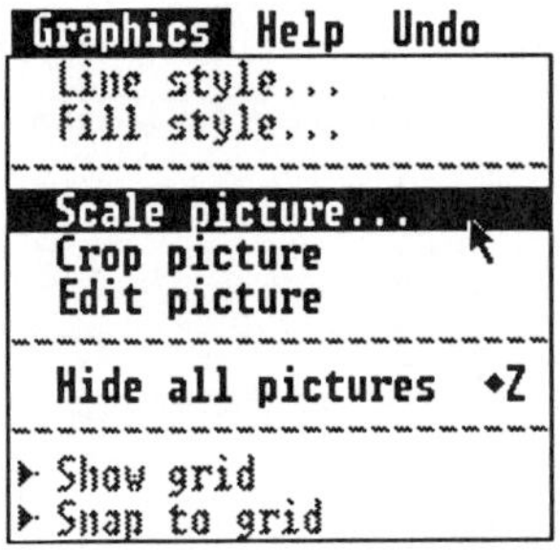

on <Paste>. The frame with the tree appears somewhere on top of the previous image. The handles show that it is selected. Place the pointer on one of the center side handles and, depressing the mouse button, drag it toward the tree. Do the same with the opposite handle until the tree is in a narrow frame. Now place the pointer in the center of the frame. Holding down the mouse button, drag the entire frame to the far right, inside the border. It covers part of that border, but don't worry about that.

Figure 8-12. *The Scale Picture dialog box*

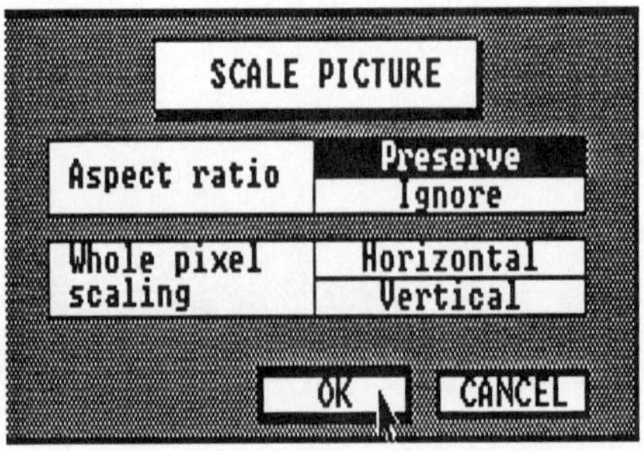

Figure 8-13. *The tree restored to its correct proportions*

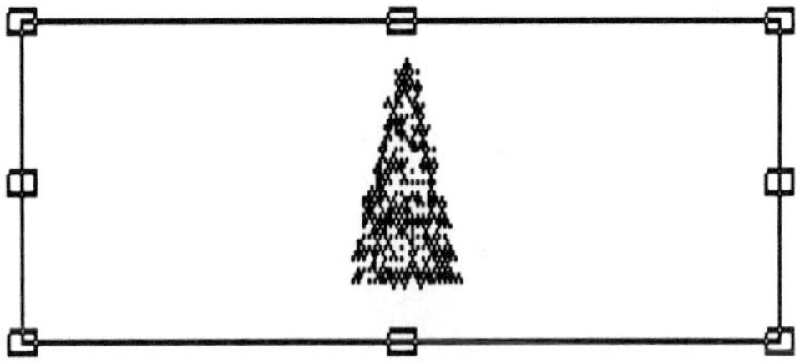

10. Access the Page menu and click on <Send to back>, as shown in Figure 8-14. The frame reappears in its entirety and the tree disappears.
11. Access the Options menu and click on <Frame tint>. When the dialog box shown in Figure 8-15 is displayed, click on <Clear> and <OK>. The tree reappears without interfering with the border.

Figure 8-14. *The <Send to back> option in the Page menu*

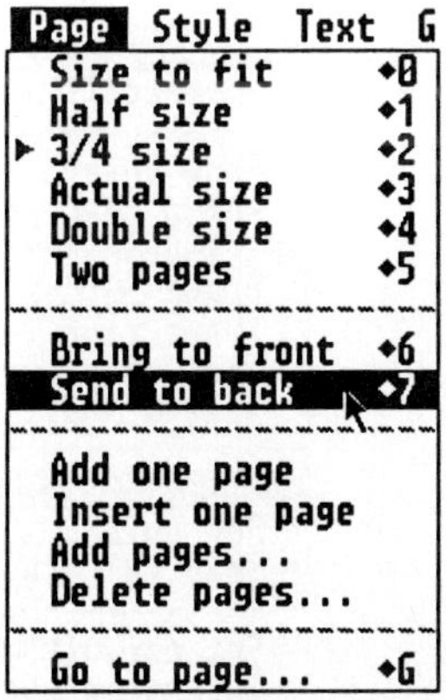

Figure 8-15. *The Frame Tint dialog box*

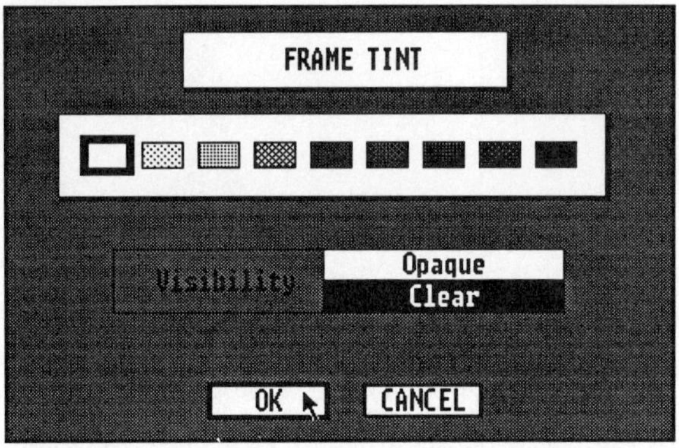

12. To see what you have created so far, access the Options menu and click on <Show frames & cols>, as shown in Figure 8-16. What results is a clear picture, shown in Figure 8-17, of what the work looks like

Figure 8-16. *The <Show frames & cols> option in the Options menu*

Figure 8-17. *The border and tree with frames and column guides removed*

up to this point. Click on <Show frames & cols> again to return to the normal screen mode.

13. Now click on the right arrow in the <PAGE> icon to return to the second page. Create a frame into which to import the next graphic. In the File menu click on <Import picture>. In the dialog box click on <OK>, and in the Item Selector box click on <XMAS.IMG> and <OK>.
14. When the XMAS.IMG file is imported, click on <Crop picture> in the Graphics menu and use the scissors pointer to crop "MERRY CHRISTMAS" out of the rest of the picture. It is reformed immediately inside the frame, as shown in Figure 8-18.

8

Figure 8-18. *"MERRY CHRISTMAS" cropped from the clip-art page*

15. Access the Edit menu and click on <Cut>. Click on the left arrow in the <PAGE> icon to return to page 1. Access the Edit menu again and click on <Paste>.
16. The frame now covers most of the previous picture. Place the pointer on one of the corner handles. Holding down the mouse button, drag the handle diagonally toward the opposite corner until the frame has been reduced to a manageable size. Place the pointer inside the frame. Holding down the mouse button, move the frame to the place inside the border where it looks right. If some of the border is obscured by it, access the Page menu and click on <Send to back>.
17. While still in the <FRAME> mode, create two new frames, as shown in Figure 8-19, which you will use to enter text. Click on the <TEXT> icon and, with the I-beam pointer inside the larger frame, click to establish the text cursor. Click on <Font/size> in the Style menu, and select a font style and size that appeals to you (20-point Madison was used in the current example). Type your invitation into the larger frame.
18. Place the I-beam pointer into the smaller frame, and click to establish the text cursor there. Click on <Font/size> in the Style menu to select a font style and size for the second box (10-point Dutch was used in the current example), and then type the text.

Figure 8-19. *Several frames added*

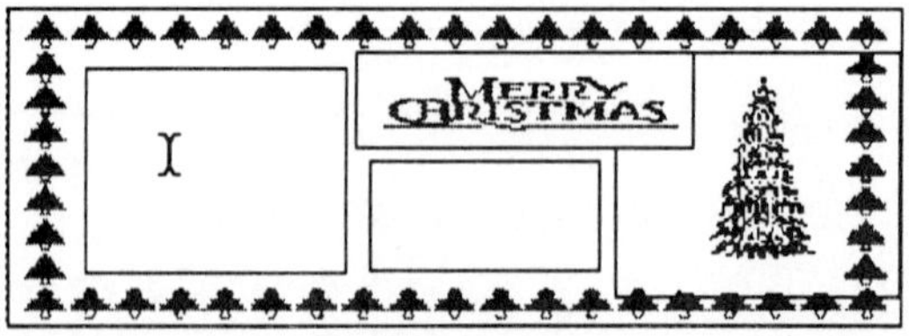

19. Click on the <FRAME> icon in the toolbox to revert to the <FRAME> mode. Click inside the smaller frame to select it. Access the Options menu and click on <Frame border>. In the resulting dialog box, click on the frame style you like and then on <OK>.
20. Access the File menu and click on <Save as>. In the Item Selector box, enter a filename with a .DTP extension (it is supplied automatically if no extension is typed).
21. In the File menu click on <Print> and choose page 1 as both the starting and the ending page numbers. Then sit back and wait until your printer prints your handiwork. Since you selected <Landscape>, your printer is going to print the picture sideways on the page (assuming it is capable of printing landscape orientation).

Improving the First Effort

There are a number of things wrong with the result. The tree doesn't seem to add much to the overall appearance. The "4:30 or so..." is too low in its frame, as shown in Figure 8-20. To take care of these problems you will remove the tree and rearrange the rest of the items accordingly.

22. In the File menu, click on <Open>. From the displayed Item Selector box, click on <XMASPRTY.DTP> (if that is the filename that was used) and on <OK>. The previous work is reestablished on the screen.
23. Temporarily move the frame holding the border far enough to expose a portion of the frame holding the tree. Place the pointer inside the frame holding the tree and click to select it. Access the Edit menu and click on <Cut>. The tree vanishes.
24. Place the cursor onto an unoccupied place inside the overall frame and click to select it. Place the pointer on the center-right handle of the frame and, while holding down the mouse button, drag it to the left until it is fairly close to the last "S" in "CHRISTMAS."
25. Click on the <TEXT> icon and place the I-beam onto the line "4:30 or so..." and click to establish the text cursor. Use one of the arrow

Figure 8-20. *The first draft of the invitation*

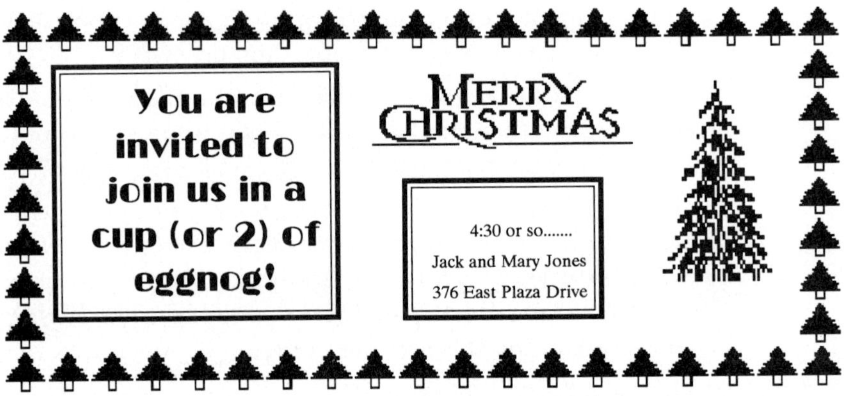

keys to move the cursor to the beginning of that line. Press ENTER to move the text down one line. Click on the <PARAGRAPH> icon and, with the pointer on the typed line, select it. In the Text menu, click on <Paragraph style> and on <Justification>. Click on <Centered> and on <OK> twice.

26. Click on the frame holding the text on the left. Access the Options menu and click on <Frame border>. In the dialog box select a border style and click on <OK>. Access the Options menu and click on <Show frames & cols> to see what your work really looks like. If you are not satisfied, make whatever improvements you think necessary.
27. Click on <Save> in the File menu and in the dialog box click on <Yes>. Then click on <Print> in the File menu. The Print Document dialog box is displayed. Since a second page was used, it will indicate that pages 1 and 2 are to be printed. Use DOWN ARROW to move the text cursor down to the next line, or simply place the pointer on the 2 and click on it to move the cursor to the position shown in Figure 8-21. Type **1** and click on <OK>, and the final result should look more or less like Figure 8-22.

Figure 8-21. *The Print Document dialog box*

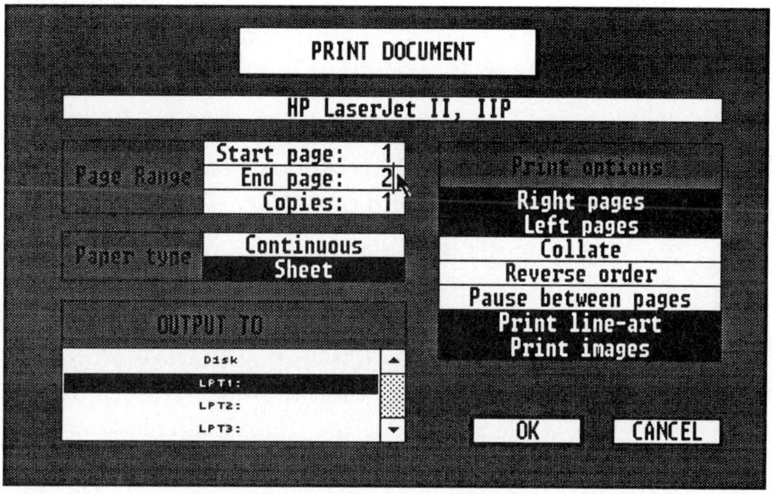

Figure 8-22. *The second version of the invitation*

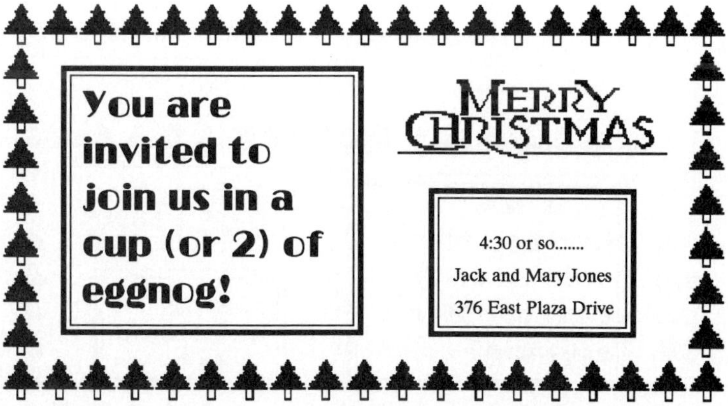

Adding Another Item to the Invitation

It may occur to you that there is something missing. The invitation doesn't tell you on what day the party is supposed to occur. To fix that after you have already exited Publish It!, take these steps:

28. Activate Publish It! in the usual manner. Click on <Open> in the File menu. In the Item Selector box, click on the filename you used when you saved the file and on <OK>.
29. When the file is displayed, click on <Half size> in the Page menu.
30. Place the pointer on an empty place in the outer frame and click to select it. Place the pointer on the center-right handle, as shown in Figure 8-23. Holding down the mouse button, drag it to the right side of the far right column guide. The frame now extends to the right, while the rest of the items inside it remain undisturbed.
31. Click on <Actual size> in the Page menu. Once the image has been reestablished, use the bottom scroll bar to view the empty portion on the right side of the frame.
32. Place the pointer outside the frame and click to deselect it. Now create a new narrow vertical frame in the empty space.

Figure 8-23. *The frame about to be stretched to the right edge*

33. Click on the <TEXT> icon in the toolbox, and place the I-beam pointer in the new empty frame. Click to activate the text cursor.
34. Click on <Font/size> in the Style menu and select a font style and size (18-point Drury Lane Caps was used in the current example).
35. Type **Dec. 25th Xmas Day**, pressing (ENTER) after each word to fill four separate lines. Since the Body Text style was already changed to a centered style and since text is by default in Body Text if no other style is specified, the text is centered automatically.
36. Click on <Save> if you want to replace the previous file. Otherwise click on <Save as>, and enter a new filename in the Item Selector box. Click on <Print> in the File menu. In the Print Document dialog box, change the end page to 1. (Alternatively you can click on <Delete a page> in the Page menu and enter the page number to be deleted.) The final result will look more or less like Figure 8-24. Notice that even though you typed those four lines using upper- and lowercase letters, everything is actually printed in uppercase because the Drury Lane Caps font does not include lowercase letters.

That takes care of preparing the Christmas party invitation. Of course, you might prefer a different look. Still, many steps involved in creating this invitation are likely to be used in different ways with considerable frequency.

Figure 8-24. *The third and final version of the invitation*

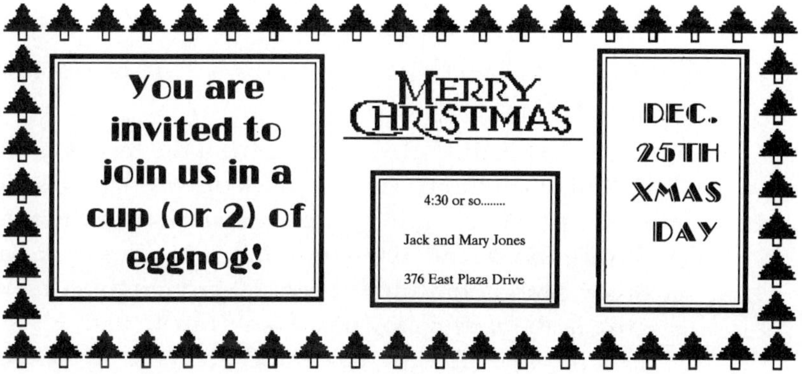

A Business Card

In the next hands-on exercise you will produce a simple business card and copy it as many times as it will fit on a page to print several at once. Business cards are usually 2 x 3 1/2 inches. Using that size, you can fit eight of them on a standard 8 1/2 x 11-inch piece of paper. Most printers can deal with sufficiently heavy stock to give the final cards some body. Seventy-pound cover stock is ideal for this purpose, and it comes in white and a variety of colors. (Some laser printers can only use paper of up to 35-pound weight.)

Here are the steps to take:

1. Access the Options menu and click on <Show rulers> to place rulers along the top and left sides of the work area. Again in the Options menu, click on <Snap to grid> to deactivate the <Snap to grid> option, allowing you to position your frames precisely.
2. In the <FRAME> mode prepare a frame that measures just under 2 x 3 1/2 inches by stretching it horizontally from the 1-inch mark to just beyond the 4-inch mark and vertically from the 1-inch mark to just above the 3-inch mark.
3. From the Options menu click on <Frame border> and in the resulting dialog box click on <All around> and on <OK> to place a narrow border around the entire frame.
4. If you are not in the Actual or Double page format, open the Page menu and click on <Actual size> or on <Double size>. Now click on the <TEXT> icon, place the I-beam pointer inside the frame, and click to produce the text cursor.
5. In the Style menu click on <Font/size>. In the resulting dialog box, click on <Dutch> and <12>.
6. Select the <PARAGRAPH> icon from the toolbox. Click on BODY TEXT in the Library window. Click on <Paragraph style> in the Text menu. If you are using an earlier version of Publish It!, click on <Justification>, and in the resulting dialog box click on <Table> and <OK>. With Publish It! version 2.0 just continue on. Click on <Set tabs> in the next dialog box. Pick <Tab 1> and select <Left tab> as the type of tab. Accept the default 0.5 as the position of the first tab

stop. Press (TAB) to move the text cursor away from the border and type your name.

7. Press (ENTER) several times to move the cursor down a few lines and press (TAB) to align the cursor more or less with the first letter of your name. From the Style menu click on <Font/size> and click on <8>. Now type your street address or post office box number.
8. Press (ENTER) to get to the next line. Press (TAB) and type the city, state, and ZIP code. Then press (TAB) and type your area code and phone number.
9. Before doing anything else, access the File menu and click on <Save as>. In the Item Selector box, type a filename, such as BUSCARD.DTP. This saves the work just in case you make some fatal error during subsequent editing.
10. Still in the File menu, click on <Print> to get a hard copy, and examine how the printer interpreted what you did. You will probably find that the copy needs to be aligned to produce a more pleasing composition.
11. Using the printout as a guide, make whatever corrections appear to be indicated and, if necessary, print it again to make sure that it is the way you want it.
12. When you are satisfied, click on the <FRAME> icon, place the pointer into the frame, and click to select it. Now access the Edit menu and click on <Copy>, as shown in Figure 8-25, and then, again in the Edit menu, click on <Paste>.

Figure 8-25. *<Copy> selected from the Edit menu*

Figure 8-26. *An offset image that can now be moved to a new location*

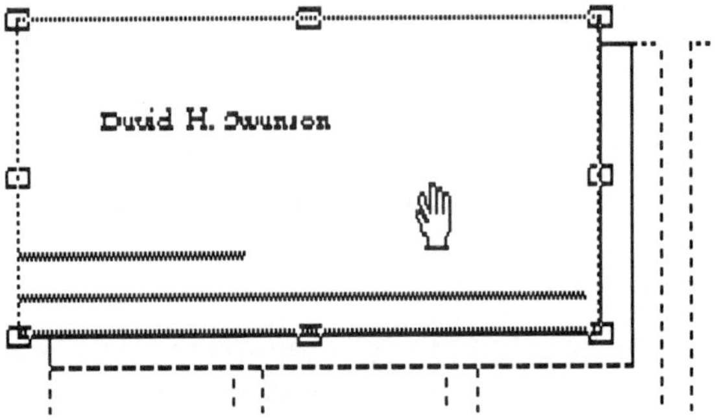

13. Place the cursor inside the new frame, which is slightly offset over the previous one, and holding down the mouse button, use the grabber hand to move the copy of the original frame to a new position on the page, as shown in Figure 8-26.
14. Repeat steps 12 and 13 six more times until you have eight copies of the business card arranged on the page, as shown in Figure 8-27.

Figure 8-27. *The business card copied seven times*

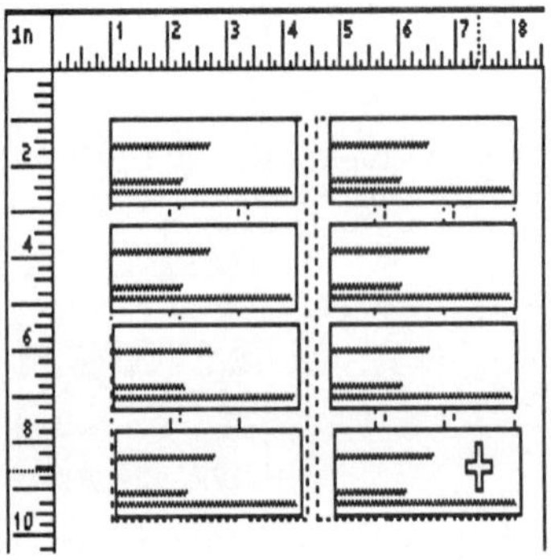

When they are all neatly arranged, you are ready to print your cards eight at a time, as shown in Figure 8-28.

Using a Graphic on a Business Card

You might want to use a logo or some kind of graphic image on your business card to produce a variation of the one shown in Figure 8-29. The steps involved here are somewhat different than in the previous procedure.

1. Create a frame of any size, preferably fairly small since it will hold graphics, and small graphic images take less time to appear on the screen than large ones. In the File menu click on <Import picture>. In the dialog box click on <GEM Paint (.IMG)> or whatever file type contains the graphic you want to use. Click on <OK>.
2. In the Item Selector box, click on the filename or the Directory line if the file is located on another directory. In this example the CAMERA.IMG clip-art page was selected.
3. In the Page menu click on <Double size> to get a good look at the graphic images. From the Graphics menu click on <Crop picture>. Use the scissors pointer to select the image, and run the pointer across it until it is enclosed in a dotted frame. Let go of the mouse button to select the cropped image, which now fills the entire frame.
4. Select the frame and, using the side and corner handles, reduce the size of the frame to approximately 1 x 1 inch (or whatever size image you want to use). You might click on <Scale picture> in the Graphics menu. In the resulting dialog box, click on <Preserve> and <OK> to preserve the original proportions.
5. Place the pointer outside the frame and click to deselect it. Now draw a new frame the size of a business card, as previously described, and place it over the previous frame, which now disappears. In the Option menu click on <Frame tint>. In the dialog box click on <Clear> and <OK>. The graphic image reappears.
6. Type the information that is to be used, arranging the placement of the copy to please yourself. You might want to adjust the tab settings, paragraph indents, or <Text runaround> settings to position your

Figure 8-28. *The eight business cards printed*

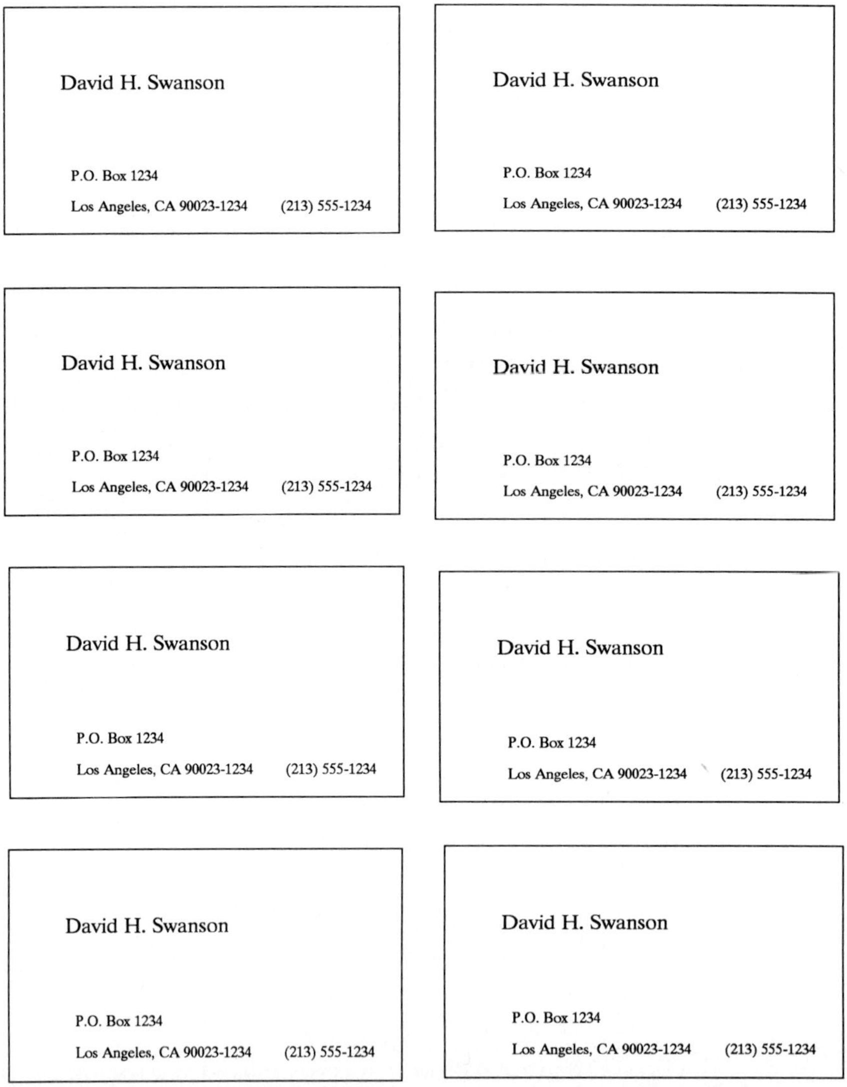

Figure 8-29. *A different business card design*

text where you want it. Be sure to save your work with a new filename, using <Save as> from the File menu. Again, print it once or possibly several times until the layout is the way you want it.

7. With Publish It! version 2.0, when you are satisfied, select both frames and use the <Copy> and <Paste> commands in the Edit menu to copy the text and graphic simultaneously. If you have an earlier version, select the larger frame, and click on <Copy> and <Paste> in the Edit menu. Using the grabber hand, move the copy to a new location on the page. The typed copy has moved, but as Figure 8-30 shows, the graphic image did not move with it.
8. In the card on the left, place the cursor inside the small frame containing the graphic image and click to select it.
9. In the Edit menu click on <Copy> and <Paste>. Use the grabber hand to move the graphic frame into the correct position in the card on the right, and let go of the mouse button. Figure 8-31 shows that the graphic now is included in both copies of the card. The text has been rearranged to its original positions.
10. Repeat the copy and paste actions for the card frame and the graphics frame individually until the page is again filled with eight cards ready to be printed.

Figure 8-30. *When the card is moved to a new location, the graphic image does not come along*

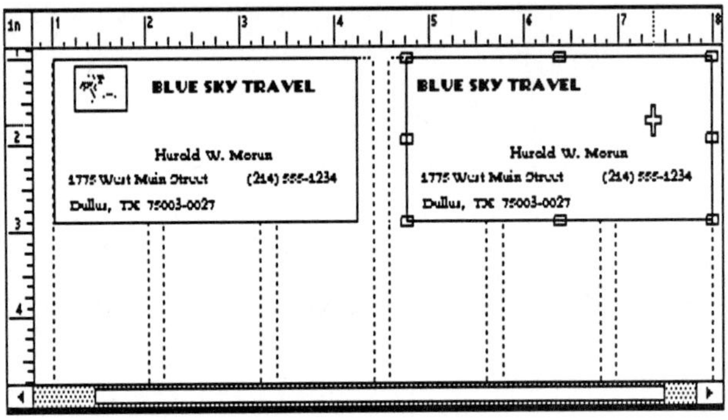

A Two-Page Product Description

The next project is a two-page document, such as an illustrated article or product description, dealing with a software package aimed at consumers interested in railroads, both model railroads and the real thing. The document's title is *Design Your Own Train,* and it demonstrates how you can

Figure 8-31. *The graphics frame must be copied and moved separately*

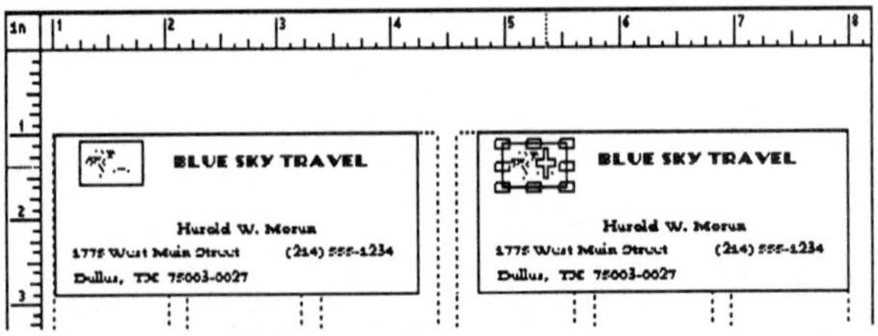

design a train layout, run several trains on your layout, and test it for practicality. Figures 8-32 and 8-33 are the first and second pages of the completed document.

Instead of the text and graphics described here, you can use any text and graphics that are readily available to you.

The individual components that make up this document are

- The software title
- The graphic showing a locomotive and a car
- The headline
- The body text
- A group of bulleted lines
- Three figures, each of which is a screen display obtained when running the software program

To assemble *Design Your Own Train,* follow these steps:

1. The text that constitutes the body of the copy used in the two-page document is in a file called DESIGNX.MAG, written in WordPerfect 5.0 and contained on a floppy disk. To prepare it for use in Publish It!, the individual paragraphs were labeled as shown here:

   <subtitle>Is This Any Way to Run a Railroad?
   <body text>A new computer program called *Design Your Own Train* . . .
   <bullet>Erase

   with all text paragraphs labeled <body text> and all bullet lines labeled <bullet>.
2. To start, click on <Import text> in the File menu and, in the resulting Item Selector box, enter the path in the Directory line where the file is located and click on <DESIGNX.MAG> and on <OK>. DESIGNX.MAG appears in the Library window.
3. Now design the basic layout for the first page, as shown in Figure 8-34.

Figure 8-32. *The first page of the two-page product description*

Design Your Own Train

Is This Any Way to Run a Railroad?

A new computer program called *Design Your Own Train* is intended especially for railroad buffs. It offers a fairly fascinating new approach to designing and then debugging a track design. To demonstrate, the program was used to design a fairly simple one-station layout that permits running several trains, causing them to leave the yard and then to run continuously before eventually returning to it.

Fig.1

For the purpose of designing the layout, the program displays the different track components shown in Fig.1. From top to bottom each rectangle represents:

- Erase
- Horizontal track section
- Vertical track section
- 90-degree crossing
- Right turn section
- Left turn section
- Right turn section
- Left turn section
- Horizontal track with right turnout forward
- Horizontal track with right turnout backward
- Horizontal track with left turnout forward
- Horizontal track with left turnout backward
- Vertical track with left turnout forward
- Vertical track with right turnout forward
- Vertical track with left turnout backward
- Vertical track with right turnout backward
- Stop

By placing the mouse arrow on the desired selection, clicking the mouse button and then moving the arrow where the track section is to be installed, and clicking again, the track appears on the selected location. This sounds a lot more complicated than it is. It only took less than 20 minutes to create the layout shown in Figures 2 and 3.

Once you have created a layout in this manner, using the **CREATE LAYOUT** option, you use the **LABEL SWITCHES** option to place a letter of the alphabet next to each switch by pointing to the switch with the arrow, pressing the **spacebar** and then typing any letter (all displayed letters appear lower case, even if you enter upper case). Once that's been done, use the **SAVE** option from the **FILE** menu.

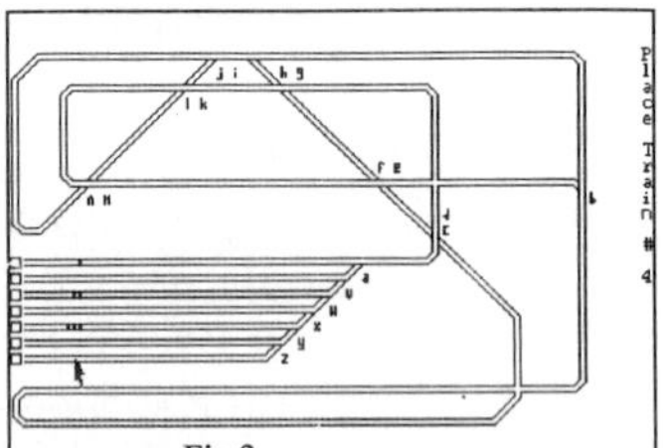

Fig.2

You're now ready to run your trains. Use the **RUN** option from the main menu which asks you to determine at which speed you want your trains to run, how many trains you

Figure 8-33. The second page of the two-page product description

want to run (4 maximum), how many cars on each train (1,2,3 or 4), and whether your trains are to represent a switcher, a local freight, a way freight or an express.

Next your layout is displayed once more and you're asked to tell the program where to place the train(s) by indicating the location with the arrow, as in Figure 2, and indicating the direction of travel by using the arrow keys or for diagonal track the home, end, PgUp or PgDn keys as in Figure 3.

After that, hitting any key starts the action. Pressing the number key for any train stops it. Pressing that number again, restarts it. Pressing the slash key (/) stops all trains, then pressing a number, restarts that train in the opposite direction. Pressing a letter key changes the direction of that particular turnout.

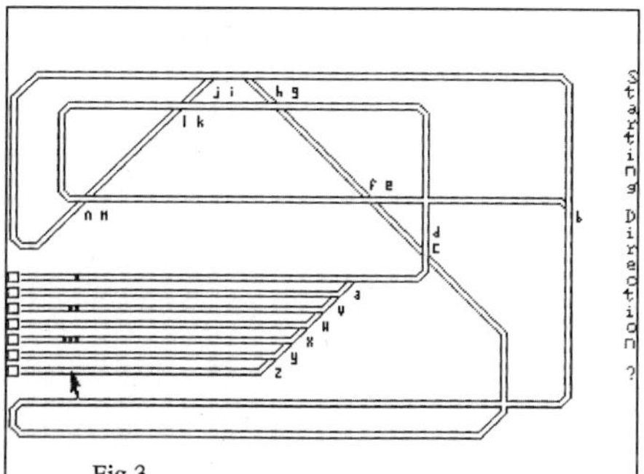

Fig.3

To start with, select one train and slow speed and watch it go through your layout and check to make sure that you haven't come up with a design that makes it impossible for the train to get back to where it came from.

What follows represents a specific exercise designed to check for shortcomings in the layout. The idea is to start with four trains: Train #1 with one car in the spur marked **a**. Train #2 with two cars in the spur marked **v**. Train #3 with three cars in the spur marked **w**. And train #4 with four cars in the spur marked **z**. Figure 2 represents this initial condition.

The exercise calls for getting all four trains out of the station and setting up the turnouts in such a way that they can run continuously without the need to reset switches. Once that has been accomplished, return to trains to the station, but this time put train #1 into spur **z**, train #2 into spur **y**, train #3 into spur **v** and train #4 into spur **a**.

To start with, immediately after starting the action (press any key), press 2,3 and 4 to stop those trains until #1 is out on the main line. Then press **a** and **v** to reset those switches and press 2 to start train #2. When it is clear, press **w** and 3 to get train #3 moving and when it is clear, press **x**, **y** and **z** and 4 to get the last train moving.

Now before train #1 get to switch **b**, be sure to set it as shown in Figure 3 where trains #1, #2 and #3 have already passed through the **b** turnout and train #4 is about to do so.

Now reset the following switches: **c**, **d**, **e**, **f**, **g**, **l**, **n** and **m** as shown in Figure 4. Also reset switch **b** and all four trains can now run continuously with no further help from the operator (unless two collide in the crossing).

In Figure 5, train #4 is already in the barn. This was achieved by changing switches **i**, **j**, **h** and **c**.

In Figure 6 train #3 is on its way back to the barn and only switch **h** must be reset once it has passed through it. When it is safely home, switches **i**, **j**, **h** and **c** must be reset to permit unobstructed passage by train #1. What is left is to repeat the above, first for train #2 and finally for train #1. The final result, with all four trains home on their assigned tracks is shown in Figure 7.

While building pikes and running trains in this manner may not duplicate the satisfaction that can be derived from the real thing, it can actually be quite a bit of fun, not to mention that it can serve a practical purpose by making it possible to pre-test a new track design.

Figure 8-34. *Page layout for the first page*

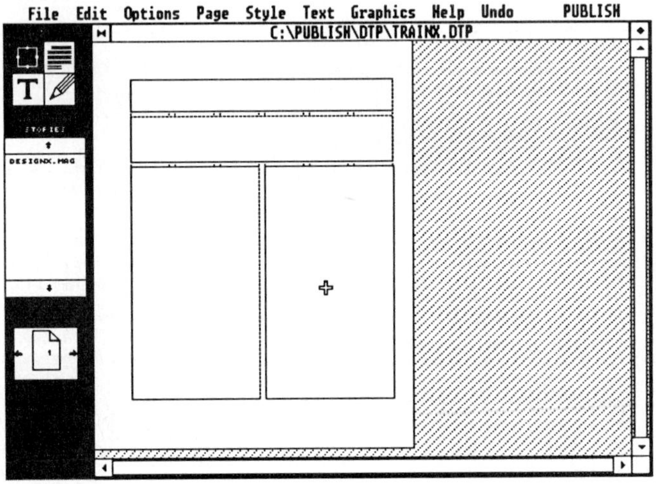

4. Next design the basic layout for the second page, as in Figure 8-35.
5. Click on the left arrow in the <PAGE> icon to return to the first page. Click on <Actual size> in the Page menu.
6. Select the <TEXT> mode in the toolbox and click inside the top frame. Type **Design Your Own Train.**
7. Select the <PARAGRAPH> mode in the toolbox and click anywhere on the line you have just typed. In the Library window click on HEADLINE to change the typed line into a headline, centered in its frame.
8. Click on the <FRAME> mode in the toolbox and select the frame with the headline.
9. Click on <Frame border> in the Options menu and click on the double line and on <OK>.
10. Click on <Frame tint> in the Options menu and click on the second gray and on <OK>. Figure 8-36 is the result.

Figure 8-35. *Page layout for the second page*

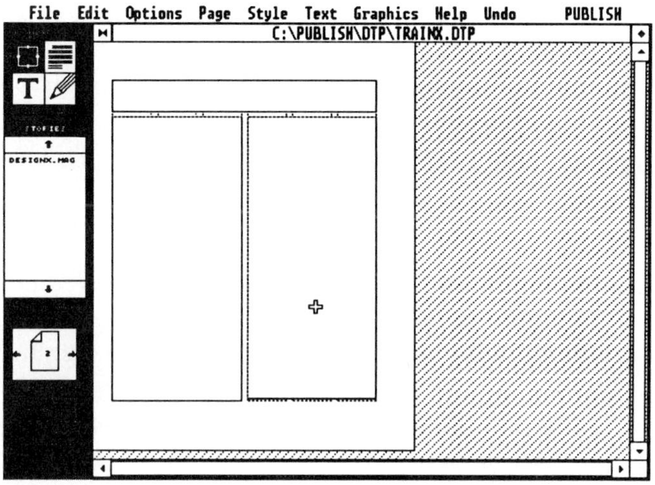

Figure 8-36. *Frame border and tint used with the headline*

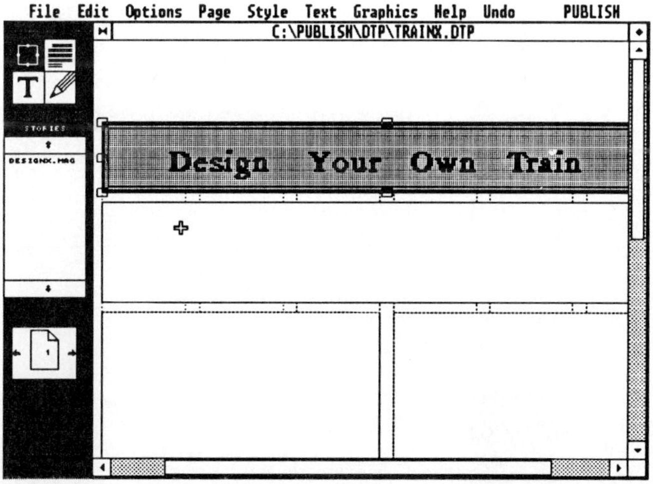

8

11. Click on <3/4 size> in the Page menu. For the moment ignore the frame under the headline and select the left column frame. Click on DESIGNX.MAG in the Library window to pour text into the left column, as shown in Figure 8-37.
12. Return to the first page. Select <PARAGRAPH> mode in the toolbox and click anywhere on the first line of text in the left column.
13. In the Text menu click on <Paragraph style> and in the resultant dialog box click on <Font & size> and select <Dutch> (<Serif>) and <20> and click on <OK>.
14. Now click on <Justification> and click on <Centered> and then on <OK> twice. In the Library window SUBTITLE is now highlighted. The line has changed to its new parameters. Because the paragraph label for the bulleted lines is <bullet>, which is a style supplied automatically by Publish It!, all those lines are already bulleted, as shown in Figure 8-38.

Figure 8-37. *Text imported into the first column*

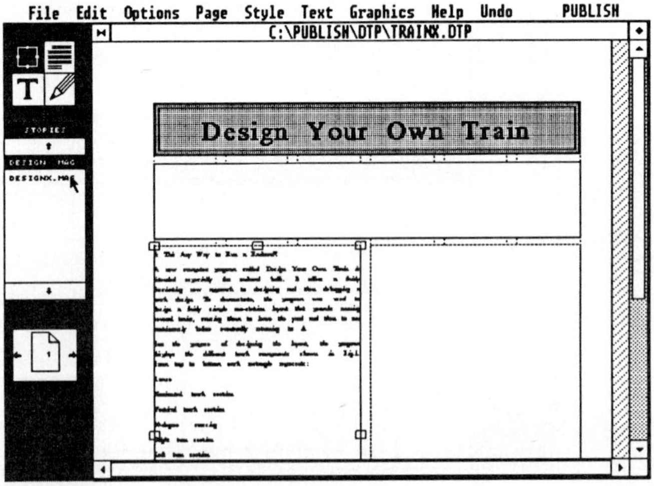

Figure 8-38. *Bulleted items in the first column*

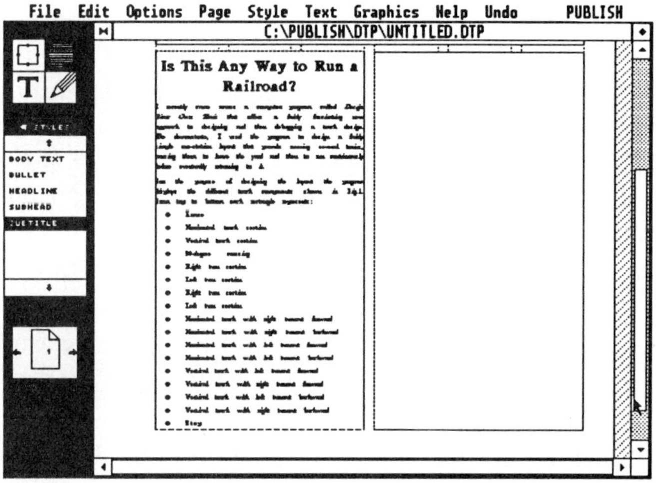

15. Select <FRAME> mode in the toolbox and select the frame for the right column. Click on DESIGNX.MAG in the Library window and watch the text pour into the right column.
16. Repeat the previous step for both columns in the second page. The right column is going to remain empty for the moment.
17. For reasons that will soon become apparent, click on the right arrow in the <PAGE> icon and click on <YES> to create a temporary third page.
18. Click on <Import picture> in the File menu and on <PC Paintbrush (.PCX)> in the dialog box. (The graphics for the three figures inside the text columns were created in .PCX format using the screen-capture program PizazzPlus. They were then inverted, using PictureEze inside Windows version 3.0 and the resulting files are DESIGN1.PCX, DESIGN2.PCX, and DESIGN3.PCX located on the C:\WINDOWS directory.) In the Item Selector box change the Directory line to C:\WINDOWS*.PCX, highlight DESIGN1.PCX

and click on <OK>, as shown in Figure 8-39. DESIGN1.PCX appears in the Library window.

19. In the 3/4-page size create a large frame. Select it and click on DESIGN1.PCX in the Library window. The result is shown in Figure 8-40. Now the reason for creating a temporary third page becomes apparent. All that is needed is the group of symbols along the far right edge of the frame. Performing the various <Crop picture> actions necessary to get the desired result would have been messy on the first page on top of all that text.
20. Click on <Scale picture> in the Graphics menu and on <Preserve> and <OK> in the dialog box. Then click on <Crop picture> in the Graphics menu and crop away everything except the symbols. (This may take several <Crop picture> tries.) Figure 8-41 shows the cropped result.
21. Select the frame. Click on <Cut> in the Edit menu.
22. Use the <Go to page> option to go to the first page. Click on <Paste> in the Edit menu. The graphic frame appears much too large on the page, as shown in Figure 8-42.

Figure 8-39. *DESIGN1.PCX is selected from the WINDOWS directory*

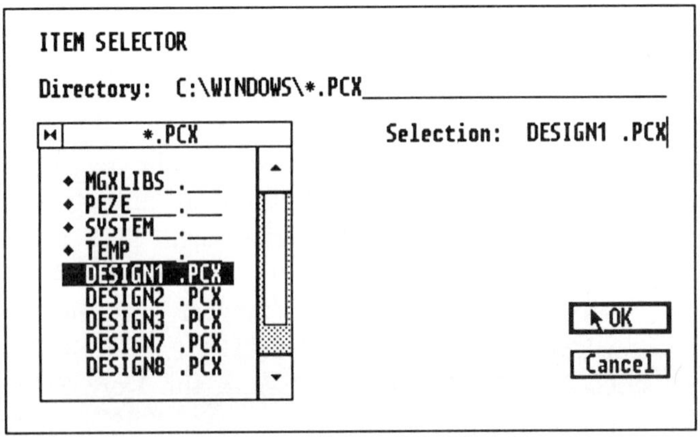

Figure 8-40. The DESIGN1 graphic ready for cropping

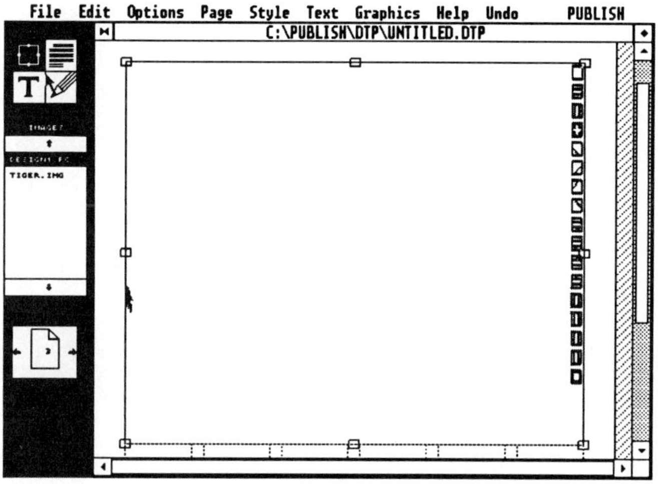

Figure 8-41. DESIGN1 cropped and ready for use

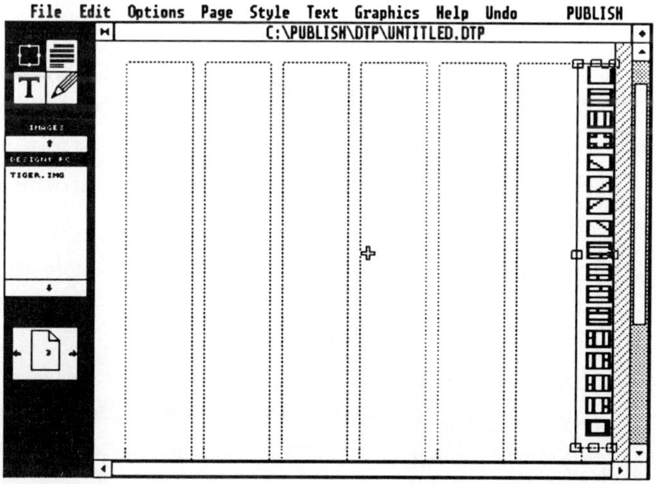

8

Figure 8-42. *DESIGN1 moved to the first page*

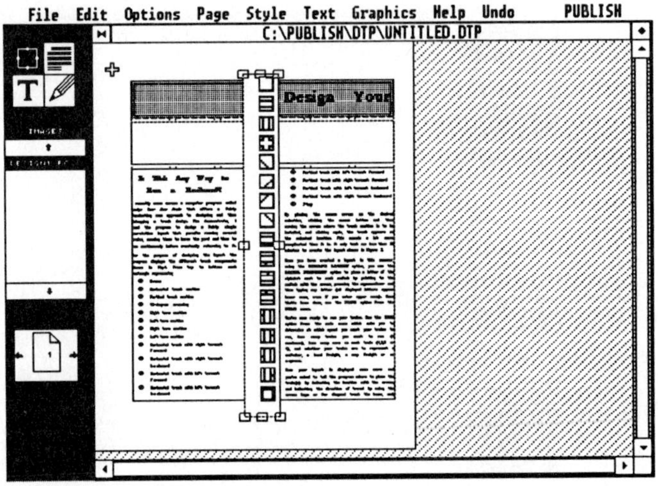

23. Reduce the frame to about a quarter of its size. Go to 3/4 page and manipulate the frame until the graphic looks the way it does in Figure 8-32. Draw a small frame where the caption "Fig.1" is to appear, and in the <TEXT> mode, type it. Then move and adjust that small frame to place the copy just where you want it.
24. Draw a rectangular frame in the lower portion of the right column, select it, and click on <Import picture> and <OK>.
25. In the Item Selector box, click on DESIGN2.PCX and on <OK>. Figure 8-43 shows your entire first page in the <Size to fit> format as it looks right now.
26. Now go to the second page, create a frame somewhere in the lower middle, select it, and import DESIGN3.PCX using the routine just described.
27. Inside the frames holding DESIGN2.PCX and DESIGN3.PCX on the two pages, use the routine described in step 23 to place the captions "Fig.2" and "Fig.3" into a convenient place inside the two frames.

Figure 8-43. *The first page with most components in place*

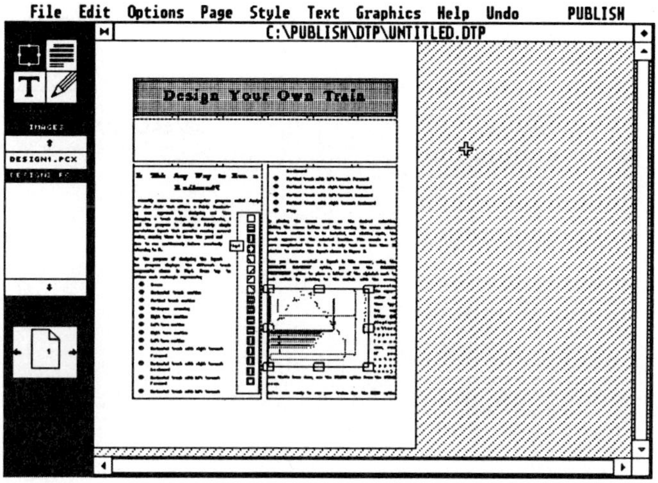

28. Again on both pages, select the frames holding figure 2 and figure 3 and, using <Frame border>, place a narrow border around each.
29. You will now want to do a bit of manipulating of those two frames. changing their sizes and positions enough to have a visually pleasing result and to cause the end of the text on the second page to fill the right column to the bottom.
30. What is left now is to import and manipulate tne graphic of the locomotive and its car. It is file SA0221.PCC (.PCX format) from the Publisher's PicturePak collection, located on a floppy disk in drive A. Click on <Import picture> and on <OK> and reconfigure the Directory line in the Item Selector box to read A:*.PCC. Press (ENTER). Highlight <SA0221.PCC> and click on <OK> as shown in Figure 8-44. The result, Figure 8-45, is not what you want at all.
31. Select the frame and click on <Cut> in the Edit menu. Go to the temporary third page and click on <Paste> in the Edit menu. The graphic reappears.

8

Figure 8-44. *Clip-art file SA0221.PCC is selected from the A drive*

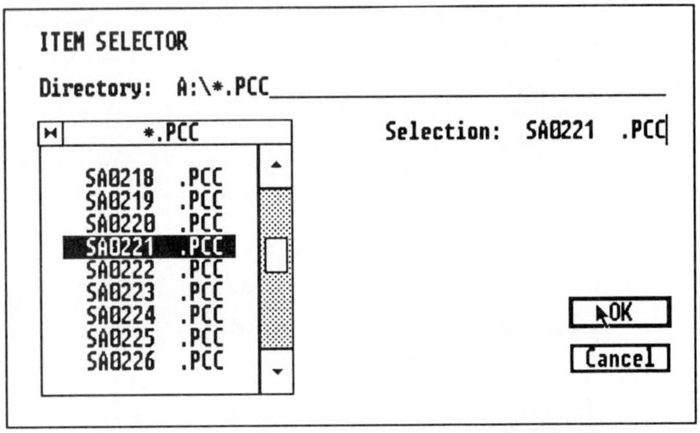

Figure 8-45. *The imported clip-art image is distorted*

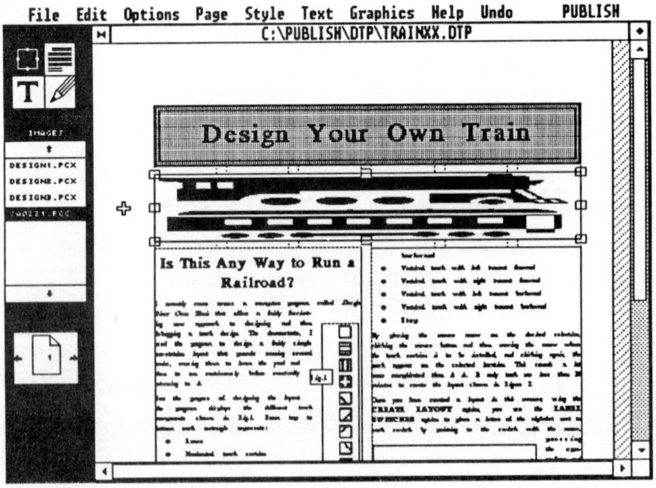

32. Make the frame much fatter so that the proportions of the images look more natural. Click on <Copy> and on <Paste> in the Edit menu and place the two identical frames below one another, as shown in Figure 8-46.
33. Use <Crop picture> to crop the car out of the top picture, leaving only the locomotive, and crop the locomotive out of the bottom picture, leaving only the car.
34. Use <Scale picture> and <Preserve> to return the images to their correct proportions.
35. Reduce the two frames and place them next to one another as in Figure 8-47 and click on <Select all> in the Edit menu.
36. Click on <Cut> in the Edit menu. Go to the first page and click on <Paste>. Set both frames to <Clear> (in the <Frame tint> dialog box) and manipulate them until they look right on the page. Create another frame over that area, give it a frame border, and click on <Send to back> in the Page menu.

Figure 8-46. *The graphic moved to the temporary page and copied*

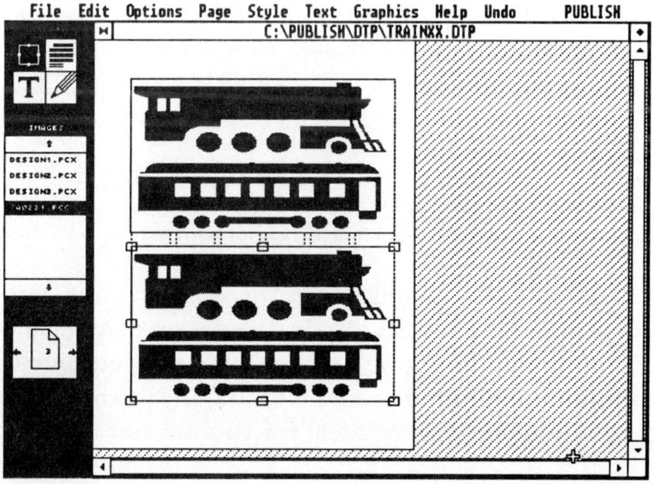

Figure 8-47. *The graphic cropped and resized*

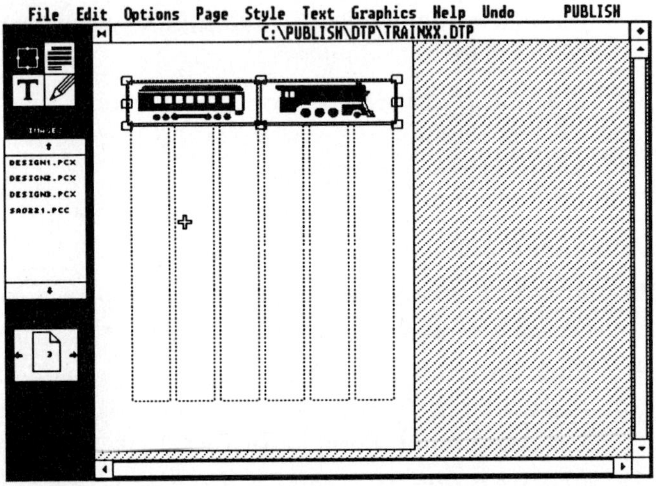

37. While holding down the SHIFT key, click on the three frames to select all three. Click on <Copy> in the Edit menu.
38. Go to the second page, click on <Paste>, and move the graphic into its place at the top. Click on <Save as> in the File menu and give your effort a name. The result should look more or less like Figures 8-32 and 8-33.

Stationery Samples

In this section you will create three letterheads: one with text only and the other two with graphics. Again, the design of letterheads is a very personal thing, and it should not be assumed that the ones included here represent ideal designs. Actually, there is no such thing as an ideal in design. Any layout that appeals to you may be ideal for you but not necessarily for anyone else.

Letterhead Number 1

The letterhead shown in Figure 8-48 uses a person's name and the name of the company at the top of the page and the address and phone number across the bottom. Follow these steps to produce this letterhead:

1. You can use a word processor to type the name, address, and phone number shown in Figure 8-49. Use separate labels for each item to simplify the task of assigning different font styles and sizes to each.
2. Use the <Import text> option from the File menu to import the text, saved as LETHEAD1.DOC in WordStar format.
3. Put the display in the <Size to fit> format to see the complete page. Place two skinny frames across the top and three small ones across the bottom. Click on the filename in the Library window, as shown in Figure 8-50, to import the text.
4. Using the <Actual size> option from the Page menu, click on the <PARAGRAPH> icon to access the <Font/size> option in the Style menu. For this example, <Drury Lane> and <30> were selected as the font style and size by clicking on them and <OK>.
5. Selecting the name by placing the pointer on it and clicking allows you to access the <Paragraph style> option in the Text menu. Center the name on the page by clicking on <Justification>, <Centered>, and <OK>.
6. Repeat steps 4 and 5 for the name of the company, except you can choose a different font style and size. For this example, <Madison> was selected as the font style.
7. The three items in the bottom frame were given <Dutch> (<Serif>) and <10> as the font style and size for this example. After making sure that they are placed correctly, save the entire page as LETHEAD1.DTP and then print it.

This printout, assuming that a quality printer was used, becomes the camera-ready mechanical that any commercial print house can use to produce letterheads in quantity.

Figure 8-48. *A simple letterhead design*

ELIZABETH BROWNING

Apex Decorating Company, Inc.

6675 Park Avenue Atlanta, GA 30331 (404) 555-5678

Figure 8-49. *Each item on the letterhead is given an individual label*

<name>Elizabeth Browning
<company>Apex Decorating Company, Inc.
<address>6675 Park Avenue
<city>Atlanta, GA 30331
<phone>(404)555-5678

Letterhead Number 2

This letterhead uses the same copy as the preceding one, but the placement and font styles and sizes were changed and a logo was added, as shown in Figure 8-51. After importing the same text file used for the first letterhead, a number of frames were placed onto the page in strategic locations. The text

Figure 8-50. *The basic design used for first letterhead*

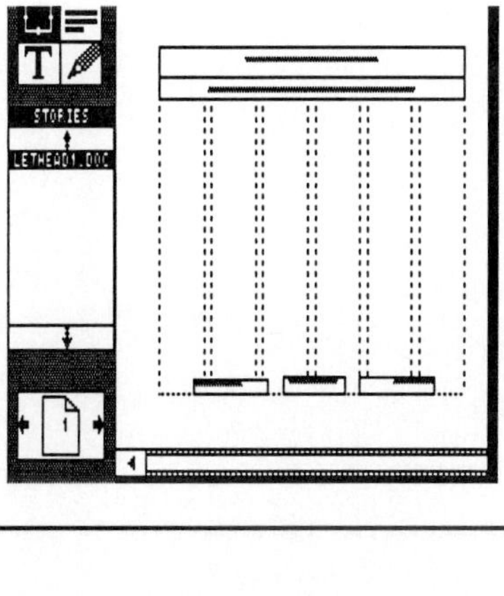

Figure 8-51. *A second letterhead design with logo*

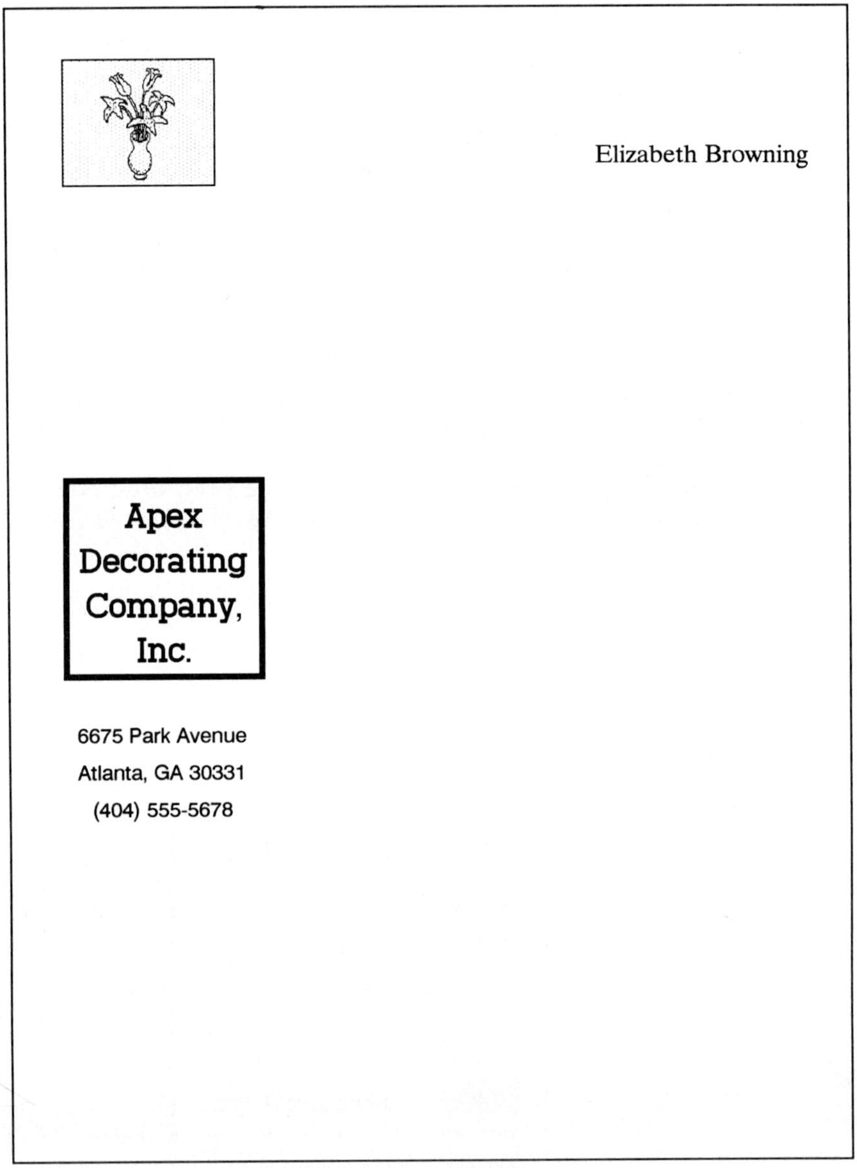

was manipulated with the page in the Actual Size format. To add the graphic, follow these steps:

1. Place a frame of any size anywhere on the page.
2. Use the <Import picture> option from the File menu. In the dialog box select <GEM Paint (.IMG)>, and in the Item Selector box select PLANTS.IMG to pour the entire clip-art page into the frame.
3. Increase the size of the frame to simplify the task of cropping one item out of the group. Click on the <Crop picture> option in the Graphics menu, and crop out the vase with flowers so it fills the entire frame.
4. Reduce the size of the frame to a square approximately the size of one frame guide. The resized frame was moved to the upper-left corner of the page.
5. Create a new frame the same size as the one containing the picture, momentarily obscuring it.
6. Select the <Frame border> option from the Options menu and click on <All around>. Select <Frame tint> and a light tint, and then click on <Clear> and <OK> to produce a narrow frame and a light tint over the entire picture, as shown in the upper-left frame in Figure 8-52.

Letterhead Number 3

The third letterhead uses copy saved as LETHEAD3.DOC in WordStar format. Figure 8-53 shows the text and graphics used in the layout. At first you might be tempted to try using the <GRAPHICS> mode to draw the line by clicking on the <GRAPHICS> icon in the toolbox. That will turn out to be exceedingly difficult to manipulate. Instead, draw a line in the text file, as shown in Figure 8-54. Then import it along with the text and manipulate it in the same way. Once the text is imported, create a number of frames and place them into their respective places on the screen. You can also generate this line using a frame border set to <Below> only.

Import the SYMBOLS.IMG clip-art page, and crop the computer symbol from it. Using the <Scale picture> option from the Graphics menu, select

Figure 8-52. *The page design for the second letterhead*

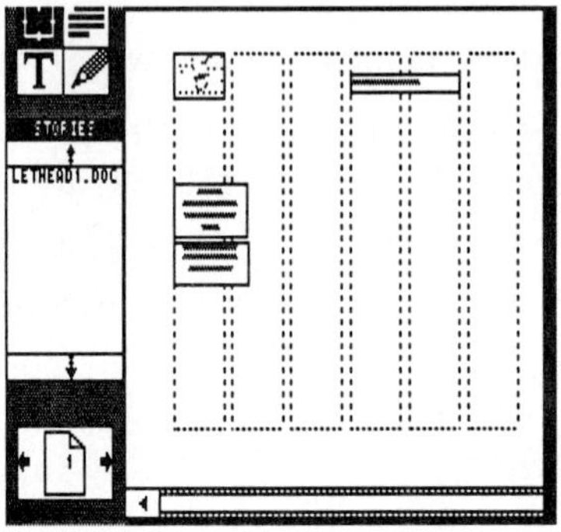

<Preserve> to retain the original proportion. Center the picture under the text frames, as shown in Figure 8-55.

As these three examples demonstrate, it is simple to produce just about any kind of letterhead in a minimum of time. Problems can arise when special graphics or logos are required, making it necessary to import material from external sources. That subject is discussed in Chapter 9, "Using External Files."

An Odd-Size Multipage Document

In this exercise you will produce documentation for a software package consisting of a group of games such as roulette, dice, blackjack, and others. It is shipped on a 5 1/4-inch disk, and in order to fit the documentation into the disk mailers, the documents are 5 x 5 inches and the cover is 5 1/4 x 5 1/4 inches. Also, you will design the documentation in such a way that it can be printed on both sides of each page, like a regular booklet. A cover is included to be used in the conventional manner or, if printed on large enough stock, it can be made into a folder to hold the pages.

Figure 8-53. A third letterhead design

DESKTOP PUBLISHING USER GROUP, INC.

1168 Main Street
Dallas, TX 75001

(214) 555 3456
Telex 6503 765432

Figure 8-54. *The text file and labels used for the third letterhead*

<company>DESKTOP PUBLISHING USER GROUP, INC.
<line>____

<address>1168 Main Street
<addrsss>Dallas, TX 75001
<phone>(214) 555 3456
<phone>Telex 6503 765432

The Text File

Use a word processor to prepare the file containing the text for the document. Add labels to control the font styles and sizes being used.

<fun>FUN CITY
<adult>A COLLECTION OF GAME PROGRAMS FOR ADULTS
<text> (this label is used for all body copy)
<block> (this label is used for all program titles)

Figure 8-55. *The page design for the third letterhead*

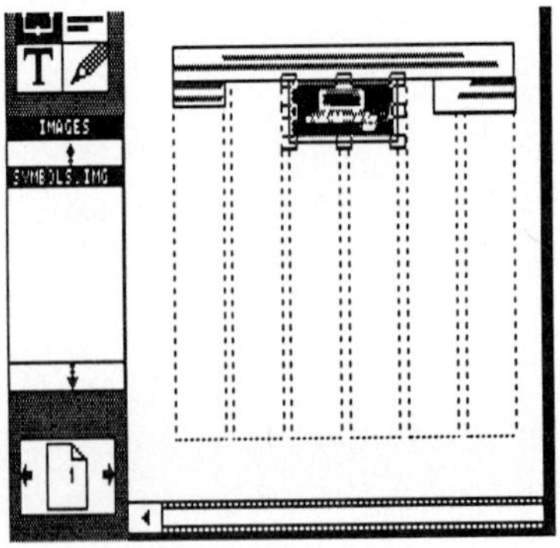

With these labels you can consistently use four different font styles, sizes, and paragraph formatting styles throughout the document.

The Graphics Files

Before starting to work on the document itself, you should probably create a number of graphics files containing the screen displays that represent what appears on the screen when the individual programs are activated. One is of the main menu, one of the roulette table, one of the table showing the odds available in roulette, and one showing the display that appears when the dice game is played. You create each using the HiJaak screen-capture facility that produces .PIX files. You then convert the two text-screen images, the menu, and the table with the odds to .TXT files using the HiJaak conversion facility. The files are then converted to GEM Paint .IMG files. The other two are graphics screens, and you convert them directly from .PIX files to .IMG files.

Page Formatting

The steps used to control the formatting of all pages are as follows:

1. In the File menu click on <New>, and in the resulting dialog box select <No> in response to the style sheet prompt. In the Page Format dialog box, click on <Left & right> and <OK>, as shown in Figure 8-56.
2. In the Page menu click on <Go to page>, and in the dialog box click on <Master pages> and <OK>.
3. In the Page menu click on <Two pages>. When the two pages are displayed, create the two identical frames, 5 1/4 inches square, shown in Figure 8-57.

   If you are working with Publish It! version 2.0, you can also do this by clicking on <Custom size> in the Page Format dialog box and changing the dimensions of the pages in the <Height> and <Width> boxes, as shown in Figure 8-58. Click on <OK> and Publish It! now

Figure 8-56. *The Page Format dialog box*

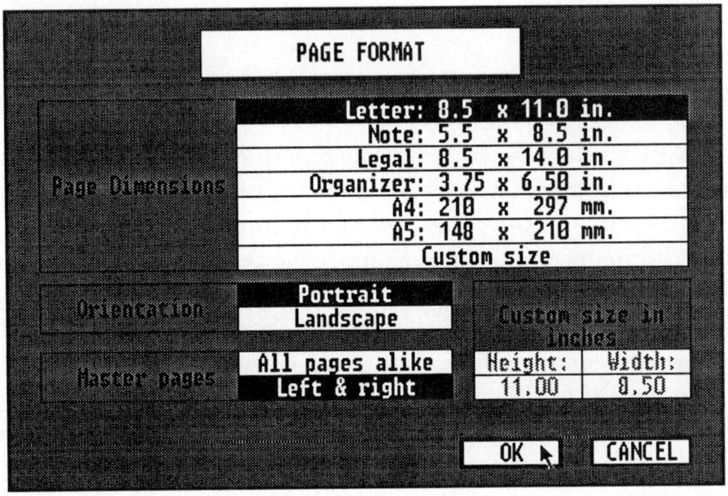

Figure 8-57. *The master pages for the new document*

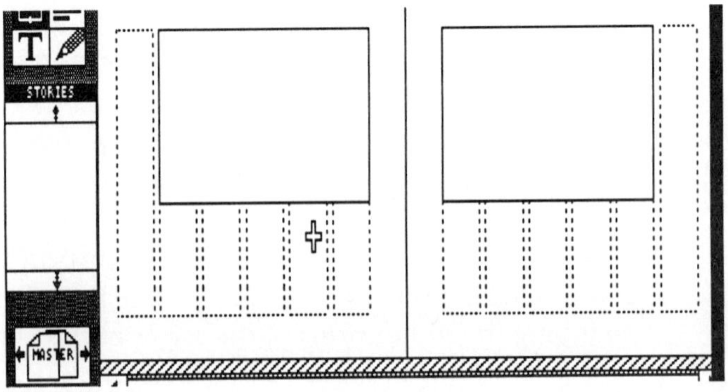

Figure 8-58. *Changing the page dimensions in the Page Format dialog box*

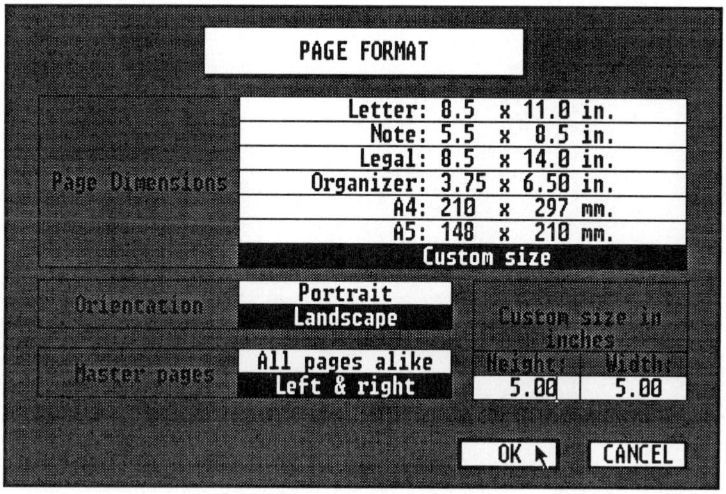

displays two pages in the desired dimensions, as shown in Figure 8-59.

4. Click on the first frame to select it. In the Options menu click on <Frame border>, and in the dialog box click on <All around> and <OK>. Repeat this for the other frame. This will cause the outer border to be displayed automatically on each page.
5. In the Page menu click on <Go to page>, type **1**, and click on <OK>.

Using the Text and Graphics Files

The following steps position the text and graphics in the formatted pages:

1. In the Page menu click on <Actual size>. In the File menu click on <Import text>, and in the resulting dialog box click on <WordStar>, if that is the format of the text file. In the Item Selector box, click

Figure 8-59. *Two pages with the new dimensions*

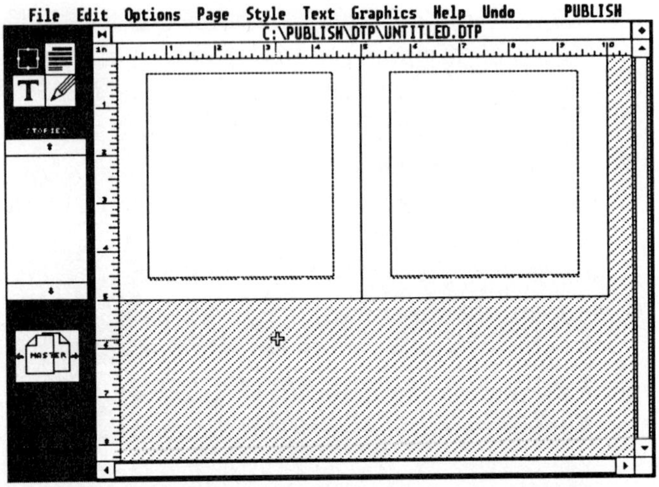

on <FUN.DOC>, assuming that is the name of the text file to be imported.

2. Inside the displayed border at the top center, create a small frame, and then click on FUN.DOC in the Library window. The first portion of the text is poured into the frame.
3. Click on the <PARAGRAPH> icon, place the pointer anywhere on "FUN CITY," and click to select it.
4. In the Text menu click on <Paragraph style>. In the resulting dialog box, click on <Font/size>. Select <Madison> and <18>, and then click on <OK>. The preceding dialog box reappears. Click on <Justification> and then on <Centered> and <OK>. When the document screen reappears, "FUN CITY" is centered in the frame.
5. Place the pointer anywhere on "A COLLECTION OF GAME PROGRAMS FOR ADULTS" and click to select it.

6. In the Text menu click on <Paragraph style>. In the resulting dialog box, click on <Font/size>, select <Dutch> (<Serif>) and <14>, and click on <OK>. The preceding dialog box reappears. Click on <Justification> and then on <Centered> and <OK>. When the document screen reappears, the paragraph is centered in the frame. If one of the words is hyphenated, adjust the size of the frame until the hyphenation disappears.
7. Now add a wide frame below the one just made and click on FUN.DOC in the Library window. Several lines of additional text are poured into the new frame. In the example used here, the frame is made smaller by moving the bottom-center handle upward until the last line remaining in the frame is "following display:".
8. In the File menu click on <Import picture>. In the dialog box click on <GEM Paint (.IMG)>, and in the Item Selector box, click on <FUN1.IMG> and <OK>.
9. Draw a frame to fill most of the remaining border and click on FUN1.IMG in the Library window. The graphic image representing the main menu is poured into the frame. The <Crop picture> option in the Graphics menu can be used to eliminate unwanted empty space, and the frame can be resized and repositioned to fill the outer border nicely.
10. Create a small frame and place it at the lower-left corner inside the outer border. Click on the <TEXT> icon, place the I-beam pointer inside the small frame, and click to activate the text cursor. In the <Font/size> option from the Style menu select <7> and type **1**, and then reposition the digit where it looks right.

This finishes the first page of the document, shown in Figure 8-60. The remaining five pages, shown in Figures 8-61 through 8-65, are included only as suggestions regarding layout and design. They were produced using the same method described earlier but you probably understand the method sufficiently without having to actually go through the hands-on exercise of creating these pages yourself.

Figure 8-60. *Page 1 of the document*

FUN CITY

A COLLECTION OF GAME PROGRAMS FOR ADULTS

There are nine separate programs on this disk, some of which will work only if the computer system being used is equipped with some type of graphics adapter.

To start any of the programs, type MENU and press **ENTER** which produces the following display:

```
                         FUN CITY
                         --------
              A COLLECTION OF GAMES FOR ADULTS
              --------------------------------
COM FILE NAME | DESCRIPTION
------------------------------------------------------------
              |
     Z        | A colorful block of letters
     A        | An Electronic Trivia Game
     B        | Roulette
     C        | A Challenging Word Game
     D        | Blackjack (21)
     E        | Another Challenging Word Game
     F        | A Dice Game (Craps)
     G        | A Roulette Analysis Program
     H        | Display all Trivia questions and answers
     I        | Patterns in color
              |
------------------------------------------------------------
     X        | Program information and explanations
------------------------------------------------------------
ress SPACE bar.  Then, with the DOS prompt A> type the letter and press ENTER
------------------------------------------------------------
```

1

Cover

Finally, the cover is designed to use 8 1/2 x 14-inch paper that can be used as an actual cover or folded to produce a folder that can hold the individual pages in the event that no actual binding is anticipated.

1. Click on <New> in the File menu. In the resulting dialog box, which asks whether you want to load a style sheet, click on <Yes>. In the

Figure 8-61. *Page 2 of the document*

A COLORFUL BLOCK OF LETTERS

This game simply consists of a large number of letters in different colorsthatgra-duallyforma solid block in random consecutive order. This game

serves no practical purpose unless you feel like placing a bet as to thelength of time it takes for all spaces in the block to be filled.

The game has no automatic end. It will go on until Ctrl C is pressed

AN ELECTRONIC TRIVIA GAME

This game consists of a large number of trivia questions which are displayed in random consecutive order. You may type the answers in upper, lower or mixed upper and lower case letters. The game is designed to be played by up to six players, and it keeps score of the right and wrong answers for each player.

The game has no automatic end. It will go on indefinitely, eventually repeating some of the questions. To quit the game, type Q as a CAPITAL letter.

ROULETTE

ROULETTE TABLE

0	RED 3	BLACK 6	RED 9	BLACK 12	RED 15	BLACK 18	RED 21	BLACK 24	RED 27	BLACK 30	RED 33	BLACK 36
	BLACK 2	RED 5	BLACK 8	RED 11	BLACK 14	RED 17	BLACK 20	RED 23	BLACK 26	RED 29	BLACK 32	RED 35
0 0	RED 1	BLACK 4	RED 7	BLACK 10	RED 13	BLACK 16	RED 19	BLACK 22	RED 25	BLACK 28	RED 31	BLACK 34

2

8

Item Selector box, click on <LANDSCAP.STY> and <OK> as shown in Figure 8-66.

2. The Page Format dialog box appears. Click on <Legal: 8.5 x 14.0 in.> and <OK>, as shown in Figure 8-67.

   Alternatively, if you are working with Publish It! version 2.0, you can click on <Landscape> and <Custom size> in the Page Format dialog box and change the dimensions of the pages in the <Height>

Figure 8-62. Page 3 of the document

This is a slightly modified roulette game. It displays the roulette table and the player has the option of playing one number, two numbers, three numbers, four numbers, one of threeentire rows of numbers, red or black, or odd or even. (This game requires a graphics adapter.)

The odds are:

```
          You have the following choices:

1            Play one number                (Odds: 35:1)
2            Play two numbers               (Odds: 17:1)
3            Play three numbers             (Odds: 11:1)
4            Play four numbers              (Odds:  7:1)
5            One row, 12 numbers            (Odds:  2:1)
6            Play red/black or odd/even     (Odds:  1:1)

0            Quit the game

Which?                  5
```

The program displays your winnings or losses after each round, based on the amount of your wager.

3

and <Width> boxes as shown in Figure 8-68. Click on <OK> and Publish It! now displays two pages in the desired dimensions, as shown in Figure 8-69.

3. When the horizontal page is displayed, click on <Show rulers> to simplify the task of placing frames into the appropriate places. Add two frames in the approximate position shown in Figure 8-70. Select the frame on the right.

Figure 8-63. *Page 4 of the document*

A CHALLENGING WORD GAME

This game displays three letters at random, asking that you type as many words of six letters or less that you can think of, with each word including all the three displayed letters. This program checks whether or not your words contain all three letters and whether any word is longer than the three-letter maximum.

The program keeps a running score. There is no automatic end to the program. To quit the game, follow the displayed directions.

BLACKJACK (21)

The purpose of the game is to collect cards in order to get as close to 21 as possible, without going over. All number cards are worth their face value and all face cards are worth 10 while aces may be counted as either 1 or 11.

Coming up with 21 in two cards (ace + face card or + 10) is called Blackjack and it pays one and a half times the player's wager. At all other times if the player wins, the payoff is even money, if the player loses, the wager is lost. If player and dealer have the same total, it's referred to as PUSH and no money changes hands.

The player can take as few or as many cards as he or she thinks is advisable. The dealer, on the other hand, must draw an additional card when the total is 16 or less, and he or she must stand fast on 17 or more.

4

4. Click on <Import text> in the File menu. In the resulting Item Selector box, click on <FUN.DOC>, which inserts the first few lines of the document into that frame.
5. Click on the <PARAGRAPH> icon, place the pointer on "FUN CITY," and click to select it.
6. In the Text menu click on <Paragraph style>. In the successive dialog boxes, click on <Font/size>, <Madison>, <18>, and then on <OK>.

Figure 8-64. *Page 5 of the document*

ANOTHER CHALLENGING WORD GAME

This game consists of 26 key words and it is the job of the player to find as many words as possible that can be made up of any of the letters that make up the key word.

The player plays against the computer and the program keeps a running score. Any player with a fairly good vocabulary should easily be able to beat the computer in this game.

A DICE GAME (CRAPS)

This is a typical dice game played with two dice. (This game requires a graphics adapter.) If the first throw results in a 2, 3 or 12, the player loses the wager. If the first throw results in a 7 or 11, the player wins the amount of the wager.

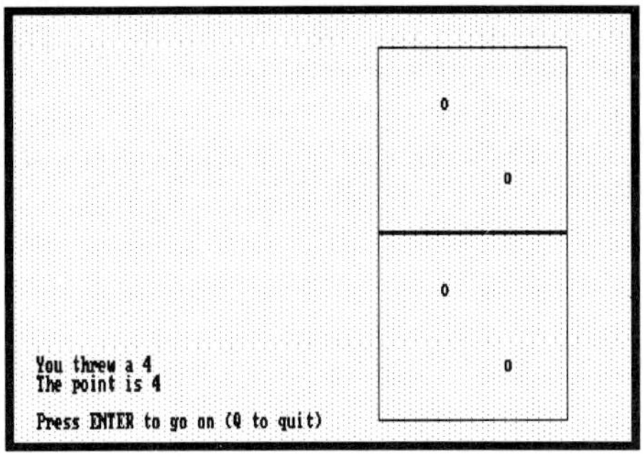

5

7. Click on <Justification>, <Centered>, and <OK> twice. "FUN CITY" now appears centered in the new font style and size.
8. Place the pointer onto "A COLLECTION OF GAME PROGRAMS FOR ADULTS," and click to select it.
9. In the Text menu click on <Paragraph style>. In the successive dialog boxes, click on <Font/Size>, <Rockface>, <18>, and then on <OK>.
10. Next click on <Justification>, <Centered>, and <OK> twice. The selected paragraph now appears centered in the new font style and size.

Figure 8-65. The last page of the document

If the first throw produces a 4, 5, 6, 8, 9 or 10, then that number becomes the "point" and the player must try to match it to win before throwing a 7 which would result in the loss of the wager.

A ROULETTE ANALYSIS PROGRAM

This program determines the number of successive wins that are needed when playing **ONE, TWO, THREE, FOUR NUMBERS, a ROW OF NUMBERS** or **RED/BLACK** or **ODD/EVEN** in order to reach a given amount with a specified initial wager, assuming that the winnings are left on the table for the next round.

The program asks that you key in the amount of the wager and the total winnings that you're looking for and it will then display the number of successful winning rounds are needed to achieve the desired result.

DISPLAY ALL TRIVIA QUESTIONS

This program simply displays all Trivia questions along with the answers that the program expects.

PATTERNS IN COLOR

This program simply scrolls some designs across the screen, displaying all available colors. It is meaningless unless the system is equipped with a color monitor. The program has no end. Press **Ctrl Scroll Lock** to quit.

6

11. Click on the <TEXT> icon in the toolbox, place the I-beam pointer anywhere inside the small frame on the left, and click to activate the text cursor.
12. In the STYLE menu click on <Font/size>, select <7> as the point size, and click on <OK>. Type the name and address of the company on three lines. The result is shown in Figure 8-71.

That completes the odd-sized booklet. In the next section you will create a four-page newsletter.

Figure 8-66. *Selecting the LANDSCAP.STY style sheet*

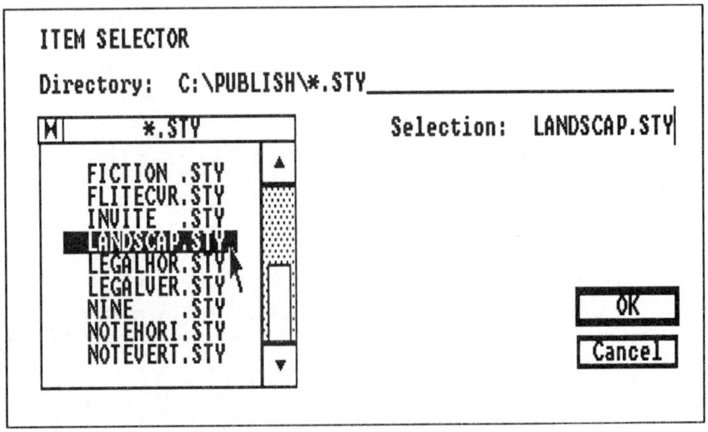

Figure 8-67. *Page Format dialog box with <Landscape> and <Legal: 8.5 x 14.0 in.> selected*

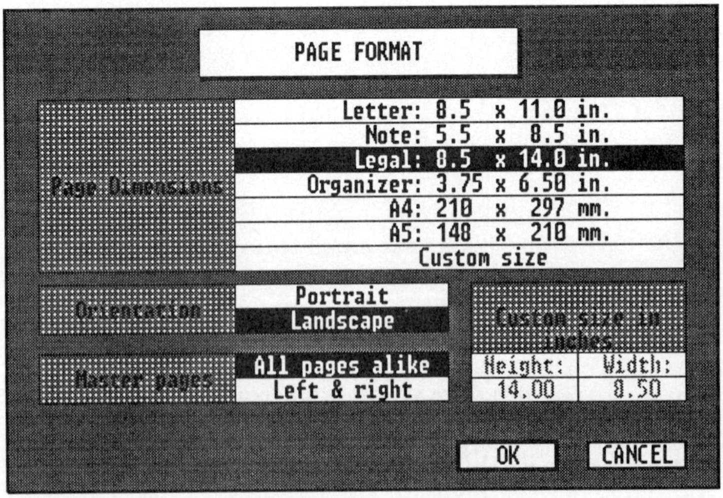

Figure 8-68. *Changing the dimensions in the Page Format dialog box*

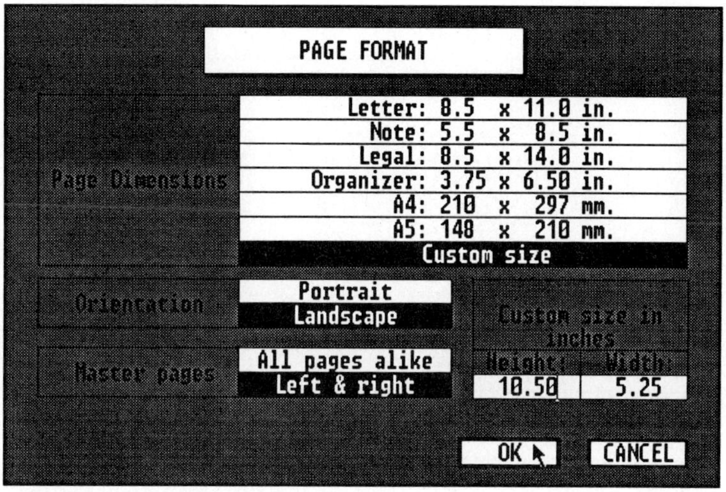

Figure 8-69. *Two pages showing the new dimensions*

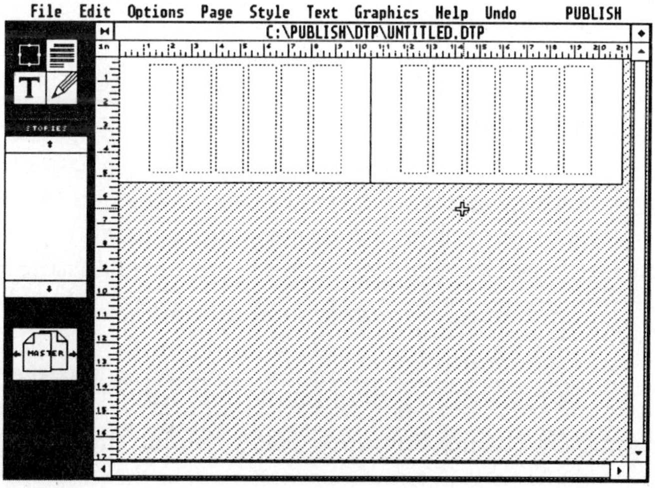

Figure 8-70. *Two frames placed on the horizontal page*

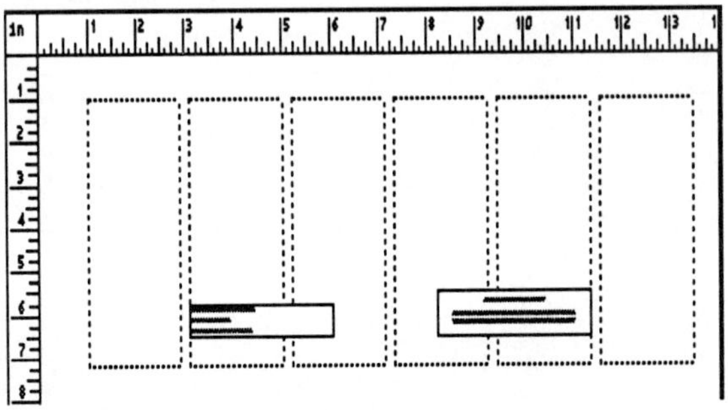

A Four-Page Newsletter

The newsletter, titled "Programmer's Forum," is shown in Figures 8-72, 8-73, 8-74, and 8-75. The text is written in WordPerfect version 5.0 and can be used as is by Publish It! versions 1.2 and 2.0. If you are working with Publish It! version 1.1 the text must be converted to WordPerfect 4.2 using the CTRL-F5 Text Out option, or if you prefer, it can be converted to WordStar version 3.3 using WordPerfect's CONVERT.EXE program.

The newsletter uses a total of four different paragraph styles: one for the title of the newsletter, one for the article title, and two styles for the article itself, one for the primary body copy and another for the smaller copy dealing with the different variables in the program that is the subject of the article. The "Programmer's Forum" header on pages 2, 3, and 4 is typed in using the <TEXT> mode.

The date and the volume information is typed in ASCII format and converted to a graphics file with an .IMG extension, using the HiJaak program. The same program is used to obtain the illustrations of the program source code and of the pull-down menus that become available when the program is run.

Figure 8-71. *The cover for the document*

FUN CITY

A COLLECTION OF GAME PROGRAMS FOR ADULTS

ABC Software Corporation

P.O. Box 6713

Santa Fe, NM 87504-6713

Figure 8-72. *Page 1 of the newsletter*

PROGRAMMER'S FORUM

ADDING MOUSE OPERATION TO LOTUS 1-2-3

May 15, 1990 — Volume 17 No. 5

Lotus 1-2-3, like most other popular applications programs, wase not designed with the idea of using a mouse. On the other hand, there are a number of reasons why using a mouse could produce some advantages in terms of operating convenience. In order to make that possible, what is needed is a mouse that includes software that can be used to write programs that then control the results produced by mouse manipulation.

The C7 Mouse from Logitech is one of several that fill that bill. The standard software that includes the MOUSE.COM program that is needed for its operation, also includes two programs that can be used to produce customized pulldown menus. These programs are MENU.COM and NEWMENU.EXE. NEWMENU.EXE. is simply a compiler that compiles source code that can be written with any text editor or word processor. (The source code shown in Figs.1, 2 and 3 was produced using the Turbo Pascal text editor.) MENU.COM is the program that is used to place a compiled mouse program into RAM for actual use. The computer language used in writing the source code is called LOGIMENU and it is unique with this system.

Figs.1, 2 and 3 represent the source code for a program

```
MidB:    MENU "Special keys used by Lotus 1-2-3",1,24,11
         OPTION "Help screens........",f1
         OPTION "Edit................",f2
         OPTION "Name................",f3
         OPTION "ABS.................",f4
         OPTION "Goto................",f5
         OPTION "Window..............",f6
         OPTION "Query...............",f7
         OPTION "Table...............",f8
         OPTION "Calc................",f9
         OPTION "Graph...............",f0
         OPTION "Backtab.............",st
         OPTION "Compose.............",af1
         OPTION "BigLeft.............",c4
         OPTION "BigRight............",c6
         OPTION "End Down............",ed
         OPTION "End Left............",el
         OPTION "End Right...........",er
         OPTION "End Up..............",eu
         OPTION "End Home............",eh
         OPTION "Cancel, no selection",no
         MEND

RightB:  MENU "Macros",1,20,11
          OPTION "This is a sample macro                ",sm1
          OPTION "This is another sample macro          ",sm2
          OPTION "______________________________________"
          OPTION "Currency format, 2 decimal places     ",cf
          OPTION "______________________________________"
          OPTION "Call up the other pop-up menu         ",om
          OPTION "______________________________________"
          OPTION "Cancel, no selection                  ",no
          MEND

dos:     TYPE "CD",92,"123",ENTER,"123",ENTER
access:  TYPE "CD",92,"123",ENTER,"LOTUS",ENTER
file:    TYPE "CD",92,"123",ENTER,"123",ENTER,"/","F","R"
main:    TYPE "CD",92,"123",ENTER,"123",ENTER,"/"
enter:   TYPE "CD",92,"123",ENTER,"123",ENTER,"/",ENTER,ENTER
sy:      TYPE "CD",92,"SYM",ENTER,"SYM",ENTER
ws:      TYPE 92,"WS4",92,"WS",ENTER
db:      TYPE "CD",92,"DBASE",ENTER,"DBASE",ENTER
quit:    TYPE 27,"/","Q","Y"
f1:      TYPE 0,59
f2:      TYPE 0,60
f3:      TYPE 0,61
f4:      TYPE 0,62
f5:      TYPE 0,63
f6:      TYPE 0,64
f7:      TYPE 0,65
f8:      TYPE 0,66
f9:      TYPE 0,67
f0:      TYPE 0,68
st:      TYPE 0,15
af1:     TYPE 0,104
c4:      TYPE 0,115
c6:      TYPE 0,116
ed:      TYPE 0,79,0,80
el:      TYPE 0,79,0,75
er:      TYPE 0,79,0,77
eu:      TYPE 0,79,0,72
eh:      TYPE 0,79,0,71
no:      TYPE ENTER
sm1:     TYPE "This is a sample macro ",ENTER
sm2:     TYPE "This is another sample macro ",ENTER
cf:      TYPE "/RFC2",ENTER
```

```
BEGIN LeftB, MidB, RightB

LeftB:MENU "Left: This Menu || Middle: Special Keys || Right: Macros",1,10,11
        OPTION "Call 1-2-3 from DOS, READY screen  ",dos
        OPTION "Call 1-2-3 from Access             ",access
        OPTION "Call 1-2-3 for file retrieval      ",file
        OPTION "Call 1-2-3 display main menu       ",main
        OPTION "Call 1-2-3 display global menu     ",enter
        OPTION "___________________________________"
        OPTION "Quit 1-2-3                         ",quit
        OPTION "___________________________________"
        OPTION "Symphony                           ",sy
        OPTION "___________________________________"
        OPTION "WordPerfect version 5.0            ",ws
        OPTION "dBASE IV                           ",db
        OPTION "___________________________________"
        OPTION "No selecion or other menus         ",no
        MEND
```

Figure 8-73. Page 2 of the newsletter

PROGRAMMER'S FORUM

that is designed as an example or template for programs to be used with Lotus 1-2-3, and it can easily be modified to fit any individual requirements.

The first line:

BEGIN LeftB, MidB, RightB

uses the reserved word **BEGIN** to start the program. The next three words **LeftB, MidB, RightB** are variables or labels that are used to identify subsequent sections in the program. Any other identifying words could just as well have been used.

Next there is a line that starts with **LeftB** followed by the reserved word **MENU** and some information in quotation marks and finally three sets of digits. The **LeftB** is the label that causes the menu that follows to be displayed when the LEFT mouse button is clicked. The data in the double quotes are shown in the top line of the menu when it appears on the screen (Fig.4). The digits at the far end of the line represent the position of the menu on the screen and the color being used. The first **1** identifies the vertical (Y) position of the upper left-hand corner of the menu. The second number **1** represents the horizontal (X) position of that corner. And the **11** causes the menu to be displayed in light blue.

What follows are a number of **OPTION** lines followed by data in double quotes and a variable at the end of each line. The first six options deal specifically with using 1-2-3, while the rest of the options can be used to call other applications programs from any currently active directory. The material enclosed by the double quotes is displayed in the menu as the available choices (Fig.2) and dragging the mouse either up or down will highlight one line at the time, producing a given series of actions when the mouse button is clicked. **OPTION** is a reserved word and at the end of this section, the reserved word **MEND** identifies the end of this menu.

Next there are the **MidB** and **RightB** labels that represent the menus that are displayed when the middle or right mouse button is pushed (Figs.5 and 6). Here each **OPTION** is again associated with a variable, the value of which is declared in the bottom portion of the program.

The final portion of the source code (Fig.3) contains the information that is responsible for what happens when a given selection is made by highlighting it and clicking the mouse button:

dos: causes the program to type the letters CD followed by the symbol associated with the ASCII code 92 (\) followed by 123, ENTER and 123 and ENTER once more. The words **TYPE** and **ENTER** are reserved words that are self-explanatory. What happens is this: Typing CD followed by 123 and ENTER causes the computer to CHANGE to the \123 DIRECTORY and then, typing 123 followed by ENTER again calls up the 1-2-3 program directly from DOS.

access: performs the identical function except that it is used to call up the program via the access screen.

file: takes the process several steps further. The sequence of "\","F","R" causes 1-2-3 to go through the steps of calling up the main menu (\), selecting File (F) and Retrieve (R), causing the menu that includes the available WK1 file names to be displayed, ready for you to make your selection.

main: simply opens 1-2-3 and causes the Main menu to be displayed.

enter goes past the main menu and causes the Global menu to be displayed.

sy: calls and opens SYMPHONY, assuming that it is located on a directory called \SYM.

ws: calls and opens WordStar, assuming that it is located on a directory called \WS4.

db: calls and opens dBASE III Plus assuming that it is located on a directory called \DEBASE.

tp: calls the Turbo Pascal (version 3.0) text editor, located on the root directory and called T.COM, and it goes through several steps to come to rest with the display asking that the Work File name be entered.

tb: calls and activates the Turbo BASIC text editor, located on the \BASIC directory.

tc: does the same thing for Turbo C, located on the \TURBOC directory.

tl: does it for Turbo Prolog, located on \PROLOG.

ut: activates a menu that displays a selection of utility programs located on the \USE directory

lp: activates the Logitech Publisher desktop publishing program on the \PUB directory.

vp: activates the Ventura Publisher desktop publishing program which, though located on \VENTURA and \TYPESET, can be called from any directory.

xp: activates the Personal Consultant Easy expert system located on \PCEASY.

ww: calls and activates Microsoft Windows located on \WWW.

Figure 8-74. *Page 3 of the newsletter*

PROGRAMMER'S FORUM

quit: uses the ASCII code for Esc (27) followed by "/", "Q", and "Y" to quit 1-2-3 and return to DOS.

By the way, these sequences such as "/ ","F","R" and "/", "Q", "Y"were written this way to add clarity. They would work just as well if written as "/rf" and "/qy", or one could have used all ASCII codes: 47,82,70 and 47,81,89. The choice is strictly up to the programmer.

F1: through **f0:**, **st:**, **af1:**, **c4:**, **c6:**, **ed:**, **el:**, **er:**, **eu:**,and **eh** use the appropriate extended ASCII codes for the 10 function keys and the other key combinations that produce the results called for in the second OPTION section.

no: simply uses ENTER to get rid of any of the menus without making a selection.

ac:, **pl:**, **sp:**, **ps:** and **pr:** cause the program to print some sample macros. These can be replaced and more can be added, depending entirely on the needs of the user. The program will simply cause the data inside the double quotes to be printed and the ENTER will cause the text to be transferred to the field in which the cursor is currently located.

cf: uses the keystroke sequence "/RFC2",ENTER to activate the currency format with two decimal places. When this selection is clicked, 1-2-3 asks that you enter the range throughout which the new format is to be used.

```
Special keys used by Lotus 1-2-3

    Help screens........
    Edit................
    Name................
    ABS.................
    Goto................
    Window..............
    Query...............
    Table...............
    Calc................
    Graph...............
    Backtab.............
    Compose.............
    BigLeft.............
    BigRight............
    End Down............
    End Left............
    End Right...........
    End Up..............
    End Home............
    Cancel, no selection
```

```
Left: This Menu || Middle: Special Keys || Right: Macros

    Call 1-2-3 from DOS, READY screen
    Call 1-2-3 from Access
    Call 1-2-3 for file retrieval
    Call 1-2-3 display main menu
    Call 1-2-3 display global menu
    -------------------------------------
    Quit 1-2-3
    -------------------------------------
    Symphony
    -------------------------------------
    WordStar Professional 4.0
    dBASE III Plus
    -------------------------------------
    No selecion or other menus
```

Pulldown menus like this remai RAM resident, available for ir stant use, as long as the compute remains turned on. The only tim they're wiped out is when a prc gram is used that causes certai high-resolution graphics modes t be activated.

When the source code for such program has been written, it mu: be saved in a file with a .DE extension. This one was saved o disk as 123.DEF. The next ste involves compiling the sourc code in order to produce a executable program. This requirе

Figure 8-75. *Page 4 of the newsletter*

PROGRAMMER'S FORUM

Macros

This is a sample macro
This is another sample macro

Currency format, 2 decimal places

Call up the other pop-up menu

Cancel, no selection

that the NEWMENU.EXE program be available. Type:

NEWMENU 123 ENTER

using whatever file name you're comfortable with in place of 123. The compiler creates a compiled version with an .MNU extension, in our case 123.MNU, assuming that it finds no errors in the source code. If errors are detected, the error(s) along with the number(s) of the offending line(s) are displayed and compilation is terminated. If compilation is successful the program displays a line reading "no errors" and another "PopUp menu loaded" which tells us that we're ready to start clicking mouse buttons.

Click the left button and the main menu (Fig.4) is displayed over whatever has been on the screen before. Click the middle button and the Special Keys menu appears and clicking the right button produces the Macros menu. Each of these menus includes one "No Selection" option which is important for a very simple reason. If you should activate one of the menus while active in 1-2-3 or a wordprocessor, text editor or other program, and the click the appropriate button on any selection other than one that can actually be executed by the currently active program, the series of key strokes associated with the selection will simply be printed on the screen. For instance, if I would click "Call 1-2-3 for file retrieval" from the main menu while active in WordStar, busy writing this article, the result will be:

CD\123

123

/FR

which is the series of key strokes represented by the variable **file:** in the program. Nothing bad has happened. That unwanted text can easily be erased. But if that happened while you're active in some portion of 1-2-3, you'd find that some unwanted text was written into the currently active field, something that could easily be overlooked, causing havoc at a later date. Therefore, when wanting to get rid of a menu without making a valid selection, always use the "No Selection" option.

Future issues will cover in-depth analyses of the following software:

- **WordPerfect 5.0 and 5.1, Advanced techniques**
- **dBASE IV from Ashton-Tate**
- **Quatro Pro from Borland International**
- **Publish It! from Timeworks, Inc.**

Figure 8-76. *A simple layout for a full-page advertisement*

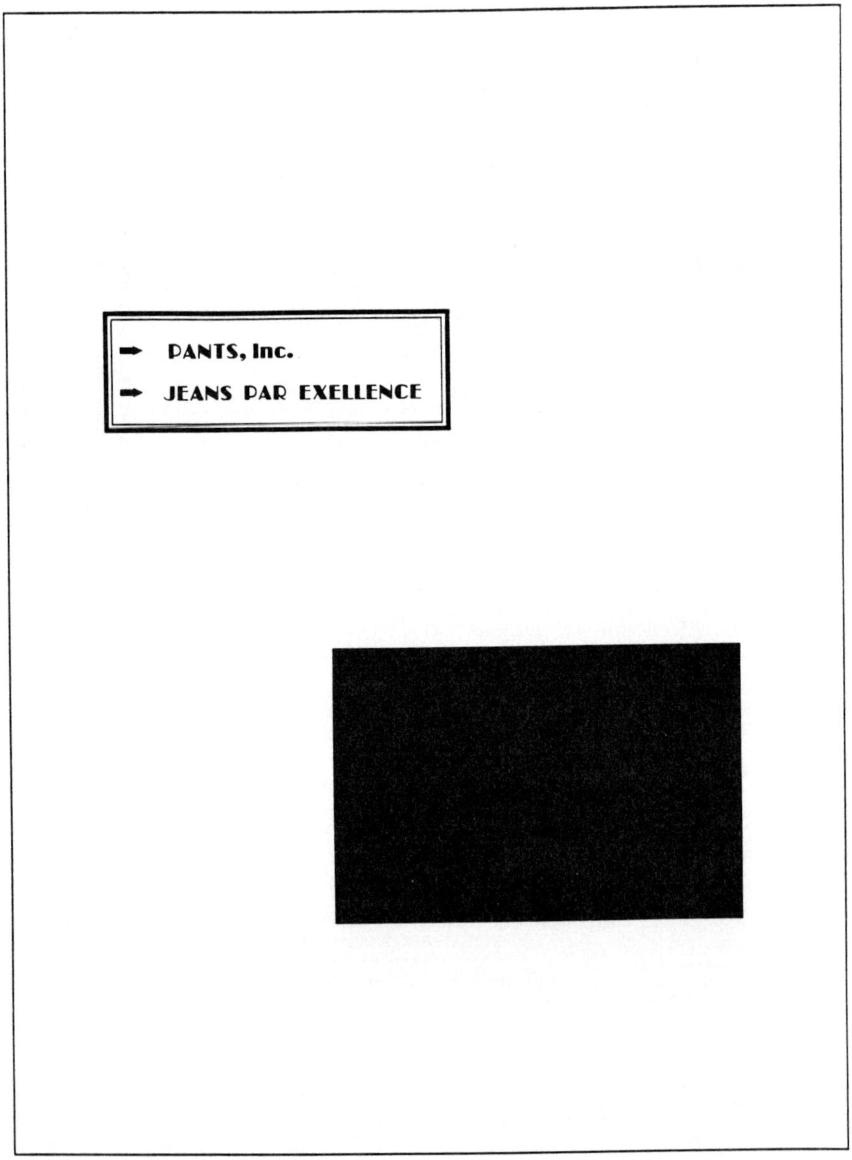

Each illustration in the newsletter consists of two frames. One frame contains the illustration itself. The second frame, placed on top of the first, is equipped with a border, a tint, and the <Clear> option. As a result, the images show through the tint.

A Full-Page Ad Layout

The final hands-on example in this chapter is the layout for a full-page ad with lots of white space, shown in Figure 8-76. Many of the more elegant ads in the better fashion magazines use a minimum of copy.

The black rectangle is where a photograph will be stripped in, and the copy itself is simply the name of the manufacturer and three words dealing with the product. The arrows are the result of using the Bullet paragraph style with the arrow shape selected. For some print shops you might want to use a bordered frame with instructions for your printer in place of the black frame used here. If a scanner is available, you can use a scanned approximation of the photograph that your print shop will replace with the actual photograph.

The chapters that follow discuss using Publish It! in conjunction with graphics and other material that is imported from external files.

9

Using External Files

Publish It!, like all desktop publishing programs, must be used in conjunction with material produced by other software, such as text and graphics files, to demonstrate its nearly unlimited versatility. Use of external files primarily involves text files created either with one of the word processors supported by Publish It! or in the ASCII format using any of the text editors available with DOS and with programming language software. The other types of files commonly used in preparing Publish It! documents are graphics files produced by a wide variety of graphics programs or contained in clip-art libraries.

Word Processing Programs

Word processing programs vary considerably in terms of available options. The latest versions of some of the more popular word processing programs, such as WordPerfect versions 5.0 and 5.1, WordStar 6.0 and 2000, and others, are beginning to approach some of the basic desktop publishing capabilities by offering a wide choice of fonts, font styles and sizes, plus the ability to include graphics in their documents. Only a few of these special features can be imported directly into Publish It!. Such font attributes as bold, underline, italic, superscript, and subscript may be recognized, but the actual selection of font styles and sizes must be made from within Publish It! itself.

Graphics must always be imported separately. Among the sources for such graphics files are programs, such as Paintbrush, available as part of Windows version 3.0 or separately as PC Paintbrush, PaintShowPlus, and others. Then there is a wide variety of CAD (computer-aided-design) programs. And for ready-to-use graphics there are the many clip-art libraries. In determining which programs or libraries to use, the deciding factor should be the file type. Is it one of the file types that can be imported directly into your version of Publish It!? If not, do you have access to a file-conversion program that is capable of converting the files in question to a format that Publish It! can use? Some of the more popular file-conversion programs are HiJaak and InSet from Inset Systems, Inc., The Graphics Link Plus from PC Quik-Art, HotShot from Symsoft Corporation, and the PaintShow or PaintShowPlus conversion program that converts .TIF files to .PCX files and vice versa.

Screen-Capture Programs

When you want to import a graphics file that happens to be in a format for which no convenient conversion is available, you may have to resort to the screen-capture option, meaning that you take an electronic snapshot of your screen. First display the image you want to capture on your screen. Then use one of the different screen-capture utilities that are available. WordPerfect versions 5.0 and 5.1 include a screen-capture program called GRAB, which produces graphics files with a .WPG extension that must still be converted. Logitech's PaintShow and PaintShowPlus offer one called CATCH, which creates files with the .TIF extension that can be used directly by Publish It! version 2.0. Another is PizazzPlus from Applications Technologies that is extremely versatile and can produce files with .PCX and .TIF extensions among many others. PictureEze, from the same company, is a graphics enhancement program, including among its many options the ability to perform file conversions among any of these formats: .BMP, .CUT, .DIB, .EPS, .GIF, .IFF, .IMG, .LBM, .MAC, .MSP, .PCX, .PIC, .PZI, .SC?, .TGA, .TIF,

.VMG, .WIN, and .WPG. All of these programs, with the exception of PictureEze, must be loaded into RAM, where they remain in the background (RAM-resident), ready to be called by the use of certain key combinations. They are unloaded from memory once the computer is turned off.

Most of the screen-capture utilities just described are capable of capturing and converting graphic screens into graphics files, but only a few are able to capture actual text displayed on the screen—meaning text produced by a word processor or text editor, not the kind of graphic text that is produced when you type text directly from within Publish It!. Two of these programs are HiJaak, and PizazzPlus. Both will capture text screens and convert them to graphic images that you can then import into Publish It! documents using the <Import picture> option from the File menu. Since most text of this type appears on the screen as white (or light) lettering on a black (or dark) background, you should use the <Invert> (with HiJaak) or <Reverse> (with PizazzPlus) options to produce black letters on a white background. PictureEze, too, performs a very fine job of inverting images. These new graphic images can then be treated like any other graphic image in terms of enlarging, reducing, stretching, compressing, cropping, and so on.

External Graphics Programs

This section deals with several different types of external programs. The software that is used is typical of each program type. In each instance, you may prefer to work with a different program than the one described here, but the principles of operation are probably similar.

Clip-Art Libraries

The number of software manufacturers offering clip-art libraries is large and growing. Figures 9-1 and 9-2 show some typical clip-art images used in electronics and logic. Figure 9-3 is a collection of images dealing with space exploration. All three of these samples give just an inkling of the scope and variety of clip art available in the Diagraph/2000 software from Computer

Figure 9-1. *Electronics and logic clip-art symbols*

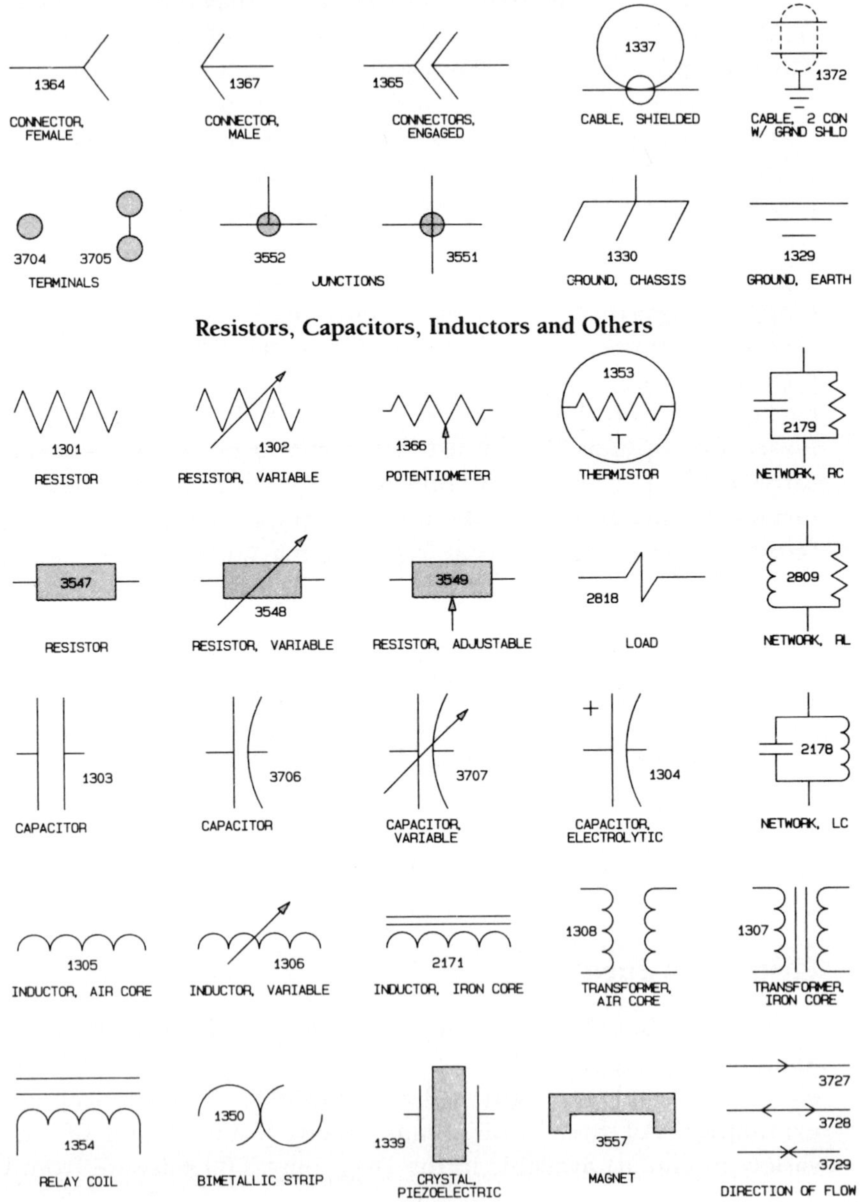

Figure 9-2. More electronics and logic clip-art symbols

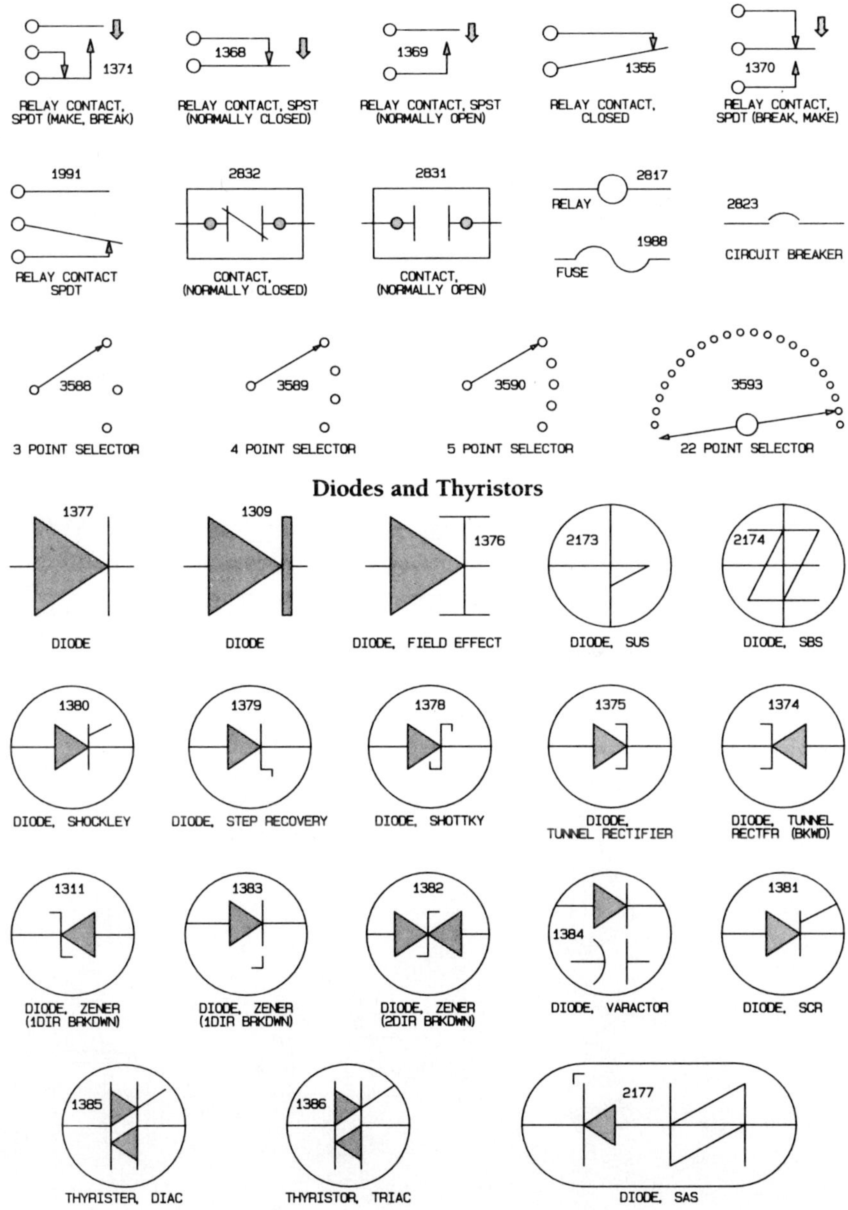

Figure 9-3. *Space-related clip art*

Support Corporation. Figure 9-4 represents different font styles and sizes available in the Halo DPE graphics program from Media Cybernetics.

You should approach purchasing any clip-art library with caution, keeping these factors in mind:

- Is the file format, usually determined by the file extension, compatible with Publish It!? If not, can it be converted by the file-conversion program available to you? The screen-capture option, available as a last resort, is not an ideal solution. The quality of screen-capture files is limited by the resolution of your monitor.
- Do you feel that the images contained in the library conform to the style of artwork that fits into the document(s) you are working on?
- Does the selection include the subject matters that you are interested in? Each of these libraries includes a manual with illustrations of every image (if it does not, don't even consider it). Examine the illustrations carefully to make sure they serve your purposes.

If you have Publish It! installed on a hard disk, you might be tempted to create a separate directory to hold your clip-art library. Don't give in to the temptation. Graphics files use large amounts of memory. A full-page halftone graphics file can use as much as 500,000 bytes. Instead, make copies on floppy disks, store the originals in a safe place, and access the files from the floppy-disk copies.

Publisher's PicturePak

Publisher's PicturePak, offered by Marketing Graphics, Inc., consists of separate libraries that concentrate on specific subjects such as Executive & Management, Finance & Administration, Sales & Marketing, and others. Each library includes approximately 180 images. The programs are available in the .CGM and .PCC file formats to be compatible with all possible software and hardware. If you plan to use Publisher's PicturePak, select the version with the .PCC extension. It is identical in format to the .PCX file format and is compatible with Publish It! without conversion.

Once you have imported a picture, it can be cropped and otherwise manipulated using the options available from the Publish It! Graphics menu.

Figure 9-4. *Font styles from a graphics program*

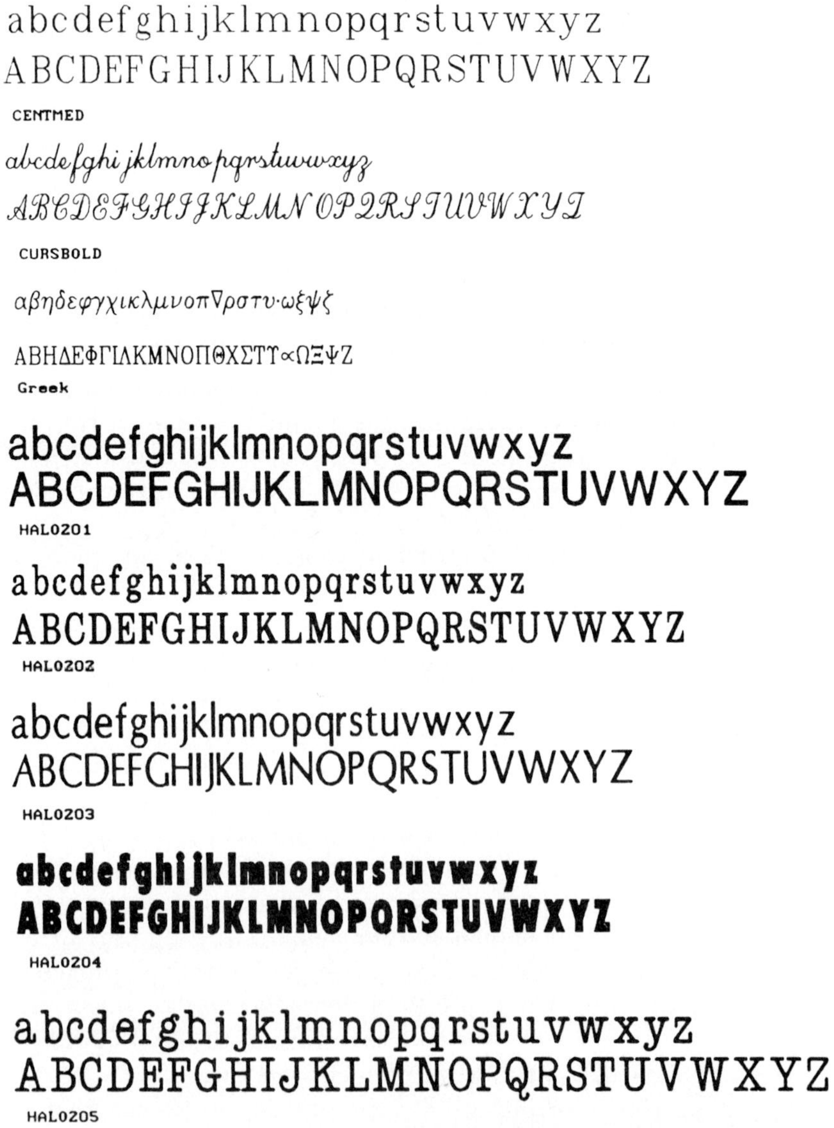

Figures 9-5 and 9-6 are clip-art pictures. You can import them into Publish It! by following these steps:

1. With Publish It! loaded in the usual manner, while in the <FRAME> mode, draw a frame into the upper-left quarter of the screen.
2. Select <Import picture> from the File menu. From the resulting dialog box click on <.PCX>.
3. Click on the Directory line in the Item Selector box to place the text cursor on that line. Press ESC to delete the line. Type something like **B:*.PCC** if your .PCC files are on the disk in drive B. Click on the filename that represents the graphic image you want to import. Click on <OK>.
4. Be patient. It takes a while for the picture to be drawn into the frame. Once it is there, it can be edited, copied, moved, and distorted, and text can be written into it.

Figure 9-5 is a picture of the White House (file SA0192 from the Publisher's PicturePak Sales & Marketing collection). It was first imported into the frame at the upper-left corner of the screen. It was then copied and reduced, enlarged, and manipulated as needed by changing the dimensions of the frame holding the graphic, using the <Copy> and <Paste> options from the Edit menu. The pointing hand pointers and grabber hand were used to distort and move the picture.

Figure 9-6 is a picture of a computer and a mouse. In the clip-art collection these are two separate files. In the upper-left corner the two were combined. In the large center picture, text was added to the computer screen. First a new frame was drawn inside the screen. Then the <TEXT> mode was selected by clicking on the <TEXT> icon. The text cursor (the I-beam) was placed into the frame. From the <Font/size> option in the Style menu, <12> and <Dutch> were selected. Then text was typed. After that, the <FRAME> mode was reselected by clicking on the <FRAME> icon. The frame inside the screen was selected by clicking on it. Then the <Frame tint> option was selected from the Options menu, and a light tint was selected by clicking on it and on <OK>.

Figure 9-5. A clip-art image manipulated five ways

Figure 9-6. *Clip-art images combined with text*

Math and Science Symbols

A number of programs on the market can be used to produce mathematical and scientific symbols that are not part of the standard ASCII character set. A typical program is EXACT, manufactured by Technical Support Software, Inc. It includes an optional subprogram called the EXACT Desktop Publishing Support Kit.

Both programs must be installed in accordance with the instructions in their manuals. If installed on a hard disk, they produce directories called EXACT and DTP. (Make sure that you don't already have a C:\DTP directory. The C:\PUBLISH\DTP directory will not be affected.) While the procedures you must follow to use the programs in combination with Publish It! may seem complicated, they are worth it if you need mathematical or scientific symbols in your document. (WordPerfect 5.1 includes an equation option in its Graphics mode. While it produces the symbols perfectly, they are ignored when the document is imported into Publish It!, leaving only the text.) What follows is an EXACT practice session.

1. From the DOS prompt type **CD\EXACT** and press ENTER to move into the EXACT directory. Then type **EXACT** and press ENTER, and the screen shows unimportant information for a moment. It then tells you that EXACT has been installed correctly. The C> prompt shows that you are back in DOS.
2. Activate your word processor or text editor and type the text that will contain the mathematical or scientific formula in the normal manner. When it is time to enter the formula itself, type **$/HEAD/** or **$/HE/**. On a new line, type the EXACT commands, which can be entered directly from the word processor or text editor if you are thoroughly familiar with them. If you're not, go to the next step.
3. Press LEFT SHIFT-F7 to display the EXACT editing screen without exiting or in any way disturbing the word processor. You can now enter the EXACT commands and at the same time see the symbols you are creating. This makes it easy to correct any errors immediately.
4. When the formula is finished, press LEFT SHIFT-F10. The command characters are inserted in your document at the exact place where you left the cursor before.

5. Type **$/FOOT/** or **$/FO/** to indicate the end of the formula. Then continue typing your text. When you send the finished document to the printer, it will print your text and the mathematical formula in the correct format. But this format cannot be imported directly into Publish It!. To do that, the formula must first be converted to a graphics file.
6. The EXACT Desktop Publishing Support Kit can work with ASCII text files only. If your document was created with a word processing program, you will have to convert the formula itself to ASCII code. Save the formula portion as a separate ASCII file.
7. From the DOS prompt type **CD\DTP** and press ENTER to enter the DTP directory. Now type **EXACT**, press ENTER, type **EXACT2DT**, and press ENTER again. This produces a display asking that you key in the name of the file to be converted.
8. Type **C:*PATH**FILENAME.EXT*** and press ENTER. Note that you substitute your own information for the italicized text here. *PATH* is the disk/directory on which the file to be used is located. The rest is the name and extension under which the formula is saved. After a moment you should be informed that the file was successfully converted and saved. The file is saved on the DTP directory under the filename EXASC001.PCX. If there are several formulas contained in the same text file, they are stored with increasing consecutive numbers such as EXASC002.PCX, EXASC003.PCX, and so on.
9. You can now import the .PCX file directly into Publish It! using the <Import picture> option from the File menu. Since this is a graphics file, you can change its size in any way you like.

Figure 9-7 is a text file that displays the regular text and the group of EXACT commands in the top box. The mathematical formula is displayed in the bottom box.

In addition to producing mathematical and scientific symbols, the program can produce unusual text in graphics format. It can print extremely small text, and it can print text vertically, on its side. The available options

Figure 9-7. *Mathematical formula imported into Publish It!*

USING EXACT

A Program that Permits Printing Math and Scientific Symbols

For instance, the mathematical formula for something described as

normal distribution,

one of the fundamental concepts in statistics, can be created using your word processor by typing the following commands:

```
$/HEAD/
F(x) = $/FR/1$,$/RA/2$p$.$. $=
$J$*%-$I$**$+$#x $=
e$*#-$/FR/1$,2$.y$#2$** dy
$/FOOT/
```

These commands embedded in the text produced by the word processor activate EXACT which translates them into a formula which is saved as a .PCX graphics file and which looks like the one shown below:

$$F(x) = \frac{1}{\sqrt{2\pi}} \int_{-\infty}^{x} e^{-\frac{1}{2}y^2}\, dy$$

are too many and varied to be described here. Figure 9-8 demonstrates how a file containing text but saved in a graphics format can prove useful. The following ASCII file is created:

$/HE/
Graphic TEXT
$/FO/

This ASCII file is treated in the same manner as the mathematical formula. The result is a file called GRAXT001.PCX, which is imported into Publish It! where it produces the very small text shown in the upper-left corner of Figure 9-8. By stretching the frame vertically, the next image is created. Then, using the <Copy> and <Paste> options from the Edit menu, it is moved and vastly enlarged by stretching the frame. The <Crop picture> option from the Graphics menu is used to crop out the word "TEXT." The same routine is

Figure 9-8. *Text imported as a graphics file*

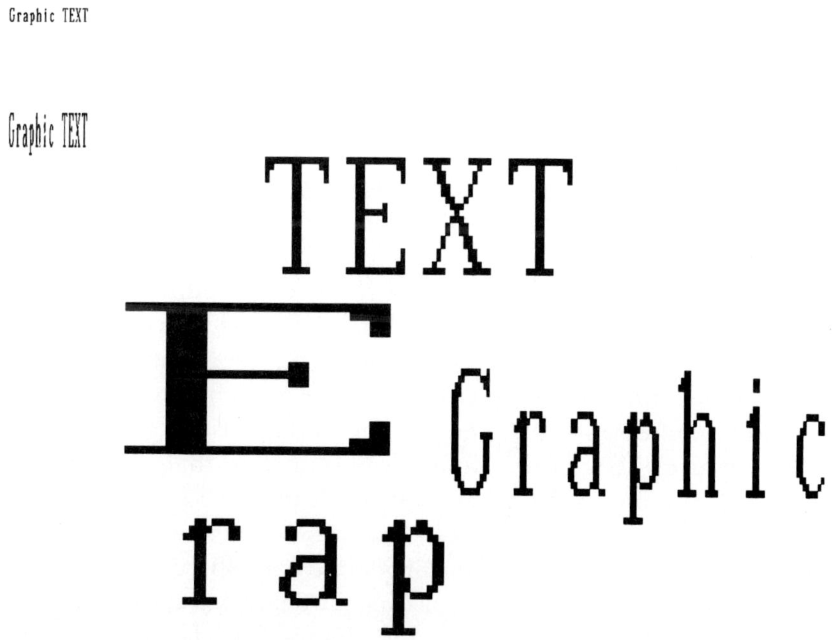

used to crop the letter "E" out of the word "TEXT" and the letters "rap" out of the word "Graphic."

By creating graphics files that contain text, it is possible to produce a wide variety of font sizes and effects that are not readily available directly from Publish It!. If you use mathematical or scientific formulas in your business or profession, you will find this type of program useful.

Graphs and Charts

Many programs used in business create bar charts, line graphs, pie charts, and the like. You may find it convenient to include such graphs and charts in newsletters and other documents you produce using Publish It!.

The demonstration graphics used here were created using a program called EnerGraphics. In this type of program, you enter the numbers that represent the values to be illustrated as vertical or horizontal bars, slices of a pie, or curved lines. You then tell the program what type of chart you want to create. The choices include two-dimensional or three-dimensional bar, line, or pie charts. With the information keyed into the computer, the program takes over and creates what you asked for.

Figures 9-9 through 9-13 were produced using the EnerGraphics program. This program produces bit-mapped graphics files that are higher in quality than the vector-type files produced by Lotus 1-2-3, Quattro, Quattro Pro, and others. Each file was saved in the .IMG format and is available to be imported into Publish It!. Figure 9-9 is a two-dimensional bar chart representing aircraft data, where "%" represents the percent of power used, "kts" represents the true airspeed in knots, "gph" represents gallons of fuel burned per hour, "nm*10" represents the range available in nautical miles times 10, and hours represents the endurance under various power settings.

Figure 9-10 is a three-dimensional bar chart that compares different types of business and personal aircraft. It illustrates the 3-D option available with EnerGraphics. It also shows what can happen when such charts are not carefully planned to avoid having some bars obscuring others.

Figure 9-11 is a two-dimensional pie chart that shows the annual operating costs of a business aircraft, and Figure 9-12 is the same chart in three dimensions. Figure 9-13 is another example of a two-dimensional bar chart.

Figure 9-9. *Two-dimensional bar graph*

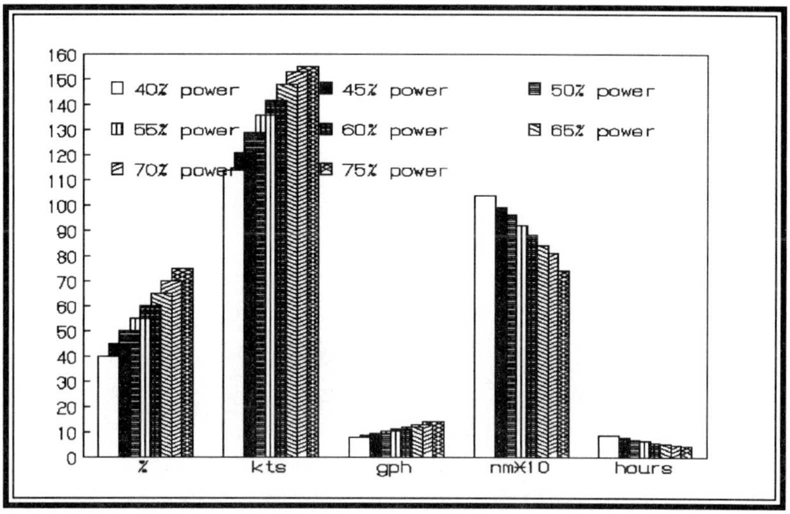

Figure 9-10. *Three-dimensional bar graph*

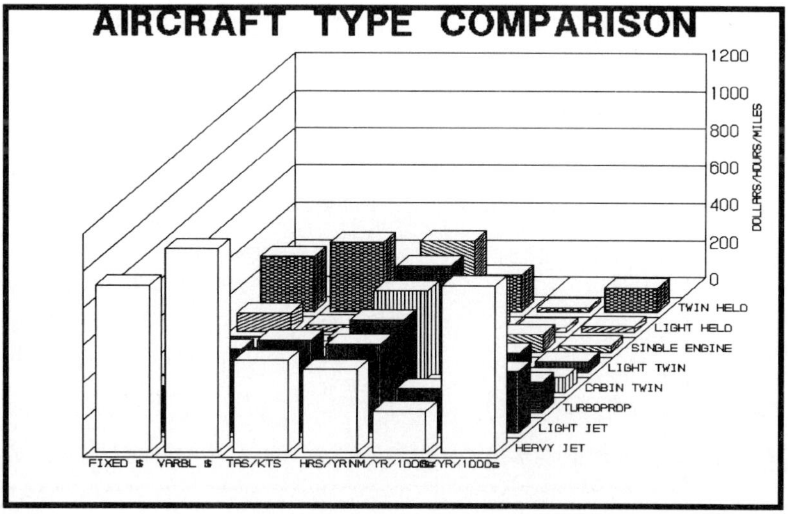

Figure 9-11. *Two-dimensional pie chart*

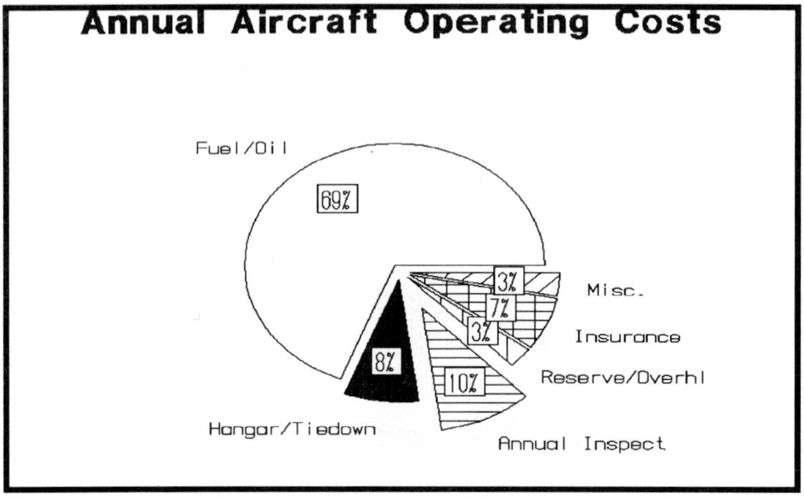

Figure 9-12. *Three-dimensional pie chart*

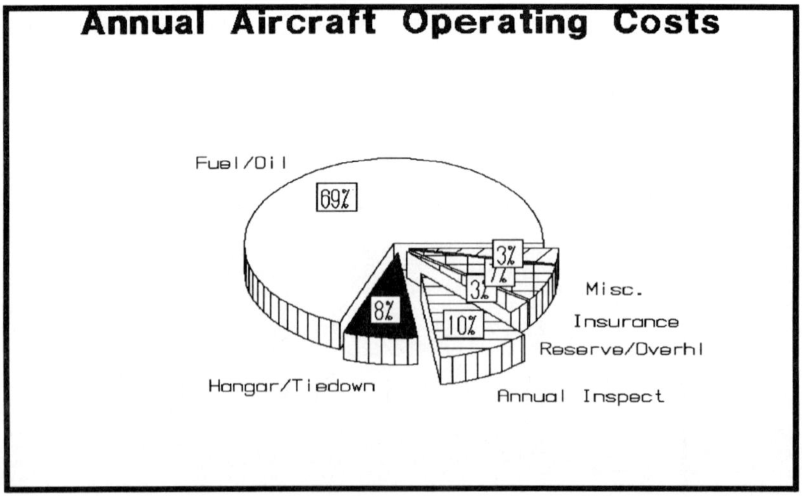

Figure 9-13. *Bar chart*

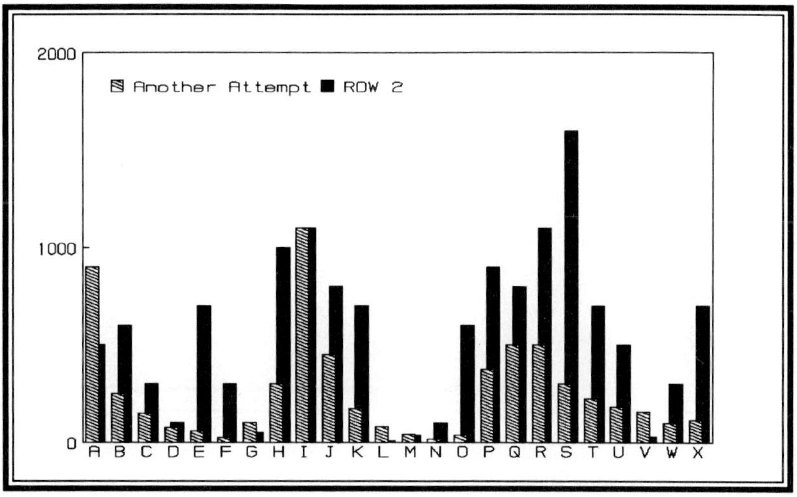

These charts are imported into Publish It! as graphics files. As such, they can be enlarged, reduced, stretched, and manipulated in the same way as other graphic files. Portions can be cropped and used separately.

Since Publish It! includes a <Lotus 1-2-3 (.PIC)> option in the Import Picture dialog box, any graph that is produced by the Lotus 1-2-3 spreadsheet program can be imported directly without conversion. In addition, the Quattro and Quattro Pro spreadsheet programs from Borland International also include the option to save graph and chart files in the identical .PIC format compatible with Publish It!.

9

A SoftCraft Font-Manipulation Program

SoftCraft, Inc. is the manufacturer of a number of font programs that serve different purposes. One of the more interesting is called Spinfont. It is used to produce text in circles of various kinds—as the spokes of a

Figure 9-14. *Curved text inside a double ring*

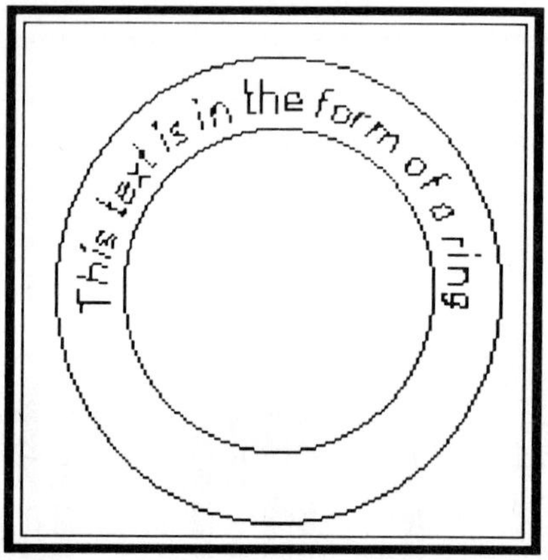

wheel, at angles, copied onto itself, and more. Figures 9-14 and 9-15 are two examples. The curved text in both figures and the two circles in Figure 9-14 were produced using Spinfont. The program produces graphics files with .PCX or .TIF extensions. The .PCX option was selected, and the files were

Figure 9-15. *Curved text*

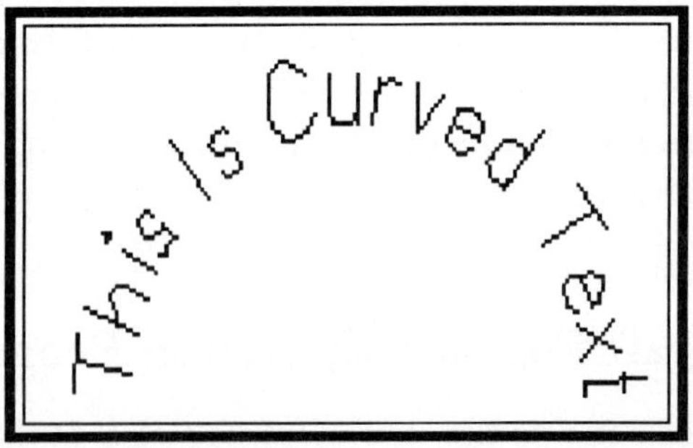

imported into Publish It!. The <Frame border> option was used in Publish It! to place the borders around the frames into which the images were imported.

The Spinfont program uses the BFG.EXE file, which is included with the Fontware program that is available free of charge from WordPerfect, Microsoft Word, and other programs. It is also included with GEM Desktop.

VP-Graphics

VP-Graphics is a low-cost graphics program developed by Paperback Software International. It combines the usual freehand drawing aids with graph and text options. In any mode the images, either graphics or text, can be flipped horizontally and vertically, rotated 90 degrees in either direction, and copied or moved. In the Text mode you can choose from several font styles, including an impressive Old English style. All fonts are available in sizes from 9 to 36 points.

Graphic files that contain graphics or text are automatically saved with a .VPG extension that cannot be used by Publish It!. To use VP-Graphics files you must use one of the screen-capture programs plus a conversion program to arrive at a file that Publish It! can work with.

Figure 9-16 is text typed in Old English typeface. It was imported into Publish It! once with the <Invert> option active to produce white letters on black and once without the <Invert> option. Figure 9-17 consists of two lines of text typed in the Blocktype face. It was copied several times, flipped horizontally and vertically, and rotated 90 degrees.

PaintShow Plus

The graphics files that produced the text in Figures 9-18, 9-19, and 9-20 were created using Logitech's PaintShowPlus graphics program. Figure 9-18 used that program's Old English font. Figure 9-19 used a Roman font in the Shadow font style, greatly enlarged after it was imported into Publish It!. In the center frame in Figure 9-20, a Script font was used in the Shadow font style. The single-line frame around that text was also created in PaintShowPlus. The symbols above that frame were produced by typing the 9

Figure 9-16. *Imported Old English font*

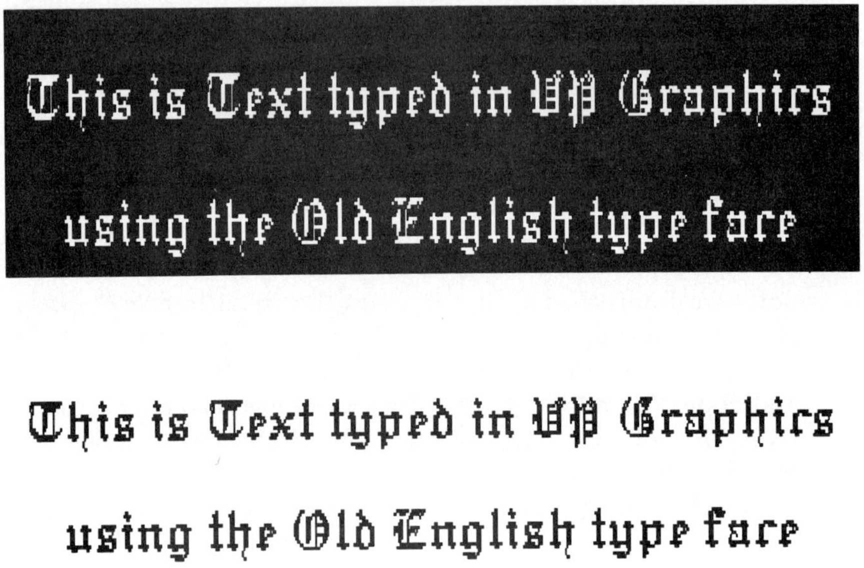

letters "A" through "Z" in the Symbols font style. The letters below the frame were produced by typing the letters "A" through "M" in the Greek font style. In all three illustrations, the final size of the text was adjusted after it was imported into Publish It!. The double-line frames were also produced by Publish It!.

PaintShowPlus files are saved with a .TIF extension and must be converted to the .IMG or .PCX format using the conversion option that is part of the PaintShowPlus program. Type **TIF2IMG** ***FILENAME*** and press (ENTER). *FILENAME* is the name under which you saved the graphics file, minus the extension. As another alternative, you can use the conversion programs that are available with HiJaak, InSet, and several other programs.

Figure 9-17. *Text flipped and rotated*

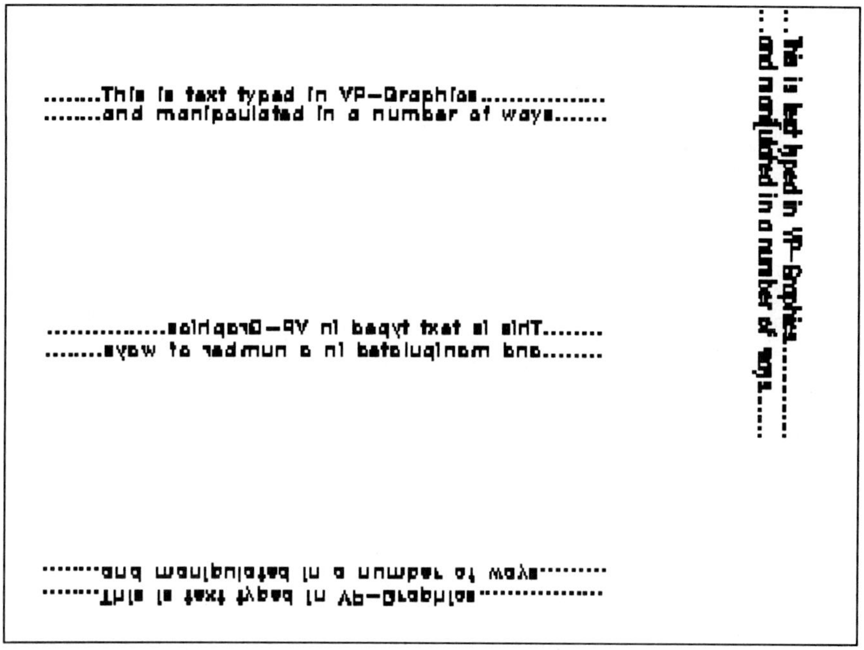

Figure 9-18. *Old English from a different program*

Figure 9-19. *Shadow font style*

Figure 9-20. *Several font options from a graphics program*

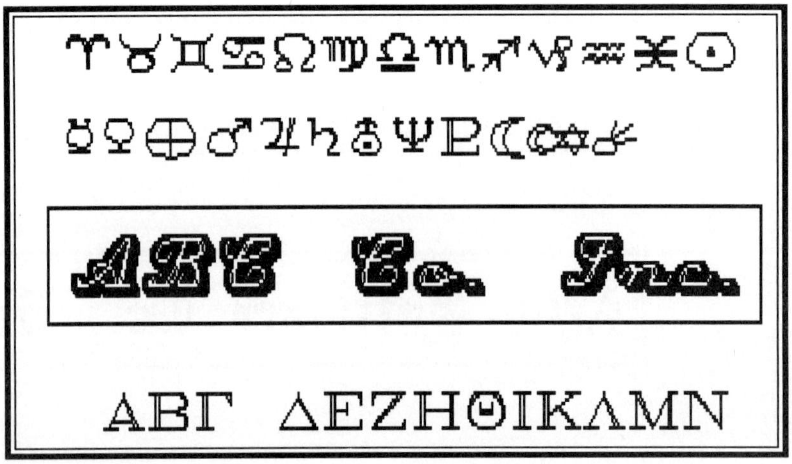

AutoSketch

The AutoSketch program, from AutoDesk, Inc., includes special and useful options. Text can be slanted forward or backward. It can be typed horizontally, vertically, diagonally, or at any other angle. The text and the vertical rectangular box in Figure 9-21 were created using this program. The slant of the letters was set at 45 degrees and the angle of the base line of the text was set at 90 degrees. The text was then typed starting at the bottom and continuing toward the top. Since that program produces files in .SKD or .DXF formats for which no ready file-conversion program appears to exist, a screen-capture program was used to produce a file in a format compatible with Publish It!.

Figure 9-21. *Vertical text slanted 45 degrees*

Scanners

A scanner is a combination of hardware and software systems designed to convert printed material, text, drawings, photographs, or anything that can be found on the printed page into graphic files. These files, usually in the TIFF format (tagged image file format) with a .TIF extension, can be imported directly into Publish It! versions 1.2 and 2.0, but must be converted to .IMG files to be used with the earlier versions of Publish It!.

Scanners are available at a wide variety of prices. Some are hand-held systems that you drag manually across the image to be scanned. Depending on the model, some are limited to covering areas not wider than four inches, while others can handle full pages.

Sheet-fed scanners mechanically drag a single sheet of printed material across the scanning head. They can only be used for individual sheets of paper and cannot scan the pages of books, magazines, or other bound publications unless the pages are physically removed.

Flatbed scanners are the most costly. They use a moving scanning head under a glass surface and can be used to scan almost anything. Some scanning systems, the combinations of hardware and associated software, are better than others at text recognition, and some do a better job of handling halftones or converting color images to black-and-white halftones.

You should be aware that files of photographs or similar halftone graphic images produced by scanners frequently take up a huge amount of disk space. For instance, the scan file that produced Figure 9-22, created from an original 4 x 5-inch black-and-white photograph, uses 68,742 bytes.

For most purposes, photographs are best prepared for your camera-ready layout by a print shop. Files of this size take forever to import and often overload earlier versions of Publish It!. If you must scan an image, try to scan at a resolution no higher than that of your printer. Also, try not to scan extremely large areas unless absolutely necessary.

If you plan to produce many scanned image files, save them on separate floppy disks to retain ample free space on your hard disk or the floppy working disks.

Figure 9-22. *Scanned image of a black-and-white photograph*

The scanned image in Figure 9-22 was produced using the flatbed Hewlett-Packard ScanJet and the associated ScanGal scanning gallery software. The resulting .TIF file was converted to an .IMG file using the HiJaak file-conversion utility.

10

Computer-Generated Artwork

If your drawing needs are simple, and you only want to create very basic graphics, you can use the tools in the Publish It! toolbox.

If you need to create complex or technical drawings, if your documents contain graphics on mechanical objects, architecture, scientific applications, and soon, you'll want to investigate some of the software available that lets you draw advanced graphics. We'll discuss the software shortly–first let's look at the toolbox in Publish It!.

Toolbox Tools

Publish It! includes the <GRAPHICS> mode in the toolbox. When you click on it, the pointer turns into an open arrow. In the area normally occupied by the Library, eight graphics tools are displayed, as shown in Figure 10-1. These tools can be used to create your own artwork.

Figure 10-1. *The eight graphic tools in the Publish It! toolbox*

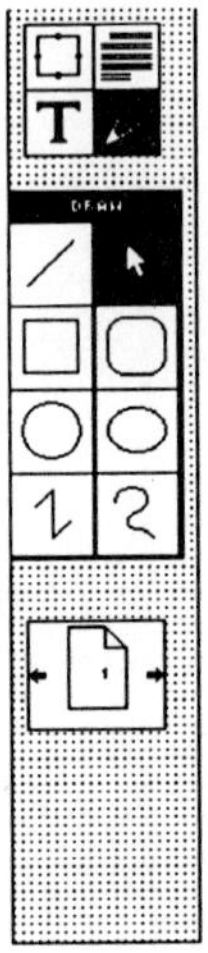

The Line Tool

The diagonal line at the top left of Figure 10-1 is the line tool. To use it to draw a line:

1. Access the <FRAME> mode, create a frame and select it.
2. Access the <GRAPHICS> mode.
3. Click on the line tool. The pointer turns into a hairline cross. Place it inside the frame and, holding down the left mouse button, drag it from one position to another. A line appears from the original point to the current location of the pointer.
4. Let go of the mouse button. The line appears surrounded by a new frame, with handles that indicate that it is selected, as shown in Figure 10-2.

Figure 10-2. *Using the line tool*

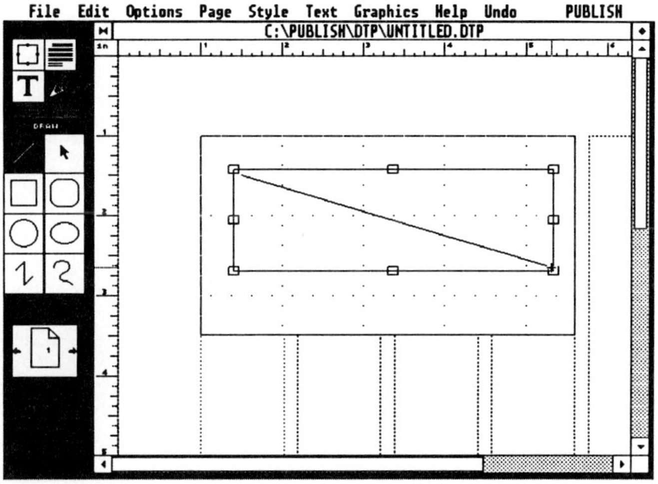

The Arrow Tool

5. Click on the arrow tool shown in the upper right of Figure 10-1.
6. Place the point of the arrow on one of the handles of the selected frame. Move it and watch as the frame changes shape, taking your line with it, as shown in Figure 10-3.

The Box Tool

1. Click on <New> in the File menu to start with an empty page.
2. Repeat steps 1 and 2 under "The Line Tool."
3. Click on the box tool, the second one down on the left in Figure 10-1. The hairline cross replaces the pointer.

Figure 10-3. *Using the arrow tool to manipulate a frame*

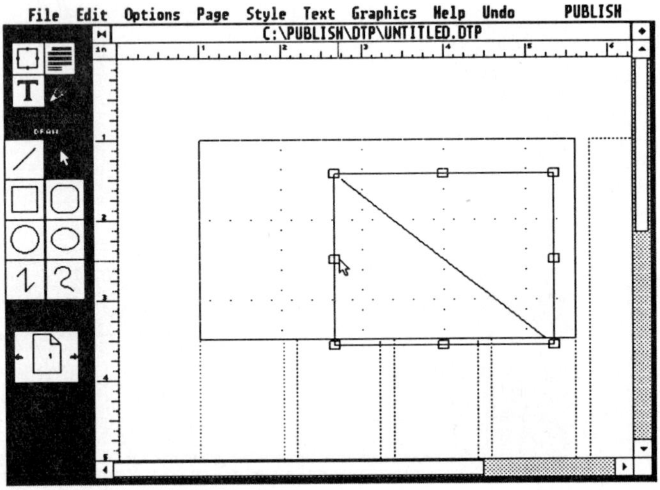

4. Holding down the mouse button, drag the mouse and watch a rectangular box being drawn. Draw several such boxes, as shown in Figure 10-4.
5. You can use the arrow tool to reshape the selected box containing the last rectangle.

The Rounded Rectangle Tool

1. Click on the rounded rectangle tool, the second tool down on the right side in Figure 10-1.
2. Holding down the mouse button, draw the rounded-corner boxes shown in Figure 10-5.

Figure 10-4. *Drawing boxes with the box tool*

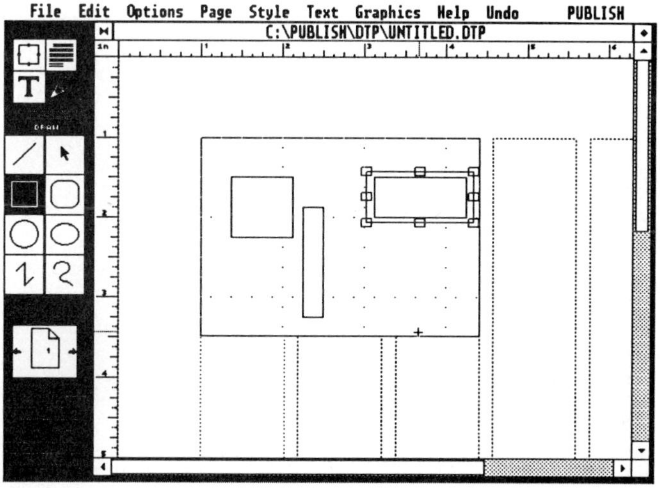

Figure 10-5. *Drawing rounded-corner rectangles*

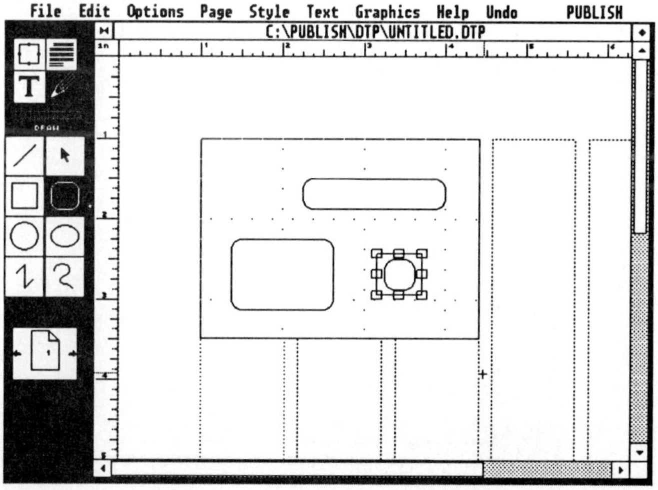

10

The Circle Tool

1. Click on the circle tool, the third tool down on the left side in Figure 10-1.
2. Holding down the mouse button, draw circles like the ones shown in Figure 10-6.

The Ellipse Tool

1. Click on the ellipse tool, the third tool down on the right side in Figure 10-1.
2. Holding down the mouse button, draw ellipses as shown in Figure 10-7.

Figure 10-6. *Drawing circles with the circle tool*

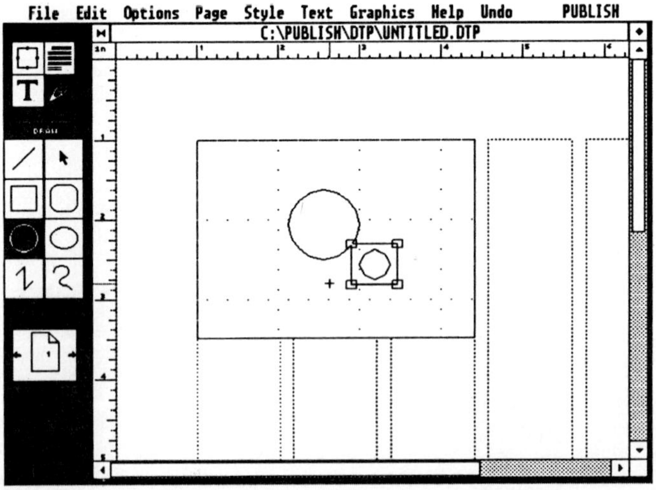

Figure 10-7. *Drawing ellipses with the ellipse tool*

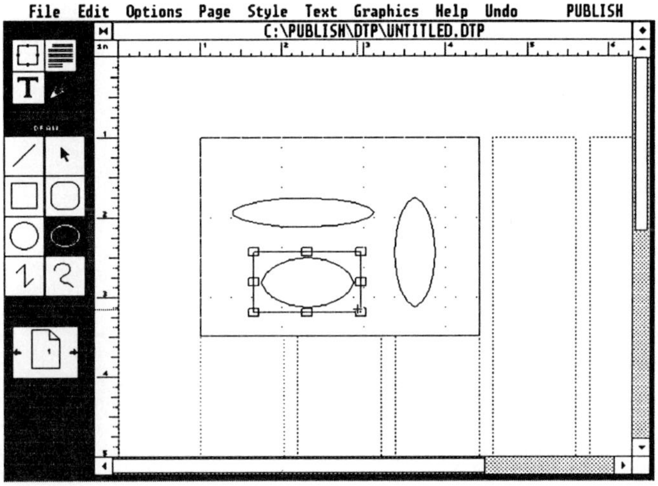

The Polygon Tool

1. Click on the polygon tool (on the bottom left of Figure 10-1).
2. Draw a series of connected straight lines, letting go of the mouse button each time you want to change direction. When you've finished, double-click, and a selected frame appears around your work as shown in Figure 10-8.

The Freehand Tool

1. Click on the freehand tool (the squiggle on the bottom right of Figure 10-1).
2. Draw a free-form line. When you let go of the mouse button, your work is again enclosed in a selected frame that can be reshaped using the arrow tool. The usefulness of this tool is limited only by your

Figure 10-8. *Drawing a series of connected lines with the polygon tool*

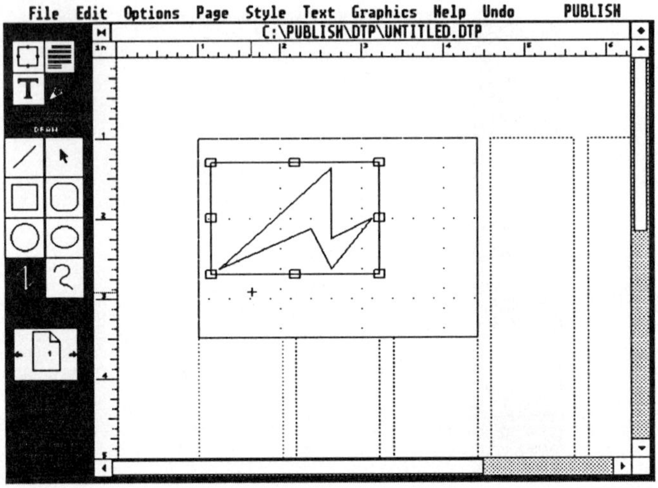

ability to draw whatever shapes you're interested in, like the odd-shaped abstract form in Figure 10-9.

While using any of these tools you can access the Graphics menu and select one of the available line-style options by selecting <Line style>.

1. Select a fat line and the arrow option, as shown in Figure 10-10.
2. Click on <OK> to return to the <GRAPHICS> mode.
3. Draw a straight line. As you let go of the mouse button, the new line takes on the attributes selected in the Line Style dialog box, as shown in Figure 10-11.

You can also "fill up" any contained areas in your graphics by selecting the Fill Style dialog box from the Graphics menu, shown in Figure 10-12.

1. Select a fill style you like.
2. Click on <OK> to return to the <GRAPHICS> mode.

Figure 10-9. *Using the freehand tool*

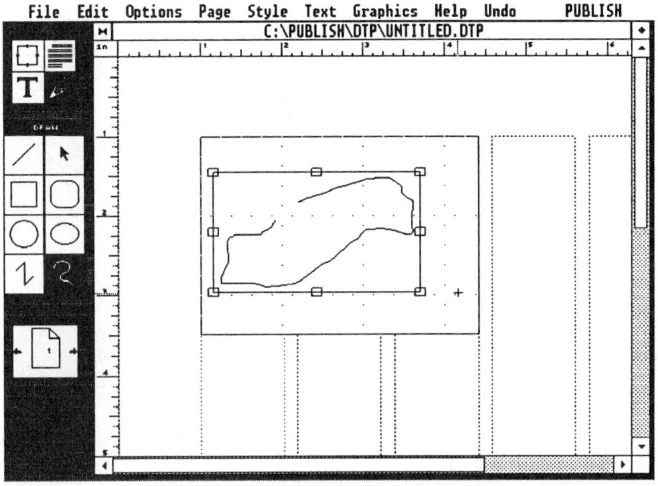

Figure 10-10. *Selecting from the Line Style dialog box*

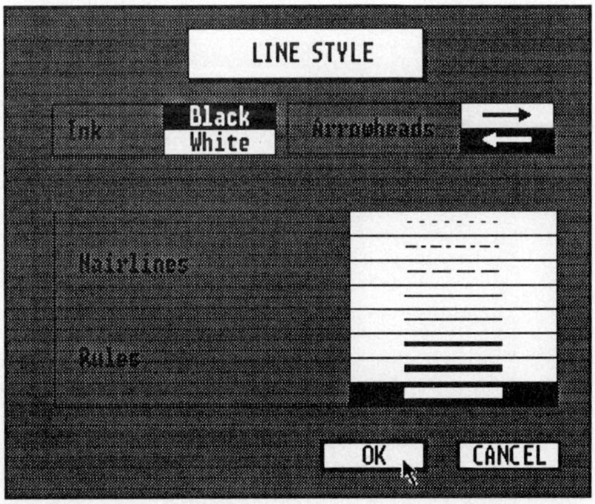

Figure 10-11. *The line drawn takes on the attributes selected in the Line Style dialog box*

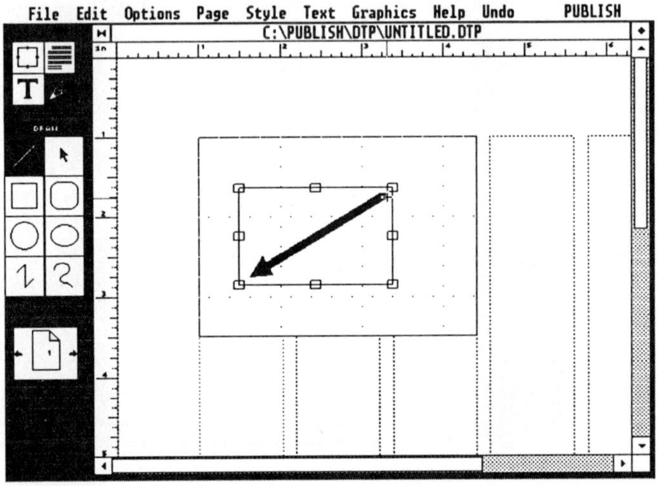

Figure 10-12. *The Fill Style dialog box*

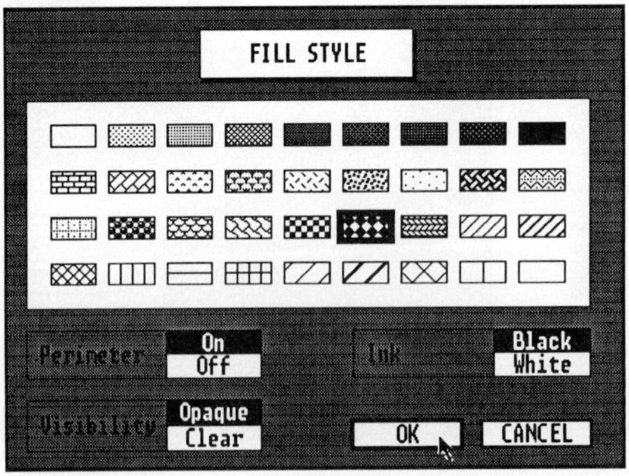

3. Draw a rectangle. As you let go of the mouse button, your new rectangle is filled with the selected pattern, as shown in Figure 10-13. Note that the fill function will not work with the freehand, line, or polygon tools.

The graphics tools available with Publish It! are fairly limited. They suffice for simple drawings, but to create more advanced artwork, you may want to use one of the paint programs available for that purpose.

The software market offers a number of programs designed to simplify the task of creating original artwork. These programs fall into two fairly broad categories. The first category consists of programs that provide a collection of tools that are used to produce freehand drawings. These drawings may be limited to geometric shapes, or can be free-form images. No matter which of these programs you use, the final result depends entirely on your talent, skill, and patience.

The second category consists of CAD (computer-aided-design) programs, which are used to produce two- and three-dimensional drawings, usually of mechanical, technical, architectural, or similar subjects. These programs offer different types of tools to assist you. Many of the three-dimensional CAD

Figure 10-13. *A rectangle filled with the pattern you selected*

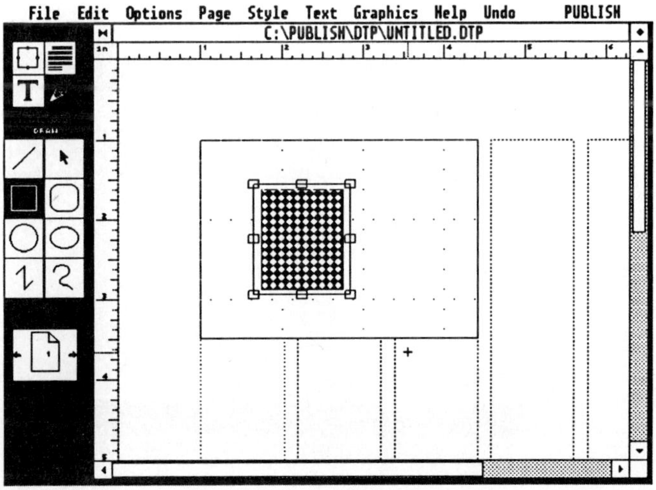

programs include the option of drawing a subject in three dimensions and then observing it from many different points of view. If you are involved in producing technical drawings, using images produced by these CAD programs may prove valuable.

Paint Programs

One of the oldest and most widely known programs in the freehand category is the PAINT.EXE program that was part of the earlier versions of Microsoft Windows (see Figure 10-14). Today the Windows 3.0 version has replaced that program with the full-fledged Paintbrush program, PBRUSH.EXE, (also available separately as a stand-alone program) that is capable of producing color graphics. The resulting files are saved with either the .MSP or .BMP extensions, but can easily be converted.

Files created using the older PAINT.EXE program must be converted using one of the functions that convert negative images to positive ones (and

Figure 10-14. *The Microsoft Windows PAINT.EXE screen drawing tools*

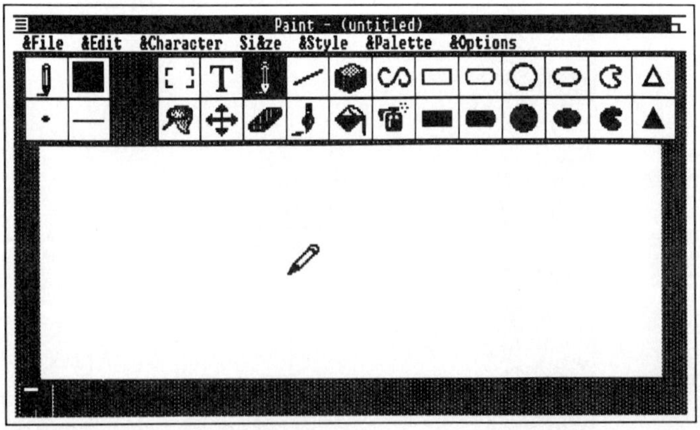

vice versa). If that is omitted, the resulting image is the negative of the one displayed on the screen.

Three other programs in the freehand category are PC Paintbrush from ZSoft, and PaintShow and PaintShowPlus from Logitech, Inc. The drawing tools available with these programs are all virtually identical. Figure 10-15 shows the screen presented by PaintShowPlus. PC Paintbrush files are saved with the .PCX extension, which Publish It! can use without conversion. PaintShow and PaintShowPlus files are saved as .TIF files, but the programs include a file-conversion utility that converts these files to the .PCX format. That utility is used by typing **TIF2PCX *FILENAME*** and pressing (ENTER), where *FILENAME* is the name (without its extension) of the file to be converted

Figure 10-16 shows the screen display of the Sled Image Processor program from VS Software. Instead of the graphic tool icons used with the other programs, this one displays the drawing style options in written form in one of the seven pull-down menus. Files produced by Sled can be saved in a number of formats, including .IMG and .PCX, which can be imported into Publish It! without conversion.

Figure 10-15. *The PaintShowPlus screen drawing tools*

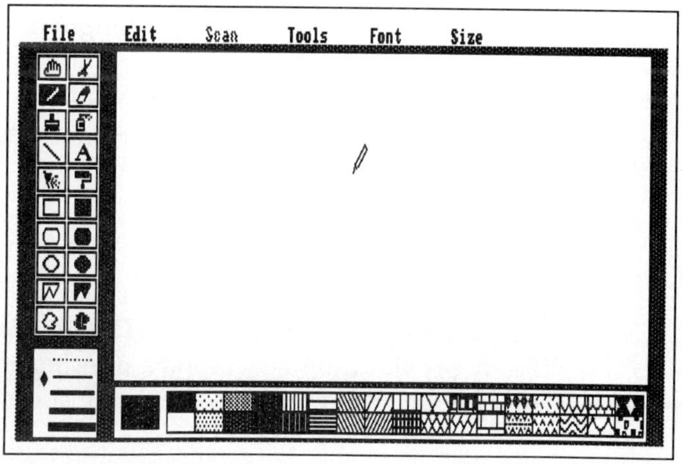

Figure 10-16. *The Sled Image Processor screen drawing menu*

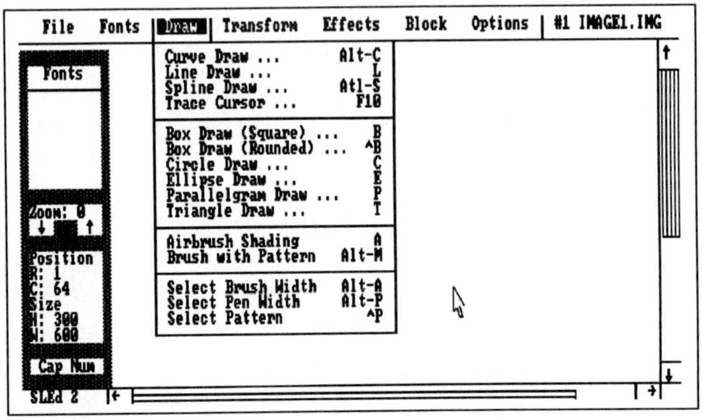

Computer-Aided-Design Programs

CAD programs range from those available for about $100, adequate for relatively simple two-dimensional applications, to such astronomically expensive advanced programs as those used by designers of automobiles and airplanes. The simplest ones produce only two-dimensional images, such as architectural floor plans or the elevations of buildings, machinery, and the like. For illustrations that must display depth data, you need to use programs that specialize in three-dimensional artwork.

Two-Dimensional CAD Programs

One fairly easy-to-use two-dimensional CAD program is AutoSketch from AutoDesk, Inc. It provides ample graphics drawing aids for the average two-dimensional presentation. The degree of sophistication you achieve with the program depends on the amount of time you take to practice. Figure 10-17 is one of the sample files included with the program, showing what AutoSketch is capable of producing. Files produced by this program are vector graphics that convert to .PIC or .GEM file formats.

EnerGraphics from EnerTronics, Inc., includes a two-dimensional and limited three-dimensional CAD option. Figure 10-18 is one of the sample two-dimensional drawings included with the program. Files produced with EnerGraphics can be saved in several different formats, including the .IMG format, which can be imported into Publish It! without conversion.

Among the more sophisticated two-dimensional CAD programs is CADD Level3 from Generic Software, Inc. Figure 10-19 shows the floor plan for a house that is included among the program's sample files. It appears here as it does on the screen, with text greeked as dots. Files produced using CADD Level3 are saved with a .DWG extension and must be converted in order to be compatible with Publish It!.

Figure 10-17. *A two-dimensional drawing made using AutoSketch*

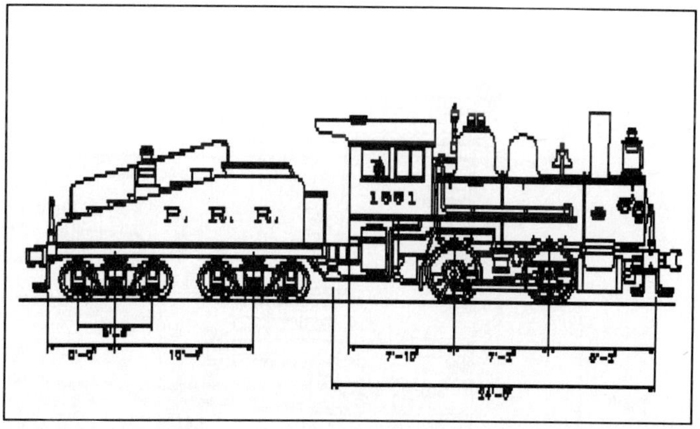

Figure 10-18. *A two-dimensional drawing made using EnerGraphics*

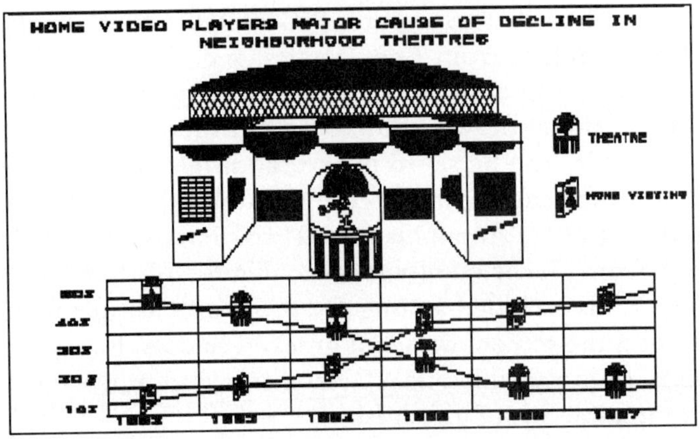

Figure 10-19. *A two-dimensional drawing made using CADD Level3*

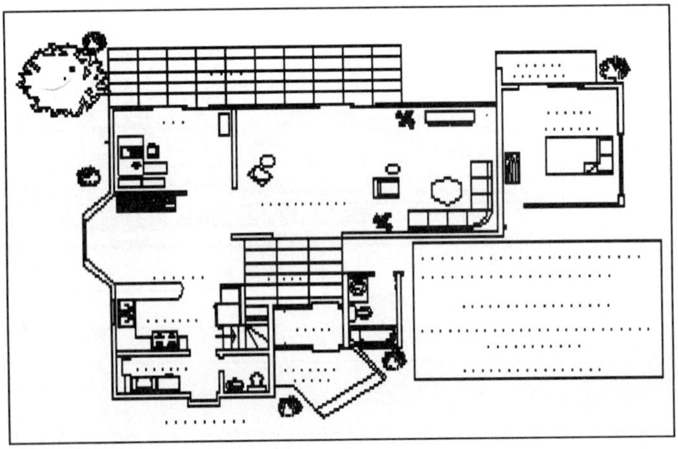

Three-Dimensional CAD Programs

Figures 10-20 through 10-28 illustrate the basic principle on which most of the three-dimensional CAD programs operate. For these examples, 3D Drafting from Generic Software, Inc., was used. First the simple line in Figure 10-20 was drawn in just a few minutes, using the straight line and the 2-point arc options. Next a Surface of Revolution command was combined with the vertical (Y) axis—this is the axis around which the drawing will revolve. All the program needed to know in addition were the degrees of revolution (360) and the number of segments (10). The program did the rest, drawing the three-dimensional object shown in Figure 10-21.

Another command was used to straighten out the drawing, as shown in Figure 10-22. The hidden lines, the features that an observer would not see in a normal opaque object, were removed, resulting in Figure 10-23. To get the flat two-dimensional representation shown in Figure 10-24, the View Flat command was entered. Figures 10-25, 10-26, and 10-27 represent the results of different view and perspective commands, and in Figure 10-28 the hidden lines were removed once more.

Figure 10-20. *A single line that produces a three-dimensional drawing using 3D Drafting*

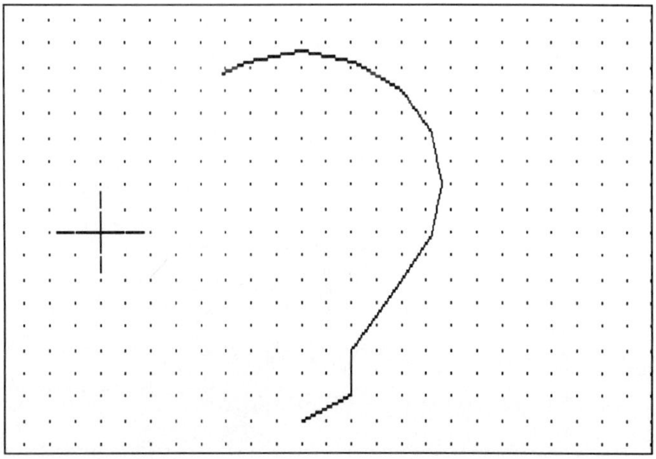

Figure 10-21. *The three-dimensional drawing, original view*

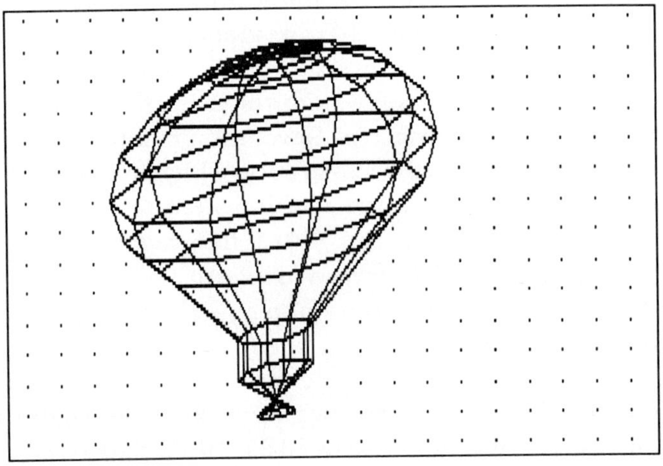

Figure 10-22. *The three-dimensional drawing, straightened*

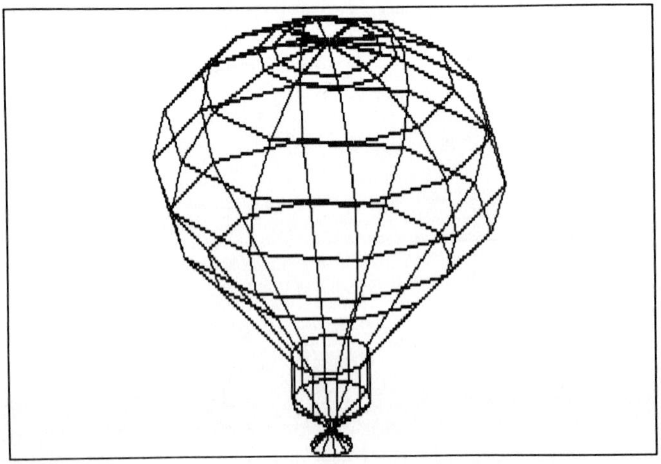

Figure 10-23. *The three-dimensional drawing with hidden lines removed*

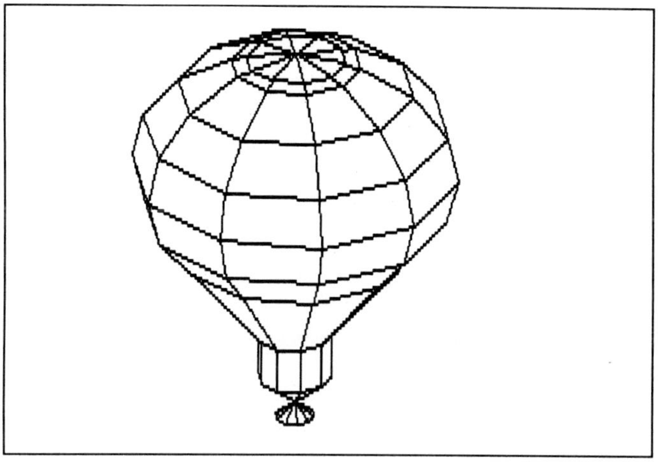

Figure 10-24. *The three-dimensional drawing in a flat view*

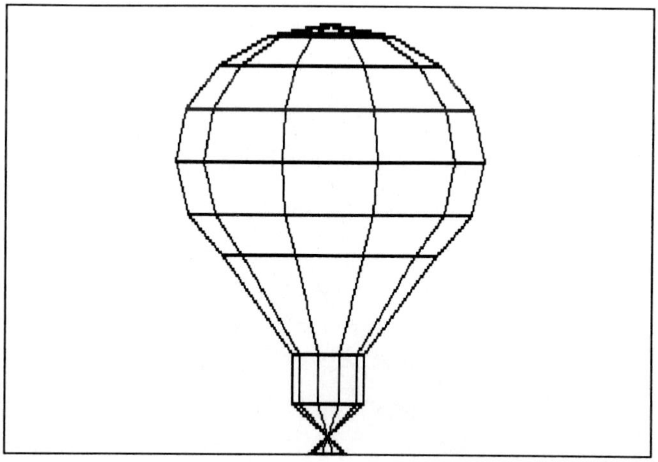

Figure 10-25. *The three-dimensional drawing viewed from above*

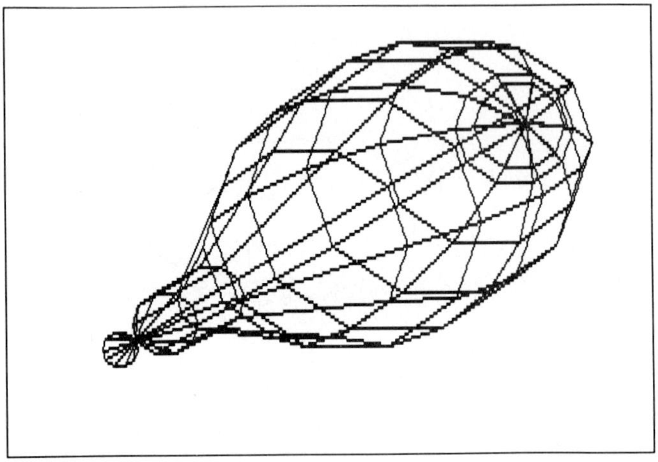

Figure 10-26. *The three-dimensional drawing from a different view*

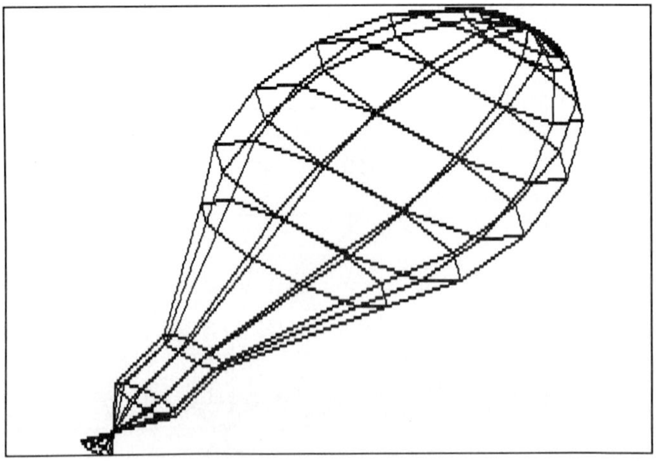

Figure 10-27. *The three-dimensional drawing from yet another viewpoint*

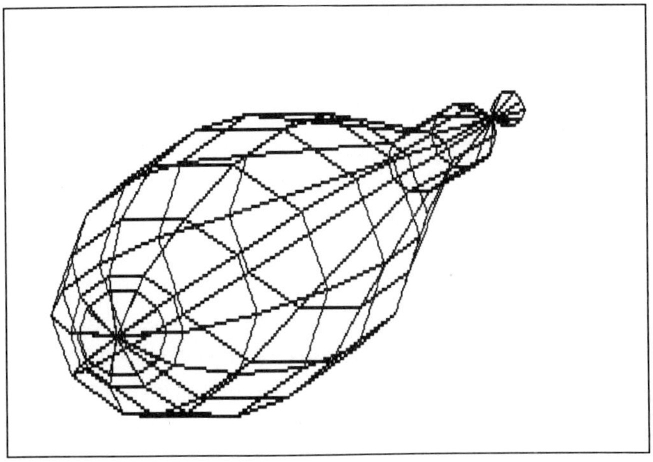

Figure 10-28. *The three-dimensional drawing with hidden lines removed*

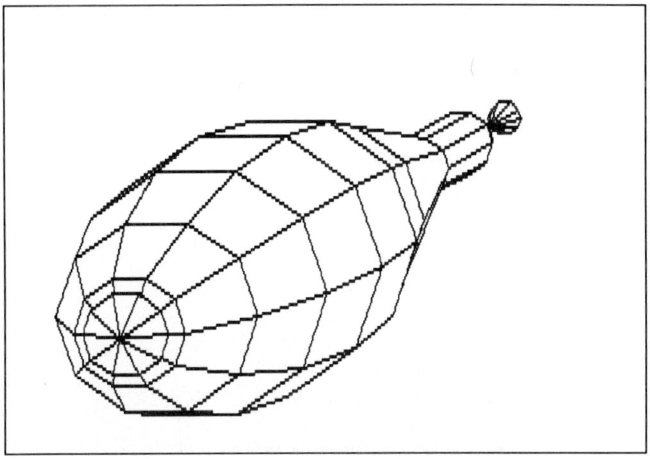

All of this was the result of drawing a single line and then using the program to do the rest. The important advantages of using three-dimensional CAD programs are obvious: The programs can produce the correct perspective from any vantage point, they can rotate the three-dimensional subject to present views from different angles, and they can display or hide the details located on the back side of the three-dimensional object.

Figure 10-29 shows four different views of a three-dimensional metal part. A single drawing was made using the EnerGraphics Draw option. As different commands are entered with reference to the different axes, the program redraws the image in a new perspective with no additional effort on your part.

Design CAD 3-D from American Small Business Computers, Inc., is another program designed to generate both two- and three-dimensional drawings. Figure 10-30 shows a screen that displays the main view of two gears in the center of the work area. To the left are three smaller views from three different points of view. In the bottom right of the work area is the 3-D cursor representing the X (horizontal), the Y (vertical), and the Z (depth) axes. Figure 10-31 is the final drawing of the gears that was sent to the printer.

Figure 10-29. *A three-dimensional drawing made using EnerGraphics*

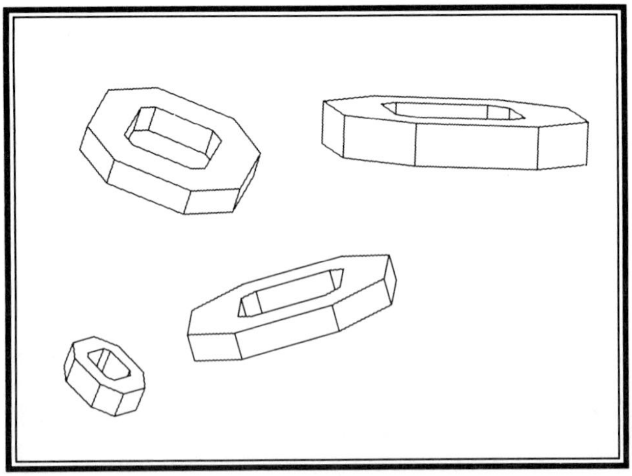

Figure 10-30. *The screen display from Design CAD 3-D*

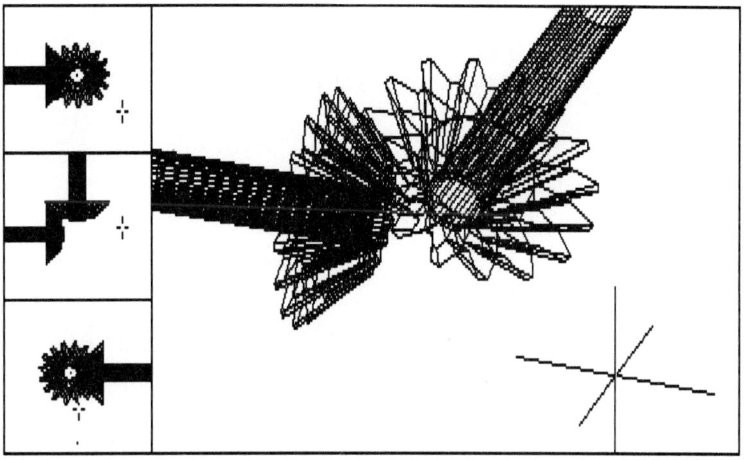

Figure 10-31. *The final drawing of the gears printed by the printer*

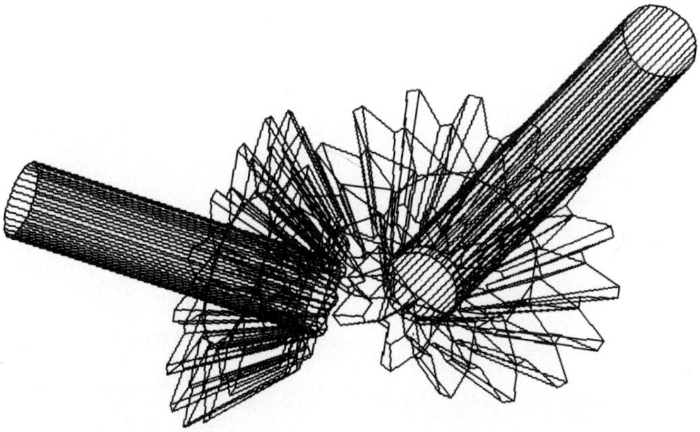

The graphics programs mentioned in this chapter represent only a tiny portion of what is available. Once you know exactly what it is you want to accomplish, examine as many of the graphics programs as possible, including the three GEM programs, GEM Paint, GEM Draw, and GEM Graph, and then select the one that does the best job for you.

11

Special Tricks and Techniques

As you spend more time with Publish It!, you will become aware of certain idiosyncracies, some good and some not so good. This chapter describes some of the less obvious features and functions that have surfaced during our work with Publish It!.

Text Versus Graphics

Publish It! makes very firm distinctions between frames that hold text and those that hold graphics. All text, whether it is imported from word processing programs or text editor files or is typed directly into a frame using the <TEXT> mode, can be manipulated only in terms of the font styles and sizes available with Publish It! or Publish It Lite!. Unlike graphics, text cannot be squeezed or stretched by changing the size and shape of the frame. If the size of the frame is reduced, the text that can no longer fit into the smaller frame is simply stored and made available later to be poured into a new frame. The availability of additional text is indicated by a dashed bottom border on the frame.

Text Frames

How a change in frame size affects text depends on whether the frame is enlarged or reduced horizontally, vertically, or diagonally. Figures 11-1 through 11-5 demonstrate the effects of manipulating the size of a frame containing text.

Figure 11-1. *A portion of text imported into a frame*

Lotus 1-2-3, like most other popular applications programs, was not designed with the idea of using a mouse. On the other hand, there are a number of reasons why using a mouse could produce some advantages in terms of operating convenience. In order to make that possible, what is needed is a mouse that includes software that can be used to write programs that then control the results produced by mouse manipulation.

For 1-2-3 users, a mouse can minimize the number of key strokes and the often hard-to-remember key-stroke combinations that are required in order to produce a given result. For instance, one click of the mouse button can take the place of

CD\123 ENTER 123 ENTER / F R

to move to the \123 directory and then to access 1-2-3, activate the main menu and select **F**ile **R**etrieve from it, producing the display of available files. Alternately, it is possible to activate most or all of 1-2-3's special key combinations and standard macros as well as any number of macros that you might have created yourself, by displaying the list of available macros on a pop-up menu and clicking the mouse button on the desired one.

Figs.1A and 1B represent the source code for a program that is designed as an example or template for programs to be used with Lotus 1-2-3, and it can easily be modified to fit any individual requirements or to be used with Symphony instead.

Figure 11-2. *The frame squeezed to half its previous width*

Lotus 1-2-3, like most other popular
applications programs, was not
designed with the idea of using a
mouse. On the other hand, there are
a number of reasons why using a
mouse could produce some advan-
tages in terms of operating con-
venience. In order to make that
possible, what is needed is a mouse
that includes software that can be
used to write programs that then
control the results produced by
mouse manipulation.

For 1-2-3 users, a mouse can minim-
ize the number of key strokes and
the often hard-to-remember key-
stroke combinations that are
required in order to produce a given
result. For instance, one click of the
mouse button can take the place of

CD\123 ENTER 123 ENTER / F R

to move to the \123 directory and
then to access 1-2-3, activate the
main menu and select **F**ile **R**etrieve
from it, producing the display of
available files. Alternately, it is pos-
sible to activate most or all of 1-2-3's
special key combinations and stan-

In Figure 11-1 a portion of an article is poured into a frame of arbitrary proportions. The text is justified (by default), and hyphenation is provided automatically by the program. In Figure 11-2 the frame is squeezed horizontally to approximately half its original width. Notice that the text to the right was not cut off but rather wrapped around to the next line. Thus, only text at the bottom of the frame was lost from the frame and stored. If the frame is now extended vertically, the missing text will flow back into it. If the text

Figure 11-3. *The frame changed to square proportions*

Lotus 1-2-3, like most other popular applications programs, was not designed with the idea of using a mouse. On the other hand, there are a number of reasons why using a mouse could produce some advantages in terms of operating convenience. In order to make that possible, what is needed is a mouse that includes software that can be used to write programs that then control the results produced by mouse manipulation.

For 1-2-3 users, a mouse can minimize the number of key strokes and the often hard-to-remember key-stroke combinations that are required in order to produce a given result. For instance, one click of the mouse button can take the place of

CD\123 ENTER 123 ENTER / F R

to move to the \123 directory and then to access 1-2-3, activate the main menu and select **F**ile **R**etrieve from it,

was imported from a word processing program, a new frame can be drawn and the remaining text poured into it.

Figure 11-4. *The frame reduced in size*

Lotus 1-2-3, like most other popular applications programs, was not designed with the idea of using a mouse. On the other hand, there are a number of reasons why using a mouse could produce some advantages in terms of operating convenience. In order to make that possible, what is needed is a mouse that includes software that can be used to write programs that then control the results produced by mouse manipulation.

For 1-2-3 users, a mouse can minimize the number of key strokes and the often hard-to-remember key-stroke combinations that are required in order to

Figure 11-5. *The frame enlarged*

Lotus 1-2-3, like most other popular applications programs, was not designed with the idea of using a mouse. On the other hand, there are a number of reasons why using a mouse could produce some advantages in terms of operating convenience. In order to make that possible, what is needed is a mouse that includes software that can be used to write programs that then control the results produced by mouse manipulation.

For 1-2-3 users, a mouse can minimize the number of key strokes and the often hard-to-remember key-stroke combinations that are required in order to produce a given result. For instance, one click of the mouse button can take the place of

CD\123 ENTER 123 ENTER / F R

to move to the \123 directory and then to access 1-2-3, activate the main menu and select **F**ile **R**etrieve from it, producing the display of available files. Alternately, it is possible to activate most or all of 1-2-3's special key combinations and standard macros as well as any number of macros that you might have created yourself, by displaying the list of available macros on a pop-up menu and clicking the mouse button on the desired one.

Figs.1A and 1B represent the source code for a program that is designed as an example or template for programs to be used with Lotus 1-2-3, and it can easily be modified to fit any individual requirements or to be used with Symphony instead.

The first line:

BEGIN LeftB, MidB, RightB

uses the reserved word BEGIN to start the program. The next three words LeftB, MidB, RightB are variables or labels that are used to identify subsequent sections in the program. Any other identifying label names could just as well have been used. Here these variables represent the three mouse buttons.

Next there is a line that starts with **LeftB:** followed by the reserved word **MENU** and some information in quotation marks and finally three sets of digits. The LeftB is the label that causes the

In Figure 11-3 the frame is squeezed from the bottom up while the original width is retained. The lines in the upper portion of the frame are again restored to their original length, but the text at the bottom is simply eliminated and stored for later use. In Figure 11-4 the frame is squeezed diagonally from the lower-right corner toward the upper-left corner, reducing width and length simultaneously. Again, all new hyphenation is produced by the program, and the front portion of the text is retained in the new format while the bottom portion simply disappears.

In Figure 11-5 the width of the original frame is extended to fit nearly an entire page. Suddenly the frame now includes not only the text that was contained in the original frame, but also additional text that was part of the original word processor file.

Graphics Frames

Frames containing graphics behave differently from those containing text. In the <GRAPHICS> mode, when the size of a frame is changed, the entire image is retained in different proportions. No part of a graphic image can ever be lost by manipulating the frame size or proportion. The only way to eliminate a portion of a graphic image is by using the <Crop picture> option from the Graphics menu, available only when the frame that contains the to-be-cropped picture has been selected. Figures 11-6 through 11-11 use the same graphic image but show different effects by manipulating the frame and using the Graphics menu options.

In Figure 11-6 the graphic image, which is included with Publish It! under the filename SKYLINE.IMG, is depicted in approximately its original proportions. Figure 11-7 is the same image in changed proportions that result from squeezing the frame horizontally to approximately half its original width.

In Figure 11-8 the frame is stretched horizontally to about one and one half times its original width; all the buildings end up short and fat. In Figure 11-9 the frame is first returned to its original proportion, and then the <Crop picture> option is used to crop the buildings on the left side of the original picture. The uncropped portion automatically fills the entire frame, eliminating the cropped portion altogether.

Figure 11-6. *The original skyline image*

Figure 11-7. *The image squeezed horizontally*

There are two ways in which the resulting picture can be returned to its original proportions. In Figure 11-10 the <Scale picture> option from the Graphics menu is invoked, and in the resulting dialog box the <Preserve> aspect ratio option is selected. The image returns to its original proportions inside the wider frame. In Figure 11-11 a similar result is achieved by simply narrowing the frame.

Figure 11-8. *The image stretched horizontally*

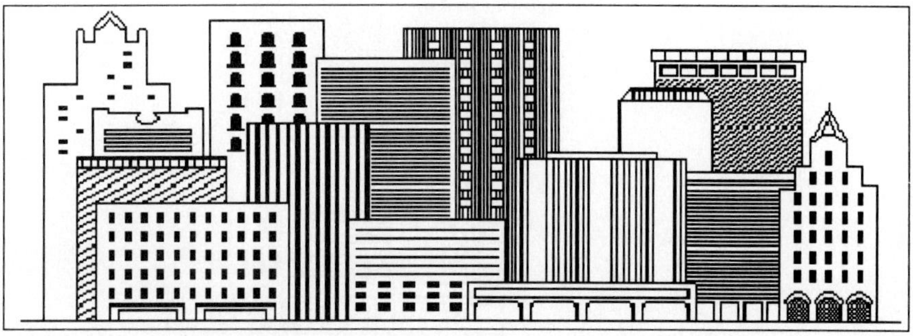

Figure 11-9. *A portion of the image cropped from the original*

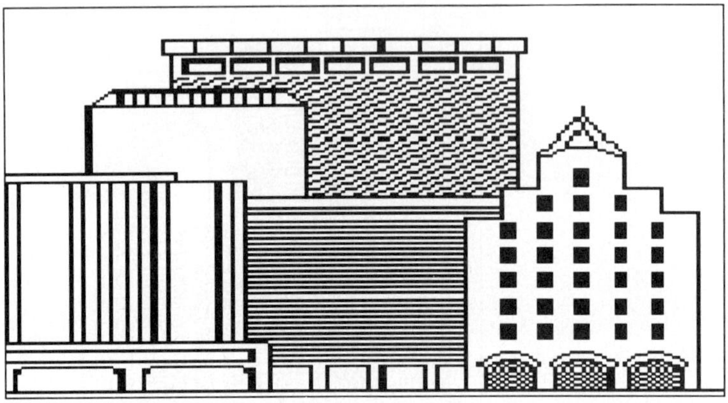

In several rather cumbersome ways, text can be translated into a graphic format and then manipulated as a graphic. More details on this topic are given later in this chapter.

Figure 11-10. *The portion restored to its correct proportions*

Figure 11-11. *The image proportion controlled by resizing the frame*

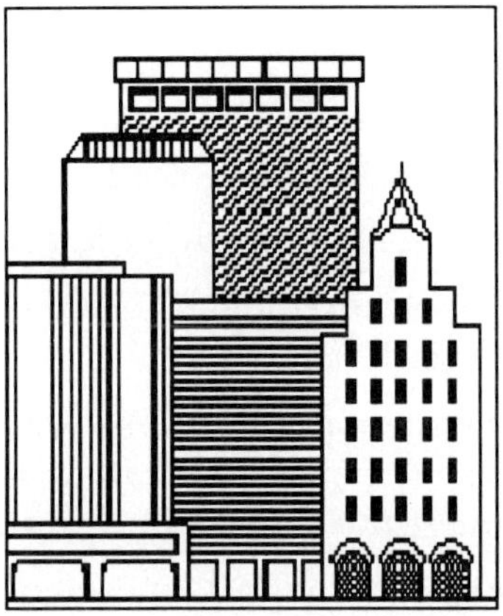

Combining Documents

Sometimes you'll want to combine into one file several Publish It! documents created earlier and originally saved under individual filenames with the usual .DTP extension. With Publish It! version 2.0 there is a simple means of doing this. Follow these steps:

1. Use the <Open> option in the File menu to retrieve the first of the documents to be combined.
2. Click on a frame containing text.
3. Click on <Export text> in the File menu.
4. In the Item Selector box a filename similar to the one that was exported is displayed with an .ASC extension. You can change the filename to anything you want, but retain the .ASC extension. Click on <OK>.
5. Repeat steps 1 through 4 for each of the .DTP files that you want to combine.

You now have several files with .ASC extensions that contain the text (not the graphics and not the font styles and sizes) from the documents you want to combine.

6. Select <New> from the File menu and click on whatever options you want to use in the dialog boxes.
7. Create a frame on the empty screen and select it.
8. Select <Import text> in the File menu and in the resulting dialog box click on <ASCII> and <OK>.
9. All files with an .ASC extension, including the ones you have just created, are displayed in the Item Selector box. Click on one and on <OK>. The text is poured into your frame(s).
10. Repeat steps 7 through 9 for each of the documents to be combined. Save the new combined document under a new .DTP filename.

You will now have to again import any graphics you want to use, and you may want to edit text and format the files to produce an acceptable final result.

If you are using an earlier version of Publish It!, then the <Export text> feature is not available. Combining documents is still possible, but somewhat more arduous. The difficulty is that you cannot open more than one document at a time. There is another way. It's not perfect, but it's sometimes very useful:

1. Select <Import text> from the File menu and in the resulting dialog box highlight <Word Writer> and click on <OK>.
2. In the Item Selector box click on the Directory line and type .DTP for the file extension. Click on <OK>. After a pause (the length of the pause depends on the length of the file) the name of the file will appear in the Library window.
3. In the <FRAME> mode create the frames necessary to hold the contents of the file.
4. Click on the name in the Library window. The contents of the file are poured into the frames. You are going to find that there are some extraneous characters at the beginning and possibly interspersed with the text. You can easily eliminate those.

5. Click on the right arrow in the <PAGE> icon and select <Add a page> from the resulting dialog box.
6. With the new blank page displayed, click on <Import text> in the File menu and select the next document to be added to the first.

You can repeat this procedure as often as you like. You can edit the resulting text, add text in the <TEXT> mode to bridge the individual items, and when you're satisfied with the result, use the <Save as> option from the File menu and give the file a new name.

Experiment with the options available in the dialog box displayed when you click on <Import text> to determine which of the available word processor formats does the best job with importing .DTP files.

If the imported text files include graphic images, they are likely to show up as a bunch of meaningless ASCII codes. Simply delete the contents of those frames before attempting to import the .DTP file. Then import the graphics file that was used in creating the original document and place it into a new frame. Any graphic image that was saved as a .DTP file cannot be imported as either text or graphics. With <Import text> the file becomes gibberish, and with <Import picture> nothing happens at all, regardless of the file format selected from the dialog box.

Some file-viewing programs or filters can be used to strip out text from a file. They change a .DTP file into a straight ASCII file that can then be imported into another Publish It! file.

The following alternative method permits copying only selected portions of one file into another file:

1. Access the file from which a portion is to be copied into another. Select the frame containing the portion of material to be copied.
2. In the Edit menu click on <Copy>.
3. In the File menu click on <Open>, and when asked whether to abandon the current document, click on <Yes>.
4. In the Item Selector box, click on the filename representing the document into which you want to copy the material from the other file.

5. With the document displayed on the screen, access the Edit menu and click on <Paste>. The material from the earlier document is copied into the current one in its selected form.
6. Now move the frame to the place in the document where you want to use the copied material.

You can import only one item of a given type at a time. The buffers that retain text, graphics, or frame data are designed to retain only one such item. The <Paste> option can be used more than once to copy the item into different places in the document. If additional material of the same type is to be imported from one file to another, you have to go back to the original file and repeat the procedure.

Remember, files containing text that has been typed directly into Publish It! and frames containing graphics can be copied directly. Frames containing text that has been imported from a word processor are probably best copied by importing the text into the new document directly. Still, portions of text can be copied by moving into the <TEXT> mode, selecting the text with the pointer, and then using <Copy> and <Paste> from the Edit menu.

Eliminating Material from Imported Text

After importing text into Publish It!, you might decide to get rid of a portion of it, such as a paragraph or a block of text. This can be a bit tedious. You can enter the <TEXT> mode, place the text cursor at the head of the text that you want to delete, and then press the DEL key, which will delete the text to the right of the cursor one character at a time. Alternatively, place the text cursor at the end of the block of text to be deleted and press BACKSPACE, deleting the text to the left of the cursor one character at a time. A simpler way is to drag the text pointer across the portion of text and then use the <Cut> option from the Edit menu. This works for any block of text up to the size of the frame.

It may simplify your task to make the text frame the size of the entire page for the purpose of editing and adding or deleting text. The frame can subsequently be returned to its original proportions.

These methods may be a bit laborious. An alternative would be to exit Publish It!, activate your word processing program and edit the file that contains the text in question. Once the text block has been deleted from the file, save the file as before. Activate Publish It! and use <Import text> from the File menu to import the new version of the file with the offending block of text deleted.

The <Delete style> option from the <Paragraph style> selection in the Text menu cannot be used to delete actual text. It deletes paragraph styles (except Body Text), but the text itself remains intact.

Adding Material to a Document

If you want to import new material into an existing document or a document that is currently being worked on, it is sometimes a good idea to add a page to the end of the existing document by either clicking on the right arrow in the <PAGE> icon or by selecting the <Add pages> (<Add a page> in earlier versions) option from the Page menu.

Import the item, be it text or a picture, into a frame prepared for that purpose on the extra page. Then use the <Cut> and <Paste> options from the Edit menu to move the material to where it belongs in the document. This method is less likely to temporarily mess up the original document than when you import the material directly into its final place. It also speeds up the redrawing function of the program if most of the changes are made on a fairly blank page.

To avoid having a blank page printed at the end of the document because the program believes that your document is one page longer than is actually the case, use the <Go to page> option from the Page menu and go to the final page. Then select <Delete pages> and in the resulting dialog box enter the current page number in the <First page number> and <Last page number> boxes to get rid of the extra page that is no longer needed.

Text as Graphics

There are times when it is desirable to create some special types of text that may not be readily available using the <Font/size> option available from Publish It!. For instance, you might need to create an enormous letter or a special logo that uses characters in a unique way. Such special treatments are possible when you create graphics files that actually contain text, although it does require some fairly roundabout routines.

Since it is not possible to create text and save it as a graphics file using Publish It! alone, it is necessary to use an external program. There are several possible routines that you can use to accomplish this purpose. One involves the use of screen-capture programs, which capture whatever is written on the screen and save it as a graphics file. (See Chapter 9, "Using External Files," for more on screen-capture programs.)

Not all screen-capture programs capture text screens. For instance, the GRAB.COM program that is included with the later versions of WordPerfect does an outstanding job with graphics screens, but it cannot capture any text screen, no matter by what means it was produced.

The capture programs included with the HiJaak and InSet software, both from Inset Systems, Inc., do capture text screens, but the final result depends on the manner in which the text screen was created. If you use a color monitor, there may not be sufficient contrast between the text and the background to view the file easily. You may need to change the background color to white and the color of the written text to black to produce a satisfactory result. The InSet program includes many options that may improve the final result.

To produce excellent results with text screens captured in this way, use the HiJaak CONVERT program to convert the file to an ASCII text file with a .TXT extension. Then use the same CONVERT program to change that .TXT file into a graphics .IMG or .PCX file. The result is clean, high-contrast black text on a white background that can be imported into Publish It! with the <Import picture> option.

Instead of using screen-capture programs, you can use one of the many graphics programs, and unless there is a reason to use one specific program because of its peripheral capabilities, it is easier to use a graphics program that produces files in a format acceptable to Publish It!. For instance, PC Paintbrush produces .PCX files, and GEM Paint produces .IMG files. Many other programs, such as Logitech's PaintShow and PaintShowPlus produce files with the .TIF extension, but those programs include a conversion utility to convert .TIF files to .PCX files. AutoSketch from AutoDesk, Inc., CADD Level3 from Generic Software, Inc., and many others produce files in formats that are not necessarily compatible with either Publish It! or any of the file-conversion programs included with HiJaak, InSet, and PaintShow or

PaintShowPlus. In such cases, the programs can still be used, but the text created using their graphics capabilities must be captured with one of the screen-capture programs in a format that can be used by Publish It!.

Inverting and Rotating Images

While Publish It! includes the option of typing white text onto a dark or black background, it does not include a means for you to convert a black on white graphic image into a white on black image. Similarly, while graphic images can be resized and reconfigured in many ways, they cannot be rotated, turned on their side, turned upside down, or reversed into a mirror image.

These options *are* available in most graphics programs. If such features are needed, the image file may have to be converted to a format that is compatible with whatever graphics program you use. For instance, to turn the daytime skyline image in Figure 11-6 into a nighttime image, you have a number of options. If HiJaak or InSet is available, the process is simple: Use the CONVERT program and convert SKYLINE.IMG to SKYLINE.PCX with the <Invert> option set to <On>, and then import the newly created .PCX file into Publish It! to produce the new picture shown in Figure 11-12.

Figure 11-12. *The skyline printed as a night scene*

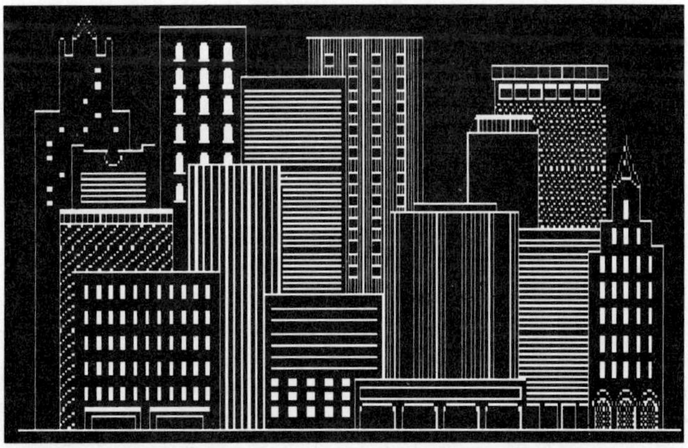

You can achieve the same result by importing the SKYLINE.IMG file into any other graphics program, assuming that a file-conversion program is available to convert it to a format compatible with the program being used, such as .TIF if PaintShow or PaintShowPlus is used. Then use the <Invert> (also often called <Reverse>) option in the graphics program, save the new file, and convert it to a .PCX format.

Templates

Sometimes after you have created a document, you may wish to retain its basic layout to be used again. You can do this by removing all text and graphic items, retaining only the features and format you might want included in future documents. Figure 11-13 is one of the sample documents available with Publish It!. To retain it as a template follow these steps:

1. Click on the <TEXT> mode in the toolbox.

Figure 11-13. *Saving a sample document as a template*

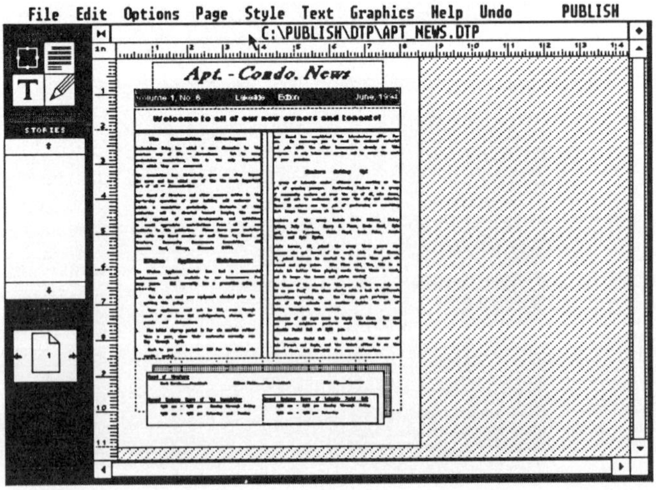

2. Drag the cursor across all text in the frame to be deleted. That text should now be highlighted, as shown in Figure 11-14.
3. Press the (DEL) key or click on <Cut> in the Edit menu. The text disappears.
4. Repeat this for all text to be deleted.
5. If the document includes graphics, they too must be removed. Follow these steps:
   a. Draw a frame over the frame containing the graphic, exactly matching the original frame. The new frame should cover and hide the graphic.
   b. In the Page menu, click on <Send to back>. The graphic reappears.
   c. Click on the graphic to select its frame and to deselect the one you just drew.
   d. In the Edit menu, click on <Cut>. The graphic disappears with its frame, leaving in its place the empty frame you just created.

Figure 11-14. *Highlighting text to be deleted*

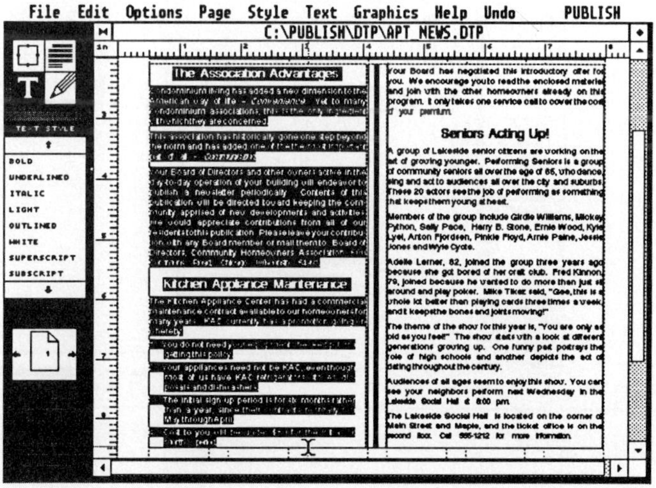

6. When you have removed all extraneous text and graphics in this manner, the basic format remains, as shown in Figure 11-15. Here the boilerplate copy in the bottom frame and volume/issue information in the second frame from the top were retained because the boilerplate copy remains unchanged and the volume number and issue date can easily be changed when the template is used again.
7. In the File menu select <Save as>. Give the template a new name without any extension. Click on <OK>. The new template is saved with a .DTP extension, as shown in Figure 11-16, and can be reactivated at any time. (Do not attempt to save the template using the <Save style sheet> option. It does not work.)

Figure 11-15. *Only the basic format remains visible*

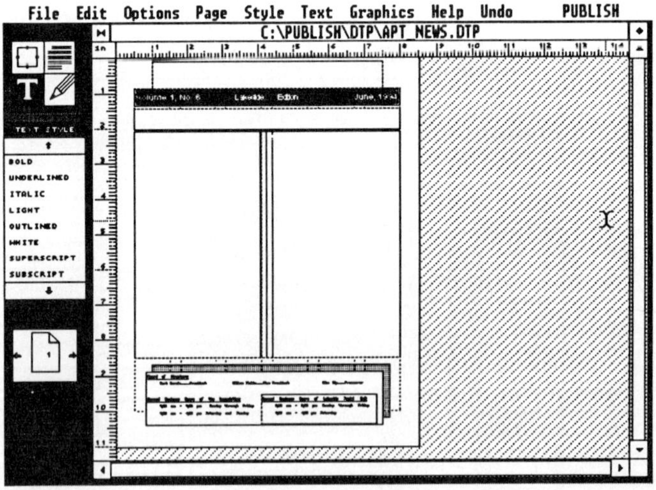

Figure 11-16. *Saving the new template*

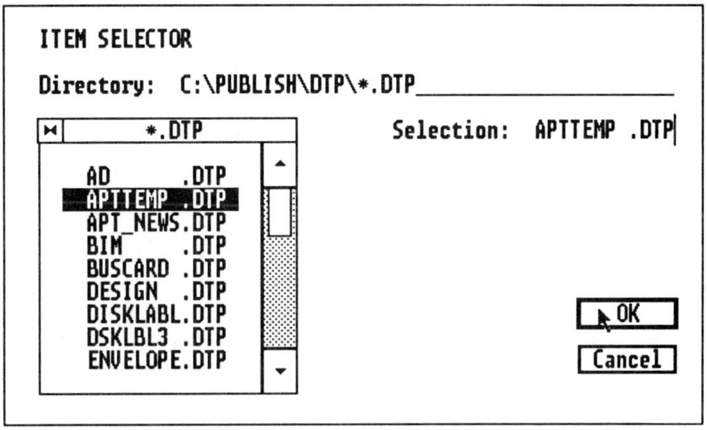

Experimenting with <Frame Tint> and Graphics <Fill Style>

There are many ways to combine the options available with Publish It! version 2.0 (and in many cases the earlier versions) to produce special effects. Figures 11-17 through 11-21 illustrate the wide variety of output that results from the combined uses of different functions.

Follow these steps to achieve the result shown in Figure 11-17:

1. Create a lightning-shaped frame using the <Text runaround> option in the Options menu.
2. Use the <Frame tint> option to add the tint inside that custom frame.
3. Use the <Frame border> option to create the border around the original frame in which the custom frame was created.

Figure 11-17. One result of combining several Publish It! options

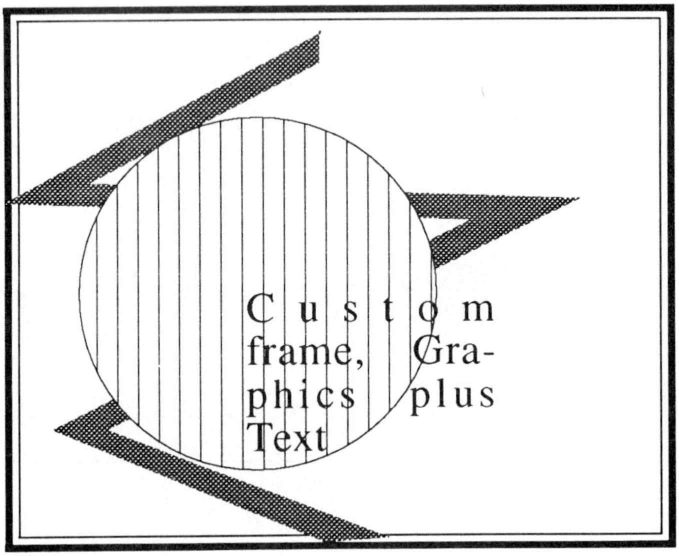

4. Select the <GRAPHICS> mode in the toolbox and the circle tool from the Library window.
5. Draw a circle. Size the resulting graphics frame holding that circle to make the circle the desired size. Move the frame until the circle is in the desired location.
6. Use the <Fill style> option in the Graphics menu and select the desired fill style.
7. Create a new frame in the text area.
8. Using the <TEXT> mode (entered in the toolbox) type the text into the new frame.
9. Using the <PARAGRAPH> mode (selected again from the toolbox) highlight the text.

10. Select <Font/size> from the Style menu and <Dutch> and <16> from the resulting dialog box.
11. Select the <FRAME> mode from the toolbox and then select the frame containing the text.
12. Select <Frame tint> from the Options menu and <Clear> from the resulting dialog box. The results are shown in Figure 11-17.

To get the Mona Lisa shown in Figure 11-18, follow these steps:

1. From the toolbox select the <GRAPHICS> mode and select the rectangle tool from the Library window.
2. Draw four narrow rectangles and move them to create the frame.
3. Select <Fill style> from the Graphics menu and pour the desired fill style into the four frames.
4. Select the <FRAME> mode from the toolbox and draw a new frame to fill the space inside the graphic frame.

Figure 11-18. *A modified Mona Lisa*

5. Select <Import picture> from the File menu, and select .IMG as the style.
6. In the Item Selector box select MONALISA.IMG.
7. Select <Crop picture> from the Graphics menu and crop the image until it fills the frame to your satisfaction. Figure 11-18 shows the results.

You'll create six frames to get the image shown in Figure 11-19:

1. To start with, create first the outer frame, then the next three. Then create the vertical narrow frame.
2. With that narrow frame selected, click on <Send to back> in the Page menu to place this frame behind frame number four.
3. Add a sixth small frame for the tiger's head graphic.
4. Use the <Frame tint> option from the Options menu to add different tints to each of the individual frames.

Figure 11-19. *A six-frame-and-graphic combination*

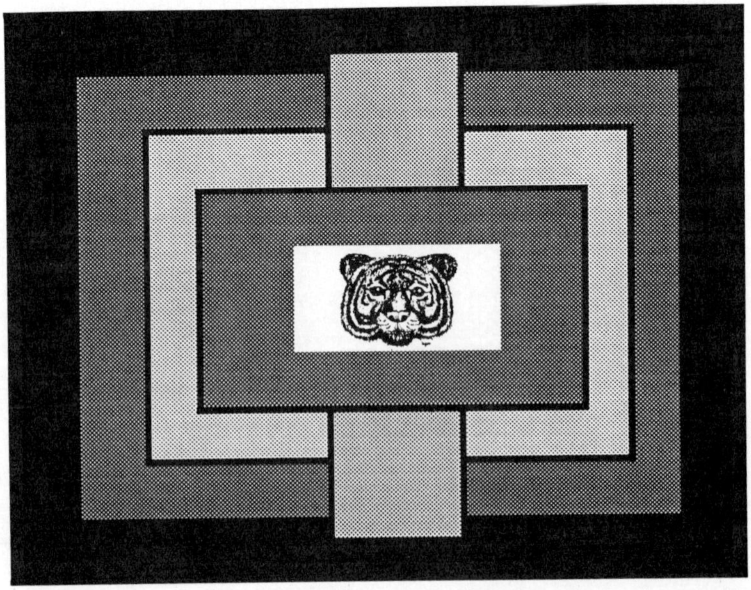

5. Select the small center frame and use <Import picture> from the File menu to import TIGER.IMG into the frame.
6. Use <Scale picture> and <Preserve> to retain the correct proportion for the tiger's head, as shown in the final Figure 11-19.

To create the abstract art shown in Figure 11-20, you use the same group of frames. Add circles and ellipses in the <GRAPHICS> mode, and use the <Fill style> option to place patterns into the circles and ellipses.

Figure 11-21 shows the same group of six frames with yet a different design.

1. Place a large circle behind the group of frames in the <GRAPHICS> mode and use <Fill style> to add the pattern.
2. In the <FRAME> mode create a new frame in the text area.
3. In the <TEXT> mode type the text.

Figure 11-20. *The same group of frames with a different graphic*

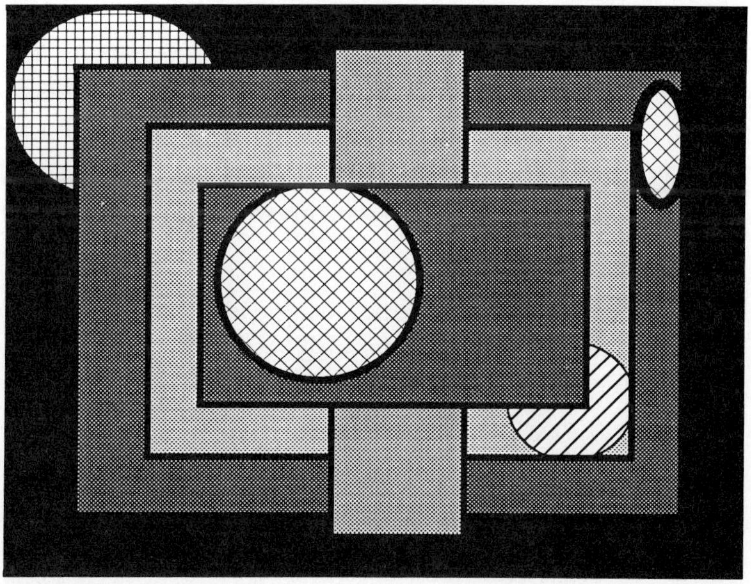

Figure 11-21. *Another variation on the six-frame theme*

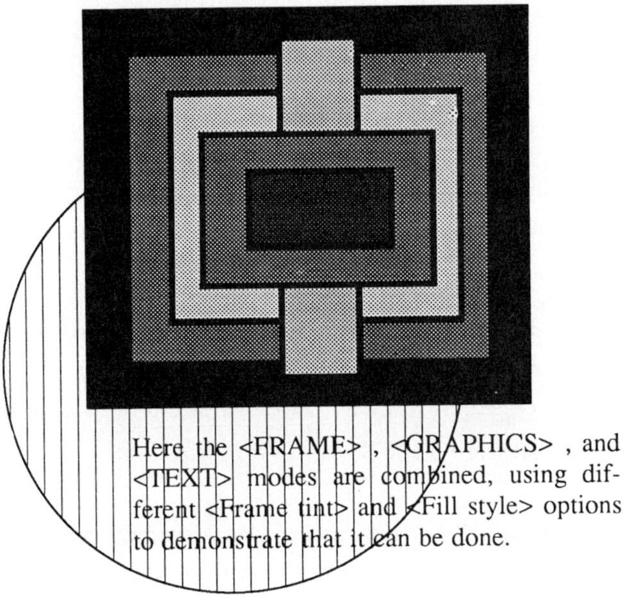

4. In the <PARAGRAPH> mode highlight the text. Access <Font/size> in the Style menu and select <Dutch> and <16>.
5. In the <FRAME> mode select the text frame. Access <Frame tint> and select <Clear> to produce the final product shown in Figure 11-21.

A little time spent experimenting with what your version of Publish It! has to offer will present you with all kinds of possibilities that are not necessarily readily apparent.

IV

Publishing

12

Layout and Design

The layout and design of a document largely depend on the proficiency, taste, and talent of the designer. Nonetheless, there are certain basic guidelines. The considerations involved in the design of a magazine page differ from those of designing the pages of a book. Newsletters, brochures, advertisements, and all kinds of other documents each involve specific constraints that affect the layout and design.

This chapter surveys books, magazines, newsletters, display advertisements, and a range of other commercial documents. Depending on the type of documents you plan to produce with Publish It!, you might want to concentrate on the portions of this chapter that deal with the issues that you are likely to encounter.

Books

In both fiction and nonfiction books you are likely to find a considerable variety of layouts and designs. This section simply provides some suggestions and general guidelines.

Fiction

The average hardcover fiction book page is approximately 6 1/2 x 9 inches. The typefaces used may differ considerably; among the typefaces available with Publish It! and Publish It Lite!, 10-point Dutch is a good choice. In terms of margins, an inch all around is a reasonable starting point. Page numbers may be at the bottom or at the top of the page, and each page usually includes a header identifying the chapter or the book title in a type size that differs from the body text.

Figure 12-1 shows a fairly typical page in a fiction book. The frame represents the physical size of the page and is not printed. To add the book or chapter title in the form of a header, click on the <Headers & footers> option in the Text menu. Figure 12-2 shows the resulting dialog box. If you enter the header and page number given in Figure 12-2, you'll get the results shown in Figure 12-1.

Alternatively, the header copy can be entered into a frame of its own on the master page and can then be copied automatically to all subsequent pages that use that same master page. If the header copy is the title of the book, then the entire book can use the same master page. If it is the title of a chapter, a new master page must be created for each chapter. Save each chapter as a separate file and use the automatic page numbering feature described in Chapter 4, "The Menus."

When preparing a book using Publish It!, design master pages for the pages that contain the body text. Use the <Two pages> option from the Page Format dialog box that is displayed when <New> is selected from the File menu. After that, when laying out the master pages, use the <Two pages> option from the Page menu to see how the facing pages relate to one another.

In addition to laying out text pages, book design requires a plan for title pages, part title pages, chapter title pages, copyright pages (including Library

Figure 12-1. A typical fiction book page

FOOL'S PARADISE 213

The fellow sitting on the bench looked to be in his later twenties. He wore jeans and a sport shirt open at the neck. His hair was longish and not too clean, but not exactly repulsive either. On the bench next to him lay a satchel, apparently containing whatever luggage he had decided he needed for the trip.

"Hi, there, fellow," Dick said.

"You talkin' to me?"

"Seems that way. I don't see anyone else around."

"Okay..."

"I understand you're looking for a ride."

"That's right."

"I'm going to Atlanta. That help you any?"

"Sure does. When're you plannin' on goin'?"

"Right now. If that's okay. Follow me."

"Thanks. I appreciate that."

"You're welcome. By the way, my name is Dick Brown."

"Homer Attenbury."

They shook hands and then Dick led the way to his airplane which was parked at the far end of the ramp.

"Here we are. You climb in and put your seatbelt on while I check the oil. Here," he reached for the fellow's satchel, "might as well put that in the back."

"Uh uh." Homer held onto it as if it contained something of irreplaceable value.

"Suit yourself."

While Dick checked the oil and performed the usual preflight, Homer strapped himself into the right seat and, once settled in, placed the satchel on his lap and put both arms around it.

With the preflight done, Dick strapped himself into the left seat, made sure that both doors were firmly closed, and then started the engine.

"You ever been in a little airplane before?" he asked.

"Uh uh, no."

"Relax. It'll be a nice flight." He turned on the radio and switched to ground control. "Ground, Cessna Triple Three Delta Bravo ready to taxi, VFR Atlanta."

"Three Delta Bravo, cleared to Runway Two Niner, wind two eight zero degrees at seven, altimeter two niner niner one."

Dick released the brakes and turned into the taxiway. He performed

Figure 12-2. *Information in this Headers and Footers dialog box gives the results in Figure 12-1*

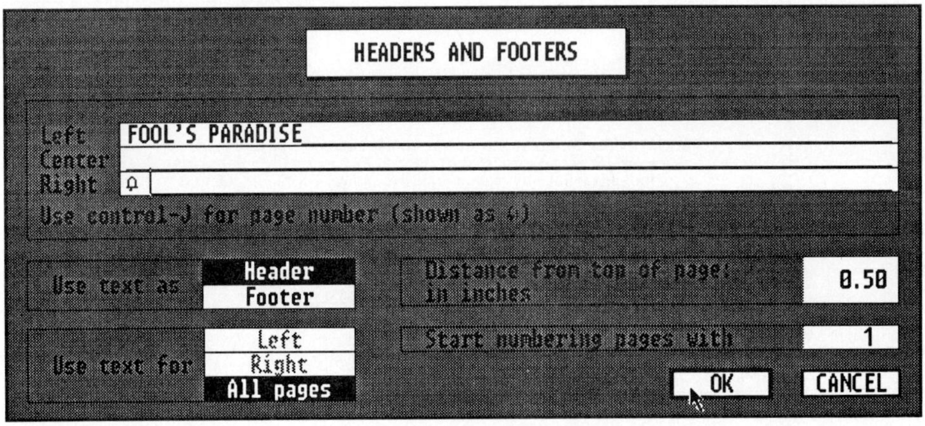

of Congress and ISBN, or International Standard Book Number, information), dedications, lists of other books by the author, acknowledgments, and tables of contents. Each of these has its unique characteristics and must be planned with the rest of the book pages. Because printers work with forms (called *signatures*) of a fixed number of pages, inserting pages after the fact is a very difficult procedure.

Usually the very first page of the book displays only the title. Turning that page you are likely to find a list of other books written by the author.

The next page is probably the actual title page with the title, the name of the author, and the name of the publisher. Figure 12-3 is an example of such a page. The text on this page was created with an external word processing program and imported into Publish It!. The <Paragraph style> options were then used to center each line and determine the font style and size. Turning that page you might find the copyright page, and the page facing that might contain a dedication.

Finally, there is the first chapter page that is identical to all subsequent pages that start a new chapter. Figure 12-4 shows such a page. These chapter pages do not necessarily need to display a page number, as long as the text pages that follow are numbered as if the chapter page had its own page

Figure 12-3. *The main title page of a fiction book*

FOOL'S PARADISE

A NOVEL BY

JOHN SMITH

ABC PUBLISHERS, LTD.

New York

Figure 12-4. *The first page for each chapter of a fiction book*

Chapter

23

The pilot's name was Dick Brown. His single-engine airplane was parked on one of the general aviation airports in the Miami area and he was in the flight service station checking the prevailing conditions for a VFR flight to Atlanta. The forecast called for ample ceiling and visibility throughout most of the day, with possible thunderstorms and rain showers during the late afternoon and early evening. He wrote out his VFR flight plan and handed it to the specialist on duty.

"Okay, call us when you're off," the specialist said.

"Will do."

"Oh, by the way, there's some fellow who's been hanging around looking for a ride up in that direction. Don't know who he is. Thought I'd mention it in case you like company."

"Fine with me. I don't care. Where is he?"

The flight service specialist looked out of the window toward the ramp outside. "There, that's him." He pointed. "Sitting on that bench over there."

"Okay. If he decides to come along, you better change the flight plan from one to two persons on board."

"Sure thing. Have a good flight."

"Thanks. See you."

number. You can make separate first-pages files. Although chapters generally begin on the right page, if your design also allows for left-hand chapter openers, design one separate master page each for left and right pages, as you won't know on which pages chapters will begin. Use the appropriate master page for each chapter heading and follow that page with the master pages for the body text.

This book design outline is not intended to represent hard and fast rules. It is a basic template of the kind of page designs most often associated with a fiction book. There can be many variations, and you are certainly encouraged to use your own taste and imagination.

Nonfiction

Nonfiction books include many diverse categories. Popular nonfiction, such as biography and popular history, is often designed with the same considerations as works of fiction. The primary difference is the use of photographs or illustrations, which either can appear throughout the book or can be grouped and printed on a different type of paper. Another difference is the inclusion of an index and sometimes a bibliography, both at the end of the book.

Nonfiction books on technical subjects are a different matter. Readers of such books don't usually start at page 1 and continue to the end. They pick and choose, looking for the specific subjects that are of interest. Books of that type use many different styles and designs. The book that you are holding in your hand is an example. What follows is just one idea for an instructional book.

Two facing pages are shown in Figures 12-5 and 12-6. The actual printed pages are 5 1/2 x 8 1/2 inches and might be put together with spiral or regular binding. The top of the page identifies the subject discussed on the page and possibly some type of specific identification represented by the large "XX" and "YY", for which separate frames with individual borders were created. The one line across the top is a separate frame with a light tint but no border.

The wide column contains text in 10-point Dutch and an illustration. The frame for this text column continues underneath the picture to the bottom of the page. A separate frame creating white space was placed on top of the fame and another separate frame was placed on the white space to hold the picture. If you encounter problems with one frame obscuring something that

Figure 12-5. *An even-numbered nonfiction book page*

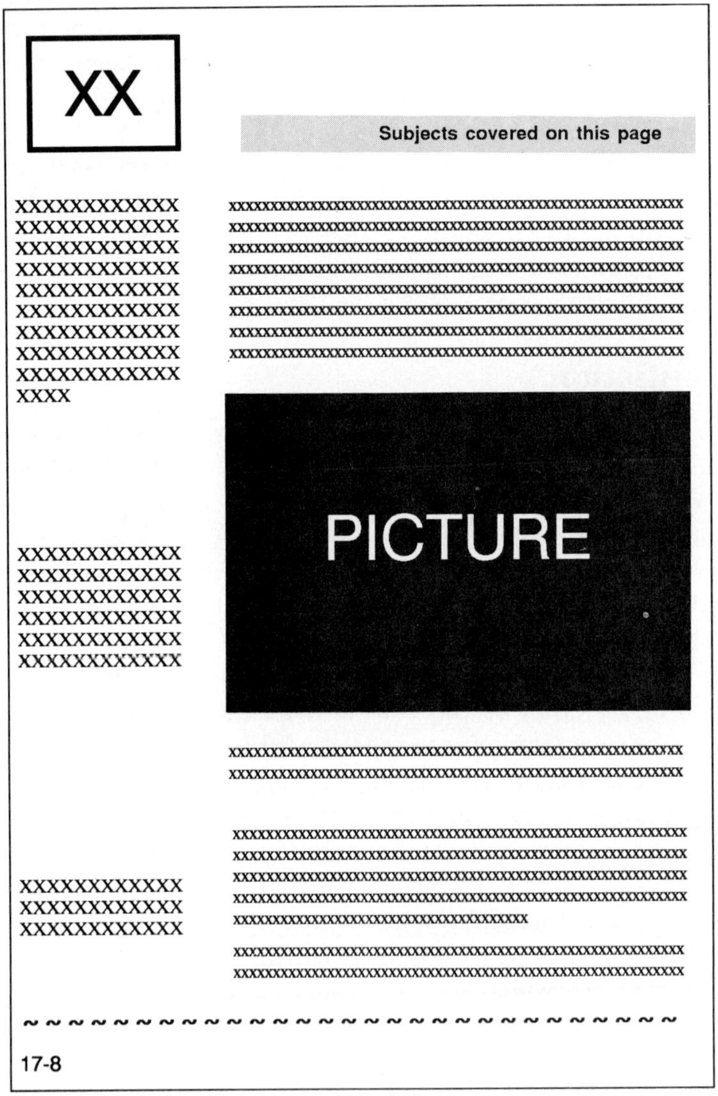

should be seen, use the <Clear> option from the Frame Tint dialog box in the Options menu.

Figure 12-6. *An odd-numbered nonfiction book page*

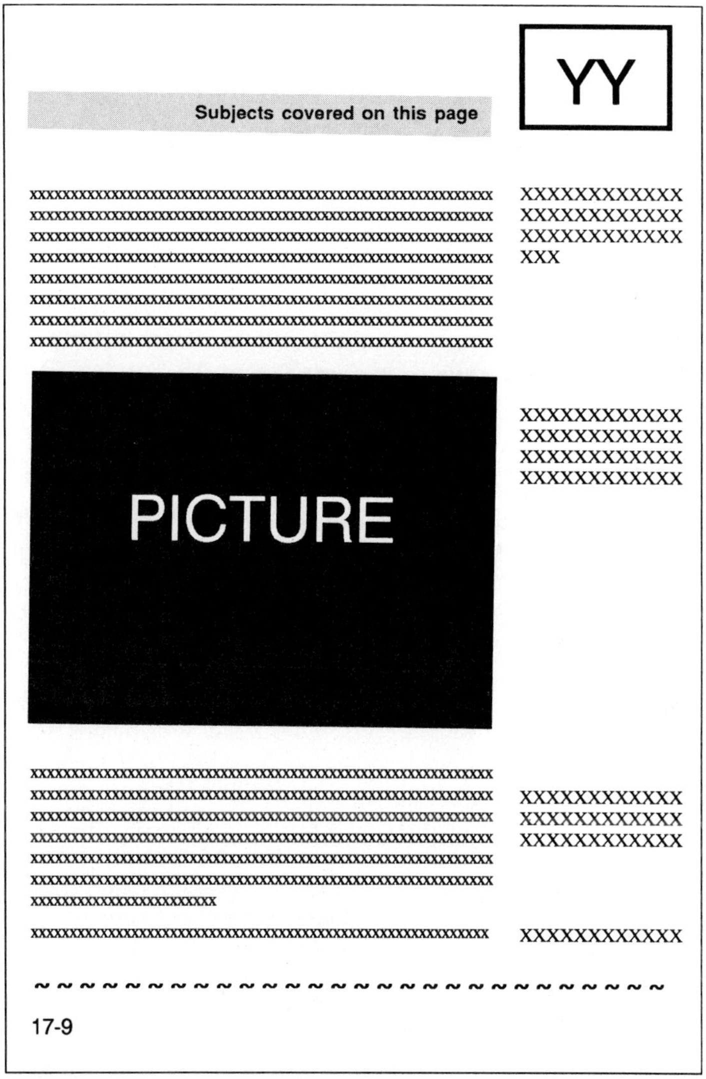

The narrow column, printed in 10-point Swiss and in all capital letters, contains key phrases that relate to the text and/or picture, drawing attention to what is being described. If the text contained in this column consists of individual blocks, use separate frames for each of the text blocks.

Many books that expect the reader to actually follow through with some actions that are described and illustrated use this two-column design. It gives the reader the option of either actually reading the full detailed text or just skimming the key phrases in the narrow column. The text in the narrow column may also be printed in a different color, setting it off from the rest.

Tables

In books dealing with technical subjects, it is often necessary to include tables. The data for such tables can be prepared several ways. For a short table with just a few items, you might want to simply type the material into the columns that you have prepared. Figure 12-7 shows a short table produced in this manner.

WordPerfect 5.1 includes a Tables option in the Columns/Tables ((ALT)-(F7)) function. It can create tables with up to 32 columns and up to 32,765 rows. If you attempt to import a file containing such a table into Publish It!, only the text, quite unformatted, is imported, but the table format is disregarded.

Figure 12-7. *The table typed in the <TEXT> mode in Publish It!*

Program	Manufacturer	Type
=============	=============	============
dBASE II, III+, IV	Ashton-Tate	Database
Lotus 1-2-3	Lotus Development Corporation	Spreadsheet
Symphony	Lotus Development Corporation	Spreadsheet/Database
VP Graphics	Paperback Software International	Graphics
VP Expert	Paperback Software International	Expert System Shell
WordPerfect 4.2, 5.0, 5.1	WordPerfect Corporation	Word Processor
Exact	Technical Support Software, Inc.	Scientific Symbol Utility
HiJaak	InSet Systems, Inc.	Screen Capture Utility
Publish It!	Timeworks, Inc.	Desktop Publishing Program
Publish It Lite!	Timeworks, Inc.	Desktop Publishing Program

Tables usually contain a great deal of material, so it would be tedious to type large amounts of data. You would probably want to prepare such lists using your word processor or text editor. You will face some problems, 1
however. Publish It! ignores extra spaces or tabs that you might have used to produce the desired spacing. Publish It! also ignores formatting commands available with some of the better word processing programs—functions that are used to produce parallel columns. One way to solve these problems is to prepare separate text files, each containing the data for just one column. In that way you can import each file separately into the appropriate frame.

Figure 12-8 is a file originally produced by a word processing program. It is part of an alphabetical list of the aviation navigation aids known as VORs. (The STATION column is the station name, the ID column is the two-letter state ID, FIX is the three-letter station identification, FRQ is the radio frequency, LAT is the latitude, LONG is the longitude, VAR is the magnetic variation, and ELEV is the elevation in feet above sea level.)

To import the file into Publish It!, each column is saved as a separate file. Publish It! is prepared to receive the text using the <Set column guides> option from the Options menu to produce nine columns. Then the first frame is created, covering the left two columns. After that each column is turned into a frame. The <Import text> option is used to import the eight individual text files, one for each column.

The frame for the sixth column—LONG, containing the longitude data—is too narrow, so Publish It! writes each item across two lines. To correct the problem, the VAR column is made narrower and the LONG column wider.

One other way to solve the problems is to prepare the file in ASCII format and to use the HiJaak file-conversion utility that converts ASCII files of any length into graphics files. Those graphics files then can be imported with the <Import picture> option from the File menu. Figure 12-9 is the same list, this time converted to a graphics file and imported into Publish It!.

Publish It! offers another method by which lists of this type can be imported, and this method may actually be the simplest of all. Activate Publish It! as usual, and then take the following steps:

1. In the Page menu click on <Size to fit>. Select the <PARAGRAPH> mode from the toolbox and in the Library window click on BODY TEXT.

Figure 12-8. *A table saved as individual columns and imported*

STATION	ID	FIX	FRQ	LAT	LONG	VAR	ELEV
ABERDEEN	SD	ABR	113.0	45-25.1N	098-22.1W	10E	1300
ABILENE	TX	ABI	113.7	32-28.9N	099-51.8W	10E	1810
ACTON	TX	AQN	110.6	32-26.1N	097-39.8W	09E	848
AINSWORTH	NE	ANW	112.7	42-34.7N	099-59.6W	11E	2580
AKRON	OH	ACO	114.4	41-06.5N	081-12.7W	04W	1200
AKRON	CO	AKO	114.4	40-09.3N	103-10.8W	13E	4620
ALAMOSA	CO	ALS	113.9	37-21.0N	105-48.9W	13E	7530
ALBANY	NY	ALB	117.8	42-44.8N	073-48.2W	13W	270
ALBANY	GA	ABY	116.1	31-39.3N	084-17.6W	01E	280
ALBERT LEA	MN	AEL	109.8	43-41.0N	093-22.1W	05E	1253
ALBUQUERQUE	NM	ABQ	113.2	35-02.6N	106-49.0W	13E	5740
ALEXANDRIA	MN	AXN	112.8	45-57.5N	095-13.9W	07E	1380
ALEXANDRIA	LA	AEX	116.1	31-15.4N	092-30.0W	07E	80
ALICE	TX	ALI	114.5	27-44.4N	098-01.3W	09E	170
ALLEGHENY	PA	AGC	110.0	40-16.7N	080-02.5W	05W	1290
ALLEN COUNTY	OH	AOH	108.4	40-42.4N	083-58.1W	02W	980
ALLENDALE	SC	ALD	116.7	33-00.7N	081-17.6W	01W	190
ALLENTOWN	PA	ABE	117.5	40-43.6N	075-27.3W	10W	680
ALLIANCE	NE	AIA	111.8	42-03.3N	102-48.2W	11E	1925
ALMA	GA	AMG	115.1	31-32.2N	082-30.5W	00	200
ALPENA	MI	APN	108.8	45-05.0N	083-33.4W	04W	680
ALTOONA	PA	AOO	108.8	40-19.5N	078-18.2W	07W	1630
ALTUS	OK	LTS	109.8	34-31.2N	099-16.5W	10E	1330
AMARILLO	TX	AMA	117.2	35-17.3N	101-38.3W	11E	3550
AMEDEE	CA	AHC	109.0	40-16.1N	120-09.1W	17E	4006
ANDREWS	MD	ADW	113.1	38-48.4N	076-52.0W	07W	266
ANTHONY	KS	ANY	112.9	37-09.5N	098-10.2W	10E	1390
ANTON CHICO	NM	ACH	110.0	35-06.7N	105-02.4W	12E	5450
APPLETON	OH	APE	116.7	40-09.1N	082-35.3W	02W	1360
ARCATA	CA	ACV	110.2	40-58.9N	124-06.4W	19E	190
ARDMORE	OK	ADM	116.7	34-12.7N	097-10.1W	09E	930
ARMEL	VA	AML	113.5	38-56.1N	077-28.0W	08W	291
ASHLAND	WI	ASX	110.2	46-33.0N	090-55.0W	02E	820

2. Access the Text menu and click on <Paragraph style>. If you are using Publish It! version 2.0, click on <Set tabs> and in the resulting

Figure 12-9. *The table converted to an .IMG file and imported*

STATION	ID	FIX	FRQ	LAT	LONG	VAR	ELEV
ABERDEEN	SD	ABR	113.0	45-25.1N	098-22.1W	10E	1300
ABILENE	TX	ABI	113.7	32-28.9N	099-51.8W	10E	1810
ACTON	TX	AQN	110.6	32-26.1N	097-39.8W	09E	848
AINSWORTH	NE	ANW	112.7	42-34.7N	099-59.6W	11E	2580
AKRON	OH	ACO	114.4	41-06.5N	081-12.7W	04W	1200
AKRON	CO	AKO	114.4	40-09.3N	103-10.8W	13E	4620
ALAMOSA	CO	ALS	113.9	37-21.0N	105-48.9W	13E	7530
ALBANY	NY	ALB	117.8	42-44.8N	073-48.2W	13W	270
ALBANY	GA	ABY	116.1	31-39.3N	084-17.6W	01E	280
ALBERT LEA	MN	AEL	109.8	43-41.0N	093-22.1W	05E	1253
ALBUQUERQUE	NM	ABQ	113.2	35-02.6N	106-49.0W	13E	5740
ALEXANDRIA	MN	AXN	112.8	45-57.5N	095-13.9W	07E	1380
ALEXANDRIA	LA	AEX	116.1	31-15.4N	092-30.0W	07E	80
ALICE	TX	ALI	114.5	27-44.4N	098-01.3W	09E	170
ALLEGHENY	PA	AGC	110.0	40-16.7N	080-02.5W	05W	1290
ALLEN COUNTY	OH	AOH	108.4	40-42.4N	083-58.1W	02W	980
ALLENDALE	SC	ALD	116.7	33-00.7N	081-17.6W	01W	190
ALLENTOWN	PA	ABE	117.5	40-43.6N	075-27.3W	10W	680
ALLIANCE	NE	AIA	111.8	42-03.3N	102-48.2W	11E	1925
ALMA	GA	AMG	115.1	31-32.2N	082-30.5W	00	200
ALPENA	MI	APN	108.8	45-05.0N	083-33.4W	04W	680
ALTOONA	PA	AOO	108.8	40-19.5N	078-18.2W	07W	1630
ALTUS	OK	LTS	109.8	34-31.2N	099-16.5W	10E	1330
AMARILLO	TX	AMA	117.2	35-17.3N	101-38.3W	11E	3550
AMEDEE	CA	AHC	109.0	40-16.1N	120-09.1W	17E	4006
ANDREWS	MD	ADW	113.1	38-48.4N	076-52.0W	07W	266
ANTHONY	KS	ANY	112.9	37-09.5N	098-10.2W	10E	1390
ANTON CHICO	NM	ACH	110.0	35-06.7N	105-02.4W	12E	5450
APPLETON	OH	APE	116.7	40-09.1N	082-35.3W	02W	1360
ARCATA	CA	ACV	110.2	40-58.9N	124-06.4W	19E	190
ARDMORE	OK	ADM	116.7	34-12.7N	097-10.1W	09E	930
ARMEL	VA	AML	113.5	38-56.1N	077-28.0W	08W	291
ASHLAND	WI	ASX	110.2	46-33.0N	090-55.0W	02E	820

dialog box, click on <Yes>. Then continue with the second half of step 4. With earlier versions of Publish It!, click on <Justification> and continue with step 3.

3. In the new dialog box, click on <Table> and <OK>.
4. In the next dialog box click on <Set tabs>, and then set your tab positions to fit your list. For the example list, enter the following tab positions:

Tab #1 left 2.00
Tab #2 left 2.50
Tab #3 left 3.00
Tab #4 left 4.00
Tab #5 left 5.00
Tab #6 left 6.00
Tab #7 left 6.50

When all tabs have been set, click on <OK> twice.

5. When you're back in the work screen, click on the <FRAME> icon to return to the <FRAME> mode. Then create and select a single full-page frame.
6. Now click on <Import text>, and click on the appropriate text type, based on the word processing program you used to produce the original list file.
7. In the Item Selector box, click on the filename and <OK>. After a short pause you will see your list appear on the screen arranged in accordance with the tab stops that you entered.
8. In the File menu click on <Save as>, and when you have entered a new filename, the list has been imported and is ready for use within Publish It!.

Magazines

With literally thousands of magazines displayed on our newsstands month after month, the variations in layout and design are much too great to be examined here. All that can be done within the context of this book is to mention a few basic guidelines.

Today most, though not all, magazines are printed in the 8 x 10 3/4-inch format. Some are smaller, such as *Reader's Digest* or *TV Guide,* and others are larger, such as *LIFE.* For the purpose of this discussion, only the standard size periodicals will be considered.

All magazines, in order to comply with postal regulations, must have a masthead somewhere in the front of the issue. In addition, nearly all have tables of contents, also located among the first few pages. The remaining pages are, in most instances, a mix of editorial material and advertisements. The trick is to satisfy the reader by producing a magazine that does not give the impression of being all advertisements and, at the same time, satisfy the advertisers by placing their ads in visible positions. Always keep in mind that the lion's share of revenue for the average magazine comes from the advertisers, not the subscribers or newsstand buyers.

Figure 12-10 is a page design that combines the masthead and the publishing company address and other data with an editorial printed across two columns. A page containing this information is usually found before or immediately after the table of contents. Three separate frames were created for this page design. The text should probably be in separate paragraph styles for each frame. This simplifies manipulating it to fill the available space.

Figure 12-11 is a table of contents page, with the article information printed across two columns and, on the left, small reproductions of illustrations used inside the magazine, added for emphasis. When the pictures used in this manner are photographs, use the frames in a light color and enter information for the printer regarding which picture to use in the specified frame. In the figure, the magazine name was given the Headline paragraph style, which automatically centered it in an invisible frame stretched across the top of the page from edge to edge.

Figure 12-12 is a typical three-column text page with a line between the columns. These vertical lines are produced by creating separate frames with the <Frame border> option activated and either <Left> or <Right> selected. Then, with the frame itself being sent to the back, only the vertical line representing either the left or right side of that frame remains. Headlines for individual stories and subheads may extend across more than one column, and boxes with bold text may be inserted to emphasize some major points made in the story.

Figures 12-13 through 12-16 show the placement of advertisements on the pages of magazines. Ads are generally provided by the advertiser or the advertising agency in camera-ready format. Each frame representing an ad should include the necessary instructions for the printer.

In some cases the advertiser expects the publication to actually typeset the ad, based on copy provided by the advertiser. In such instances, you can use Publish It! or Publish It Lite! to produce the ad yourself and include it with the page makeup.

Figure 12-10. *A magazine masthead page*

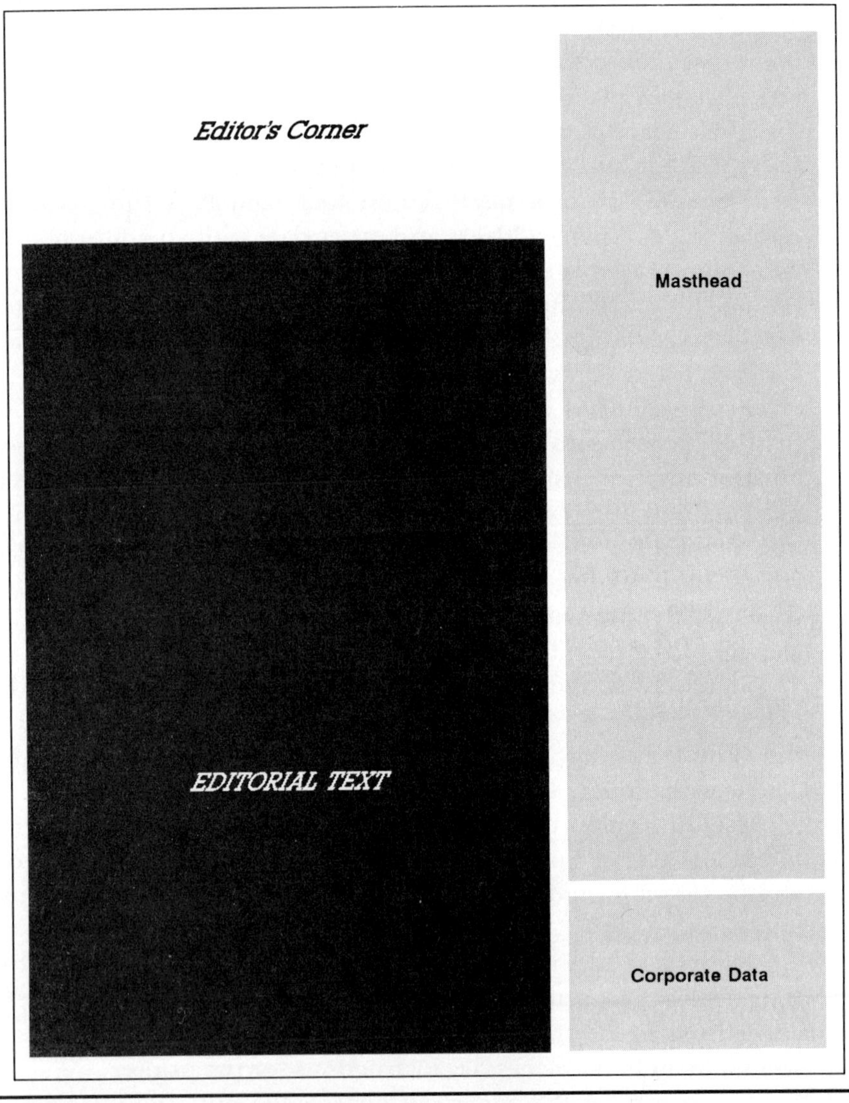

Figure 12-13 is a text page with a one-third page ad. Such ads are always placed on the outside of the page with the text columns occupying the portion

Figure 12-11. *A magazine contents page*

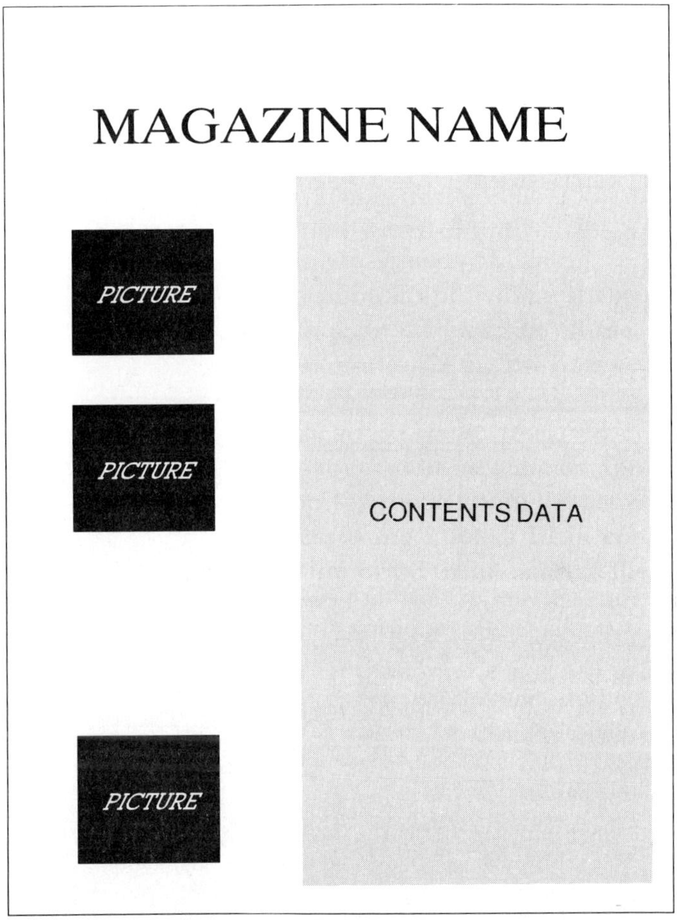

of the page close to the gutter. Again, the vertical line is one border side of an invisible frame. Figure 12-14 is a similar page, this one with a two-thirds

Figure 12-12. A three-column magazine text page

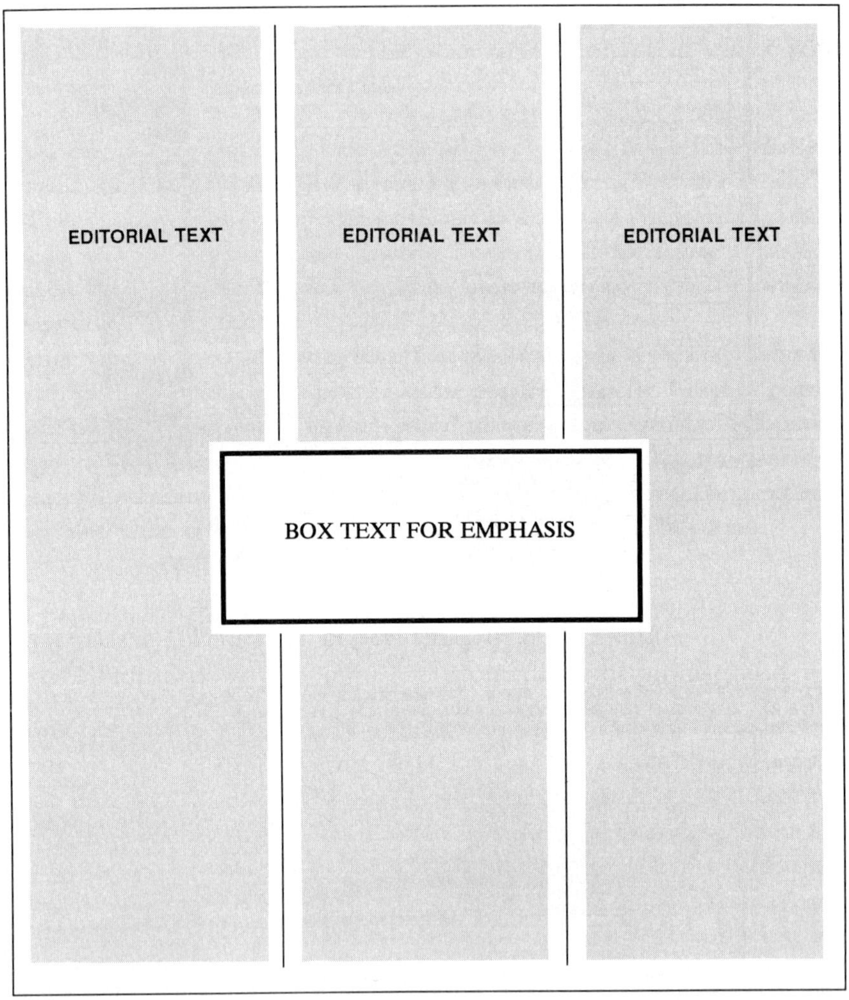

page ad. In Figure 12-15 two one-third page ads occupy the outside two columns, and in Figure 12-16 a half-page ad occupies the bottom half of the

Figure 12-13. *A one-third page magazine ad*

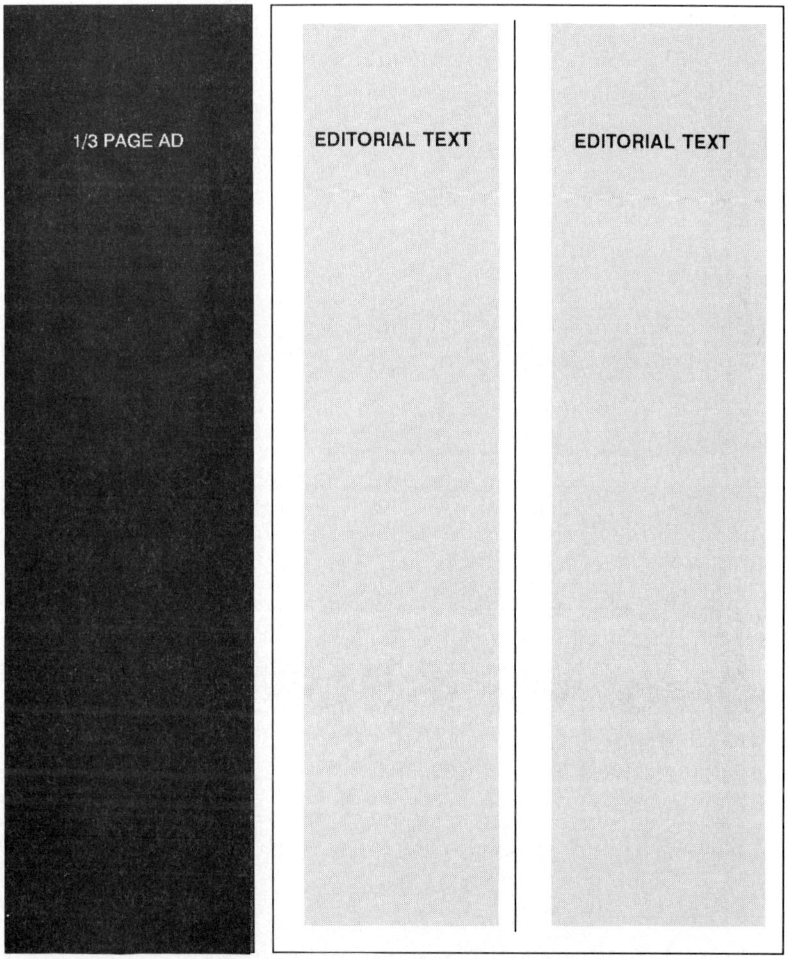

page. In this three-column page format, it is not possible to accommodate vertical half-page ads. If necessary, a two-column format can be introduced.

Figure 12-14. *A two-thirds page magazine ad*

Figure 12-15. *Two one-third page magazine ads*

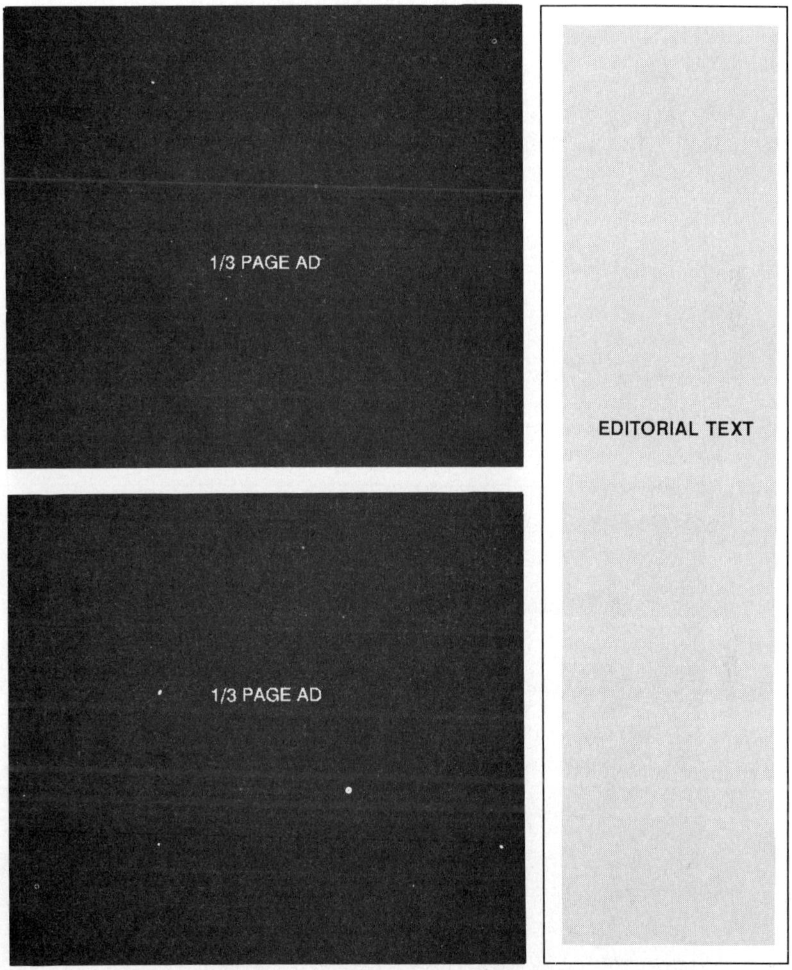

Figure 12-16. A half-page magazine ad

There is no hard and fast rule that says that two- and three-column formats cannot alternate, as long as they are not mixed within a single article.

Newsletters

Newsletters do not necessarily follow any standard design format. They are usually printed on 11 x 17-inch paper and folded to produce 8 1/2-inch wide pages. As a result, the page design can be in the standard 8 1/2-inch format. In most instances, each page in a newsletter will carry a large amount of text. It is often advisable to print text flush left or flush right but not justified. Text printed in that manner allows for a certain amount of white space, making the page look less forbidding.

Figure 12-17 is a sample design for the front page of a newsletter. Here an invisible frame is placed beneath the Text or Graphics Box frame to produce a white border. Figure 12-18 represents an inside page in the two-column format, and Figure 12-19 is an inside page in the three-column format, with a separate box containing a large photograph and the text associated with it. A large more-or-less square frame is created inside the page format, and that frame is given its own border, thus tying the photograph and the accompanying text together. Figure 12-20 is the back page that includes space for the address of the subscriber and a subscription coupon. Since the bottom portion of this page is a standard that is repeated with each issue, you might consider storing it in a separate file that can be imported in its entirety.

Display Advertisements

When using Publish It! to produce camera-ready copy for display advertisements, keep in mind that you probably cannot produce full-page bleed ads because the average laser printer does not print all the way to the edge of the paper. But the printing company that uses your mechanicals can enlarge or reduce them to fit into a given space.

In most cases, ads that include a lot of white space—a single eye-catching graphic and a minimum of copy—get more attention than those that demand a lot of reading. A few suggestions are shown in Figures 12-21 through 12-23.

In Figure 12-21 the large "Help" was imported from Publisher's PicturePak, as was the package at the bottom. The balance of the text was typed in the <TEXT> mode.

Figure 12-17. *A newsletter title page*

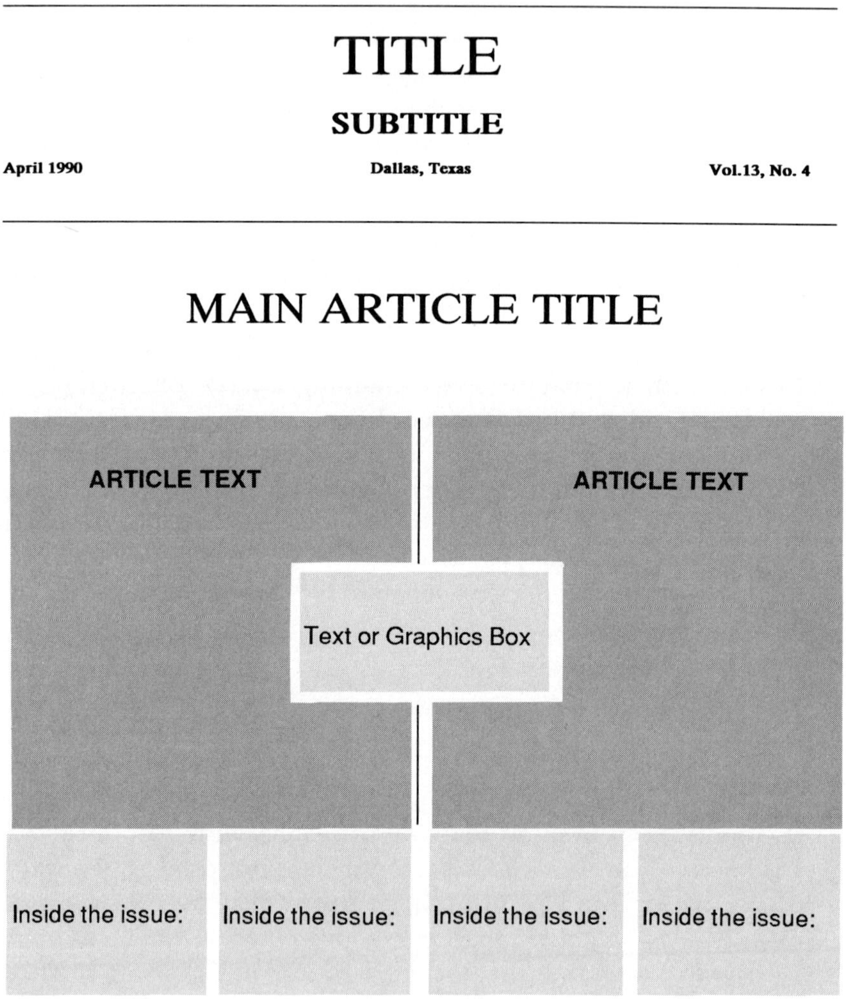

In Figure 12-22 the dollar sign was also imported from Publisher's PicturePak and then was repeated using the <Copy> and <Paste> options from

Figure 12-18. *A two-column newsletter page*

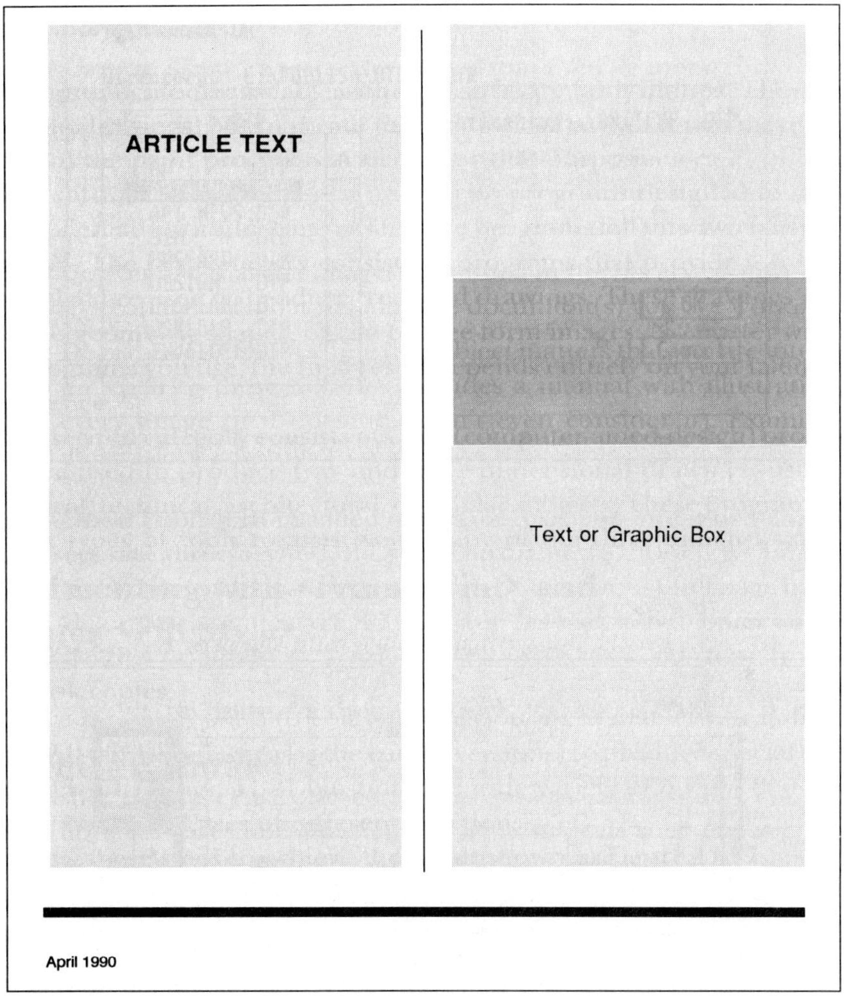

the Edit menu. The sizes were changed by adjusting the frame sizes. The text was typed in the <TEXT> mode.

Figure 12-19. *A three-column newsletter page*

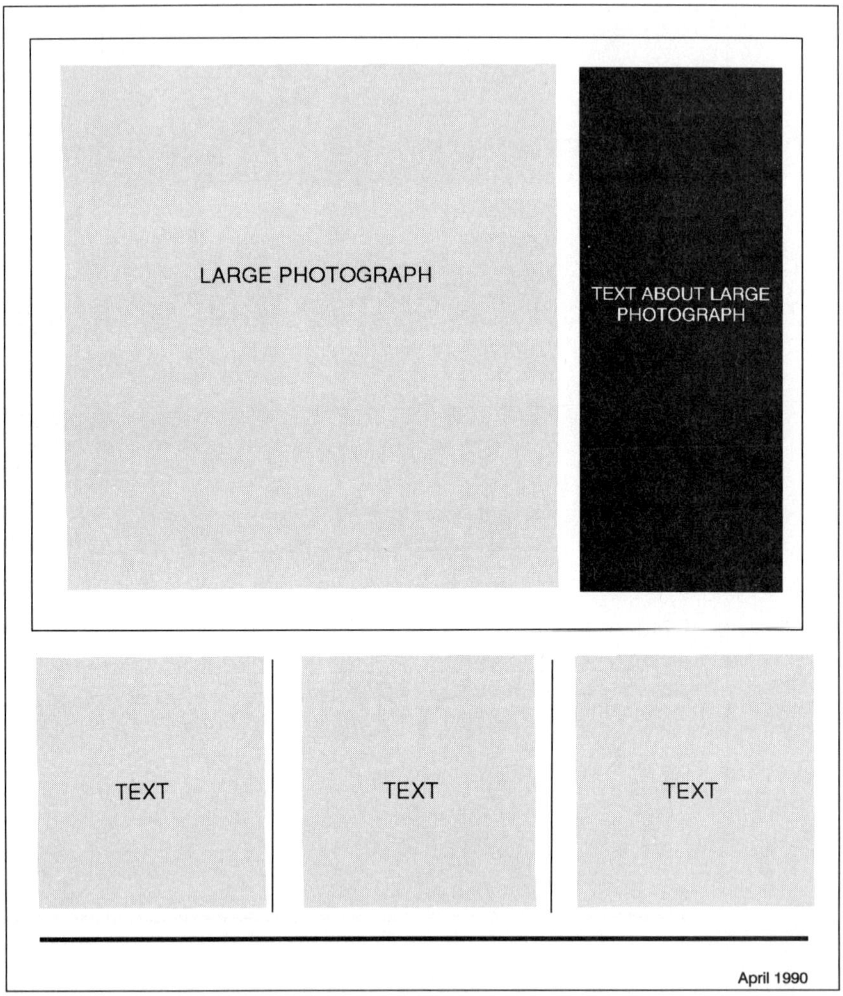

In Figure 12-23 the two rectangular areas representing a single photograph would actually be a single open frame with instructions to the printing service.

Figure 12-20. *A newsletter back page*

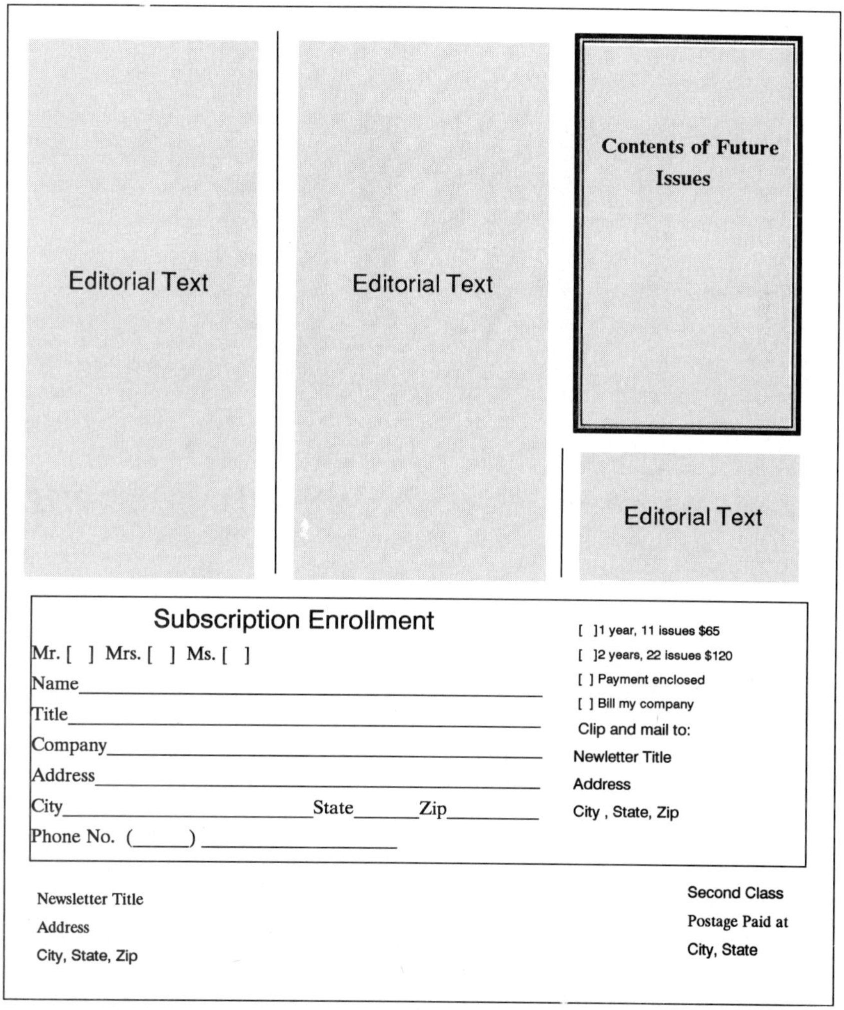

For other ideas, look through some of the magazines on the newsstands, and copy the layout and style of an ad that you believe to be effective.

Figure 12-21. *A display ad*

Advertising agencies are paid large amounts of money to develop effective advertisements; don't hesitate to follow their lead. In fact, most professional publications are fairly well designed. Always be on the lookout for pleasing

Figure 12-22. *Another display ad*

layouts and designs. Study them, learn from them, and figure out ways to apply their lessons to your work with Publish It!. If your final product will be widely distributed, take care not to infringe on copyright laws.

Figure 12-23. *A third display ad*

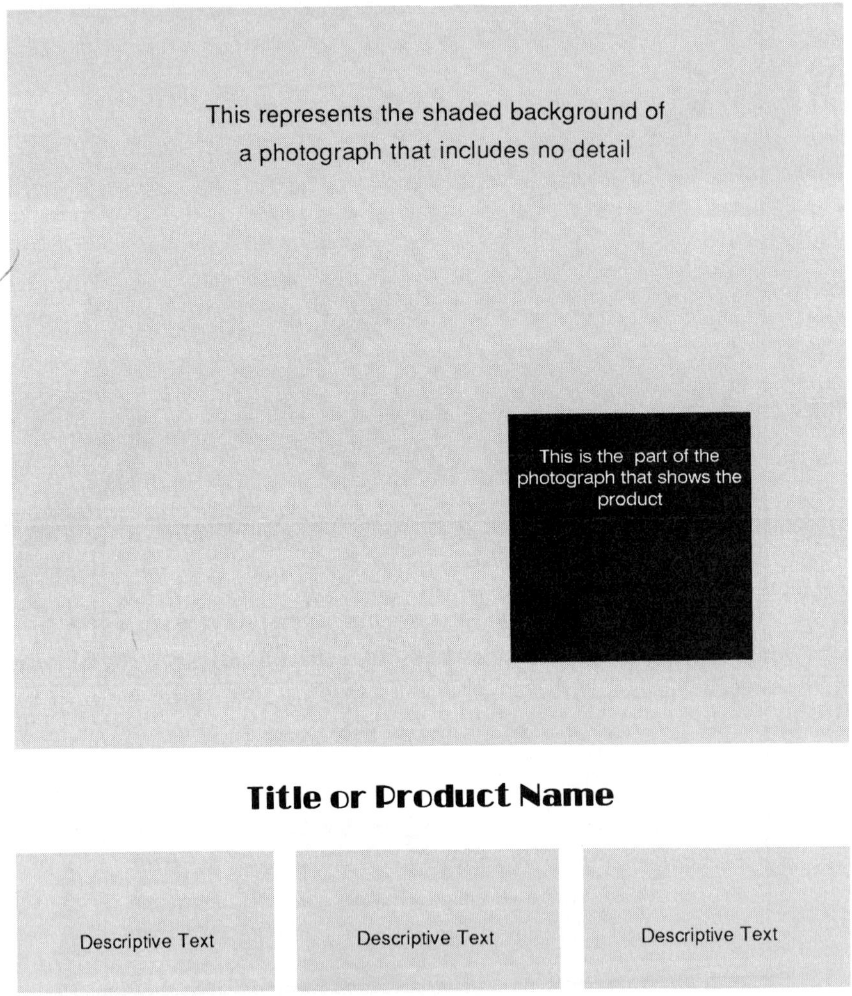

Other Applications

When we talk about publishing, we're generally talking about books, magazines, newspapers, and regularly issued newsletters. Other types of publications include catalogs, brochures, and a variety of direct mail material.

Figures 12-24 through 12-33 are sample forms of various publications and special purpose pieces that might be used in one variation or another in different business situations. The graphic illustrations used are those available from the clip-art files of Publisher's PicturePak.

In Figure 12-24 the horizontal lines in the Message and Reply columns are underlines created in the <TEXT> mode and then placed using the <Centered> justification option. The graphic is from Publisher's PicturePak, as is that fellow with the cluttered desk in Figure 12-25 and the horn in Figure 12-26. In both illustrations the text was typed in Publish It! <TEXT> mode using different paragraph styles to vary font styles and sizes.

Figure 12-27 combines two different clip-art images, and the text was typed into three separate frames: flush left, centered, and flush right. Figure 12-28 combines three separate clip-art images, the horse and buggy, the "Welcome" in script, and the garland at the bottom, with the balance of the text typed into a single box in centered Ravinia font. In Figure 12-29 a box of text was added to a single clip-art image, and the same is true for Figure 12-30.

Figures 12-31, 12-32, and 12-33 are the cover and two representative pages of an annual report. Figure 12-31 might be the title page. The "Advanced Information Systems" copy was produced using the VP-Graphics program in Roman font and then imported into Publish It! as a graphic file in the .IMG format. It was then resized and, using the <Crop picture> option, divided into three separate frames. Next the "A" in "Advanced" was cropped out, copied, and greatly enlarged to give the impression of being created by a group of building blocks. Finally, the balance of the text was typed directly in Publish It! in the <TEXT> mode.

Figure 12-32 is a sample first page of an annual report that provides details about the worldwide operations of the company. The map of the world was

Figure 12-24. *Express message form*

URGENT MESSAGE

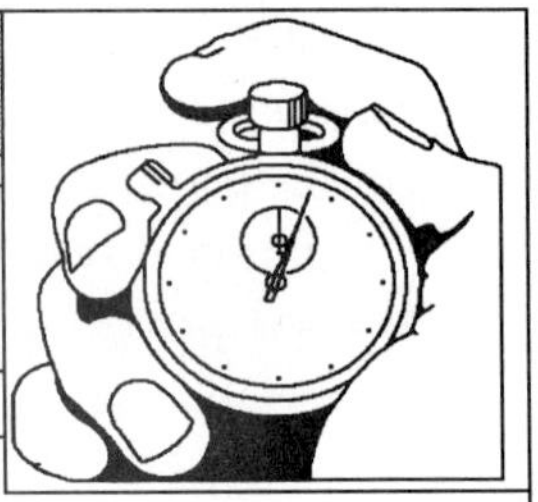

Please mail response within one work day!

From:

To:

Message:

Signature:

Reply:

Signature:

imported from Publisher's PicturePak, and an invisible frame around the frame holding the map produced the white border between the text and the border of the graphic image.

Figure 12-25. *Flier for a computer sale*

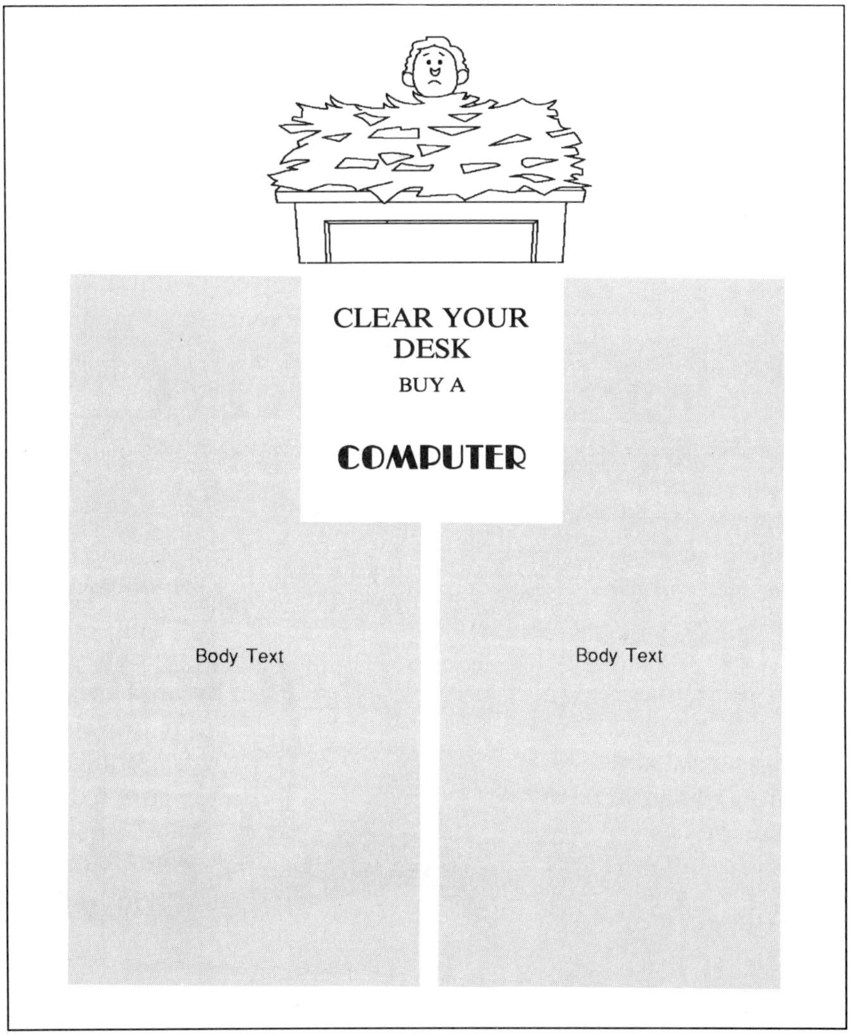

Figure 12-33 is one of the subsequent pages in the report, detailing some of the financial data. The pie chart was created originally as a .PIC file using

Figure 12-26. *Announcement for a new play*

Lotus 1-2-3. It was then imported into EnerGraphics where it was greatly enhanced and then saved as an .IMG file that could be imported into Publish It! without further conversion.

Figure 12-27. *Airline ad*

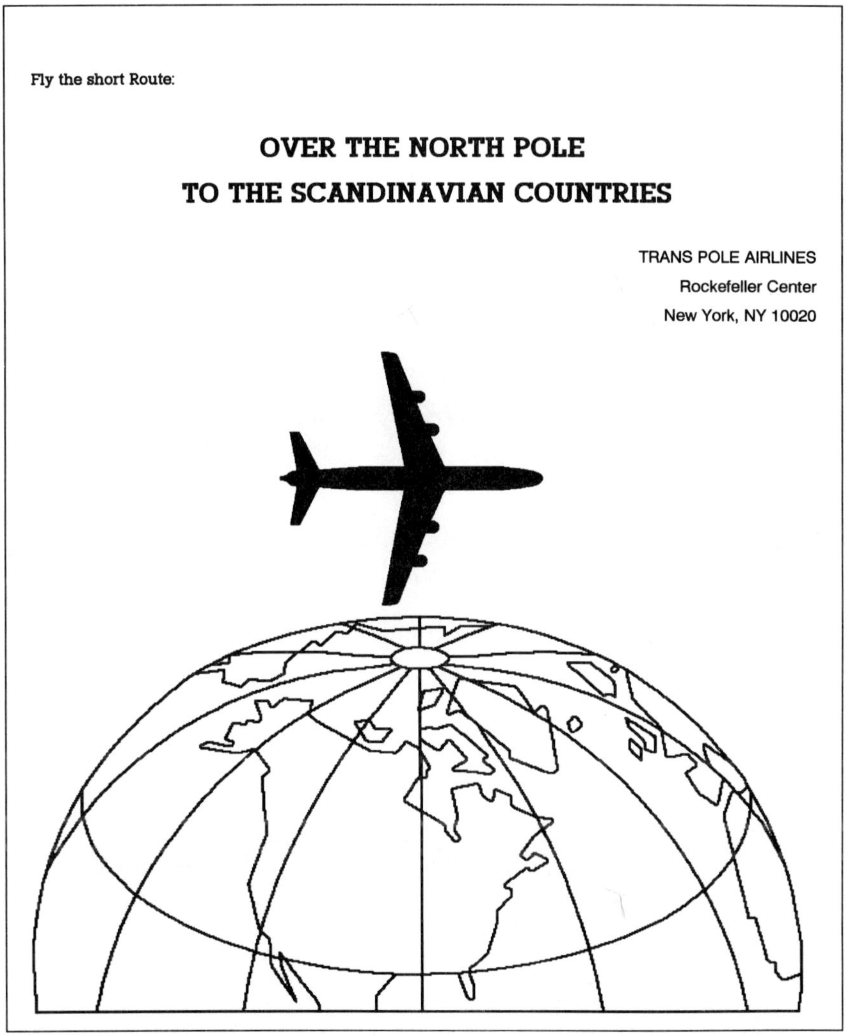

A page like Figure 12-33 would probably be printed in several colors, with the text in one color, the pie chart in another, and the labels identifying the pie slices in a third. Figures 12-34, 12-35, and 12-36 represent the mechanicals

Figure 12-28. *Convention program cover*

for the page shown in Figure 12-33. After the complete page was created in Publish It!, the <Copy> and <Paste> options from the Edit menu were used to move the individual frames onto the three pages that represent the

Figure 12-29. *Award announcement*

mechanicals. The two + marks on either side of each page are the registration marks used by the printer to control the placement of the separate mechanicals. They are not printed.

Figure 12-30. *First page of sales meeting program*

Figure 12-31. *Annual report cover page*

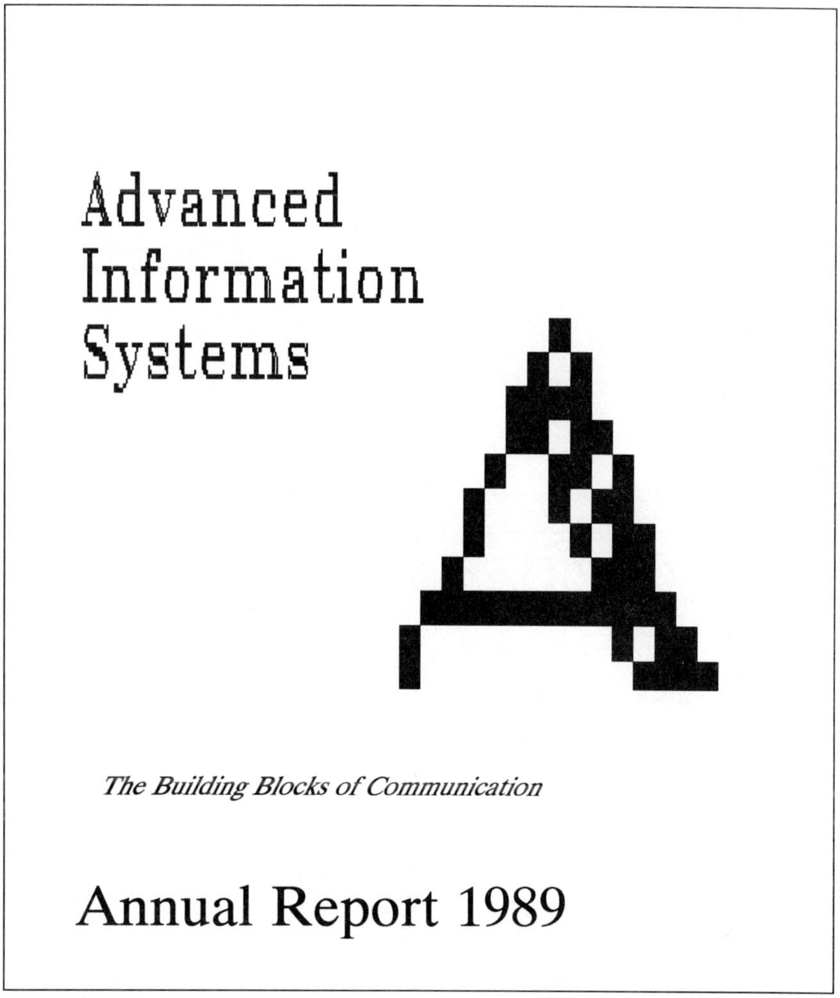

Figure 12-32. First page of annual report

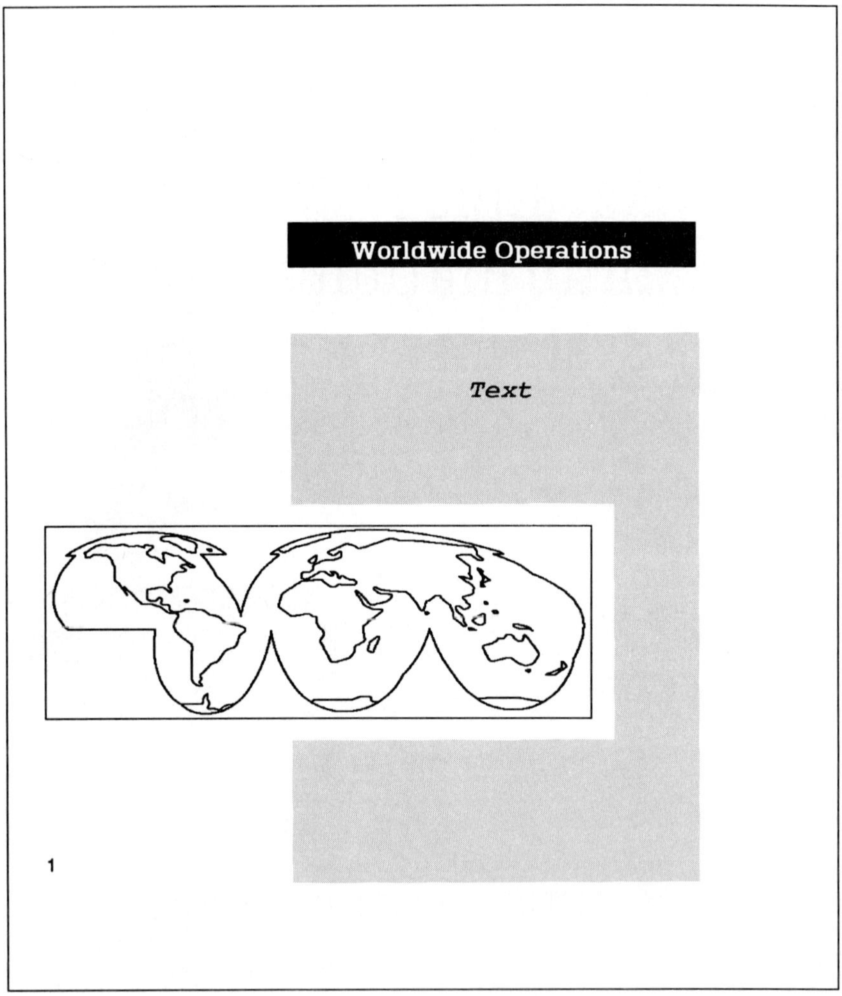

Figure 12-33. *Body page of annual report*

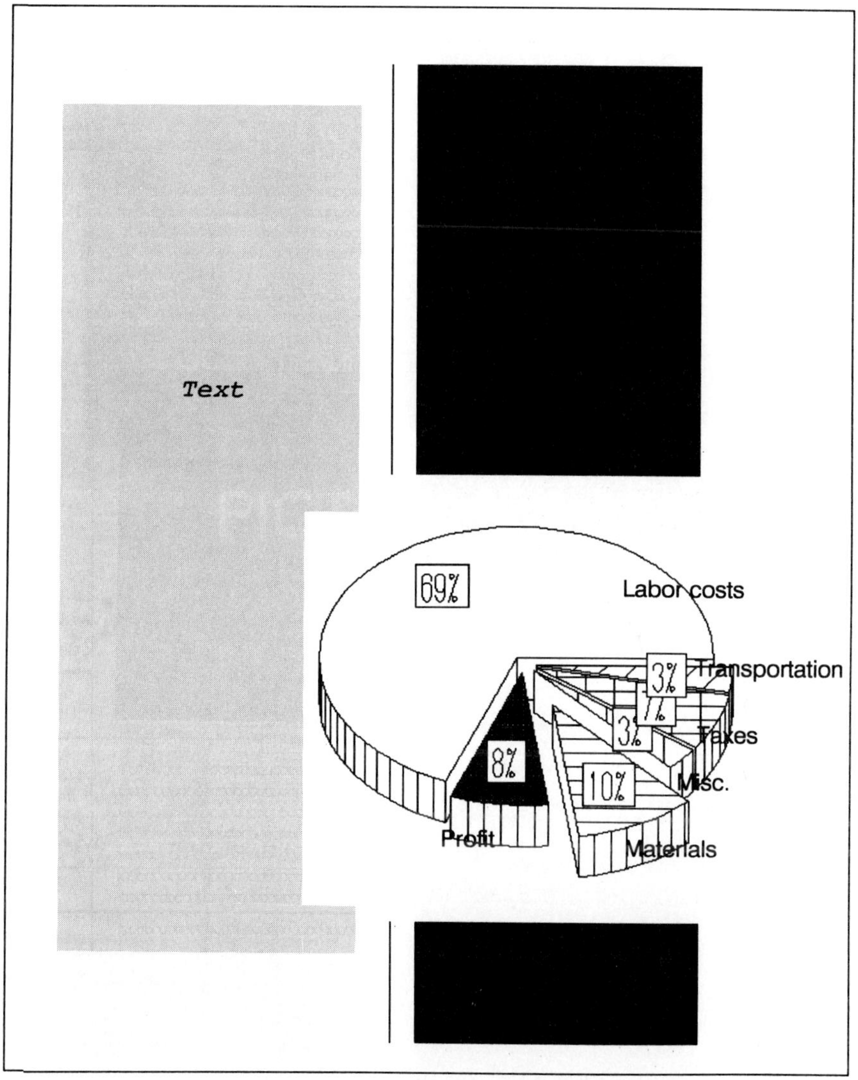

Figure 12-34. *First color mechanical*

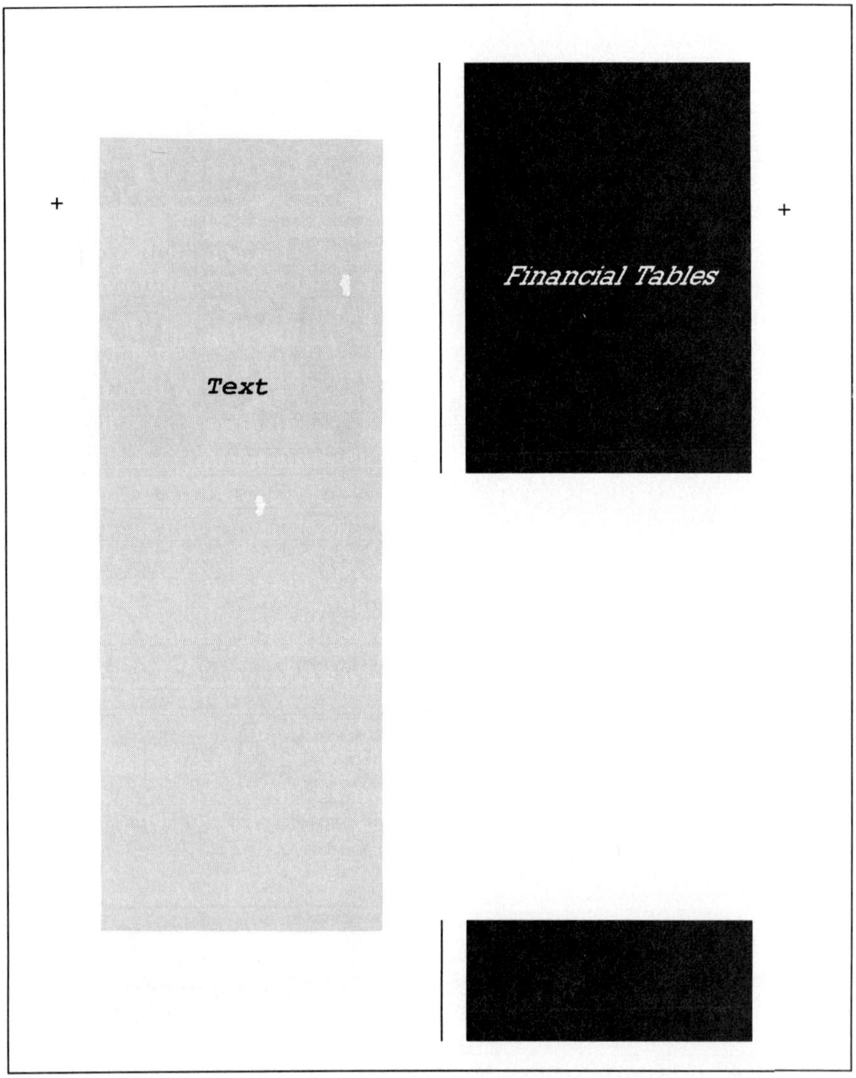

Figure 12-35. *Second color mechanical*

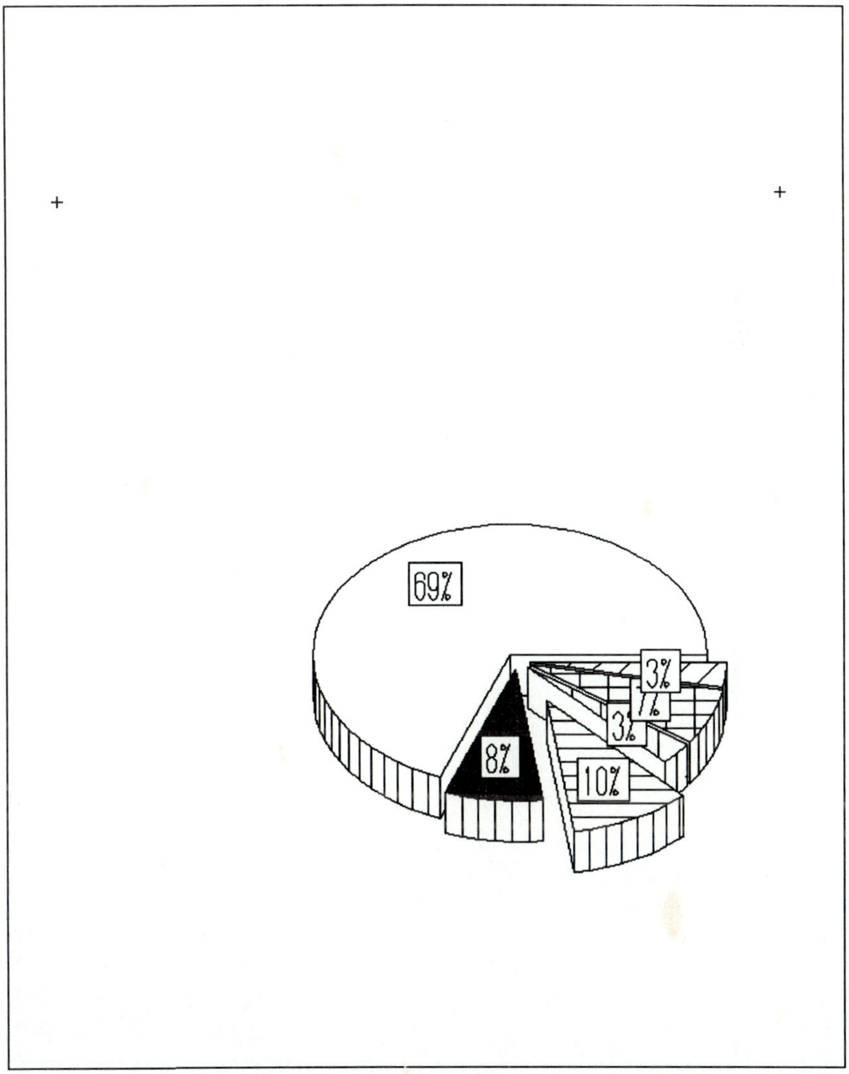

Figure 12-36. *Third color mechanical*

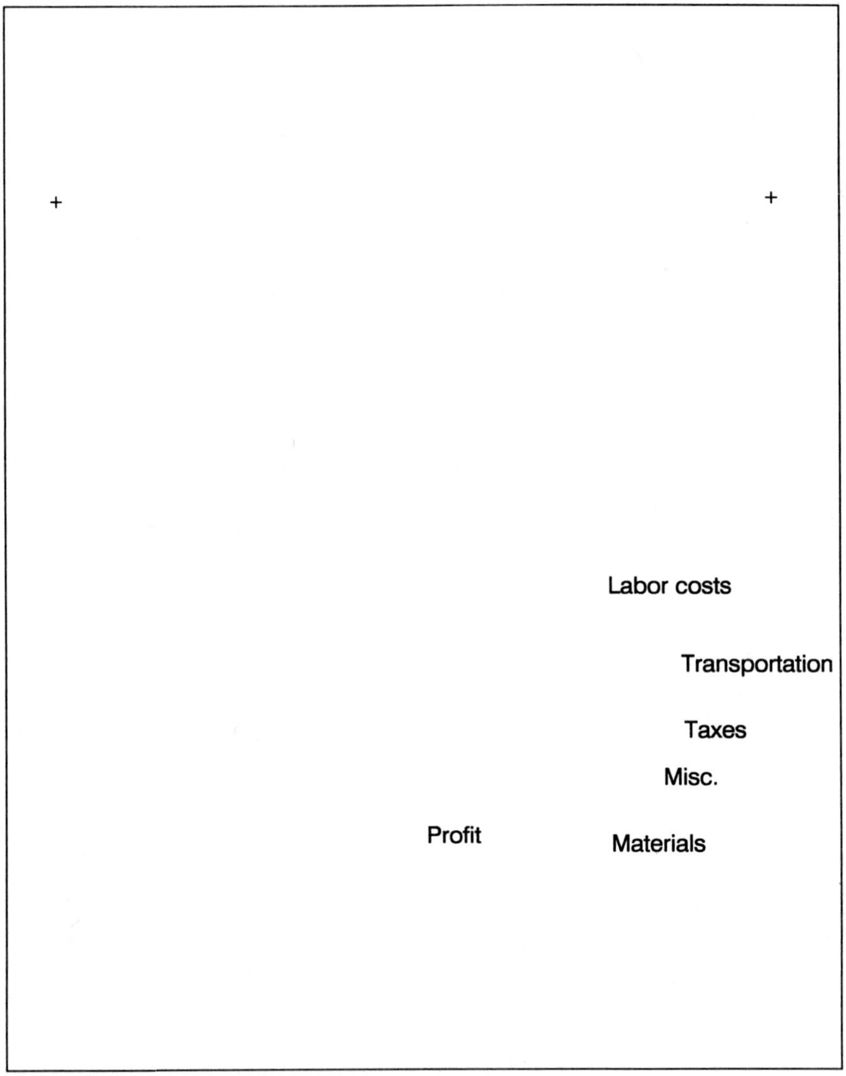

13

Peripheral Publishing Requirements

The primary subject of this book is *desktop publishing*–the preparation of camera-ready material. While that is a big part of the entire publishing picture, it is by no means all of it. The process is like preparing a meal. The greatest recipe in the world isn't worth a thing until it's completely prepared, ready to be eaten. Once the camera-ready copy has been prepared with Publish It!, there is the task of selecting a printer if a large number of copies is needed. Then there is the question of how best to distribute your work. And finally, if you intend to reach a large audience, that audience must be apprised of what you have to offer, which means advertising.

Printing

Whether you have produced a single-page flier or a 300-page book, it is still only one single copy of the document. In most instances you will need a large number of copies. Producing more than a few copies of such a document on your own printer, while possible, may not be practical. Desktop publishing documents, even if they contain only text, are graphic documents, and printing graphics takes time, quite possibly a lot of time, depending on your computer system and on your printer.

With Publish It! you can instruct your printer to print up to 99 copies of a given document. To fit two digits into the Number of Copies line on the Print Options screen, first press (ESC) to clear the line. Printing the first copy of each page of the document can take as much as an hour, depending on what is on the page. The additional 98 copies don't take any time if you use a laser printer, but then if you want to print another 99 copies, the entire process must be repeated.

If your document is designed to be distributed to a limited audience, such as the department heads in your company, then it is possible for you to make all the multiple copies on your own printer. When you need really large numbers of copies, however, you will find that it is better to turn to a professional printing establishment.

A word about using photographs: When using original black-and-white photographs, provide the printer with clear 8 x 10-inch glossy prints with good contrast. Be sure to include all the necessary placement and size information for the reproduction on your original copy or on a separate sheet of instructions. Try to avoid using color photographs, either prints or transparencies, for black-and-white reproductions. The results are rarely satisfying.

For color reproduction, some printers prefer the original transparencies, while others can work from color prints. Assuming that the original color photograph is a transparency, it is usually better to let the printer work from it, as color prints frequently lose some of the finer definition.

Single-Page Documents

To obtain multiple copies of a single-page document, it is probably most economical to go to one of the fast-print establishments. They use your camera-ready mechanical to run off as many copies as you like in little time and at a reasonable price.

Unless you specify a certain type and weight of paper, the document will probably be printed on 20-pound plain white stock, which is ideal for documents that are to be mailed. If other uses are anticipated—uses that do not call for folded pages—you may need a heavier paper stock. Before you make a decision, have the printing salesperson show you what is available in paper weight, surface texture, and color.

Your paper selection can prove to be of considerable importance. Some papers can give your product a touch of elegance, while others seem cheap and ordinary. There is, of course, a price difference, but letting your firm's message be undervalued by selecting a cheap paper stock just to save a few dollars would be false economy. Even printers with very high resolution, such as 300 x 300 dots per inch, often produce unsatisfactory results on brightly colored or patterned paper stock. It is best to stick to white, beige, or gray paper, unless you're going to use offset printing.

Newsletters

Newsletters are usually printed on 11 x 17-inch paper stock, 34-pound or heavier. Most print shops can fold, bind, and trim the pages, so that what you finally pick up is the finished newsletter, ready to be mailed.

You may want to have the name of your newsletter printed in a different color from that used in the rest of the document. This adds to the cost and may increase printing time, but it may also add a touch of professionalism that could be worth the extra expense.

Magazines

Magazines that include advertisements, the mechanicals of which are provided by the advertiser or by advertising agencies, are usually printed on coated stock on sheet-fed or rotary presses. After the editorial portion of the issue has been prepared using Publish It!, quite a bit of work will have to be done to integrate the ads into the pages. Unless you have some experience with magazine publishing, don't hesitate to get advice and help from professionals.

The printing establishments that handle this kind of work usually operate on predetermined schedules. If your magazine is weekly or monthly or published at some other regular interval, make arrangements to schedule your printing on predetermined dates. It is then up to you to have the dummy and all the materials that make up the issue ready in time.

The printing presses, especially rotary presses, not only print the issue but also collate, bind, and trim it so that plain white paper is fed in on one end and the finished magazine comes out at the other.

The type of binding used depends largely on the number of pages. The two popular methods are *saddle stitching* and *perfect binding*. Saddle stitching refers to staples placed where the pages are folded. *Time* and *People* magazines use this method. Perfect binding is a gluing process that produces a hard, square spine. When it is used, the publication consists of several sections of folded paper that are collated, held tightly, and have about an eighth of an inch sliced off the spine to create separate pages. The pages are glued together at the back and enclosed in the heavier stock that becomes the cover. Perfect binding is used in magazines like *Byte* and *PC Magazine*. Magazine issues consisting of up to approximately 100 pages can usually be saddle-stitched. Once they get much larger, perfect binding is preferred.

Books

Getting advice from professionals is even more important when you produce a book. Books may be in hardcover or paperback. Hardcover books require the preparation and printing of dust jackets as well as the design and production of the covers themselves. Paperback books require the design and printing of the paperback cover, usually in color.

When selecting a printing company, consider its experience with book production. The process involves not only the actual printing but also book binding, which requires expertise and special machinery.

Unless you have made arrangements for the distribution of your book, find out whether the printing company is willing to store your books and for how long. Books are heavy and take up a lot of room. For example, if you've ordered a print run of 5000 copies of even a small 200-page paperback, the cartons may take up the better part of a room in your house or apartment.

Distributing

The distribution of your work is no less important than the production of the work itself. You must make your document available to its intended audience for it to be of any value.

Newsletters

Newsletters usually focus on specific subjects or disciplines and are aimed at a defined audience. Depending on the type of audience, you can buy mailing lists. If your newsletter demands a paid subscription, you may have to send some type of flier to the names on such a mailing list.

You can obtain the services of professionals who will handle the distribution for a fee, or you can do it yourself. Either way, you will have to obtain the appropriate postal permit, and you will be expected to prepay the postage for the number of copies that are to be distributed.

Magazines

Magazine distribution requires the services of a professional organization. Virtually all major subscription magazines are distributed by specialists. Newsstand copies are distributed by local, regional, or national organizations, depending on the area in which the periodical is sold. All of this costs money. As a general rule, new magazines don't produce a profit for at least a year.

Books

Some book publishing companies will accept for distribution a book that is prepared for publication by the author. If they do, they will probably also perform the typesetting, printing, binding, and related operations themselves. (Vanity presses will charge a fee for these services.) Books that are completely self-published and distributed seldom produce a meaningful profit. A rare few have become best-sellers, but those are the exceptions.

Advertising

To make a profit, you must find an audience for what you have produced. Don't expect people to beat a path to your door just because you think you've produced something of outstanding value. You must advertise.

The available means of advertising are direct mail, newspapers, magazines, Yellow Pages, radio, and television. Direct mail advertising has the advantage of being aimed toward a selected audience. You can buy mailing lists for all conceivable audiences. Prices vary depending on the number of names in the list and on the source selling the list. The average response is usually in the 2% to 3% range. This means that if you send out 5000 mailers, you may end up with between 100 and 150 sales.

Newspaper advertising is predominantly regional, reaching an audience in one specific city and its environs. In newspapers you have the choice of display or classified advertising. Remember, daily newspapers are just that, daily papers, and on the second day your ad may end up in the trash.

Many communities have weekly newspapers that are distributed to an enormous audience free of charge. They are geared to serve a specific community or specialized audience. The cost of advertising in this type of publication is generally fairly reasonable.

Magazines may be general-audience or special-audience periodicals, national or regional. Most offer display advertising, and some include classified advertising. The cost is nearly always high. Make sure that the magazine you select reaches the audience you want to target. Some of the better magazines will not accept display ads unless they are prepared by an accredited advertising agency.

Radio and television advertisements should be prepared by professionals. Whether you use a network that reaches a national audience or a local station, broadcast advertising is quite specialized and expensive. For this reason this book does not discuss the details of broadcast advertising.

Yellow Pages advertising is good for a year, but as a general rule, the type of ads that people look for in the Yellow Pages are for service establishments, restaurants and such.

In conclusion, it is important that you be aware that the work that you do with Publish It! or Publish It Lite! is just the beginning. Be prepared to use and pay for the best professional services available to do justice to your creation.

V

Appendixes

A

Installation

All versions of Publish It! and Publish It Lite! can operate on any IBM PC XT, AT, PS/2, or compatible computer. Version 2.0 requires a minimum 640K random access memory (RAM), while earlier versions can operate with 512K RAM, although here too, 640K is recommended. Version 2.0 requires one hard disk and one (or more) floppy drives, either 3 1/2- or 5 1/4-inch (or both), while earlier versions can operate on dual floppy systems.

The programs require that any one of the many available graphics adapters and a monitor compatible with that graphics card be installed. EGA and VGA graphics cards result in a display in color while CGA and most other graphics adapters produce a monochrome display when working with Publish It! or Publish It Lite!.

A mouse, while not an absolute necessity, is recommended. Using the keyboard for all command and option selections and for moving the different types of pointers and cursors, while possible, is extremely time-consuming and inefficient.

Publish It! and Publish It Lite! support a long list of printers, including dot-matrix, ink-jet, and laser printers. (Daisywheel printers cannot be used with desktop publishing programs.) Some of the 24-pin dot-matrix printers, such as the Epson LQ series, print 180 x 180 dots per inch. They produce acceptable results that can be used as camera-ready copy, except when large areas of solid black are included in the document. Such areas are likely to need additional work before printing satisfactorily.

For truly outstanding results, laser printers are preferred. The Hewlett-Packard LaserJet Series II printer, which prints 300 x 300 dots per inch, is the industry standard. Most other laser printers, such as the Epson EPL 6000 and the Toshiba PageLaser 6 that were used to produce the camera-ready copy for the illustrations in this book, have the ability to emulate the Hewlett-Packard LaserJet Series II printer. This is important because nearly all graphics and font software is designed to ideally be used with that type of printer.

Publish It! version 2.0 can export its work directly to PostScript printers. When a PostScript printer is selected, the available fonts are those of that printer rather than those customarily provided by Publish It!, and when the <Font/size> option is selected from the Style menu or the <Paragraph style> function in the Text menu, the fonts listed are the 11 fonts available with the Adobe PostScript printer, shown in Figure A-1.

If PostScript printers are to be used with earlier versions of Publish It!, then PostScript files must be printed to disk. They can then be taken to a service capable of printing encapsulated PostScript files (.EPS).

In selecting a printer, remember that the basic idea of desktop publishing is to produce camera-ready copy that can then be reproduced and multiplied by conventional printing means. Thus, it is the quality of that camera-ready material that determines the quality of the final printed work.

The Installation Procedure

Publish It! and Publish It Lite!, like all other applications programs, must be installed before they can be used. The installation tells the program what system parameters and peripheral hardware it has to deal with. The installa-

Figure A-1. *Two screens showing a total of 11 fonts available with Adobe PostScript printers*

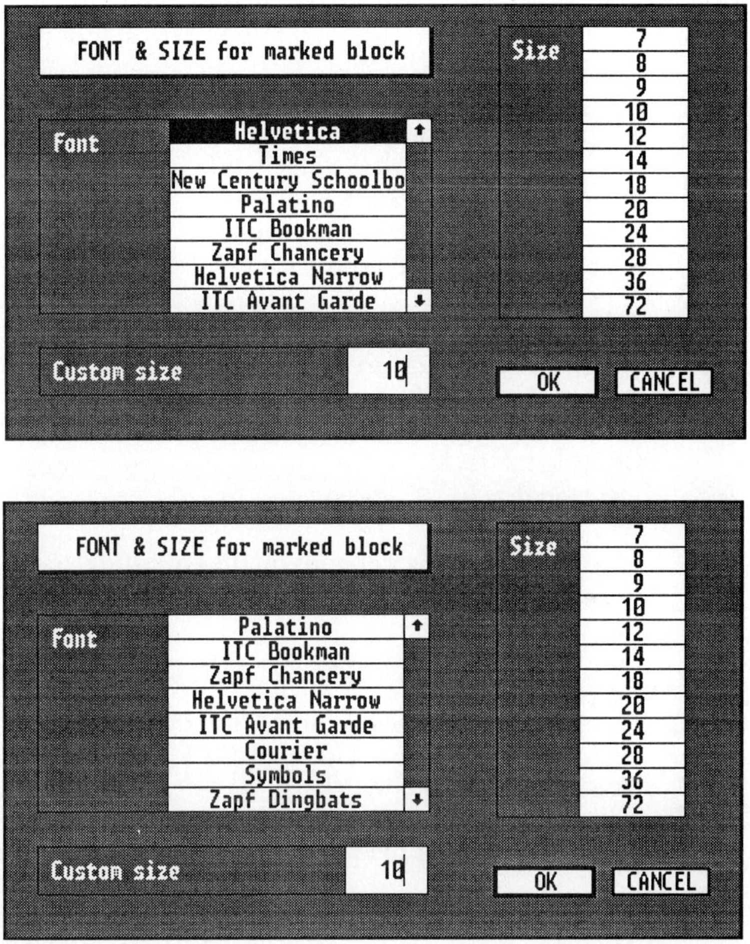

tion procedure varies, depending on whether GEM/3 Desktop is installed on your system.

Making Backup Copies

Before doing anything else, make backup copies of all disks. Use only those backup copies, and store the originals in a safe place.

To make backup copies with dual floppy drives, follow these steps:

1. From the DOS prompt, type **DISKCOPY A: B:** and press ENTER. The following prompt is displayed:

   ```
   Insert SOURCE diskette in drive A:
   Insert TARGET diskette in drive B:
   Press any key when ready...
   ```

2. Place the first original program disk into drive A. Place a blank disk, either formatted or unformatted, into drive B, and press any key. The display changes to something like this:

   ```
   Copying xx tracks
   x sectors/tracks, 2 side(s)
   ```

   where the value of *x* depends on the type and size of disk being used. If the blank disk was not formatted, the display includes

   ```
   Formatting while copying
   ```

3. When the disk has been copied, the display changes to

   ```
   Copy another diskette (Y/N)?
   ```

   Type **Y** and repeat the procedure with each of the remaining disks.

If you want to copy a disk to another in the same drive, drive A in this example, type **DISKCOPY A: A:** and press ENTER. Then follow the instructions displayed on the screen.

If you plan to install the program on a hard disk, skip to step 3 in the next section. If you plan to use the program on a two-drive system, regardless of whether it uses 3 1/2- or 5 1/4-inch disks, you will have to format five blank disks and label them as follows:

Startup
Fonts
Printer Driver
Overlays
Data

During the two-drive installation procedure, you will be asked to insert these disks at specific times.

Publish It! version 2.0 requires a hard disk with a minimum of 1.5 megabytes free disk space on that drive if the sample and artwork files are to be installed. If not, slightly more than 1 megabyte of free disk space is required. The information in the previous section applies only to earlier versions.

Installation

This is the installation procedure to follow if you do not intend to install GEM/3 Desktop separately.

If you are planning to install Publish It! version 2.0 and you have Publish It! version 1.1 or 1.2 already installed on your hard drive, back up any documents (.DTP), style sheets (.STY), and any other files you might have imported to or created on the PUBLISH directory or one of its subdirectories onto a floppy disk or any other directory on your hard disk. Then delete all files from PUBLISH and from all its subdirectories, and remove these directories with the DOS RD command. Now proceed with the installation described next. It applies to all versions of Publish It!.

To successfully complete the installation you will need to know the following:

- The kind of video card and display your system includes, such as VGA
- The pointing device you use, such as a Logitech serial mouse.

If you are using a Microsoft mouse that uses MOUSE.COM, select "Bus Mouse" from the displayed options.

- The make and model of the printer(s) you intend to use with Publish It!, such as Epson LQ 850 or Hewlett-Packard LaserJet Series II. You can install up to four printers, although only one can be operative at any one time. (For more on this, see the upcoming section, "Changing Your Configuration.")
- The designated printer port, such as LPT1.

Do not be perturbed if the Publish It! installation does not use all master disks. Your printer selection(s) determine which disks are used.

1. Insert your copy of Master Disk 1 into drive A. Type **A:** and press (ENTER) to make drive A the selected drive.
2. Type **INSTALL** and press (ENTER), and follow the instructions displayed on the screen. The INSTALL procedure will sense your drive configuration automatically, and if there is more than one possible installation location, such as two hard drives, the program asks for more information and then automatically transfers files to the appropriate location. It also asks about the graphics card, monitor, printer, and mouse. If the displayed options don't exactly match the equivalent in your system, use the option that is the closest.

Changing Your Configuration

You can change your configuration at any time if you change your hardware, install a new printer or mouse, or for whatever reason.

1. Start the INSTALL program again as described in the previous section.
2. From the displayed choices, select <Reconfigure an existing installation>.
3. In the next screen select <Change configuration>.

You can now make the appropriate changes.

After completing the installation or after changing your configuration, you must run the FONTWID program. It may be activated automatically as the installation procedure concludes. If not, access your DOS root directory (type **CD** and press ENTER) and type **FONTWID** and press ENTER. This program generates the font width tables used by Publish It! to position characters on the screen. The initial FONTWID screen, shown in Figure A-2, lists the printer(s) that were installed during the installation or reconfiguration process. Click on the printer you intend to use. The screen changes to the one shown in Figure A-3, giving a succession of messages about what is happening. Finally the screen changes to Figure A-4 telling you the program has completed.

If your mouse refuses to move, you have used the wrong mouse information, such as "Microsoft Serial Mouse" instead of "Bus Mouse." You will need to rerun the INSTALL program.

Figure A-2. *The initial FONTWID screen*

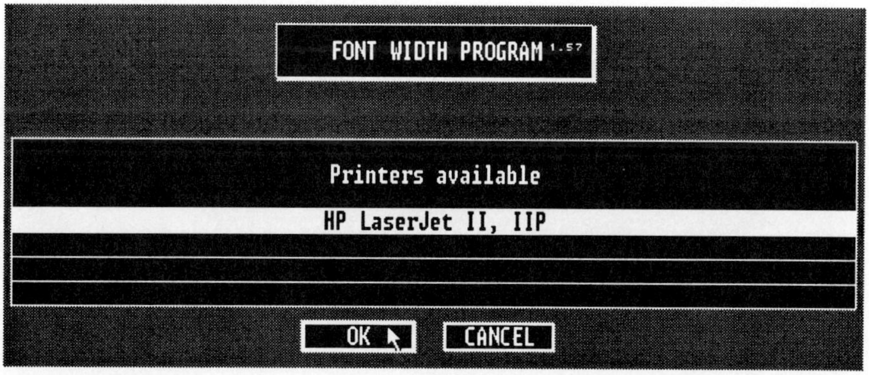

Figure A-3. *The second FONTWID screen*

Figure A-4. *The final FONTWID screen*

The Publish It! version 2.0 installation creates a number of directories on your hard disk:

- \PUBLISH
- \PUBLISH\ARTWORK
- \PUBLISH\CLIPBRD
- \PUBLISH\DTP
- \PUBLISH\FONTS
- \PUBLISH\GEMSYS
- \PUBLISH\PICTURES
- \PUBLISH\SAMPLES
- \PUBLISH\STORIES

Copying the Samples and Artwork

If you decided not to copy the samples and artwork files during the installation process, you can do so at a later date by following these steps:

1. Type **CD** and press ENTER to move to your DOS root directory.
2. To copy the artwork files, type **CD\PUBLISH\ARTWORK**.
3. Insert the copy you made of the master disk that contains the file ARTWORK.EXE into drive A (or B) and type **A:ARTWORK** (or **B:ARTWORK**) and press ENTER.
4. To copy the samples files, type **CD\PUBLISH\SAMPLES**.
5. Insert the copy you made of the master disk that contains the file **SAMPLES.EXE** into drive A (or B) and type **A:SAMPLES** (or **B:SAMPLES**) and press ENTER.
6. To copy the METRO and IMAGECLB files, type **CD\PUBLISH\ARTWORK**.
7. Insert the copy you made of the master disk that contains the files METRO.EXE and IMAGECLB.EXE into drive A (or B) and type

A:METRO (or **B:METRO**) and press (ENTER), and **A:IMAGECLB** (or **B:IMAGECLB**) and press (ENTER).

Typografica

Publish It! version 2.0 includes Typografica, a font-generation program. In it you can generate fonts in any point size from 6 to 72, and it includes font styles not routinely available in Publish It!. Typografica must be installed separately. Before doing so, be sure that you have at least 600K of free space on your hard disk. To install Typografica, take these steps:

1. Insert your Typografica master disk into drive A (or B) and type **A** (or **B**) and press (ENTER).
2. Type **TYPOGRAF** and press (ENTER). The Typografica main menu appears, as shown in Figure A-5.

Figure A-5. *The Typografica main menu*

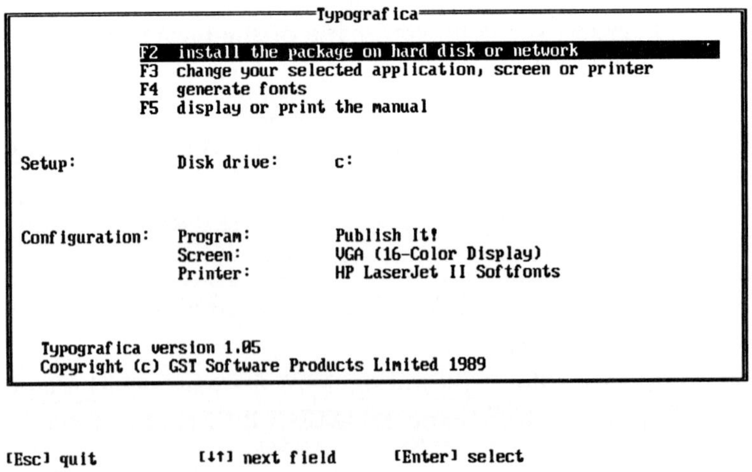

3. Press the F2 key to install the program on C:\TYPOGRAF. The screen in Figure A-6 shows what is happening.
4. Press the F10 key to accept the files.
5. Press ESC to return to the main menu. Press the F3 key. The screen changes to one that asks you to identify which application you will use. The top line reads "Application: none." Press ENTER to see the available choices. Highlight Publish It! to select it.
6. Figure A-7 shows the result. Press ENTER to accept the selection.
7. Press ESC to return to the main menu. Press the F4 key. The screen changes to one that asks you to select typefaces. The top line reads "Typeface: none." Press ENTER to see the available choices.
8. Figure A-8 shows the result. Highlight the typeface you're interested in and press ENTER to accept the choice.
9. In the next screen select the style (<Normal>), the device (<Screen and Printer>), the orientation (<Portrait>), the point sizes (<8>, <10>, <12>, <14>, and <16> in this example), and the width expansion or

Figure A-6. *The Typografica Install menu*

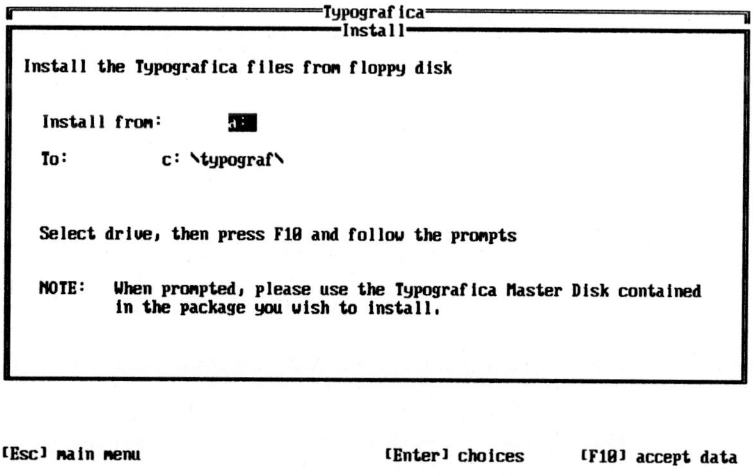

Figure A-7. *Selecting an application on the Typografica Configuration menu*

```
Typografica
Configuration

Application:   Publish It!

Screen:        VGA (16-Color Display)

Printer:       HP LaserJet II Softfonts

Directories (you will only need to change the information below if your
            application is installed in a non-standard way)

Screen fonts:
   c:   \publish\fonts\
Printer fonts:
   c:   \publish\fonts\
Width tables:

Control file:
                                                          :

[Esc] main menu    [↓↑] next field    [Enter] choices    [F10] accept data
```

Figure A-8. *Selecting a font on the Typografica Fonts menu*

```
Typografica
Fonts

Typeface:   none        ATM Autumn
                        BRW Brushwood
Styles:     - Normal    COU Courier
            - Bold      DIA Diamond
            - Italic    SAN Sans
            - Bold itali SGE Sage
                                        ↓↓
Point sizes (between  6 and  96 inclusive):


Width expansion or compression (25-200%):  100 %

Character set:     GEM/3 US ASCII Character Set

[Esc] abandon     [↓↑] next field     [Enter] accept choice
```

compression (<100%>), which results in the screen shown in Figure A-9. Press the F10 key to accept your choices.

10. Press ESC and ENTER to quit.

After using Typografica to generate font styles and/or sizes, you must once more run the FONTWID program described earlier. It then adds your new font styles and sizes to those available in the <Font/size> option in the Style menu and the <Paragraph style> function in the Text menu.

Fonts, especially those in large point sizes, take time to generate (Typografica tells you how long it is going to take, asking whether or not to go on), and use a large number of bytes. For that reason you might want to generate only those fonts and sizes that you expect to be using. To see a list of fonts, access the \PUBLISH\FONTS directory, type **DIR/P**, and press ENTER. All fonts, including those that you generated with Typografica, will be displayed. The Typografica manual, supplied with Publish It! version 2.0, explains how to recognize the typefaces by their filenames. To save space on

Figure A-9. *Selections made on the Typografica Fonts menu*

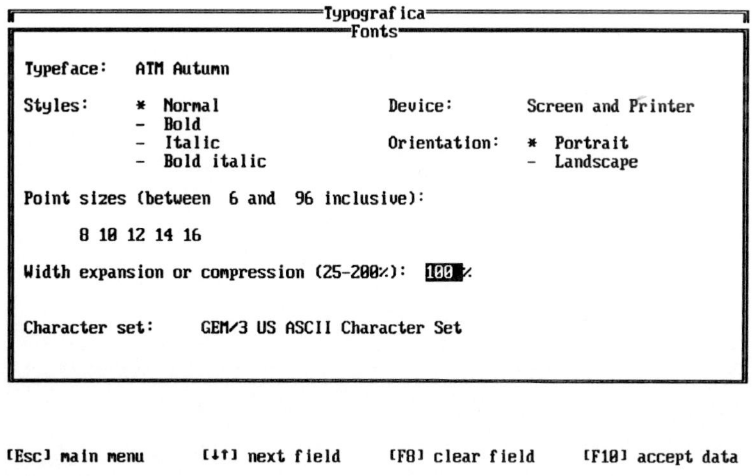

your hard disk you might want to delete those that you don't expect to need in the near future. You can always generate them again if you need to.

Running the Program

At the C:\> DOS prompt, type **PUBLISH** and press ENTER. And that's it! The program should be up and running.

Publish It! is a fairly large program that makes considerable demands on your random access memory. Therefore you may find that it is a better idea to remove such RAM-resident programs as SideKick from memory before attempting to create any sizeable document, particularly if you're using a high-resolution printer or video system.

B

Glossary of Publish It!, Publish It Lite!, and Computer Terms

Alert box A message box on the screen containing a question to be answered by clicking on one of the displayed replies.

Array A series or collection of related data or objects arranged in a pattern.

ASCII Acronym for American Standard Code for Information Interchange. It is a computer code representing letters, numbers, and symbols. Text editors produce ASCII text; word processors do not. But most can convert files to this format when saving.

Aspect ratio The ratio of height to width of the pixels that make up an image on the screen.

Baseline An imaginary line connecting the bottoms of capital letters and all other letters that do not include descenders, such as "p," "y," and "g."

BASIC A high-level programming language. The acronym stands for Beginners' All-purpose Symbolic Instruction Code. *See also* High-level language.

Binding margin Extra space added to the inside of a printed page to allow for punching or binding. Usually the left side of odd-numbered pages and the right side of even-numbered pages. Also called *gutter.*

Bit The smallest unit of information used by computers. Each bit stands for either 0 or 1, right or wrong, yes or no, and so on.

Bit-mapped Composed of individual pixels (dots) on the screen or stored as an array of bits. *See also* Vector graphics.

Body text The body of text in a document, other than headlines, subheads, and so on.

Boilerplate Text or graphics used again and again in different documents without change.

Bold The weight of characters printed with heavy type.

Buffer A temporary area in memory used to hold specific data, such as frames, text, or graphics that have been cut or copied before they are pasted elsewhere.

Bullet A heavy dot or other symbol used for emphasis before a paragraph or items in a list. Known in typesetting circles as a "dingbat."

Button A word in a dialog or alert box representing a choice. Click on it to select it.

Byte Any unit of information consisting of eight bits. Most individual letters, digits, or symbols occupy one byte.

C A high-level programming language. *See also* High-level language.

CAD Computer-aided design.

Centered text Text positioned halfway between the left and right margins of a page or frame.

Character Any single letter, digit, or symbol.

Clear A frame that is transparent rather than opaque, allowing frames beneath to be seen through it.

Click A press followed by a release of a mouse button to execute a function or command.

Close box A small square in the upper-left portion of the work screen. Clicking on it closes the work in progress without saving changes. A warning box is displayed to avoid inadvertent deletions.

Column guides Dotted lines visible on the screen to assist in positioning frames. They do not print.

Compiling The action of a program that translates source code into an executable program. *See also* Source code.

Coordinates The X coordinate specifies a horizontal location, the Y coordinate a vertical location, and in 3-D the Z coordinate specifies a depth location.

Crop To select part of a graphic image, eliminating unwanted areas.

Cut To remove a block of text, a frame, or graphics from the document. The cut item is placed into a memory buffer and can subsequently be pasted.

Decimal tab A type of tab stop that aligns decimal points rather than the beginning of a string of data.

Default The condition that exists automatically but can be changed by the user.

Delete To remove text, pages, styles, files, or other items from the document, disk, or directory.

Desktop The basic screen display that displays menus, icons, scroll bars, boxes, and windows in Publish It!.

Dialog box A box that is displayed on the screen to present a number of choices or ask for additional information.

Dimmed Menu options appear dimmed when they are unavailable in the present working mode.

Dingbat *See* Bullet.

Directory A named division on a hard or floppy disk used to store related files.

Drag To press and hold down a mouse button while moving the mouse to move the pointer, such as when moving or reformatting a frame.

Em A unit of measure equivalent to the width of the uppercase letter "M" in any active typeface or size.

File A collection of data. Files can contain text, graphics, pictures, programs, lists, or any other computer-generated material.

Fixed space A space used to keep words together on the same line. It is never stretched during justification. *See also* Variable space.

Flush To format text so it aligns at the left or right margin.

Font A complete set of characters and symbols in the same size in a given typeface.

Footer A line of copy that is inserted automatically at the bottom of every page or alternate pages.

Format The appearance of a page of text–its size, shape, margins, and type characteristics.

FORTRAN A high-level programming language. *See also* High-level language.

Frame A rectangular box used to hold text or graphics.

Full box A small box in the upper-right corner of the screen. It is used to extend the size of the work area window to the full screen width. It is a toggle action.

Grabber hand The pointer that appears when a selected frame is being dragged.

Graphic A line, shape, or filled shape created by using the Publish It! graphic tools or the graphic tools available with other software.

Greeking A method of representing text by a series of lines or meaningless symbols when text is too small to be displayed on the screen.

Grid A display inside graphics frames that resembles graph paper. When you draw or when you move drawn shapes, your work is fastened to the grid points.

Handle Small open squares on the corners and sides of frames, which indicate the frames are selected. You use handles to adjust the size and proportion of frames.

Hanging indent A type of paragraph with the first line flush with the left margin and subsequent lines indented. Also referred to as "outdent." *See also* Flush.

Hard copy The printout of computer-generated data.

Header A line of text designed to automatically appear at the top of every page or alternate pages. The header at the top of this page gives either the part or appendix title.

High-level language All programming languages other than assembly and machine language. High-level languages fall into two categories: procedural languages, such as BASIC, Pascal, C, and FORTRAN, and declarative languages, such as Prolog and LISP.

Highlight To emphasize a menu item or other data, usually by making it reverse video. *See also* Reverse video.

Hourglass A GEM icon that appears in place of the pointer to indicate that the computer is busy and unable to accept input.

Hyphenation Placing a hyphen where a word has been split at the end of a line. Publish It! and Publish It Lite! do an excellent job of automatic hyphenation.

Hyphenation hot zone An invisible area at the end of every line in the ragged text mode. Long words at the end of a line in the hot zones will be hyphenated, if possible.

Icon A small picture on the screen that activates a function of the program when it is clicked on. Icons are pictorial representations of the functions they represent.

Image file A picture consisting of pixels (dots), created with one of the painting or design programs or by a scanner.

Import To load text or graphics produced by another program.

Indent The space between the margin and the start of a line of text.

Item Selector box A screen that allows access to text and graphics files, enabling you to save and open files and view the contents of directories from within GEM in Publish It!.

Italic A style of text in which the letters slant to the right. *See also* Roman.

Justified Text that is spaced automatically to be flush at both sides of the page.

K or Kbyte 1024 bytes.

Kerning Adjusting the space between any two characters for a more pleasing effect.

Leader A row of characters, usually dots, used to guide the eye to the beginning of a line of text.

Leading The distance in points from the baseline of one line of text to the baseline of the next.

Letter spacing When text is justified, extra spaces are inserted between words and, if necessary because of user-defined limits, between characters.

Library A window on the left side of the screen, displaying imported text or graphics files, paragraph styles, typefaces, or graphics tools.

Light text A character weight in which the character lines are very thin, appearing gray in print.

Line-art file A picture consisting of lines, curves, circles, and so on, created with a drawing program.

LISP A high-level programming language. *See also* High-level language.

Marked block A highlighted section of text that can be cut or copied. It can also be given a new font style or size.

Master page A single- or double-sided page that acts as a template for any new pages added to the document. Master pages are not printed. *See also* Template.

Menu The lists of program options that drop down from the titles in the menu bar across the top of the screen.

Menu bar The menu titles across the top of the screen.

Opaque The opposite of clear. A frame is opaque when it cannot be seen through.

Open To load a previously saved file from disk onto the screen.

Outdent *See* Hanging indent.

Page layout The arrangement of text, graphics, and pictures on a page.

Paragraph style A specific set of features—font style and size, justification, bullets, and indentation—applicable to a specific paragraph or a group of paragraphs with the identical paragraph style identification.

Pascal A high-level programming language. *See also* High-level language.

Paste The menu option used to insert into a document text, graphics, or a frame that has been placed into the memory buffer by the <Cut> or <Copy> options.

Pica A unit of typesetting measurement equal to one sixth of an inch.

Picture format The kind of file, such as line art or image, in which a picture is stored.

Pixel A graphics element or dot. The text and graphics displayed on the monitor consist entirely of individual pixels. On most monitors they are rectangular, taller than wide.

Point A unit of typesetting measurement equal to one seventy-second of an inch.

Point size The height of a font measured in points.

Pointing hand The pointer displayed when a frame is being sized. It appears when clicking on any of the handles of a selected frame.

Polygon Connected line segments that may form a closed figure.

Prolog A high-level programming language. *See also* High-level language.

Quick key The combination of the ALT key and another key to execute a command. At times using quick keys may be faster than pulling down menus and clicking on the option. (See Appendix D, "Quick Keys.")

Ragged Text that is flush with either the left or right margin and uneven at the opposite side.

RAM Random-access memory. The memory buffer available in a computer system for the temporary storage of data. RAM sizes are measured in kilobytes (640K, for example).

Resolution The number of pixels (dots) per square measure determines the resolution capability or the clarity of images and text appearing on a monitor or printer.

Reverse video Black and white are reversed on the screen to produce a negative image. *See* Highlight.

Right-aligned text Text that is flush right and ragged on the left.

Roman A style of text in which the characters are displayed in a vertical position. *See also* Italic.

Rubber banding A term used primarily in computer-aided-design and in paint programs. It relates to the flexible line appearing on the screen when dragging the mouse.

Rubber box When a picture is being cropped, the rubber box encloses the portion that remains.

Rulers Guides that are calibrated in inches, picas, or centimeters and located along the top and left edge of the working window.

Sans serif A typeface that has no ornaments or cross strokes at the bottoms or tops of letters.

Save The command to save the edited version of a previously saved file.

Save as The command that asks that a file be named before it is saved for the first time.

Scale The increase or decrease in size of an image file within a frame.

Scroll bars The bars along the right and bottom edges of the screen, used to scroll the image on the screen either horizontally or vertically.

Serif The ornaments or cross strokes used on many typefaces. *See also* Sans serif.

Shade The underlying tint or pattern of a frame.

Slab Serif A typeface with bold serif.

Sliders *See* Scroll bars.

Snap The command option that makes a frame or picture only positionable on the column guides or ruler divisions.

Soft hyphen A hyphen inserted by the user. It overrides any automatic hyphenation by the program. A soft hyphen placed at the beginning of a word prevents the word from being hyphenated.

Source code The text of a computer program in any of the high-level languages before the program is compiled.

String A series of characters, words, or phrases of any length.

Style sheet The master page data, paragraph styles, and other information for a given document.

Subscript Text in a reduced point size, dropped below the baseline of surrounding text.

Superscript Text in a reduced point size, raised above the baseline of surrounding text.

Tab stop Marked position for aligning text in columns.

Template A basic design or layout used as a guide for others of a similar nature to follow.

Text cursor A thin vertical line indicating where the next typed character will appear or where editing can take place.

Text runaround To make text wrap around the outline of an overlying frame.

Text style The characteristic of text printing that can be toggled off or on such as bold, underline, or italic.

Toggle An option like a push-button switch. It turns the option alternately on or off.

Toolbox A group of four icons in Publish It! or three in Publish It Lite! in the upper-left portion of the screen. Clicking on the icons selects one of the three or four available modes.

Typeface A family of fonts that share the same characteristics but vary in size and style.

Variable space A space inserted by pressing the spacebar. Variable spaces may be stretched during justification. *See also* Fixed space.

Vector graphics Graphics that use a fill pattern composed of dots connected by lines occurring at regular intervals. Vector graphics can be scaled to different sizes.

Visibility The clear or opaque condition of a frame. *See also* Opaque and Clear.

Whole pixel scaling A method of scaling an image file so that all of the dots are scaled equally. The result will be a picture two or three times larger than the original.

Window A portion of the screen area designed for a specific purpose.

Word spacing The adjustment of the maximum and minimum amount of space allowed between words.

WYSIWYG Acronym for What You See Is What You Get. It refers to the ability to see on the screen what the final printed page will look like.

C

Glossary of Publishing Terms

This glossary includes terms used in the publishing, printing, and typesetting businesses. Some of the terms here are also found in Appendix B, which defined the terms as they are used in Publish It! and Publish It Lite!.

Alignment How text lines up on a page or in a column:

Align left	Flush left, ragged right
Align right	Flush right, ragged left
Align center	Ragged left, ragged right
Justified	Flush left and right

Ascender The part of type that extends above the x line, as in "b," "d," "f," and so on.

Baseline The lowermost point of letters, not including the descenders of letters like "j" and "g."

Benday A flat tone applied to line illustrations. It may be a pattern, dots, or lines.

Binding margin Extra space added to the inside of a printed page to allow for punching or binding. Usually the left side of odd-numbered pages and the right side of even-numbered pages. Also called *gutter*.

Bit map Also called raster. A graphic image formed by a matrix of dots with a specific number of dots per inch.

Bleed An illustration that runs to the edge of the page.

Body text The body of text in a document, other than headlines, subheads, and so on.

Boilerplate Text or graphics used again and again in different documents without change.

Bold The weight of characters printed with heavy type.

Buffer *See* Clipboard.

Bullet A heavy dot or other symbol used for emphasis before a paragraph or items in a list. Known in typesetting circles as a "dingbat."

Butting Placing together with no space between.

Caliper Thickness of paper or other material.

Camera-ready copy Parts of a document that can be used directly in offset printing or similar printing methods. The quality of the final printed result depends on the quality of the camera-ready mechanical.

Centered text Text positioned halfway between the left and right margins of a page or frame.

Character Any single letter, digit, or symbol.

Clipboard A holding place, or buffer, for temporarily storing text or graphics.

Cold type *See* Photo typesetting.

Color separation The separate single-color ingredients produced by using filters. When combined they produce a full-color image. Color separations are usually cyan, magenta, yellow, and black.

Copy editing Correcting errors of fact, grammar, and spelling to prepare copy for printing.

cps Characters per second. The speed with which a printer will print text documents.

Cropping Cutting off unwanted portions of an illustration.

Descenders The part of type that extends below the baseline, as in "g," "p," and "y."

Dialog box A window or other screen display that appears in response to a command. One of the displayed options must be selected.

Dingbat *See* Bullet.

dpi Dots per inch. *See* Resolution.

Dummies Rough copies of a magazine, brochure, book, or other document on which the layout for type and graphics is roughed in.

Em A unit of measure equivalent to the width of the uppercase letter "M" in any active typeface or size.

Embedded codes Codes typed directly into the text to activate type specifications. Embedded codes are not printed but do appear on the screen. *See also* Invisible codes.

Flush *See* Alignment.

Folios Page numbers.

Font One complete set of characters, including letters, digits, punctuation marks, and symbols, in the same typeface and size. 12-point Times Roman is a different font from 14-point Times Roman or 12-point Helvetica.

Footer A line of copy that is inserted automatically at the bottom of every page or alternate pages.

Footnotes Notes printed at the bottom of the page, referenced to some item on the page. Unlike footers, each footnote appears only on the designated page.

Four-color press A printing press that can print four colors at one pass.

Front matter Title page, preface, contents, and other sections preceding the actual copy or text in a book or magazine.

Galley proofs Proofs taken prior to the makeup of a book.

Generic font The screen representation of alphanumeric characters that may appear different on the screen from the way they are printed.

Glossary A list of word or phrase definitions.

Greeking The conversion of lines of text into symbolic bars or boxes that show the position of the text only, not the actual characters.

Gutter *See* Inside margin.

H and J Short for hyphenation and justification.

Halftone copy Photographic or other illustrations using a continuous gray scale. The originals may be in color or black and white.

Hanging indent A type of paragraph with the first line flush with the left margin and subsequent lines indented. Also referred to as "outdent." *See also* Flush.

Hard copy The printout of computer-generated data.

Header A line of text designed to automatically appear at the top of every page or alternate pages. The header at the top of this page gives either the part or appendix title.

Highlighting *See* Invert.

Icon A graphic representation of a command, file, function, or tool displayed on the screen. Clicking on an icon activates what it represents.

Indent The space between the margin and the start of a line of text.

Index A list of items of significance along with the page numbers where they appear.

Inside margin The left margin of a right odd-numbered page and the right margin of a left even-numbered page. Inside margins, also referred to as gutters, are often wider to allow for hole-punching or perfect binding.

Invert The opposite of the normal appearance of text or graphic. An inverted image is the negative of the normal image. Also referred to as reverse video or highlighting.

Invisible codes Codes typed directly into the text to activate type specifications. Invisible codes are not printed and do not appear on the screen. *See also* Embedded codes.

Italic A style of text in which the letters slant to the right. *See also* Roman.

Justified Text that is spaced automatically to be flush at both sides of the page.

Kerning Adjusting the amount of space between individual letters, digits, or symbols, based on the width of the individual characters.

Landscape Printing horizontally on a horizontal page. Not all printers are capable of printing in the landscape orientation. *See also* Portrait.

Laser printing Printing with one of the toner-based laser printers. Laser printers produce the best quality results for use as camera-ready copy.

Leaders Dotted or dashed lines to link items printed apart. For example: Item.............$3.75.

Leading The amount of vertical separation between the baselines of lines of text, expressed in points.

Letter spacing When text is justified, extra spaces are inserted between words and, if necessary because of user-defined limits, between characters.

Line spacing *See* Leading.

Mechanical A component of a document to be printed. A piece of camera-ready copy that consists of more than one element, arranged and marked for maximum accuracy.

Offset printing An indirect method of printing in which the ink is first transferred to an intermediate surface, and from that to the paper.

Orphans and widows An orphan is a short line, usually the last line in a paragraph, that falls at the top of a column or page. A widow is a short line, usually the last line in a paragraph, that has fewer than the required number of characters. Widows and orphans are considered aesthetically unappealing and should be avoided.

Outdent *See* Hanging indent.

Page layout The arrangement of text, graphics, and pictures on a page.

Perfect binding Holding pages together with an adhesive along the back edge after the folds are trimmed off.

Photo typesetting Producing a page image on photosensitive paper. Also referred to as cold type.

Pica A typographic unit of measurement equal to 12 points or one-sixth of an inch.

Point The smallest unit of typographic measurement. There are 72 points in an inch.

Portrait The normal vertical orientation of a page. *See also* Landscape.

PostScript printing A page description language used by Apple's LaserWriter and other high-resolution printers and typesetters.

Ragged Text that is flush with either the left or right margin and uneven at the opposite side.

Raster *See* Bit map. A graphic image formed by a matrix of dots with a specific number of dots per inch.

Resolution The number of dots per inch (dpi) used to represent a character or graphic image. The resolution of monitor screens is usually considerably lower than that available with quality printers.

Reverse Video *See* Invert.

Roman A style of text in which the characters are displayed in a vertical position. *See also* Italic.

Rules, ruled lines Lines of different styles and thicknesses that can be drawn on a page.

Run-in chapters Chapters that do not start on a new page.

Saddle stitching Holding pages together with two or three staples passed through the gutter, as in most magazines with less than 100 pages.

Sans serif A typeface that has no ornaments or cross strokes at the bottoms or tops of letters.

Scale The increase or decrease in size of an image file within a frame.

Screen Gray tone usually described as a percentage: 100 percent screen is solid black, 10 percent screen is light gray.

Script A typeface designed to resemble handwriting.

Serif The ornaments or cross strokes used on many typefaces. *See also* Sans serif.

Shade The underlying tint or pattern of a frame.

Slab Serif A typeface with bold serif.

Size To make a graphic image larger or smaller.

Subheads Section titles or headings subordinate to the chapter title.

Tab stop Marked position for aligning text in columns.

Template A basic design or layout used as a guide for others of a similar nature to follow.

Text wrap The ability to wrap text around graphic images on a page.

Text-only document Text saved without type specifications or other formatting.

Trade books Books distributed through book stores.

Typeface A family of fonts that share the same characteristics but vary in size and style.

Vertical justification The ability to adjust the spacing between lines of text in minute increments to make columns end at the same point across a layout.

Widows and orphans A widow is a short line, usually the last line in a paragraph,that has fewer than the required number of characters. An orphan is a short line, usually the last line in a paragraph, that falls at the top of a column or page. Widows and orphans are considered aesthetically unappealing and should be avoided.

D

Quick Keys

Quick keys are keystroke combinations that produce the same result as clicking on a specific item in a menu. Quick keys work only if the menu is *not* displayed. If you use the keyboard rather than a mouse for command entry you will appreciate these keys. There are quite a few, so it is a good idea to make a copy of the following table and keep it handy.

The keystroke combinations are printed as ALT-A, which means that you should hold down the ALT key and type **A** at the same time. P = Publish It!, all versions; P2 = Publish It! version 2.0 only; L = Publish It Lite!.

Keystrokes	**Action**	**P/L**	**Menu**
ALT-A	Repeat last Find or Find and Replace	P	Text
ALT-B	Bold text (toggle)	P	Style
ALT-B	Bold text (toggle)	L	Style
ALT-C	Copy frame, text, or graphic	P	Edit
ALT-C	Copy text or graphic	L	Edit
ALT-E	Show/hide column guides (toggle)	P2	Options

Keystrokes	Action	P/L	Menu
ALT-F	Find a string of text	P	Text
ALT-F	Find a string of text	L	Edit
ALT-G	Go to page	P/L	Page
ALT-H	Show/hide toolbox (toggle)	P	Options
ALT-I	Italic text	P/L	Style
ALT-J	Show/hide rulers (toggle)	P2	Options
ALT-K	Kern two characters by 0.5 point	P	Text
ALT-K	Kern two characters	L	Style
ALT-L	Light text	P/L	Style
ALT-M	Switch between frame/text/ paragraph/graphics	P	None
ALT-M	Switch between frame/text/graphic	L	None
ALT-N	Normal text	P/L	Style
ALT-O	Open document	P2	File
ALT-P	Print a document	P/L	File
ALT-Q	Quit the program	P/L	File
ALT-R	Find and replace text	P	Text
ALT-R	Find and replace text	L	Edit
ALT-S	Save file	P/L	File
ALT-T	Open font/size dialog box	P/L	Style
ALT-U	Underlined text	P/L	Style
ALT-V	Paste text or graphic in a frame	P/L	Edit
ALT-W	White text	P	Style
ALT-X	Cut out a frame, text or graphic	P/L	Edit
ALT-Z	Hide all pictures	P2	Graphics
ALT-0	Size to fit	P2	Page
ALT-1	1/2 size	P2	Page
ALT-2	3/4 size	P2	Page
ALT-3	Actual size	P2	Page
ALT-4	Double size	P2	Page
ALT-5	Two pages	P2	Page
ALT-5	Bring frame/graphic to front	L	Options
ALT-6	Send frame/graphic to back	L	Options
ALT-7	Send frame/graphic to back	P	Page

Keystrokes	Action	P/L	Menu
ALT-+	Superscript	P/L	Style
ALT--	Subscript	P/L	Style
HOME	Move insertion point to beginning of current page	P2	None
END	Move insertion point to end of current page	P2	None
SHIFT-HOME	Highlight a range of text from the insertion point to the beginning of the current line	P2	None
SHIFT-END	Highlight a range of text from the insertion point to the end of the current line	P2	None
PGUP	Move to the previous page	P2	None
PGDN	Move to the next page. If used while on the master page, moves to page 1	P2	None
CTRL-PGUP	Move to first page	P2	None
CTRL-PGDN	Move to last page	P2	None
CTRL--	Soft hyphen	L	Edit
F1	Left-justified paragraph	L	None
F2	Fully justified paragraph	L	None
F3	Right-justified paragraph	L	None
F4	Center-justified paragraph	L	None
F5	Indented, left-justified paragraph	L	None
F6	Indented, fully justified paragraph	L	None
F7	Outdented, left-justified paragraph	L	None
F8	Outdented, fully justified paragraph	L	None
F9	Bulleted, left-justified paragraph	L	None
F10	Bulleted, fully justified paragraph	L	None

The function keys F1 through F10 can be used to represent paragraph styles that you assign to them through the <Paragraph style> option in Publish It!'s Text menu.

E

External Program Sources

This appendix lists only those manufacturers and products that are actually mentioned in the book. There are many more, and careful perusal of the advertisements in computer magazines will tell you what else is available.

3-D Drafting	Generic Software, Inc. 11911 North Creek Parkway S. Bothwell, WA 98011	2-D and 3-D CAD program
AutoSketch	AutoDesk, Inc. 2320 Marinship Way Sausalito, CA 94965	2-D CAD program including a limited font library
Bitstream Fonts	Bitstream, Inc. Athenaeum House 215 First Street Cambridge, MA 02142	Fonts

CADD Level3	Generic Software, Inc. 11911 North Creek Parkway S. Bothwell, WA 98011	2-D CAD program
Design CAD 3-D	American Small Business Computers, Inc. 327 South Mill Street Pryor, OK 74361	2-D and 3-D CAD program
Diagraph	Computer Support Corp. 2215 Midway Road Carrollton, TX 75006	Clip-art library and font library
EnerGraphics	EnerTronics Electronics Research Inc. #5 Station Plaza 1910 Pine Street St. Louis, MO 63103	Business graphics and a limited 2-D and 3-D drawing program
Exact	Technical Support Software, Inc. 72 Kent Street Brookline, MA 02146	Program to produce mathematical and scientific symbols
FontGen IV, V	VS Software P.O. Box 165920 Little Rock, AR 72216	A full-font editor and generator
GEM/3 Desktop GEM Paint	Digital Research, Inc. 60 Garden Center Box DRI Monterey, CA 93942	The disk-operating supplemental program used by Publish It! and Publish It Lite! draw and paint programs
The Graphics Link	PC Quick-Art 994 S. Milledge Athens, GA 30606	Screen-capture graphics-conversion and editing program

Halo DPE	Media Cybernetics, Inc. 8484 Georgia Ave. Suite 200 Silver Spring, MD 20910	Font library and desktop publishing editor
HiJaak InSet	Inset Systems, Inc. 71 Commerce Drive Brookfield, CT 06804	Screen-capture and graphics-conversion and editing programs
HotShot	Symsoft Corp. 444 First St. Los Altos, CA 94022	Screen-capture and graphics-conversion and editing program
Lotus 1-2-3	Lotus Development Corporation 55 Cambridge Parkway Cambridge, MA 02142	Spreadsheet and business graphics program
PaintShow PaintShowPlus	Logitech, Inc. 6505 Kaiser Dr. Fremont, CA 94555	Paint programs and limited font libraries
PC Paintbrush	Microsoft Corporation 16011 NE 36th Way Box 97017 Redmond, WA 98073	Paint program and limited font library
Publisher's PicturePak	Marketing Graphics Inc. 4401 Dominion Blvd. Suite 210 Glen Allen, VA 23060	Clip-art libraries
Publish It! Publish It Lite!	Timeworks, Inc. 444 Lake Cook Road Deerfield, IL 60015	Desktop publishing programs
Quattro Quattro PRO	Borland International 4585 Scotts Valley Drive Scotts Valley, CA 95066	Spreadsheet and business graphics programs

Sled	VS Software 209 West 2nd Street P.O. Box 6158 Little Rock, AR 72216	Image processor, draw program, and limited font library
Spinfont	SoftCraft, Inc. 16 N. Carroll Street Suite 500 Madison, WI 53703	Font manipulation program
VP-Graphics	Paperback Software International 2830 Ninth Street Berkeley, CA 94710	Draw and paint program and limited font library
Windows	Microsoft Corporation 16011 NE 36th Way Box 97017 Redmond, WA 98073	A collection of utility programs including a paint program and limited font library
Word	Microsoft Corporation 16011 NE 36th Way Box 97017 Redmond, WA 98073	Word processing program
WordPerfect	WordPerfect Corp. 1555 Technology Way Orem, UT 84057	Word processing program
WordStar	MicroPro Int'l. Corp. 33 San Pablo Ave. San Rafael, CA 94903	Word processing program

F

Publish It! Version 2.0

Publish It! version 2.0 includes a sufficient number of new features, refinements, and improvements to make upgrading from any of the earlier versions an option to be seriously considered. Whatever kind of desktop publishing you might be doing, many of the new features can make your working with Publish It! easier and more efficient.

The Virtual Memory System

Publish It! version 2.0 has something described as a *virtual memory system*. It works by treating your hard drive as an extension of your computer's memory. It writes portions of the program and data that are not currently being used to your hard disk in the form of temporary files—a practice known as *data slaving*. When this data is needed, it is read from the hard disk and alternate information, not currently in use, is then written to disk. Publish It!'s virtual memory system can use up to four megabytes of disk space. Whenever you exit Publish It!, these slave files are automatically deleted, freeing your disk space for other uses. With this feature, if you are working with large documents or are using large high-resolution scanned images, try to keep at least four megabytes of disk space free and available for this virtual memory system.

Changing the Data Slaving Path

When Publish It! is installed on your C drive, you can send the slave files to a different drive. If your system includes a D drive or if your AUTOEXEC.BAT file automatically creates a RAM disk whenever your system is activated (be sure that it has at least 4MB space), you can order Publish It! to send your slave files to them. To do that, access your word processing program and load the file C:\PUBLISH\PUBLISH.SLV. You will find that the file is totally empty. Type **D:** if you want your D drive used or **E:** if your RAM disk is E. You can also use drive A or B for your floppy drives. This command will be the one and only line in that file. Save it and from now on Publish It! uses the designated disk for the temporary slave files.

Improving Performance

There are some things you can do that may improve the performance of Publish It!. One is to remove all memory-resident programs such as SideKick and any device drivers that are not needed. Also, you might want to change your CONFIG.SYS file to read FILES=15 and BUFFERS=20 unless you habitually need greater numbers to run some of your other applications.

Expanded and Extended Memory

Publish It! 2.0 is designed to utilize any available memory over and above the 640K RAM that is the required minimum. If your system is limited to 640K RAM, then skip this section and go to the "Text Autoflow" section later in this appendix.

Configuration Recommendations

If your system has extended or expanded memory to 1MB or more, the recommendations that follow should interest you.

640K to 1MB RAM If you have extended or expanded memory between 640K and 1MB, Publish It! makes use of this extra memory automatically, assuming you have a memory manager such as HIMEM.SYS or EMM386.SYS installed. To take advantage of this, access your CONFIG.SYS file in your word processing program or text editor and type **DEVICE=C:\DOS\HIMEM.SYS** as the first line in that file, if your HIMEM.SYS file is located on the C:\DOS directory. If it is located on the C:\ root directory, you should enter **DEVICE=C:\HIMEM.SYS**, or if it is on a boot disk in drive A, enter **DEVICE=A:\HIMEM.SYS**. The memory manager is thus loaded each time you start your system.

1MB RAM If you have 1MB of extended or expanded memory, create a 768K disk *cache* (in computer language this is a safe place for high-speed use of information), leaving 256K for Publish It! to use. To install a disk cache, enter a line such as **DEVICE=C:\SMARTDRV.SYS 768** for expanded memory or **DEVICE=C:\SMARTDRV.SYS 768/A** for extended memory as the first line in the CONFIG.SYS file. (If SMARTDRV.SYS is located in a place other than your C:\ root directory, make the appropriate changes in the line.) If you want to start your computer system without automatically creating a disk cache, place the DEVICE= line into a .BAT file with any other name, such as PI.BAT. Then, after booting your computer, type **PI** and press ENTER to activate the disk-caching process.

More than 1MB RAM What follows are suggestions for the most efficient methods to use extended or expanded memory of one megabyte or more:

Memory	Extended	Expanded
640K to 1MB	Automatically used; no configuring necessary	Automatically used; no configuring necessary
1MB	Create a 768K disk cache	Create a 768K disk cache
2MB	Create a 768K disk cache; 1MB is used by virtual memory	Create a 1768K disk cache

F

Memory	Extended	Expanded
3MB	Create a 768K disk cache; 2MB is used by virtual memory	Create a 2768K disk cache
4MB	Create a 768K disk cache; 3MB is used by virtual memory	Create a 3MB disk cache
5MB	Create a 768K disk cache; 4MB is used by virtual memory	Create a 768K disk cache and a 4MB RAM disk. Redirect slave files to RAM disk
MORE	After allowing 256K for Publish It! and 4MB for virtual memory create a disk cache between 768K and 3MB in size	After allowing 256K for Publish It! and 4MB for virtual memory create a disk cache between 768K and 3MB in size

Text Autoflow

This is a convenient option for creating lengthy documents. To use it, select <Autoflow text> from the Text menu and Publish It! automatically adds the necessary pages and draws all the necessary frames to hold the entire story.

Using No Master Page

If you're not using a master page, take these steps:

1. Draw the text frame on the current page. You can use multiple frames, but each succeeding page is going to be a copy of this page.
2. Click on the first frame to select it. Select <Import text> from the File menu. Select the word processing program and then the story you want to import.
3. With more than one frame on the page, click on the next text frame to select it. Click on the filename in the Library window to pour text into the next frame. If you have, say, four frames on the page but

have poured text into only two, using Autoflow pours text into only those two frames on each succeeding page.

4. Select <Autoflow text> from the Text menu. This option is available only when the text frames on the current page are filled and there is more text to come. When Autoflow finishes, the displayed page is the last one into which text was poured. Autoflow uses the insert method of adding pages. If you have created more than one page and are using Autoflow from page 1, all other pages are pushed to the end of the document.

Using Master Pages

You can use master pages that may include headers, footers, graphics, headlines, and more, giving all pages produced with the Autoflow option a uniform look.

1. Create your one- or two-page master page as usual.
2. Select <Go to page> in the Page menu, type **1** and click on <OK> to go to the first page.
3. Click on the first frame to select it. Select <Import text> from the File menu and select the word processing program and then the story you want to import.
4. With more than one frame on the page, click on the next text frame to select it, and click on the filename in the Library window to pour text into the next frame. If you have more frames on the page but have poured text into only two, using Autoflow will pour text into only those two frames on each succeeding page.
5. Select <Autoflow text> from the Text menu. This option is available only when the text frames on the current page are filled and there is more text to come. When Autoflow finishes, the displayed page is the last one into which text was poured.

Publish It! adds pages after page 1, using the format of your master page(s). If you use left and right master pages, they don't have to be identical. All added left pages will conform to the left master page and all added right pages to the right master page. You can make changes on your first page to give it a distinctive look. The added pages are not affected by such changes.

Automatic Timed Backup

The <Automatic backup> option is available in the Options menu. Selecting it saves your work at intervals that you decide and type into the dialog box. These backup files are saved by Publish It! with an .ATB extension unless you decide on another and type it into the dialog box, shown in Figure F-1. File extensions that you cannot use with this option are .STY, .DTP, and .BAK. The files created with the <Automatic backup> option are saved on the same subdirectory as the current document (C:\PUBLISH\DTP unless changed by you).

The dialog box includes a <Warning beep> option. If you select it, the files are not automatically saved. Rather, the program beeps to remind you that it is time to save your work.

Figure F-1. *The Automatic Timed Backup dialog box*

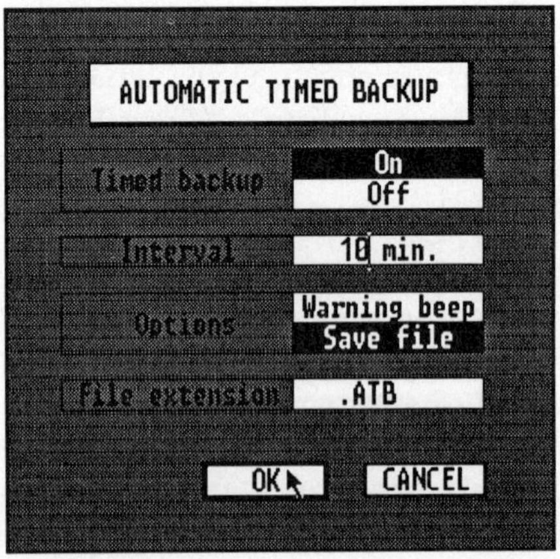

Backup Files

This option is different from the <Automatic backup> option. Instead of overwriting your earlier file every time you select <Save> from the File menu, it saves the last version in a separate file. The option is available as <.BAK files> in the <Set defaults> option in the Options menu. The Set Defaults dialog box is shown in Figure F-2. When this option is active, it saves the version of your file that existed before the last editing or changes with the .BAK extension. At the same time it saves the edited or changed version with the usual .DTP extension. These files too are saved on the currently active subdirectory. You can check on their presence by selecting <Open> from the File menu, changing the end of the Directory line in the Item Selector box to *.* and pressing (ENTER). The Item Selector box now displays all files including those with the .ATB and .BAK extensions as shown in Figure F-3.

Figure F-2. Setting the backup files option in the Set Defaults dialog box

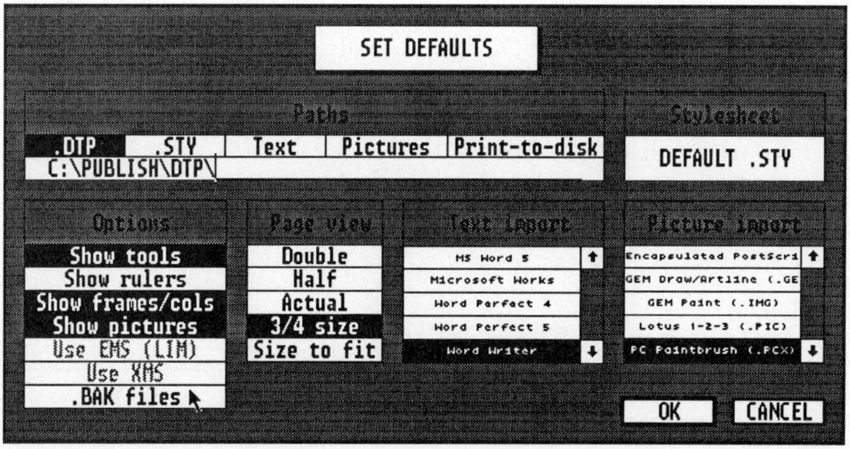

Figure F-3. *The Item Selector box displaying backup files along with .DTP files*

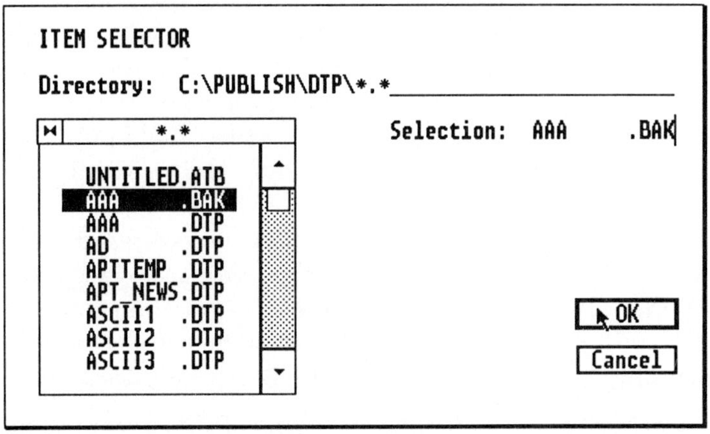

Draft Printing

Printing documents containing graphics can be a time-consuming activity. To speed up printing when all you need is a temporary hard copy of your text, select <Print> from the File menu and click on <Print images> and <Print line-art> in your Print Document dialog box as shown in Figure F-4. That will de-select both options so your printer prints only text with diagonal lines replacing the graphics on the printed page(s). You can also cause your printer to print text plus line art but no images or text plus images but no line art. Both options are toggle commands, meaning that clicking on them again selects them once more.

Selecting All Frames

The <Select all> option available in the Edit menu is an enormous improvement over earlier versions of Publish It!. In Figure F-5 only four

Figure F-4. *The Print Document dialog box with graphics disabled*

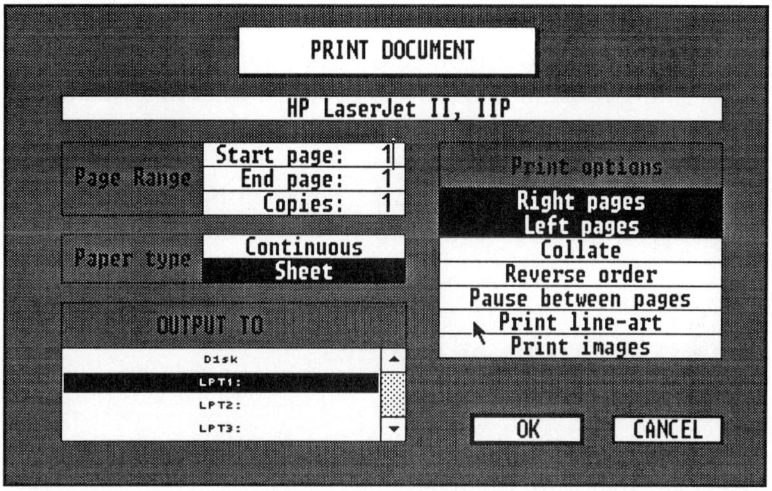

Figure F-5. *Four frames selected using <Select All> and then duplicated and moved*

F

frames of the eight shown in the figure were originally created; two holding graphics and two holding text. Then <Select all> was selected, followed by <Copy> and <Paste>, all from the Edit menu. The combined group of frames was then moved to the bottom of the frame and reduced in size as a group. Everything remained in perfect proportion to everything else except that the text was lost. It was too large to fit into the reduced frames and will have to be reduced before it will reappear.

In this manner all frames representing entire pages can be selected together, copied or cut, and then pasted onto other pages.

Select a Group of Frames

Similarly Publish It! 2.0 makes it possible to select a specific number of frames when you don't want every frame on the page to be included. Hold down the SHIFT key and click on the individual frames you want selected. Another way is to hold down the SHIFT key and drag a selection box around the frames you want selected. Let go of the SHIFT key. You can now cut or copy and paste that selected group of frames, or you can move or re-size the selected frames in unison as a group. In Figure F-6 the two text frames at the bottom were selected, moved, and then enlarged to again display the text. The <PARAGRAPH> mode can now be used to reduce the text to a size that will fit into the much smaller frames. The frames can then be reduced once more as a group and moved back into their original position.

Custom Page Sizes

In addition to the regular page sizes displayed in the Page Format dialog box when <New> is selected from the File menu, the dialog box includes the

Figure F-6. *Two text frames selected by holding down the* (SHIFT) *key*

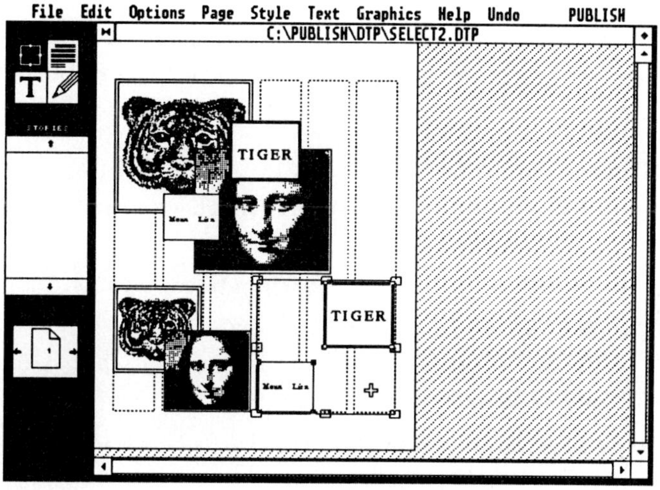

<Custom page size> option. This option can be used to create any kind of page size or proportion from a maximum of 22.5 x 22.5 inches down to business-card size or anything in between.

1. From the File menu click on <New> and on <No> in the style sheet question box.
2. In the Page Format dialog box click on <Custom size> and in the Height and Width boxes enter the dimension you want. Then click on <OK>.

If the selected size is one you expect to be using frequently, select <Save style sheet> from the File menu and give it a distinctive name. Publish It! adds the .STY extension automatically.

Customizing Defaults

This option, available in the Options menu as <Set defaults>, lets you determine the configuration existing each time Publish It! is activated. The available options in the Set Defaults dialog box shown in Figure F-7 are as follows:

- The disk\directory\path where you want your .DTP, .ATB, and .BAK files to be saved.
- The disk\directory\path where you want your .STY files to be saved.
- The disk\directory\path where you want your text, pictures, and print-to-disk files to be saved.
- The name of the style sheet (.STY) that is used to format the page when Publish It! is activated.
- The <Options> box in the dialog box contains seven toggle options that determine whether the toolbox, the rulers, the frames and columns, and pictures are shown, and whether the backup files (<.BAK files>) option is active. In addition, the options <Use EMS (LIM)> and <Use XMS> are grayed out and unavailable unless expanded or extended memory in excess of 1MB is available.
- The <Page view> option determines the page size that is active when the program is started.
- The <Text import> option determines which word processor format is highlighted initially when <Import text> is selected from the File menu.
- The <Picture import> option determines which graphic file format is highlighted initially when <Import picture> is selected from the File menu.

Click on <OK> and the new defaults remain active until you make changes in the Set Defaults dialog box.

Figure F-7. *The Set Defaults dialog box*

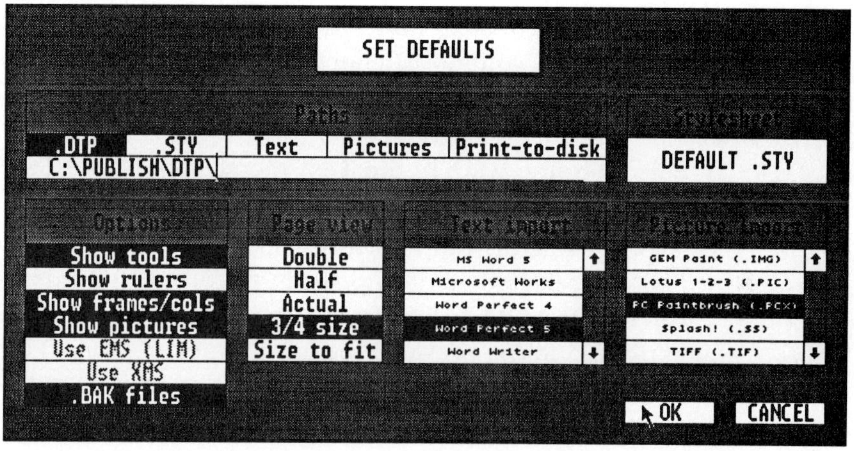

Exporting Text

Publish It! version 2.0 lets you export the text in your .DTP files into an ASCII text file with an .ASC extension that contains no formatting commands or graphics but all text is there. This text can then be entered into your word processing program for editing, or added to the data contained in other .DTP files.

1. To export text, click on the frame that holds text to be exported.
2. Select <Export text> from the File menu. In the Item Selector box give the new file a name, but accept the default .ASC extension supplied by Publish It!. Not only the text in the selected frame, but the entire story, regardless of length, is exported.

If the text in the selected frame was typed in the <TEXT> mode, then you must give it a name before it can be exported. See "Naming Text," next.

Naming Text

If you want to export text that was typed into a frame or several frames in the <TEXT> mode, you must first give it a name.

1. Select the frame containing your text.
2. Select <Name text> in the Text menu. The Name Text dialog box appears.
3. Type a name of your choice and click on <OK> as shown in Figure F-8. The selected name appears in the Stories Library window. You can now treat it like imported text and if you choose to export it (as explained in the previous section, "Exporting Text") it is treated as imported text and saved with an .ASC extension.

Figure F-8. *The Name Text dialog box*

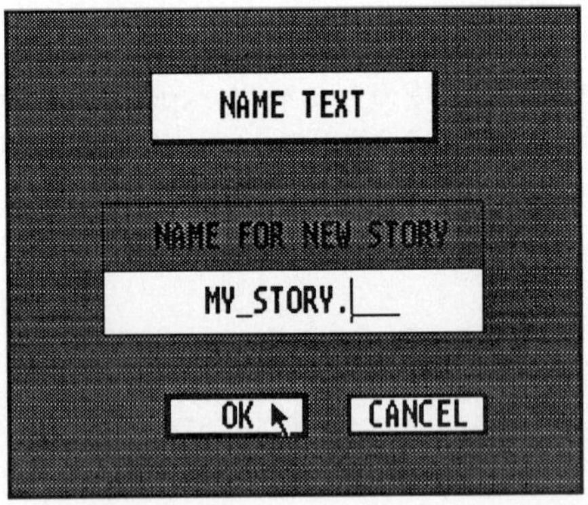

Other Improvements

There are a number of other improvements available in Publish It! version 2.0. Each is covered in considerable detail in Chapter 4, "The Menus." Following is a brief overview of the most important improvements:

- <Import text> has additional word processing program formats.
- <Import picture> has additional graphic file formats.
- <Text runaround> permits running text around odd-shaped graphics or to be typed or imported into odd-shaped frames.
- <Set tabs> is now simplified.
- Page numbering formats are available in five styles.
- Pages can be added or deleted, several at a time.
- <Box>, <Rounded box>, and <Strikethrough> are added to the <Font/size> option.
- Imported graphics added to master pages can now be saved in style sheets.
- Using Typografica, special font styles and sizes are available. (See Appendix A, "Installation.")

Index

A

B

D

E

F

G

H

I

J

K

L

M

N

O

P

Q

R

S

T

U

V

W

X

Z

Tear off for Bookmark

You're important to us...

We'd like to know what you're interested in, what kinds of books you're looking for, and what you thought about this book in particular.

Please fill out the attach card and mail it in. We' do our best to keep you informed about Osborn newest books and speci offers.

YES, Send Me a FREE Color Catalog of all Osborne computer bo

To Receive Catalog, Fill in Last 4 Digits of ISBN Number from Back of Bo (see below bar code) 0-07-881 _ _ _ – _

Name: ______________________ Title: ______________

Company: ______________________

Address: ______________________

City: ______________ State: __________ Zip: ______________

I'M PARTICULARLY INTERESTED IN THE FOLLOWING *(Check all that apply*

I use this software
- □ WordPerfect
- □ Microsoft Word
- □ WordStar
- □ Lotus 1-2-3
- □ Quattro
- □ Others ______________

I use this operating system
- □ DOS
- □ Windows
- □ UNIX
- □ Macintosh
- □ Others ______________

I rate this book:
□ Excellent □ Good □ Poor

I program in
- □ C or C++
- □ Pascal
- □ BASIC
- □ Others ______________

I chose this book because
- □ Recognized author's name
- □ Osborne/McGraw-Hill's reputation
- □ Read book review
- □ Read Osborne catalog
- □ Saw advertisement in store
- □ Found/recommended in library
- □ Required textbook
- □ Price
- □ Other ______________

Comments ______________________

Topics I would like to see covered in future books by Osborne/McGraw-Hill inclu

____

IMPORTANT REMINDER

To get your FREE catalog, write in the last 4 digits of the ISBN number printed on back cover (see below bar code) 0-07-881 _ _ _ – _